A selection of related titles published by Cassell

Marketing in Hospitality and Tourism
Teare, Mazanec, Crawford-Welch and Calver
Strategic Hospitality Management
Richard Teare and Andrew Boer
Managing Projects in Hospitality Organizations
Teare, Adams and Messenger
Hotel and Food Service Marketing
Francis Buttle
Management of Foodservice Operations
Peter Jones with Paul Merricks
Principles of Hotel Front Office Operations
Baker, Bradley and Huyton
Achieving Quality Performance
Teare, Atkinson and Westwood

An up-to-date catalogue of the full range of Hospitality and Tourism titles is available from the publisher.

SERVICE QUALITY IN HOSPITALITY ORGANIZATIONS

Edited by

MICHAEL D. OLSEN
RICHARD TEARE
EVERT GUMMESSON

CASSELL

Cassell
Wellington House, 125 Strand, London WC2R 0BB
215 Park Avenue South, New York, NY 10003

First published 1996

British Library Cataloguing-in-Publication Data
A catalogue record for this book is available from the British Library.

ISBN 0-304-32788-3 (hardback)
      0-304-32786-7 (paperback)

Typeset by York House Typographic Ltd
Printed and bound in Great Britain by Redwood Books, Trowbridge, Wiltshire

Contents

Preface

The impact of recession and better organized competition, among other developments in the international hospitality industry, has, in our view, stimulated a sustained interest in service excellence. This book aims to integrate the theory and practice associated with researching, designing, developing, implementing and sustaining service quality programmes in hospitality organizations. The broad approach is to consider both customer and operator perspectives, so as to provide an instructive and useful textbook for students and practitioners. Further, the book explores the meaning of service quality as perceived in the academic world and the practicalities of how it should be addressed in hospitality organizations. This is achieved by reviewing and applying research-based literature to underpin examples and case study illustrations drawn from a range of international hospitality and tourism organizations.

In order to fully examine the dimensions of service quality in hospitality/tourism organizations as they apply now and in the future, the book seeks to:

- Review a diverse range of service quality literature, much of which has been applied to hospitality/tourism settings by the contributors as they assess the organizational implications relating to service quality opportunities and challenges.
- Provide a concise, authoritative commentary on 'state of the art' service quality developments as they relate to the organizational context of each chapter.
- Explain and illustrate how service quality initiatives are planned, developed and implemented in commercial settings. Contributors have used a wide range of exhibits and other supporting information to illustrate the application of business principles, methods, techniques and strategies relating to service quality. This information is drawn from reports, interviews, site visits, observations and other functional and operational sources.

The book consists of four Parts which constitute the framework of the book. Part One, 'Service Quality Concepts', seeks to provide an overview of the elements of service quality and how they fit together. Part Two, 'Integrating Service Quality', aims to explore the issues relating to establishing and maintaining a service ethos and culture in organizations. Part Three, 'Organizational Perspectives on Service Quality', provides a broader perspective on the interrelationships that sustain or impede the success of service quality initiatives and programmes. Part Four, 'New Directions for Service Quality', provides a look forward at some of the ways in which service quality improvements might be achieved.

We are conscious that, to some extent, this book addresses comparatively new ground, as there are few existing texts which focus exclusively on service quality. In this regard, we are grateful to all the contributors for enabling this to happen. We would also like to thank Judith Entwisle-Baker for her encouragement and support, and also Naomi Roth, Fiona McKenzie, Huw Neill, Melissa Riley-Jones and Justine White at Cassell and David Swinden, the copy-editor.

MICHAEL D. OLSEN, RICHARD TEARE, EVERT GUMMESSON
July 1995

Contributors

Editors

Michael D. Olsen is Professor of Strategic Management, Department of Hospitality and Tourism Management, Virginia Polytechnic Institute and State University, USA. In his 30 years of industrial and academic experience, he has authored or co-authored more than 150 articles which have been published in both trade and professorial journals. He co-wrote *Strategic Management in the Hospitality Industry* (with Eliza Tse and Joseph West) and co-edited *International Hospitality Management: Corporate Strategy in Practice* (with Richard Teare). He currently serves as Associate Editor of the International Journal of Hospitality Management. He is the Founding President of the International Academy of Hospitality Research and his industrial experience includes service as a Visiting Professor in Australia, China, Finland, France, Hong Kong, Switzerland, the Netherlands and the UK.

Richard Teare is the Charles Forte Professor of Hotel Management and Executive Director of CHART International, Department of Management Studies, University of Surrey, and a Non-Executive Director of the National Society for Quality through Teamwork, UK. He is a Fellow of the Hotel, Catering and Institutional Management Association and previously worked for both national and international hotel companies. He is Editor of the *International Journal of Contemporary Hospitality Management*, Editor of Cassell's Resource-Based Series in Hospitality and Tourism Management and a member of the Editorial Advisory Boards of *International Marketing Review*, the *Journal of Travel and Tourism Marketing* and *Strategic Insights into Quality*. He has co-written and edited ten books on aspects of strategic management and marketing in service industries and most recently for Cassell, *Marketing in Hospitality and Tourism: A Consumer Focus*.

Evert Gummesson is Professor of Service Management and Marketing, Department of Business Administration, Stockholm University, Sweden. Prior to this, he was Professor and Scientific Leader at the Service Research Centre, University of Karlstad and a faculty member of the University of Gothenburg and the Swedish School of Economics and Business Administration, Helsinki, Finland. In industry, he has been Marketing Manager for the *Reader's Digest* in Sweden and a Vice-President of the Scandinavian Division of the PA Consulting Group where he worked for fourteen years. Among his many publications, he has written books on marketing, corporate strategy, quality, scientific method and the first book on services marketing to be published in Scandinavia. He currently serves on the editorial advisory board of the *International Journal of Contemporary Hospitality Management*.

Contributors

Gail Ayala is a Doctoral Candidate in marketing with an emphasis in hospitality administration at The Florida State University, USA. She received her MBA in marketing from Michigan State University and previously worked for Westin Hotels and Resorts as well as various restaurant companies, including Speciality Restaurants Inc. Her areas of research interest include service quality issues in the hotel sector and the effectiveness of promotional strategies in the hospitality industry.

Cherylynn Becker is an Associate Professor at Kansas State University, USA, where she teaches graduate and undergraduate programmes in hospitality management. Her primary research interest lies in the management and organization of service sector firms and the management of human resources in such firms. Prior to an academic career, she held management positions in a variety of hospitality organizations including hotels, restaurants, institutional foodservice and private clubs.

Sören Bergström is Associate Professor at the School of Business, Stockholm University, Sweden. His research in environmental business management started twenty years ago and he has published several books and articles in the area. As a management consultant, he has worked with the hospitality industry, the Swedish Energy Board, and the Swedish Consumer Co-operative. He also has practical experience of managing hotels and conference centres at General Manager level.

Bob Brotherton is Reader in Hospitality and Tourism Management at Blackpool and The Fylde College, UK. He has published articles, conference papers and reports on various strategic and operational aspects of the hospitality/tourism industries. He has extensive consultancy experience in the UK and overseas, particularly in Turkey, where he is currently engaged in a World Bank Educational Development Project and a collaborative research project with Bogazici University, Istanbul.

Bonnie Farber Canziani is an Associate Professor, College of Business, San Jose State University, California, USA, and Regional Editor (Americas) of the *International Journal of Contemporary Hospitality Management*. Her doctorate from the School of Hotel Administration, Cornell University, focused on organizational theory applied to the hotel sector. She spent five years as Co-ordinator of Tourism and Hospitality Training Centers for the governments of Puerto Rico and Venezuela.

Mike Coyle is a Principal Lecturer at Blackpool and The Fylde College, UK. His background includes wide experience of the hospitality industry in operational and senior management roles. His interests include all aspects of operational management and he has written a number of articles and undertaken consultancies across the spectrum of hospitality provision. Research interests include quality management in general and service management in hospitality settings.

Anne G. Dickinson is a graduate in Hotel and Catering Management from the Manchester Metropolitan University, UK, where, during her final year, she co-authored an article on recruitment and training using biodata and standardized tests. She now works for Midland Bank plc and, prior to her current role as a Business Banking Team Manager, she worked in Personnel and on Graduate Recruitment and Training programmes.

Nicholas F. Horney is President, Nicholas F. Horney & Associates, a management consulting firm. Prior to this, he held senior roles with Pizza Hut Inc. and Stouffer Hotels and Resorts. He has served on the Board of Examiners, Malcolm Baldrige

National Quality Award and he is a judge for the *RIT/USA Today* and *Sloan Management Review*/Coopers & Lybrand Quality Awards. He is currently authoring a TQM series for the American Hotel and Motel Association.

Elizabeth M. Ineson is a Senior Lecturer in the Department of Hotel, Catering and Tourism Management at the Manchester Metropolitan University, UK. Her research interests lie in the fields of undergraduate selection, employment, recruitment and hotel, catering and tourism management education. Her doctoral work explored the predictive validity of criteria used in the selection of undergraduate and graduate hotel and catering management trainees.

Nick Johns is Reader in Hospitality Management, Norwich Hotel School, City College, Norwich, UK where he has been engaged in teaching and research since 1984. He has written widely on scientific, educational and management topics and his publications include several books. He is a member of the editorial advisory board of the *International Journal of Contemporary Hospitality Management* and his research interests include quality and productivity management in the hospitality industry.

Svein Larsen is Associate Professor of Social Psychology, Department of Tourism, Finnmark College, Norway, where he is currently developing a three-year programme in hotel management. He has published papers on numerous topics, including service quality research in a cruise line organization. He previously taught at The Norwegian College of Hotel Management, where he developed leadership and personnel development programmes for public and private hospitality organizations.

Anton Meyer is Professor of Services, Retail and Industrial Marketing at the Ludwig Maximilians University, Munich, Germany. He has extensive consulting experience and is the scientific adviser of the German Customer Satisfaction Barometer. Professor Meyer has published several books and many articles in scholarly journals and he currently serves on the editorial advisory board of the *International Journal of Service Industry Management*.

Lyn Randall is a Senior Lecturer in the Department of Services Industries, Bournemouth University. She has ten years of management experience in the hospitality industry and is currently completing her doctorate, which is concerned with service quality in hospital hotel services. Recent publications include a number of articles, papers at international conferences and a management brief relating to aspects of her research.

Bengt Sahlberg began his career as a research leader at the Nordic Institute for Studies in Urban and Regional Planning, Stockholm. He later became Executive Vice-President of the Swedish Tourist Board and Vice-Chancellor of the Mid-Sweden University, Ostersund, Sweden, where he is now Professor and Head of the Department of Tourism. His current research includes destination marketing, mental maps, decision processes, travel and risks, IT in tourism and tourism development.

Eberhard E. Scheuing is Professor of Marketing, Director of the Business Research Institute and Director of Executive Education at St John's University, New York, USA. As Founder and President of the International Service Quality Association (ISQA), he co-chairs the prestigious series of international conferences on Quality in Services (QUIS). To date, he has published more than 500 articles and 22 books and he is co-editor of *The Service Quality Handbook*.

Martin Senior is Head, Business Administration, IHTTI School of Hotel Management, Neuchâtel, Switzerland. Prior to this, he worked as Project Manager for the Standards

Section at the Hotel and Catering Training Company, UK, where he was concerned with developing and implementing occupational standards and national vocational qualifications. His research interests focus on hotel service quality issues.

Edward V. Staros is Vice-President, Operations, of the Ritz-Carlton Hotel Company. He joined Ritz-Carlton in 1983 as Corporate Director of Rooms Operations and later General Manager of the Ritz-Carlton Atlanta, Georgia. In 1986, he was promoted to General Manager of the Ritz-Carlton Buckhead and became Regional Vice-President two years later. He now oversees the operations of 30 Ritz-Carlton hotels and resorts as well as taking responsibility for pre-opening planning.

Barbara E. Sutton is Human Resources Manager and UK Training Co-ordinator based at the Holiday Inn Crowne Plaza, Manchester, UK. She previously worked in Personnel and Training in the manufacturing sector and joined Holiday Inn in 1985 to assist in the opening of one of the first Crowne Plaza hotels in Europe. She subsequently assumed responsibility for the co-ordination of training throughout Holiday Inn's UK operations.

Eliza Ching-Yick Tse is an Associate Professor in the Department of Hospitality and Tourism Management, Virginia Polytechnic Institute and State University, USA, where she also completed her doctorate. She has held managerial positions and served as a consultant in both the USA and Hong Kong. Her main research interests are in the areas of strategic management and organizational policy, hospitality research and development activities, cost control and market analysis.

Joseph J. West is Chairman, Department of Hospitality Administration, College of Business, The Florida State University. He has held numerous managerial positions in the hospitality industry, including Vice-President, Operations, Spring Garden Grill and Bar/Franklin's Off Friendly restaurant company. He co-wrote *Strategic Management in the Hospitality Industry* (with Michael Olsen and Eliza Tse) and his research interests are strategic planning and quality service as a competitive tactic.

Peter Westerbarkey is a Doctoral Candidate at Ludwig Maximilians University, Munich, Germany. He studied economics at the Johannes Gutenberg University, Mainz, and has taught services marketing on undergraduate, graduate and executive level programmes. He has also published articles and case studies on aspects of services marketing and hospitality management.

Robert H. Woods is an Associate Professor, School of Hotel, Restaurant and Institutional Management, Michigan State University, USA. He specializes in human resources and management and has authored more than 40 articles and three textbooks. He is an active consultant and he also teaches executive education programmes at Cornell University. Prior to his current post, he owned and successfully operated a chain of restaurants and a hospitality consulting company.

1

Exploring the service quality paradigm: an overview

Michael D. Olsen, Richard Teare and Evert Gummesson

INTRODUCTION

The decade of the 1990s began with renewed emphasis by businesses in their thinking about improving service quality to the customer. The emphasis was upon delivering the best service possible, that is delighting customers by providing services which exceed their expectations. Firm after firm has embraced this idea and revamped the processes they utilize when interacting with the customer. In improving the quality of service delivery processes, many businesses consider this new-found orientation to quality customer service to be one of the dominant competitive methods making up their entire strategy.

At the mid-point of this decade we can now witness the successes of those firms who have emphasized service quality for some years. Further, we can expect to see a continued emphasis on service quality as an essential part of the competitive methods of high customer contact firms. Since the concept of service has become so important to industry in general and to the hospitality industry in particular, the purpose of this book is to share with the reader the current practices in the hospitality industry and to offer some insights into how service will evolve in the future.

This international contemporary look at the concept of service quality as applied to the hospitality industry has, primarily, a Western orientation and includes authors from Europe and North America. This orientation is based upon the fact that the body of literature in the field has its roots in these regions and the authors contributing to the book have drawn upon prior work. Thus, the book reflects the nature of service as influenced by Western industrial organizations and excludes, though not deliberately, the unique dimensions of service quality which a study of Asia–Pacific hospitality organizations would yield. The book extends these Western roots to applications in the hospitality industry. This extension is characterized by new conceptual insights, case histories of best practices, recommendations for further applications and suggestions for new thinking about the service paradigm as it applies to the hospitality industry.

The effective management of service quality in an organizational context is, without question, a multidisciplinary paradigm. It is anchored in the relationship between the customer and the service provider. This unique diadic relationship is dynamic, that is, service is a process. Managing the process to try to provide quality service requires a thorough understanding of concepts in such fields as organizational theory and behaviour, management functions such as human resources, operations and marketing, work process design and flow, human behaviour and expectations, quality control and information processing, to mention only a few. The literature on service quality spans a range of thought which includes ideas from basic applications to propositions of theoretical relationships. It appears at this stage of the literature development that no one archetype of service has emerged. Rather, it continues to develop in discipline-specific areas, with synthesis of thought occurring frequently.

Because of the diverse, multidisciplinary nature of the service quality literature, this book does not attempt to create an overall archetype for the service quality paradigm in the hospitality industry. Rather, it is organized with a focus upon organizational behaviour relationships. More specifically, it addresses the human element in the diadic relationship between customer and service provider. This focus has its primary emphasis in the intangibles of service quality and how they can be improved in this exchange. The importance of quality throughout the service delivery process pervades most of the discussion in this text; however, the mechanics or tangibles of service delivery are left for others to develop in a forum of their choosing. Also important in the offerings contained in this volume are some new insights on how the concepts of service quality apply to the hospitality industry and how they might be viewed differently. It is hoped that these fresh insights might push the reader to consider questioning how they are utilizing current concepts in an applied setting and to contemplate new thoughts and applications.

PART ONE – SERVICE QUALITY CONCEPTS

The goal in Part One is to establish an understanding of the basic elements of the service quality concept in the hospitality industry. An attempt is made to provide working definitions of these elements which are anchored in the general service literature and applied to the hospitality industry context. The concepts of service quality, the influence of organization culture on achieving service quality and the role of communications in accomplishing overall success are also covered.

Nick Johns develops a thorough definition of service quality with specific applications to the hospitality industry. He examines the evolution of the development of the concept of quality. This examination is done within the context of the general conditions existing within the business environment of hospitality organizations. In particular, social and economic issues are explored with regard to how they affect the competitive industry atmosphere. The impact that these issues have upon the industry leads Johns to the development of a model that identifies the strategies that industry firms will have to follow in future.

Any strategy which embodies the delivery of quality service will have to consider the human element both within the organization and external to it, in the form of the customer. The argument often made is that the employee should be viewed as the internal customer and thus should receive management's attention in equal proportions to the external customer. Both participate in the simultaneous production and consumption of the service product and therefore should be accorded the same degree of interest and respect. In order to accomplish this type of orientation, Robert Woods and Eberhard Scheuing provide a look at concepts and recommendations on how to approach this essential ingredient of service quality.

Robert Woods explores the concept of organizational culture and the many forms that it can take in achieving service quality. He addresses the need for hospitality firms to integrate the processes and procedures for service design and delivery with organizational culture. He builds his argument upon the theoretical framework of culture in organizations and applies it to both commercial and non-commercial hospitality organizations. Suggestions and implications for hospitality managers are provided as they attempt to integrate the service concept into the organization's culture.

In a similar vein, Eberhard Scheuing utilizes the concept of the value chain to identify the role of the internal customer and how an organization's culture, which recognizes the value of satisfying the expectations of this internal customer, is important in providing quality service to the external customer. He offers suggestions for creating a quality service culture, by emphasizing that it is important to delight not only the external customer but also the internal one, the employee. He recommends ways of serving the internal customer, including ideas such as exploring their expectations regarding what quality service they expect to receive from the firm and how important these expectations are. Measuring the internal customers' level of satisfaction against expectations allows the organization to then meet and exceed the internal customers' needs, which should then, in turn, improve their level of output in meeting the external customers' desires.

Organizational culture, in part, is a function of the communication system which exists within the organization. Svein Larsen reports on research which explores the role of communication in organizational climates, culture and traditions. He explores the theoretical and practical dimensions of this important ingredient of organizational life and then demonstrates its significance through reporting upon a research project which was undertaken in the context of the cruise industry.

PART TWO – INTEGRATING SERVICE QUALITY

Defining service quality and then integrating it into the organization's culture is no simple matter. In order to successfully integrate service quality as an essential competitive method, the organization must be effectively structured to accomplish this goal. This structuring must occur at all levels in the organization. The chapters in Part Two attempt to provide some guidance in this regard and offer examples of how it may take place.

A comprehensive review of the importance and role of the human resources function by Nicholas Horney sets the stage for this structuring process. His chapter provides a thorough review of the key result areas which must be re-engineered if quality service is to be provided. He presents this discussion within the context of total quality management and provides examples of its application to three well-known North American hospitality firms.

Most would argue that an effective service culture is impossible to maintain without an appropriate overall structure of the firm and its human resources function. Only then can such an organizational unit perform its role effectively and efficiently. One of the most important activities that it does perform is the selection of employees who match the organization's culture. This critical activity is discussed by Elizabeth Ineson, Anne Dickinson and Barbara Sutton. They report on research into two selection techniques to determine predictive validities in the hotel sector. This research suggests which selection criteria work best in this industry sector and draws conclusions on their relationship to service quality.

Once properly selected, the service delivery employee must undergo training. Two approaches are provided for this difficult task. First, Bonnie Farber Canziani describes a bi-phasal service diagnostics training system. This system is designed to prepare service employees as diagnosticians, problem-solvers, and designers of mini-training systems for their departments. Each phase of the training process is explained in the context of the hotel sector where pilot tests have been conducted.

The issue of training is approached differently by Lyn Randall and Martin Senior, who look at the role of the UK government in attempting to rationalize and standardize vocational training in over 160 industry sectors. The approach to training at this level is to define national quality standards for service and then design appropriate work-based learning in order to provide the opportunity for all employees to obtain a national vocational qualification for the job they do. This contribution provides an evaluation of the approach and its relevance to the provision of quality service.

PART THREE – ORGANIZATIONAL PERSPECTIVES ON SERVICE QUALITY

Organization culture must be supported by an effective human resource capability which can select and train the employee to deliver a high standard of service quality. The question often left unanswered in this statement of relationships is 'What is service quality?' While it is one of the most troublesome questions to answer, some help is provided by Anton Meyer and Peter Westerbarkey. They escort the reader through the issues surrounding the measurement and management of guest satisfaction. They offer several approaches to guest satisfaction measurement and discuss the strengths and weaknesses related to the attempt to achieve objective, valid measurements. They provide a multidimensional model of guest satisfaction measurement to assist service managers with this important ingredient in the quest to achieve maximum quality.

Communication is included in Part One, as it relates to the internal workings of the service organization, but communication is also important to the guest. In order to discuss the role of technology and its relationship to service quality, Bengt Sahlberg explores how electronic information can improve the tourist experience. He identifies which characteristics and qualities are important for information systems used by the guest in obtaining information about touristic experiences.

One of the major trends emerging as an area of importance to the hospitality provider is the role of the environmental or green movement. Understanding the role of the environment and how it affects the quality of service operations and delivery is discussed by Sören Bergström and Evert Gummesson. They provide an interesting look at how a restaurant in a research laboratory setting has addressed the important dimension of service quality. The results of this testing of the *green service quality dimension* are then translated into general green quality indicators which are relevant to the hospitality industry.

PART FOUR – NEW DIRECTIONS FOR SERVICE QUALITY

This section reflects an effort to move the quality service paradigm forward from its present state. While the earlier contributions are designed to accomplish this same goal, the authors provide a more theoretical look at expanding our understanding of what service quality is and how it can be delivered. New alternatives and models create for the reader another level of analysis with which to explore this elusive paradigm. Expanding on the idea of the quality circle, Bob Brotherton and Mike Coyle build upon their earlier work and present new perspectives and ideas relating to the issue of quality as it pertains to hospitality organizations. These authors further their work by additions to their original model of service quality. They provide what they feel to be a more accurate assessment of how the instabilities and complexities of the service environment affect the delivery of service quality.

Gail Ayala, Edward Staros and Joseph West, using an extensive review of the quality award-winning success of the Ritz-Carlton hotel chain, present a model of the role of quality in the guest's decision-making process. This model builds upon current services marketing literature and stresses the importance of quality as the guest anticipates an experience, engages the service event, and evaluates it in the post-experience framework.

Service quality is often expressed in behavioural terms with the assumption that certain behaviours are universally desirable regardless of the type of hospitality organization. Cherylynn Becker suggests that a more discriminating approach to the determination of appropriate behaviours is warranted, based upon her research into the effectiveness of various behavioural elements in different types of hospitality firms. She offers some interesting insights into new ways of accomplishing the match between service quality, strategic methods and organizational structure.

Finally, Eliza Tse extends the concept of total quality management to reflect the strategic opportunities for integrating organizational initiatives by focusing on service quality.

This text adds several new views to the service quality paradigm in the hospitality industry. While its focus is more behavioural than operational, it is our hope that it will assist the reader in applying new alternatives in the quest for service quality. Our purpose is to fill a void in the literature on service quality as it applies to the hospitality industry, and we hope that we have established a helpful framework on which to build and elaborate our understanding of the theory and practice of service quality in hospitality organizations.

PART ONE
SERVICE QUALITY CONCEPTS

2

The developing role of quality in the hospitality industry

Nick Johns

Service quality has been a major preoccupation of the hospitality industry throughout the 1980s and the early 1990s. Quality management systems have been clearly identified as a means of increasing the professionalism and social competence of staff, while developments such as customer care programmes and quality teams have produced notable improvements in the efficiency with which guests' needs are fulfilled. Service quality initiatives also have an impact upon marketing potential and upon the attraction and recruitment of quality personnel in a shrinking skilled labour market. In addition, service quality is generally viewed as a source of customer loyalty and therefore as a means of maintaining market share.

This chapter examines the development of the quality concept within the hospitality industry. It discusses social, environmental and economic pressures currently facing the industry and identifies the strategic choices available to the hospitality manager during the next decade and beyond. Two aspects of service quality are particularly relevant: the question of what it is, i.e. its definition, specification and measurement, and the question of how it may be maximized by careful management.

INTRODUCTION

Definitions of quality have become increasingly sophisticated during the past two decades. The concept of quality as 'excellence' has now been largely superseded by definitions emphasizing production or delivery contexts. Such definitions as 'conformance to requirements' (Thomas, 1965) or even 'zero defects' (Gregory, 1972) relate quality to the match between product and manufacturing specification. Others tackle quality from the customer's point of view, for example 'fitness for purpose' (Juran, 1979). An important challenge facing the hospitality industry is to reconcile the quality of the service actually produced with that perceived by the guest.

Early attempts to specify and measure hospitality quality were concerned with tangibles such as food and physical facilities; examples are the rating systems of Michelin and the Automobile Association. During the past decade, however, there has been increasing interest in specifying intangible aspects of service. For example Martin (1986) proposes nine 'conviviality factors' which include 'problem-solving' and 'tact'. There have also been attempts to measure guests' perception of service quality. Parasuraman *et al.* (1985) have suggested that the actual quality of a service is measurable as the 'gap' between the quality perceived by guests and that which they expect. They propose a ten-dimensional model of service quality which can be used for designing questionnaires to assess guests' perceptions and expectations of a service. Other psychometric techniques such as perceptual mapping have also been used in this respect (Lewis, 1985).

Development of quality management in the hospitality industry has largely followed the pattern set by the manufacturing sector. Early approaches were aimed at specifying and controlling the quality of tangible aspects such as food and accommodation. Such mechanistic approaches are suitable for systemized mass catering and therefore for in-flight meals and some public sector catering. They have also been adopted by fast-food chains, but offer little assistance to the management of the meal experience, or to getting the best from hotel service.

The hospitality industry has therefore turned successively to quality assurance (QA) models, and to total quality management (TQM). Both concepts are currently evolving to fit the industry's needs. Product-oriented concerns of manufacturing industry, such as statistical process control and 'zero defects', are of little interest to the hospitality industry, which stresses first appearances and one-off encounters between guests and employees. Service quality management therefore emphasizes training, customer care and sensitivity to guests' needs. Many proven techniques from manufacturing industry, for instance team-building and communication systems, are, however, equally applicable to hospitality organizations and are steadily being adopted.

CURRENT ISSUES IN SERVICE QUALITY SPECIFICATION

The goods/services debate still underlies much of the thinking behind the quality of hospitality service. For example, it is difficult to determine how much the tangible food product contributes to customers' appreciation of a meal experience. This is potentially important to the specification and management of restaurant service quality, yet very little research has been forthcoming. There are numerous existing theories and models of 'product' and 'service', mostly developed for use in other sectors. They have been reviewed and summarized by Shams and Hales (1989), who suggest that manufacturing and service industries form a continuum of steadily varying proportions of integral 'goods' and 'services'. The debate continues (Schwartz, 1991, 1992) as the 'service revolution' gathers momentum and more and more traditionally manufacturing-oriented organizations emphasize quality service as a differentiator in the marketplace (Berry and Parasuraman, 1992).

The ephemeral, personal nature of service quality is another important ingredient of current thinking. Modern writers stress the Herzberg-like relationship between 'motivating' and 'hygiene' quality factors. The former are capable of increasing satisfaction in proportion to their presence. The latter are only capable of decreasing satisfaction if they are absent. 'Herzberg factors' differ between hotel sectors, i.e. they are not likely to be the same in a two-star as in a five-star hotel (Balmer and Baum, 1993). They probably also change with time, as yesterday's technology and luxury give way to newer motivating factors and the older standards and styles are continually relegated to the 'hygiene' category. Whether a particular quality attribute is a 'hygiene' or a 'motivating' factor is also a matter for the individual customer. Some organizations now try specifically to identify the 'kiss off factor' (KOF) – the last straw which turns a particular individual's experience from overall positive to overall negative.

Tangible aspects of the hospitality product are more easily specified and controlled than intangibles. Hence tangible factors would arguably be the first to take the downward step from 'motivating' to 'hygiene'. Nevertheless, classifications such as star ratings, based upon tangible quality, continue to be the norm in hotels and restaurants. Callan (1989, 1990) has made some interesting studies of the relationship between the ratings of hotels and the quality perceptions of their management and guests. The general feeling that star ratings assess 'hygiene' factors rather than those contributing to 'motivation' is expressed by the current interest in quality accreditations such as BS5750 and ISO 9000 (Lee-Mortimer and Buxton, 1991). Some tourist authorities, notably the Scottish Tourist Board (Lennon and Mercer, 1993) have also introduced additional ratings based on the evaluation of service by qualified 'mystery' observers.

Quality audits, conducted by outside consultants or, within large organizations, by trained specialists, are an important means of monitoring quality in the hospitality industry (Willborn, 1986). Audits are increasingly moving from a management perspective towards greater customer orientation. One manifestation of this is the use of 'walk through' audits which follow the customer journey from the car park through the hospitality experience and back to the exit (Fitzsimmons and Maures, 1991). Guest surveys also continue to be widely employed, although they have been strongly criticized. The main objections are that guest survey cards are not generally based upon established theory (i.e. they have poor construct validity) and that the number returned is both very small and generally skewed towards dissatisfaction (i.e. poor statistical validity) (Barsky, 1992).

THEORETICAL DEVELOPMENTS

There have been several attempts to explain the nature of service quality in terms of theoretical models. Early work by Nightingale (1985) identified two 'qualities': that of the service offering, as perceived by the provider, and that of the received service, as perceived by the customer. This notion of service quality has been successively refined into the 'gap' model of Parasuraman *et al.* (1985). Gap theory identifies five discrepancies, or 'gaps', which may develop in the service supply process and interfere with the service experience. These are shown in Table 2.1.

Brogowicz *et al.* (1990) have developed the theories of Parasuraman *et al.*, and of other groups, into a general model of service delivery, an adaptation of which is shown in Figure 2.1.

As mentioned above, gap theory identifies the perception gap (no. 5) as the most important in terms of the assessment of 'actual' service quality. Parasuraman *et al.* have proposed that the gap between perceived and expected service quality be taken as the definition of service quality itself. This is justifiable on the basis that:

Table 2.1 *The five 'gaps' between service production and delivery (Parasuraman et al., 1985)*

Gap no.	Designation	Location
1	Positioning	Between management perceptions of customer expectations and the expectations themselves
2	Specification	Between management perceptions of customer expectations and the actual service specified
3	Delivery	Between the service specified and that actually delivered
4	Communication	Between the service actually delivered and that externally communicated to customers (e.g. through advertising)
5	Perception	Between the service quality perceived and that expected by the customer

- quality is always measured against expectation (thus it is possible to have an excellent hamburger stall as well as an excellent five-star restaurant);
- the service process involves the customer as a key player (thus there is no service except that perceived by the customer);
- service excellence only exists insofar as it is *perceived* as excellence by customers.

Parasuraman *et al.* (1991) have developed and successively refined a questionnaire instrument called the SERVQUAL Scale. This is designed to elicit customers' expectations and actual perceptions of a series of quality attributes. Using factor analysis, these attributes have been grouped into five categories, as shown in Table 2.2.

The SERVQUAL instrument is presently little more than a research tool, arguably too cumbersome for general use. It has been successfully applied to practical problems by a number of researchers, but it has also received some severe criticism (Carmen, 1990; Cronin and Taylor, 1992). However, its theoretical base does point the way forward for more rigorous service quality monitoring. For example, Barsky (1992) has developed hotel guest survey cards which ask guests to compare their actual perceived service with their expectations.

Other writers have also proposed structures for assessing service quality. In particular Grönroos (1983) offers a model (Figure 2.2) based on the relationship between corporate image, technical quality and functional quality. He defines the technical content of the service as the outcome received by the service customer, e.g. the quality of the haircut, banking transaction or professional advice. The functional content is the way the service is delivered, e.g. promptly, efficiently or amiably. Like Parasuraman and Brogowicz, Grönroos stresses the significance of the gap between perceived and expected quality. In another paper (Grönroos, 1988) he reviews current literature and identifies six criteria of good perceived service quality. These are shown in Table 2.3.

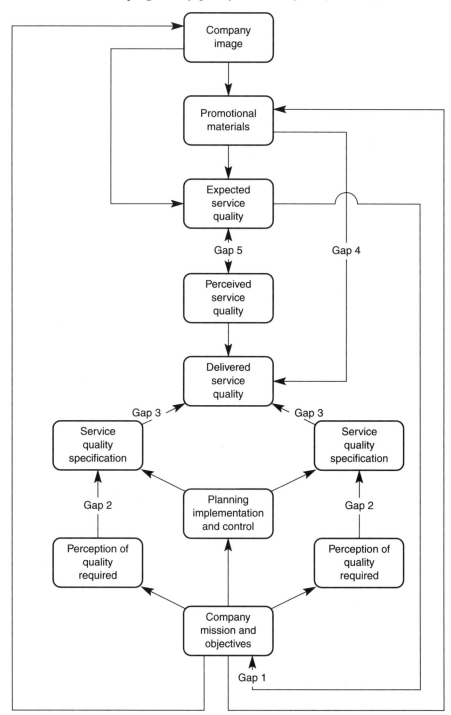

Figure 2.1   *The 'gap' model of service delivery*
Source: Adapted from Brogowicz *et al.* (1990)

Table 2.2   *The five SERVQUAL attribute categories (Parasuraman et al., 1991)*

No.	Designation	Examples
1	Tangibles*	Appearance of personnel, facilities, equipment etc.
2	Reliability	Timeliness, error-free records, service right first time etc.
3	Responsiveness	Communication promptness, helpfulness etc.
4	Assurance	Confidence, security, courtesy, knowledge etc.
5	Empathy	Individual attention, convenience, specific needs etc.

* These are the factors identified in this group's original work. In subsequent studies (e.g. the reference quoted) there was a tendency for 'tangibles' to further subdivide into aspects concerned with premises and equipment and those to do with employees.

In summary it seems that there is good agreement, if not a precise correlation, between the theories proposed by the Nordic school (Grönroos, Gummesson and their co-workers) and the North American school (Parasuraman, Zeithaml, Berry, Brogowicz and others).

Other workers have attempted to link the specification of quality to the management needs of service providers. Such proposals largely tend to be empirical observations of 'what works', unlike the elegantly substantiated theories of the Nordic and North

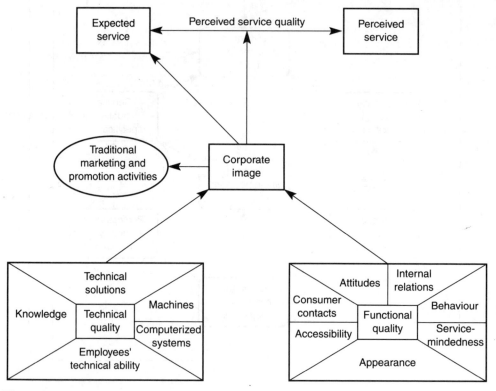

Figure 2.2   *Grönroos' model of service quality delivery*
Source: Grönroos (1983)

Table 2.3 *Six criteria of good perceived service quality*

No.	Designation	Description
1	Professionalism and skill	Customers see the service provider as knowledgeable and able to solve their problems in a professional way
2	Attitudes and behaviour	Customers perceive a genuine, friendly concern for them and their problems
3	Access and flexibility	Customers feel that they have easy, timely access and that the service provider is prepared to adjust to their needs.
4	Reliability and trustworthiness	Customers can trust the service provider to keep promises and act in their best interests
5	Recovery	Customers know that immediate corrective action will be taken if anything goes wrong
6	Reputation and credibility	Customers believe that the brand image stands for good performance and accepted values

Adapted from Grönroos (1988)

American schools. Nevertheless, these suggestions contribute to the debate. For example, Lawton (1992) compares the performance measures employed by service providers and customers as shown in Table 2.4. Lawton also explains how substitute characteristics may be used, in the absence of reliable measures of actual service. He suggests drawing up a quality table for a service product, listing measurable surrogates such as the number of help calls, waiting times etc. However, the example he chooses (a training manual) lends itself to such treatment much more than, for example, reception service at a five-star hotel.

Brown *et al.* (1990) have also studied the differences between provider and consumer perceptions of service quality. They analyse the problem strategically in terms of the two-by-two matrix shown in Figure 2.3. Quadrant A in this model indicates a large gap between experience and perception on both the supply and demand sides. In quadrant C customers are unhappy with the service and may be changing their brand allegiance, but the provider is unaware of this. Brown *et al.* (1990) advise managers to strive to move towards quadrant D, where there is an optimum balance between the perceptions of both the provider and consumer of a service. Interestingly, they make no claims for mysterious quadrant B, where in principle the customer delights in a quality which the provider perceives as poor. Nevertheless, their model begins to point the way towards

Table 2.4 *Comparison of service performance measures.*

Provider priorities	Customer priorities
Schedule	Timeliness
Standards	Certainty
Cost to produce	Cost to own

Adapted from Lawton (1992)

Service quality concepts

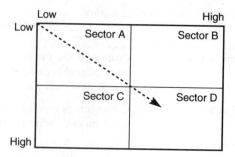

Figure 2.3   *Matrix for identifying service quality strategy*
Source: Brown *et al.* (1990)

a more substantive relationship between gap theory and quality management practice.

CURRENT ISSUES IN SERVICE QUALITY MANAGEMENT

Numerous papers have been written extolling the virtues of various aspects of quality management in the hospitality industry. These have included customer care programmes (Price, 1989), team-building exercises (Martillano, 1989), internal marketing (Lewis, 1989) and the use of information technology (Records and Glenny, 1991). It is clear, however, that these are at best only isolated facets of a successful quality management strategy. Brown (1990) warns against 'quick fix' solutions and adds that organizations often do not have a fundamental understanding of how a successful service culture may be created. Harari (1992) analyses a case study exemplifying bad service quality provision and concludes that the core problems lie with top management, not with front-line employees or middle managers. He identifies the following five typical problems:

- Top management provides employees with no priorities, or with the wrong priorities.
- Middle managers and front-line employees are not empowered to make appropriate corrective decisions on the spot.
- The environment or structure of the organization does not encourage innovation and creativity.
- Top management is complacent (i.e. attitude located in quadrant C of Figure 2.3).
- Top management is out of touch (i.e. it has lost control of one of the gaps in Table 2.1: probably delivery (gap 3) or communication (gap 4)).

Numerous other writers have arrived at similar conclusions and it is generally accepted that senior management commitment is essential to the establishment of a true quality culture.

   Hospitality organizations have responded to the quality management challenge in a number of fundamental strategic ways. Some have asked themselves what business they are really in and have made a conscious movement towards the service end of the goods/services continuum. For example, there has been a growing increase in the use of *sous vide* and other food technologies. These greatly reduce the amount of time restaurant staff spend in the product-oriented activity of food production, and emphasize service quality by freeing them to work more directly at the customer interface (Johns and Wheeler, 1991). Analogous developments are taking place in the design of accommodation and reception facilities. The aim has been to reduce servicing requirements and therefore to improve service efficiency without sacrificing any of the features which customers regard as essential (Johns, 1993). Parallel to this shift of focus towards service there has been a tendency to reduce the levels of hierarchy in organizational structures. 'Flat', or 'upside-down', organizations are appearing, which emphasize participative team work and increasingly empower employees to make decisions about their work. For example, housekeeper posts have disappeared from some hotels, and room maids are responsible for checking rooms. This reduces communication problems, increases personal feelings of commitment and encourages greater team work (Fender and Litteljohn, 1992). The term 'upside-down organization' is increasingly employed in recognition of the important role that front-line staff play in providing service quality. Larsen and Rapp (1993) recommend that the value of front-line employees should be reflected in their selection, pay and prestige, if empowerment programmes are to stand any chance of success.

Besides the shift to service and to flatter organizational structures, a number of hospitality companies have also adopted QA programmes. The principal ingredients of these are listed by Comen (1989) as:

- sponsorship by top management;
- resource allocation, i.e. budget, space and personnel;
- a good cultural fit between the programme itself and the philosophy and values of the organization;
- allocation of time for preparation and training;
- a QA director who reports directly to the person in charge of day-to-day events.

Practical examples of such systems have been reported in the literature (Fender and Litteljohn, 1992; Smith, 1991). Walker and Salameh (1990) were able to identify significant service improvements in a sample of US hotels which had maintained QA programmes for eight years, compared with a control group which had not. However, Silvestro *et al.* (1990), who studied quality monitoring and management in a range of service industries, noted that the hotel sector tended to show a reactive approach. Their evidence suggests that service quality management in the hospitality industry is in its infancy.

Numerous writers have put forward recipes for service quality management. For example, Horovitz and Cudennec-Poon (1990) list five 'commitment efforts' which are necessary to ensure quality in any service sector industry. Sharp (1990) proposes seven basic principles of quality management in the hotel industry which he calls the 'seven Cs'. Brown (1990) identifies five key areas of service management strategy, to which he gives the mnemonic 'REACH'. These three approaches are shown in Table 2.5. Several features are common to all of them, and no doubt they contribute substantially to the programmes of their authors. However, none gives more than a passing glimpse of the total service quality management picture.

Table 2.5   *Summary of three checklists for managing service quality*

Horowitz and Cudennec-Poon (1990)	'Seven Cs' (Sharp, 1990)	'REACH' (Brown, 1990)
Quality care	Comprehension	Research
Customer care	Corporate culture	Empower
'FLIP' care	No compromise	Acknowledge
(i.e. front-line	Management	Communicate
people care)	credibility	
Communication care	Controls of standards	Help
Lead care	Creativity	
	Continuity	

PRESSURES AND CHALLENGES FACING THE HOSPITALITY INDUSTRY

A number of environmental and socio-economic factors are expected to influence the development of the hospitality industry during the next decade. These include increasing competition, a greater demand for productivity, enhanced technological sophistication, demographic change, and a growing awareness of 'green' issues. All are likely to have an impact upon the perception, management and significance of service quality in hotels and restaurants.

Business competition is ever-present in the hospitality industry as in all commercial enterprise, resulting in a constant search for new ways in which to out-distance competitors. Changing fashions and legislation make it constantly necessary to upgrade the quality of the tangible hospitality product, and so too do the growing wealth and technological awareness of all market segments. For example, it has become commonplace to install data points in hotel bedrooms, and also to change complete bathroom suites on a regular basis, as new colours and styles come into fashion. Such developments are likely to intensify further in the future, yet they are also likely to be regarded more and more as 'hygiene factors'. The tangible domain is likely to decrease steadily in importance as an opportunity for developing competitive edge. However, at the budget end of the market there is no doubt scope for using the novelty value of technology as a marketing point.

Current emphasis on service excellence is expected to continue into the foreseeable future. The pursuit of quality will require development of more effective ways of specifying and measuring service quality. Targets will increasingly have to be set by management and employees, based on surrogate measures such as queuing times, speed of response to queries and paperwork processing accuracy. Accurate assessment of customer perceptions will also become more and more crucial to the success of management initiatives. The coming decade will demand a refinement of theory in this respect, plus the development of more effective measurement techniques and instruments.

Increasing competition will mean greater marketing pressure. The hospitality industry's track record is poor in terms of the development and management of its marketing concept (Lin, 1993). This deficiency tends to widen the communication gap (i.e. gap no. 4 in Table 2.1) between what is communicated promotionally to guests and what they actually receive. Plugging this gap will be an important challenge for the hospitality industry.

The present demand for productivity is likely to further intensify, in an industry which is noted for its poor track record in this respect (Witt and Witt, 1989). The traditional view that there exists a trade-off between quality and productivity is in fact only true if quality is defined as 'excellence'. Such an absolute definition is now regarded as undesirable; definitions such as 'fitness for purpose at the price' or 'meeting the customer's expectations' are more compatible with the demands of productivity. Indeed, as has been discussed above, initiatives aimed at maximizing service quality frequently also result in improved productivity.

Nevertheless it is likely that social, demographic and political changes will bring greater reliance upon technology and lower levels of staffing. For example, a recent international study (Prais *et al.*, 1989) indicates labour requirements in London hotels to be 50 per cent greater than those in equivalent units in Germany. It is unlikely that such imbalances will continue in the face of increasing European unity and international competition. The hospitality industry will no doubt find itself in the position of seeking greater revenue from ever-decreasing staffing levels. This is likely to further intensify the need for quality enhancement.

Technological change is another easily identifiable environmental challenge for the hospitality industry, though the actual nature of innovations and of their impact upon society are less predictable. Technology increases demand by accustoming guests to a widening range of day-to-day conveniences, both at work and in leisure. It also provides hospitality managers with the means to solve problems of productivity, communication and marketing. Though 'technology' is often taken as being synonymous with 'information technology', it should be remembered that the scope of technological advance is much wider than this. For instance, it encompasses the technology of food, furnishing and finishing materials and also of construction innovations. As discussed above, all of these potentially contribute to the quality of the hotel product and the efficiency of service provision.

Information technology is, however, likely to have an increasing impact on the provision of hospitality services. Developments in global reservation systems make it increasingly easier to reach customers early, to facilitate the 'service journey'. Specific customer groups may also be targeted: Far Eastern business travellers, for example, for whom a specialized guest experience can be tailored. Hotel premises management systems (PMS) are being linked to an ever-widening range of functions. This means that as well as providing general services such as individually controlled room climates and guaranteed security, the PMS can also provide guests with a personalized choice of 'extras' for which they are automatically billed. Currently available services include automatic minibars, in-room pay-per-view, video cassette players, modem and data systems and automatic central billing from bars, restaurants or fitness facilities (Reid and Sandler, 1992). The list of such services continues to grow, but each new addition tends eventually to be taken for granted as a 'hygiene' aspect of quality, rather than a 'motivator'.

Information technology will also have a growing back-of-house role to play. It is currently possible to network budgets, business forecasts, time accounting, productivity standards and other management information within one system. It is also possible to link together bookings, room status, yield management, personnel scheduling and task allocation (Records and Glenny, 1991). Such a system becomes a powerful tool for optimizing service standards because supply, demand and hence timeliness can all be managed. Other service sectors also currently use information technology to collect information about the quality of service performance (Furey, 1991). This makes it possible to gauge the progress of a service quality improvement system. It may also facilitate the reward and recognition of outstanding service by individuals or teams.

As many commentators have pointed out, the West is currently experiencing significant demographic change. The so-called 'post-war baby boomers', who are now in middle age, were followed by a slower period of population growth. During the next decade the number of young people will continue to shrink relative to increasing numbers of older individuals in their forties and fifties and above. This is likely to affect both the clientele and employees of the hospitality industry.

The needs and tastes of guests will tend to change. There will be an emphasis on comfort and convenience in rooms, and probably an increased demand for disabled facilities. Swimming pools, saunas, jacuzzis and other passive leisure installations will be more in demand than the activity equipment currently in vogue. Older guests judge hospitality services by different quality attributes and they are unlikely to regard the same aspects of quality as being important (Ananth *et al.*, 1992). Nostalgic themes, colours and designs may grow in importance. Politeness and patience will become premium attributes of service quality.

At the same time, the hospitality industry will face the growing necessity of employing older staff. This will probably be reflected in greater training requirements and perhaps in a general loss of employee flexibility. Interactions between older guests and older service personnel will be qualitatively different from those between old and young, and some care may need to be given to choreographing service encounters. The industry has the opportunity of reducing such problems by tackling the current rate of labour turnover, so that trained and experienced personnel grow old with the organization, but this too may have its drawbacks. Older employees will in general expect higher salaries and this may place a strain on both the quality and productivity of service, as discussed above.

Growing environmental awareness will also affect the development of quality within the hospitality industry. Organizations will increasingly be required to maintain the standard of their environment, through planning, construction and the use of environment technologies. For instance, tourist hotels in exotic locations are already favouring local materials and craftsmen, which minimizes the negative impact upon the built environment and economy. Use of environmental technology, such as the current measures used to protect coral reefs and rain forests from tourist pollution, will no doubt spread as the sensitivity of other situations is noted.

The near future will also see an increase in 'green' marketing. Tourist resorts will promote environment-saving aspects of their operation. Restaurants will (continue to) emphasize their moral stance on issues such as veal production, 'organic' vegetables and line-caught tuna. Guest concerns will also be reflected in an increased demand for 'green' hotel rooms, featuring purified air and drinking water (Rowe, 1992). An interesting problem is posed by waste, which tends to increase in proportion to luxury. As guests become more aware of the environmental impact of waste water, waste heat and solid wastes, hotels will increasingly face the challenge of providing luxury service in a way that is perceived as environmentally friendly. One aspect of this will no doubt include developing an organizational culture of ecological awareness among hospitality employees.

STRATEGIC DEVELOPMENTS

Three main strategic options are available to the hospitality industry in terms of quality management. These are:

- to improve the specification and provision of the service quality 'product';
- to understand the needs of customers more fully and tailor provision accordingly;
- to encourage brand loyalty, so that a better match is achieved between a specific quality of service and the perceived needs of a known customer segment.

These three strategic thrusts are not mutually exclusive and they are currently being employed by a number of hospitality organizations. There is little doubt that they will form the basis for service quality development in the foreseeable future.

The evidence discussed above suggests that quality specification and provision in the hospitality industry are being vigorously developed, but are still far from forming a practicable ideal. The industry appears to be lagging behind other service sectors in the quality race, but it is also clear that some hospitality organizations have made progress far beyond that of most of their competitors. It is likely that this gap will close with increasing competition. The 'quality leaders' will then probably seek their 'edge' through improved scheduling, communications and marketing. The industry is also poised for a much greater uptake of information technology, in line with other service sectors.

To date, comparatively little attention has been given to the design of the service encounter, which is regarded as potentially frail and subject to the whim of service staff (Lockwood and Jones, 1989). In the manufacturing sector the Taguchi approach is increasingly being used to design quality into products (Taguchi, 1981). Taguchi systems aim to build what is learned from the QA process into the design of a new product. In this way the design can be made 'robust', i.e. less sensitive to variations in materials or processing. There is no reason in principle why service systems cannot also be more robustly designed, so that they are less affected by peaks of demand, unusual individual requests, or the tiredness or inexperience of employees. However, such an approach may require greater attention to the analysis and reporting of service faults than is currently the norm.

Increasing competition and demand will also bring a greater need for hospitality organizations to demonstrate their worth by accreditation. Existing hotel award schemes are likely to become more rigorous and will increasingly be supplemented by additional schemes of service accreditation. The industry will no doubt respond by registering with the bodies offering these schemes. More organizations will apply for British and International quality standard awards BS5750 and ISO 9000 (Callan, 1992). In addition, hospitality organizations are increasingly likely to compete for national quality recognition awards, such as those of the National Society for Quality through Teamwork (NSQT), where they have hitherto been poorly represented.

It is possible that the strategy of improving quality provision may have its limitations. The tendency for tangible aspects and technological service improvements to become 'hygiene' factors has already been discussed. The same may eventually apply to the efficiency and timeliness of service if these attributes become the norm through competition. It should also be recognized that the possibilities for choreography of the service itself are not endless. Service quality is no longer the property of service industries but looks set to become the competitive battleground for most industrial sectors, as the 'service revolution' (Berry and Parasuraman, 1992) takes shape. This may eventually relegate any new service product to the scrap-heap of Herzbergian mediocrity soon after its implementation.

An alternative strategy is to develop a more sensitive awareness of the requirements of specific customer groups and to adjust service provision to these needs. Groups of foreign nationals constitute particularly attractive marketing targets. They can be reached by a combination of efficient international reservation facilities, a good reporting network and local marketing. Once in the host country they will be particularly sensitive to a service system aimed at the idiosyncrasies of their national culture. Other targetable customer groups no doubt also exist, and may be identified through detailed analysis of guest records. 'Database marketing' will no doubt assume much greater importance in the hospitality industry of the future (Francese and Renaghan, 1990).

The essence of focusing service upon customers' needs is the definition of quality as 'fitness for purpose at the right price'. Hotels and restaurants must seek to emphasize the most attractive features and to trim out amenities which customers know they are paying for, but do not want (Lewis and Nightingale, 1991). Reception and other services must be made 'robust', i.e. able to cope with cross-cultural expectations, language and other communication difficulties. Hospitality units must learn to assist customers discreetly and acceptably in choosing from the, perhaps bewildering, array of facilities they are offering.

Brand loyalty is expected to grow rapidly in importance as a basis for competitive strategy in the hospitality sector throughout the 1990s. Two main strategic thrusts are likely to be involved: 'branding' of the service itself and increasingly effective monitoring of key customer groups. Management and choreography of the service scenario are recognized techniques for generating 'branded' service quality (Lockwood and Jones, 1989). Accepted tactical approaches include aiming to 'exceed guests' expectations', and empowering employees and encouraging them to respond spontaneously to guests. Hospitality organizations are also advised to allocate funds for customer service expenses and to direct capital budgets towards implementing customers' suggestions (Kirwin, 1992).

As computer systems develop, it will become possible to store increasingly complex data about customers. Hospitality operators will have the resources to build up detailed multidimensional profiles of customers' expectations and attitudes. Knowledge of demographic, socio-economic and financial/behavioural data will make it possible to target promotions at those groups most likely to become consistently loyal customers (Francese and Renaghan, 1990). Such databases may also provide information about the preferences and dislikes of customer groups. Customer feedback data will also contribute to this process. In addition, electronic point-of-sale systems and other networked billing techniques will increasingly provide customer spending histories. By the use of this information, the hospitality service product can continuously be tailored to the needs of those guest groups identified and targeted by marketing initiatives.

BEYOND SERVICE QUALITY?

The Western world is currently in a post-industrial phase of development, in which service industries predominate over manufacturing. It seems clear that we shall continue to drift into a service culture as the 1990s progress. Manufacturing companies will increasingly concentrate on service as the key to competitive advantage, a trend largely driven by successful past quality management strategies. In many manufacturing sectors, product quality is now virtually guaranteed and largely taken for granted by the customer. This will increasingly leave service and image as the only remaining market differentiators.

The hospitality industry is moving along an analogous path to the manufacturing sector. The tangible quality of food, beverage and facilities has become less and less important as a source of competitive advantage. Service quality is becoming increasingly important and some organizations are moving to a culture which emphasizes customer service at the expense of tangible aspects. As discussed above, however, there may be limited scope for developing the service product in general terms.

This chapter has outlined ways in which service quality may develop. It will be aimed increasingly at specific customer groups and prime objectives will be to encourage return visits, to build and maintain customer loyalty. A challenge facing hospitality managers is to make service provision so flexible that it can foresee and gratify the needs of individuals and groups. It will also be important to assist customers with purchasing decisions and to remove the embarrassments or threats which accidentally occur in service encounters due to cultural or social differences. Service quality will increasingly be branded and have to live up to an image promoted to customers through the media.

All of these issues can be addressed by integration. We have seen that service quality management is a matter of integrating the elements of the service quality model and of bridging the five 'gaps' which yawn along the route of service provision. The underlying issue is to establish the appropriate resonance between company mission, corporate image, marketing concept and customer perception. Thus service quality, though very important, is not an end in itself but rather a means of bringing the organization into

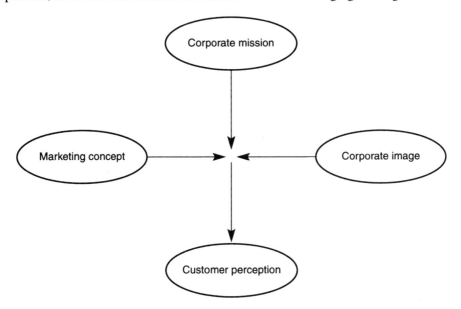

Figure 2.4 *Suggested model for the relationship between organization strategy and customer's perceived quality*

harmony: its intentions expressed in its actions and its promotion in resonance with the perceptions of its customers.

Beyond service quality lies the simple model shown in Figure 2.4. The more directly mission, policy, image and promotion can be focused upon the customers' perceived satisfaction, the more effectively business objectives will be met.

REFERENCES

Ananth, M., DeMicco, F. J., Moreo, P. J., and Howey, R. M. (1992) 'Marketplace lodging needs of mature travelers', *Cornell Hotel and Restaurant Administration Quarterly*, vol. **33**, no. 4, pp. 12–24.

Balmer, S., and Baum, T. (1993) 'Applying Herzberg's hygiene factors to the changing accommodation environment', *International Journal of Contemporary Hospitality Management*, vol. **5**, pp. 32–5.

Barsky, J. D. (1992) 'Customer satisfaction in the hotel industry: meaning and measurement', *Hospitality Research Journal*, vol. **16**, no. 1, pp. 51–73.

Berry, L. L., and Parasuraman, A. (1992) 'Prescription for a service quality revolution in America', *Organizational Dynamics*, vol. **20**, no. 4, pp. 5–15.

Brogowicz, A. A., Delene, L. M., and Lyth, D. M. (1990) 'A synthesized service quality model with managerial implications', *International Journal of Service Industry Management*, vol. **1**, no. 1, pp. 27–45.

Brown, S. A. (1990) 'Creating a service culture', *Canadian Banker*, vol. **97**, no. 5, pp. 40–2.

Brown, S. W., Haynes, R. M., and Saunders, D. L. (1990) 'Revitalizing service innovations', *International Journal of Service Industry Management*, vol. **1**, no. 1, pp. 65–77.

Callan, R. J. (1989) 'Small country hotels and hotel award schemes as a measurement of service quality', *Service Industries Journal*, vol. **9**, no. 2, pp. 223–46.

Callan, R. J. (1990) 'Hotel award schemes as a measurement of service quality – an assessment by travel industry journalists as surrogate consumers', *International Journal of Hospitality Management*, vol. **9**, no. 1, pp. 45–8.

Callan, R. (1992) 'Quality control at Avant Hotels. The debut of BS5750', *Service Industries Journal*, vol. **12**, no. 1, pp. 17–33.

Carman, J. M. (1990) 'Consumer perceptions of service quality: an assessment of the SERV-QUAL dimensions', *Journal of Retailing*, vol. **66**, no. 2, pp. 33–55.

Comen, T. (1989) 'Making quality assurance work for you', *Cornell Hotel and Restaurant Administration Quarterly*, vol. **30**, no. 3, pp. 22–9.

Cronin, J. J., and Taylor, S. A. (1992) 'Measuring service quality: a reexamination and extension', *Journal of Marketing*, vol. **56**, no. 7, pp. 55–68.

Fender, D., and Litteljohn, D. (1992) 'Forward planning in uncertain times', *International Journal of Contemporary Hospitality Management*, vol. **4**, no. 3, pp. i–iv.

Fitzsimmons, J. A., and Maurer, G. B. (1991) 'A walk-through audit to improve restaurant performance', *Cornell Hotel and Restaurant Administration Quarterly*, vol. **31**, no. 4, February, pp. 94–9.

Francese, P. A., and Renaghan, L. M. (1990) 'Data-base marketing: building customer profiles', *Cornell Hotel and Restaurant Administration Quarterly*, vol. **31**, no. 1, pp. 60–3.

Furey, T. R. (1991) 'How information power can improve service quality', *Planning Review*, vol. **19**, no. 3, pp. 24–6.

Gregory, G. (1972) 'Zero defects – Japan's quest for quality', *Quality*, vol. **1**, no. 2, p. 61.

Grönroos, C. (1983) *Strategic Management and Marketing in the Service Sector*, Report no. 83/104, Marketing Science Institute, Cambridge, MA.

Grönroos, C. (1988) 'Service quality: the six criteria of good perceived service quality', *Review of Business*, vol. **9**, no. 3, pp. 10–13.

Harari, O. (1992) 'Hotel from Hell: the analysis of the case', *Management Review*, vol. **81**, no. 10, pp. 60–1.

Horovitz, J., and Cudennec-Poon, C. (1990) 'Putting service quality into gear', *Service Industries Journal*, vol. **10**, no. 2, pp. 249–65.

Johns, N. (1993) 'Productivity management through design and operation: a case study', *International Journal of Contemporary Hospitality Management*, vol. **5**, no. 2, pp. 20–4.

Johns, N., and Wheeler, K. L. (1991) Productivity angles on *sous vide* production', in Teare, R. with Adams, D. and Messenger, S. (eds), *Managing Projects in Hospitality Organizations*, Cassell, London, pp. 146–68.

Juran, J. (1979) *Quality Control Handbook*, 3rd edn, McGraw-Hill, New York, p. 2.2.

Kirwin, P. (1992) 'Increasing sales and profits through guest satisfaction', *Cornell Hotel and Restaurant Administration Quarterly*, vol. **33**, no. 5, pp. 38–9.

Larsen, S., and Rapp, L. (1993) 'Creating the service-driven cruise line', *International Journal of Contemporary Hospitality Management*, vol. **5**, no. 1, pp. iv–vi.

Lawton, R. (1992) 'A service quality strategy that will work for you', *Journal for Quality and Participation*, vol. **15**, no. 3, pp. 38–44.

Lee-Mortimer, A., and Buxton, A. (1991) 'Beyond stars and crowns', *Managing Service Quality*, January, pp. 97–100.

Lennon, J., and Mercer, A. (1993) 'Service quality in practice: customer service in Scotland's Tourist Information Centres'. IAHMS Spring 1993 Conference on Service Quality, University of Gothenburg, Sweden.

Lewis, R. C. (1985) 'The market position: mapping guests' perceptions of hotel operations', *Cornell Hotel and Restaurant Administration Quarterly*, August, pp. 86–99.

Lewis, R. C. (1989) 'Hospitality marketing: the internal approach', *Cornell Hotel and Restaurant Administration Quarterly*, vol. **30**, no. 3, pp. 41–5.

Lewis, R. C., and Nightingale, M. (1991) 'Targeting service to your customer', *Cornell Hotel and Restaurant Administration Quarterly*, vol. **32**, no. 2, pp. 18–27.

Lin, L. (1993) 'First marketing concept, then service quality', IAHMS Spring 1993 Conference on Service Quality, University of Gothenburg, Sweden.

Lockwood, A., and Jones, P. (1989) 'Creating positive service encounters', *Cornell Hotel and Restaurant Administration Quarterly*, vol. **29**, no. 4, pp. 44–50.

Martillano, G. T. (1989) 'Participation sells and builds commitment', *Journal for Quality and Participation*, vol. **12**, no. 6, pp. 66–70.

Martin, W. B. (1986) 'Defining what service quality is for you', *Cornell Hotel and Restaurant Administration Quarterly*, February, pp. 32–8.

Nightingale, M. (1985) 'The hospitality industry: defining quality for a quality assurance programme – a study of perceptions', *Service Industries Journal*, vol. **5**, no. 1, pp. 9–24.

Parasuraman, A., Zeithaml, V. A., and Berry, L. (1985) 'A conceptual model of service quality and its implications for future research', *Journal of Marketing*, vol. **49**, pp. 41–50.

Parasuraman, A., Zeithaml, V. A., and Berry, L. L. (1991) 'Refinement and reassessment of the SERVQUAL scale', *Journal of Retailing*, vol. **67**, no. 4, pp. 420–50.

Prais, S. J., Jarvis, V., and Wagner, K. (1989) 'Productivity and vocational skills in services in Britain', *National Institute Economic Review*, vol. **130**, pp. 52–74.

Price, P. (1989) 'Customer care in licensed retailing', *International Journal of Contemporary Hospitality Management*, vol. **1**, no. 2, pp. 17–18.

Records, H. A., and Glenny, M. F. (1991) 'Service management and quality assurance', *Cornell Hotel and Restaurant Administration Quarterly*, vol. **32**, no. 2, pp. 26–36.

4Reid, D. R., and Sandler, M. (1992) 'The use of technology to improve service quality', *Cornell Hotel and Restaurant Administration Quarterly*, vol. **33**, no. 3, pp. 68–73.

Rowe, M. (1992) 'Greening for dollars', *Lodging Hospitality*, vol. **48**, no. 4, pp. 36–8.

Schwartz, M. H. (1991) 'A question of semantics', *Quality Progress*, vol. **24**, no. 11, pp. 59–63.

Schwartz, M. H. (1992) 'What do the words "product" and "service" really mean for management?', *Quality Progress*, vol. **25**, no. 6, pp. 35–9.

Shams, H., and Hales, C. (1989) 'Once more on "goods" and "services": a way out of the conceptual jungle', *Quarterly Review of Marketing*, vol. **14**, no. 3, pp. 1–5.

Sharp, I. (1990) 'Quality for all seasons', *Canadian Business Review*, vol. **17**, no. 1, pp. 21–3.

Silvestro, R., Johnston, R., Fitzgerald, L., and Voss, C. (1990) 'Quality measurement in service industries', *International Journal of Service Industry Management*, vol. **1**, no. 2, pp. 54–60.

Smith, L. R. O. (1991) 'Achieving quality in a 5-star hotel', *Quality Forum*, vol. **17**, no. 4, pp. 186–9.

Taguchi, G. (1981) *Design and Design of Experiments*, Japanese Standards Association, Tokyo.

Thomas, L. F. (1965) *The Control of Quality*, Thames and Hudson, London, p. 5.

Walker, J. R., and Salameh, T. T. (1990) 'The QA pay-off', *Cornell Hotel and Restaurant Administration Quarterly*, vol. **31**, no. 3, pp. 57–9.

Willborn, W. (1986) 'Quality assurance audits and hotel management', *Service Industries Journal*, vol. **6**, no. 3, pp. 293–308.

Witt, C. A., and Witt, S. (1989) 'Why productivity in the hotel sector is low', *International Journal of Contemporary Hospitality Management*, vol. **1**, no. 2, pp. 28–34.

The manifest level of organizational culture

The most obvious observances of culture are at the manifest level. Included in the manifestations of culture at this level are the visible and audible artifacts of the organization. These include the constructed environment (physical buildings, artwork, physical layouts, color, schemes, uniforms, trademarks), visible and audible behavior patterns (language, stories, rituals, rites, ceremonies, symbolic artifacts, conventions, customs, and norms or patterned conduct) and the public documents (memos, organizational records, profit and loss statements). The manifest level of culture is most obvious to an outside observer of a culture. However, it does not represent in total what the culture is all about. Instead, these manifestations of culture are primarily symbolic of the way managers and employees want the public to view their organization. Art in the foyer of an office building, the decor of a restaurant and the dress of employees are all examples of the manifestations that the organization wants the public to see. These manifestations represent either 'how things should be' or 'what we want the organization to be'. They do represent how things really are in the culture. Therefore, it is not practical for an outside observer to merely view the manifestations of a culture and suppose that he or she knows all there is to know about it.

The strategic level of organizational culture

The first level described above is generally visible to newcomers to a company, and often even to outsiders. The second level is less easily decipherable by those who are not members of the culture. At this second level are the organization-specific strategic beliefs that represent the manner in which a culture matches its own distinctive competencies with its available resources to differentiate itself from other cultures. These strategic beliefs do not stem from the stream of actual decisions taken over time that reveal system-wide goals and means (Lundberg, 1985). Therefore, strategic beliefs can be thought of as representing what the organization has learned about itself over time.

Beliefs at this second level represent the 'oughts' of the organization, or 'what people would say they believe in'. In effect, these are the reasons that people in organizational cultures give for rationalizing their behaviors.

There are four categories of strategic beliefs. Each represents separate important knowledge shared by the organizational members.

Strategic vision

Strategic vision is essentially the organization's long-term aspiration or what it can become and do and what it will not attempt. In essence, strategic vision is management's beliefs about what the organization is capable of accomplishing. For example, in one restaurant company used in this study the strategic vision in the organization is to dominate its home base regional market in one specific product area – fried seafoods. This company believes that it should not venture outside its market or enlarge its product line materially beyond what it already does well.

Capital-market expectations

Capital-market expectations are management's convictions about what is necessary to keep lenders and investors satisfied. One of the companies from which information used for this chapter is drawn, for instance, emphasizes a belief that most company stakeholders (lenders and investors included) want the company to retain its position as a true leader and innovator in the restaurant industry. Failure to achieve this could seriously upset the culture because it fails to agree with the capital-market expectation of the organization.

Product-market expectations

Each organization holds company-specific strategic beliefs about product-market competition. These represent 'how' and 'why' the organization can succeed in its industry. For instance, food-product innovation is the key in one US restaurant organization. Not coincidentally, the company views most of its competitors as 'followers' and itself as the product leader.

Internal approaches to management

Internal approaches to management support the other categories of strategic beliefs. Internal approaches to management cover a fairly wide range of topics, and are, therefore, very important in an organization. Included in the internal approaches to management are what activities and endeavors the organization can succeed in, what the financial goals should be for the company, how marketing is done, what are acceptable risks, what planning, control and coordination devices will work best for the company, what managing really encompasses, what structures are best for the company, which technologies are preferred, the best set of employee inducements, acceptable competitor and union–management relationships, appropriate public service and community support, and so on.

Level of deep meaning

The third level in the levels of meaning framework represents what is really important in the culture. At this level are the taken-for-granted organization-specific values and assumptions that actually determine how members perceive, think and learn. It is at this level that organizational cultures really determine actions.

It is easiest to think about culture as spreading upward and out from this level because it visually depicts how culture originates at the level of deep meaning (Figure 3.1). This deepest level of meaning in an organization's culture includes the values and assumptions that members of the organization actually live by. The values and assumptions at the level of deep meaning are largely tacit and taken for granted by organizational members. This means they are seldom talked about but widely understood. They are also invisible to outsiders. Only the insiders in a culture understand its values and assumptions.

The values of a culture include what the organization stands for, what is considered sacred in the culture and what members accept as key elements. The assumptions held at this level include such critical elements as how work is defined (doing or being), how human nature is defined (good, bad, good and bad), and which time is emphasized in the organization (past, present, future). While both manifestations of the culture and strategic beliefs provide useful meanings back downward to the level of meaning, culture originates at this deepest level.

Some of the organization-specific values may be espoused in statements of management philosophy. One restaurant company studied uses what it has identified as its key

Manifest level

Strategic beliefs

Deep meaning

Figure 3.1 *How culture works upward*

value, 'Act Guest First', very often to reinforce its importance. However, most of the values and the assumptions are 'shared' but never talked about. These taken-for-granted values and assumptions are either about external relations (e.g. how to compete and relate to constituencies, what makes for distinctive competence in an industry, how to direct the business) or they are about internal affairs (e.g. how to manage, relate to employees, deploy resources or direct the organization) (Lundberg, 1988).

Schein (1985) refers to this third level as the 'basic assumptions' and the 'theories in use' of a culture. Davis (1984) referred to the level of deep meaning as 'shared beliefs'. Regardless of the language used to describe this level, this level provides the basic building blocks upon which the first (symbolic manifestations) and second (strategic beliefs) levels are constructed. Understanding this fact is crucial.

The power of culture

As Pettigrew (1979) noted, 'It is not useful simply to point to a swirling fog and claim that it boosts performance'. One must be able to describe the fog in order to define the relationship between it and performance. Fortunately, recent research has indicated that culture affects companies in many different ways. Fifty-three organizational performance variables have been identified by scholars as 'affected by' culture (Woods, 1989). In other words, culture can affect the organizations in which hospitality managers work in 53 *different* ways. This chapter argues that culture influences performance in another way, i.e. by creating conditions in which employees are more likely to have positive interactions with their guests because of the high levels of people-focused cultural congruence in the organization.

It is useful to illustrate how congruence and interpersonal skills could influence service by briefly discussing the results of recent research linking it with various organizational performance variables.

The effect of culture on tangible performance attributes

Some organizational attributes affected by culture are difficult to measure. Service fits this description because of its intangibility. Others can be measured more directly because they are more tangible. For instance, scholars have established links between culture and tangible performance attributes for each of the following:

1. Bottom-line profitability (in restaurant companies, auto companies, service companies and banks) (Tidball, 1988; Normann, 1984; Dennison, 1989).
2. Employee productivity (Ouchi and Wilkins, 1985).
3. Job stress (Posner *et al.*, 1985).
4. The ability of companies to get new products to the market (Kunda, 1986).

The effect of culture on intangible performance attributes

Many important attributes of service companies are harder to measure. For instance, it is difficult to measure the degree of satisfaction that employees get from their work, how well employees and managers work as teams, how loyal employees and managers are to the services that they sell, and so on. Difficulty in measuring these attributes does not mean that they are unimportant. On the contrary, a strong argument can be made that intangible attributes are more important in service companies than are those that are easily measured. The following list illustrates some of the links between culture and intangible performance variables established by scholars and illustrates this point effectively:

1. Loyalty by employees and managers (Mitroff and Kilmann, 1985).
2. Positive emotional attachment by employees and managers (Dandridge, 1986).
3. Ability of companies to plan and enact sound long-term strategies (Weick, 1985; Schwartz and Davis, 1981).
4. Organizational survival (Gagliardi, 1986).
5. Establishment of positive standards of performance (Ashforth, 1990).
6. Degree of internal conflicts (or dirty politics) in organizations (Sathe, 1983).
7. Employee teamwork and sense of solidarity (Smircich and Morgan, 1982).
8. Socialization of new employees (Sutton and Louis, 1987).
9. Communication within the organization (Kanter, 1983).
10. Behavioral norm setting (Siehl and Martin, 1985).
11. Trust (Wilkins and Dyer, 1988).
12. Innovativeness (Kunda, 1986).
13. Employee and managerial attitudes about personal success (Ashforth, 1990).
14. Employee and managerial turnover (Spence, 1987).
15. Degree of congruence between how employees and managers view company goals and objectives (Tidball, 1988).
16. Ethical behavior (Waters and Bird, 1987).
17. How well company reward systems work (Kerr and Slocum, 1987).
18. Employee perceptions of managerial effectiveness (Dyer, 1985; Tidball, 1988; Harrison, 1972).
19. Degree of employee voice (ability of employees to talk about their problems) (Spence, 1987).
20. Training costs (Siehl and Martin, 1985).
21. Ability to change in response to changing customer needs and expectations (Tidball, 1988; Harrison, 1972).

While each of these intangible attributes is important to the success of any company, they are more important to hospitality organizations, because these companies rely on the one-on-one interactions between line-level employees and customers for success. For most customers, the only thing that they know about a particular company is what they learn from the few employees with whom they interact. When the interaction is positive, the customer is likely to feel positively about the company. This customer is more likely to return again. The opposite is also true.

Customers often make service decisions based on intangible factors such as the friendliness of the servers, ambience, the quiet enjoyment of their rooms, smiles, positive interactions that they see between employees and other guests, the employees' ability to deliver customer expectations or aspirations, and so on. Therefore, these intangible attributes take on special significance in the hospitality industry.

CULTURAL CONGRUENCE

Without culture people in organizations would not know how to behave. No managerial or employee manual could possibly adequately describe the acceptable behaviors or actions that a manager or employee should engage in during their many service encounters. Some organizations have attempted to script the behaviors of managers and employees. This simply does not work because of the many different branches that a service interaction could take and because of the varying emotions that servers must display during these interactions. The result of scripted service is an unfeeling 'recitation' from a server to a guest. However, culture can provide guidelines necessary for service providers that help to avoid this problem. Therefore, in a sense, culture fills the gaps between policies and procedures. For that reason culture is a very powerful force.

An example which could be used to illustrate the pervasiveness of culture involves the role of server in a restaurant. Each day these servers are called upon to make many, perhaps hundreds, of decisions for which there are no written rules. Most of the decisions involve customers and, as a result, the success of the company is on the line in each case. If these servers stopped to ask their superiors what to do each time they encountered an undefined or new situation, service would slow almost to a stop. Additionally, if the servers make decisions that go against the grain of what is important in the company then the customer will probably receive service other than what the company intended.

What restaurant companies can do to insure that their servers and other employees will make the right decisions in each of these instances is very simple – they can make sure that the servers know what is important to the culture and then encourage them to behave that way at all times, regardless of whether or not the company manual outlines specific 'rules' for such behaviors. It was previously mentioned that for a restaurant company included in a culture study, for instance, the key value of the culture is 'Act Guest First'. This value is also widely shared throughout the company. This simple key value empowers employees to do whatever is necessary to provide the best possible service to the guest. This approach would not work for all companies, of course, but it works for at least one.

Cultural congruence is the extent to which an organization's culture is shared by its members. In organizations in which the culture is widely shared, organizational members hold the same or similar opinions about important values, assumptions and beliefs. In organizations in which the level of congruence is not high, members hold varying opinions about what is important in the culture. Woods (1989) explored the importance of cultural congruence to the attainment of organizatiõnal values and found that hospitality organizations display varying degrees of congruence.

Cultural congruence plays an integral role in the delivery of service because it influences the extent to which organizationally desired services are actually delivered to customers. In organizations where congruence is low, for instance, customers often do not receive the kind of service that corporate officials planned or intended. Most companies spend considerable resources designing service delivery systems intended to provide the type of services they want to deliver.

Organizations which have taken the time to determine what is important to organizational members at various levels, and then worked to effectively spread that information throughout the organization, are less likely to experience cultural congruence problems which negatively influence service (Woods, 1989). These companies are also more likely to deliver the type of service intended.

The extent to which restaurant organizations are culturally congruent was tested using four measures: (1) the extent to which managers' and employees' job descriptions actually illustrate how things really are in the organization; (2) the extent to which how things really are depict how things should be; (3) the extent to which managers make statements which are in congruence with the shared culture of the organization; and (4) the extent to which managers are likely to live out the statements they made.[1] A series of interviews and surveys conducted and distributed among managers and employees in five restaurant organizations revealed that they displayed substantially different levels of congruence within their cultures. In one, for instance, the managers and employees held almost the same opinions about each of the four issues. In other words, reality was described in the same ways by managers and employees. The way things should be was also described in virtually the same ways; managers and employees agreed that management was very likely to make and to live out statements which were in very close agreement with the widely shared values and assumptions in the organization. An opposite condition was found in another company. In this organization, managers and employees held very different views of reality and of what should be; managers felt they made and lived out statements that were in agreement with what they understood as the key cultural elements while employees believed that the same managers were very likely to make statements that were in almost total disagreement with the key elements of the culture and that the managers were very likely to say one thing and do another. In this company very low levels of cultural congruence are obvious. The other three companies tested yielded levels of congruence between the two parameters established by these two organizations.

THE IMPORTANCE OF INTERPERSONAL SKILLS

One of the key elements in the delivery of service by front-line servers relates to the level of interpersonal skills these servers have. This issue has been explored, albeit somewhat generally, in the service literature. For instance, Sarbin and Allen (1968) pointed out that role expectations about the service encounter are largely determined by the culture of an organization. Work by Zeithaml *et al.* (1988) also identified the relationship between culture and service and noted that negative cultures form an organizational barrier which can influence the service encounter. Sparks (1994) also suggested that culture is one of the contextual variables which influence communicative aspects of the service encounter.

The importance of interpersonal skills in the service encounter has also been explored directly by a few researchers recently. For instance, Samenfink (1994) noted that an employee's interpersonal skills are an important aspect in delivering quality service. Heskett (1986) noted that interpersonal skills desirable in a service encounter should include flexibility, tolerance for ambiguity, the ability to monitor and change behavior during a service encounter and empathy for the customer. Mills (1986) noted that servers must develop environmental boundary scanning skills (an ability to respond to a variety of stimuli) in their service encounters, and Mars and Nicod (1984) found that servers must develop a variety of interpersonal skills, including verbal and non-verbal communication skills, in order to effectively deliver service.

The way in which emotions are displayed has also been investigated. Emotions are, of course, controllable through the development of interpersonal skills. Hochschild (1983) noted how the delivery of service requires emotional labor on the part of servers. Research by Rafaeli and Sutton (1987) further indicated how this emotional labor can take a toll on the ability of employees to display desirable interpersonal skills, and Romm (1989) noted how different skills are needed for differing service environments.

Samenfink (1992) further improved our knowledge of this area by laying the theoretical groundwork for using self-monitoring techniques to improve interpersonal skills and by developing a scale to test the extent to which employees used self-monitoring in the delivery of service (Samenfink, 1994).

What this research on the role of interpersonal skills in service has concluded to date is that 'good' person-to-person service interactions are, at least partially, the result of employees displaying strong positive interpersonal skills. The extent to which employees display these skills is partially a function of the personalities of the individuals (Samenfink, 1994), partially a result of the training the employees received (Woods, 1990) and partially a result of the extent to which cultural congruence exists within the organization (Woods, 1989).

Employees mirror the actions and behaviors of managers. It works like a chain reaction: middle-level managers mirror or imitate the behaviors of top-level managers, supervisors imitate middle-level managers, and employees mirror supervisors. This means that if top-level managers provide good service to middle-level managers then these middle-level managers are more likely to deliver the same kind of service to supervisors they serve. Supervisors do the same with employees. This is, of course, the basic argument behind the inverted pyramid concept. Therefore, it stands to reason that the extent to which employees mirror positive service images to the customers they serve depends at least in part on the services the employees themselves receive from their managers.

Employees undoubtedly have more direct contact with customers than do managers. If these employees have received 'good service' from their superiors they are more likely to mirror the same good services to their customers. This is why service experts say that service failure is generally the fault of the manager, not the employee. In all likelihood, employees who deliver poor service do so at least partially because they are simply mirroring the poor service that they received from others. This is where the role of culture again becomes important in service.

Cultures in which interpersonal skills are valued and widely shared emphasize managers coaching, trusting, taking pride in, listening to, training and communicating with employees, asking employees what they want and need and developing strong people skills among their employees. In these cultures the values and assumptions at the deep meaning level probably emphasize a high opinion of human nature. In other cultures the emphasis is on controlling and directing employee behaviors, monitoring employees' actions, management versus employee relationships, product-is-foremost attitudes, the belief that human nature is essentially 'bad' (e.g. employees are basically lazy), particularism (that some employees are more important than others) and so on. These are obviously examples of cultures in which interpersonal skills are not valued. The difference between these two types of cultures is that one type emphasizes managers delivering good service to their employees while the other type emphasizes managers treating employees as if they were the enemy. In the first type the employees are encouraged to mirror the good service that they receive from their managers while in the other the employees are encouraged to treat the customer better than they themselves are treated. It is reasonable to assume that in the first type customers are more likely to receive good service than they are in the second type, because of this mirroring effect. If employees in the first type deliver the same kind of service they receive, for instance, then the customer will probably be trusted, listened to and treated with dignity, just as the employees are. The second type of culture encourages treating a customer as someone who is probably trying to take advantage of the organization, someone who must be watched and controlled and someone who is, in fact, the enemy.

In person-to-person service interactions wherein the customer is a partial employee in the service interaction, these interpersonal skills become particularly important. These customers are at least partially responsible for the quality of the service delivered because of their involvement in the creation of the services they purchase. When the service provider exhibits positive interpersonal behaviors the customer is more likely to deliver similar behaviors. Rafaeli and Sutton (1987) found this to be true when they tested the concept in the service interaction in retail grocery stores. Therefore, we can extrapolate this connection to suggest that in culturally congruent organizations wherein positive interpersonal skills are valued, the customer is more likely to contribute to the service interaction positively. The same is also true in reverse. The key, then, is in developing cultures in which two elements exist. The first is a high level of cultural congruence. The second is a culture in which interpersonal skills are valued. The two must exist in tandem. Cultural congruence can, and does, exist in organizations in which people are not considered valuable assets and in which interpersonal skills are not valued, for instance. Companies which excel in service already know this important fact, of course.

THE CHALLENGE FOR MANAGERS

Managers do not simply 'control' the cultures of their organizations. Instead, all organizational members play significant roles in helping to determine what is important in their cultures. Managers can 'want' to have a certain culture but fail in their efforts to achieve it. This failure is often the result of managers believing that they can purchase, rapidly introduce, mandate or easily change organizational cultures. Cultures are far too complex and sensitive for such quick fixes to work effectively. Cultural facilitation and change depends on managers understanding and appreciating the unique cultural characteristics of their own organizations and then using this information to plan culturally sensitive managerial approaches to all organizational activities.

While managers do not control their cultures, they do play important roles in them.

Three roles identified by Lundberg and Woods (1990) are those of cultural spokesperson, cultural assessor and facilitator of cultural modification.

The principal role of a cultural assessor involves assisting a company in knowing its own culture. This can take on many forms. For instance, managers in some organizations might assist their colleagues in determining what fits the culture and what does not by encouraging internal feedback mechanisms that help them confirm what is really going on within the company. This is considered so important in one organization we studied that the top management has even developed a system wherein it regularly allows its employees to evaluate new managers on their ability to act out critical company values, beliefs and assumptions – and the company acts on these evaluations by assigning managers who do not display the right attributes to 'cultural retraining' programs. This company takes this process so seriously, in fact, that on more than one occasion new managers were 'washed out' of the company because employees reported that these managers were not living out the central cultural values of the organization.

The role of cultural spokesperson is primarily one of advocacy and education. Spokespersons help other members identify and appreciate the symbolic import and impact of events, things and actions in the culture. This role may be as simple as a manager who has been around for a long time acting as the 'knowledge source' for cultural issues. One manager in a study of five restaurant companies, for instance, has been assigned this role for two principal reasons. The first is that the manager has considerable tenure with the company. As a result, he remembers the goals established when the company was founded. The second is that the manager epitomizes what the top management in the company likes to think of as its 'ideal' company employee. While studying the culture of an engineering electronics company near Boston a few years ago, Kunda (1986) realized that the company actually employed a person whose sole responsibility it was to 'spread the culture' both inside the company and outside it. This person, known within the company officially as the 'Culture Officer', evaluated how well the company's managers and employees were living out what was important in the culture and planned 'cultural training events' to reinforce what was important.

The third role that managers play is that of cultural facilitator. Cultures change and adapt to changing goals and circumstances in organizations and, as a result, are never truly static. The role of cultural facilitator involves actively assisting the culture change and assisting culture members in adapting to the changes. To effectively enhance such changes managers must both ensure that critical elements of the past are retained and introduce elements to the culture that can assist it in becoming more effective. Cultural facilitators can also help members of the culture to think through the cultural implications of their service delivery system. The most critical role that cultural facilitators play is that of thinking about what effect proposed modifications might have on the 'cultural core', or the set of values, beliefs and assumptions that exist at the level of deep meaning in the culture. If widely shared, these issues are sacred in the culture. Attempting to change them involves careful planning and consideration of the impact.

NOTE

1. Results of the quantitative tests are not appropriate in this chapter. For a full description of the results see Woods (1989).

REFERENCES

Ashforth, B. (1990) 'Climate formation: issues and extensions', *Management Review*, vol. **10**, pp. 837–47.

Dandridge, T. C. (1986) 'Ceremony as an integration of work and play', *Organization Studies*, vol. **7**, no. 2, pp. 159–70.

Davis, S. (1984) *Managing Corporate Culture*, Ballinger, Cambridge, MA.

Dennison, D. L. (1989) 'Bringing corporate culture to the bottom line', *Organizational Dynamics*, vol. **13**, no. 2, pp. 5–22.

Dyer, W. G. (1985) 'The cycle of cultural evolution in organizations', in Kilmann, R. H., Saxton, M. J., and Serpa, R. (eds), *Gaining Control of the Corporate Culture*, Jossey-Bass, San Francisco. pp. 200ff.

Frost, P. J., Moore, L. F., Louis, M. R., Lundberg, C. C., and Martin, J. (1985) *Organizational Culture*, Sage Publications, Beverly Hills.

Gagliardi, P. (1986) 'The creation and change of organizational cultures: a conceptual framework', *Organization Studies*, vol. **7**, no. 2, pp. 117–34.

Geertz, C. (1973) *The Interpretation of Cultures: Selected Essays*, Basic Books, New York.

Harrison, R. (1972) 'Understanding your organization's character', *Harvard Business Review*, vol. **3**, pp. 119–28.

Heskett, J. L. (1986) *Managing in the Service Economy*, Harvard Business School Press, Cambridge, MA.

Hochschild, A. (1983) *The Managed Heart*, University of California Press, Berkeley.

Kanter, R. M. (1983) *The Changemasters: Innovation and Entrepreneurship in the American Corporation*, Simon and Schuster, New York.

Kerr, J., and Slocum, J. W. (1987) 'Managing corporate culture through rewards systems', *Academy of Management Executive*, vol. **1**, no. 2, pp. 99–107.

Kilmann, R. H., Saxton, M. J. and Serpa, R. (1985) *Gaining Control of the Corporate Culture*, Jossey-Bass, San Francisco.

Kroeber, A. L., and Kluckhorn, C. (1963) *Culture: a Critical Review of Concepts and Definitions*, Vintage Books, New York.

Kunda, G. (1986) 'Engineering culture: culture and control in a high-tech organization'. Unpublished doctoral dissertation, Massachusetts Institute of Technology.

Louis, M. R. (1981) 'A cultural perspective on organizations: the need for and consequence of viewing organizations as culture-bearing milieux', *Human Systems Management*, vol. **2**, no. 4, pp. 20–33.

Lundberg, C. C. (1985) 'On the feasibility of cultural intervention in organizations', in Frost, P., Moore, L. F., and Louis, M. R., (eds), *Organizational Culture*, Sage Publications, Beverly Hills, pp. 13–25.

Lundberg, C. C. (1988) 'Managing organizational transformation: understanding and influencing organizational culture', unpublished manuscript, Cornell University, School of Hotel Administration, Ithaca, NY.

Lundberg, C. C., and Woods, R. H. (1990) 'Modifying restaurant culture: managers as cultural spokespersons, assessors; and facilitators', *International Journal of Contemporary Hospitality Management*, vol. **2**, no. 4, pp. 4–12.

Mars, G., and Nicod, M. (1984) *The World of Waiters*, George Allen & Unwin, London.

Mills, P. K. (1986) *Managing Service Industries*, Ballinger, Cambridge.

Mitroff, I., and Kilmann, R. (1985) *Corporate Tragedies: Product Tampering, Sabotage, and Other Catastrophes*, Praeger, New York.

Normann, R. (1984) *Service Management: Strategy and Leadership in Service Businesses*, John Wiley and Sons, Chicago.

Ouchi, W. G., and Wilkins, A. L. (1985) 'Organizational culture', *American Review of Sociology*, vol. **11**, pp. 457–83.

Pettigrew, A. M. (1979) 'On studying organizational cultures', *Administrative Science Quarterly*, vol. **24**, pp. 570–91.

Posner, B., Kouces, J., and Schmidt, W. H. (1985) 'Shared values make a difference: an empirical test of corporate cultures', *Human Resource Management*, vol. **24**, no. 3, pp. 293–309.

Rafaeli, A., and Sutton, R. I. (1987) 'Expression of emotion as part of the work role', *Academy of Management Review*, vol. **12**, no. 1, pp. 23–37.

Romm, D. (1989) 'Restauration theatre: giving direction to service', *Cornell Hotel and Restaurant Administration Quarterly*, vol. **29**, no. 4, pp. 31–9.

Saffold, G. S. (1988) 'Culture traits, strength, and organizational performance: moving beyond "strong" culture', *Academy of Management Review*, vol. **13**, no. 4, pp. 546–58.

Samenfink, W. H. (1992) 'Identifying the service potential of an employee through the use of self-monitoring scale', *Hospitality Research Journal*, vol. **15**, no. 2, pp. 1–10.

Samenfink, W. H. (1994) 'A quantitative analysis of certain interpersonal skills required in the service encounter', *Hospitality Research Journal*, vol. **17**, no. 2, pp. 3–15.

Sarbin, T., and Allen, V. (1968) 'Role theory', in Gardner, I., and Elliot, A. (eds), *The Handbook of Social Psychology*, vol. **1**, Addison Wesley, Boston, pp. 191–223.

Sathe, V. (1983) 'Implications of corporate culture: a manager's guide to action', *Organizational Dynamics*, vol. **12**, no. 2, pp. 5–23.

Schall, M. S. (1983) 'A communication rules approach to organizational culture', *Administrative Science Quarterly*, vol. **28**, pp. 557–81.

Schein, E. H. (1985) *Organizational Culture and Leadership*, Jossey-Bass, San Francisco.

Schwartz, H., and Davis, S. (1981) 'Matching corporate culture and business strategy', *Organizational Dynamics*, vol. **10**, pp. 30–48.

Siehl, C., and Martin, J. (1985) *Measuring Culture*. USC Working Paper, G-85-11, pp. 1–44.

Smircich, L., and Morgan, G. (1982). 'Leadership: the management of meaning', *Journal of Applied Behavioral Science*, vol. **17**, pp. 114–29.

Sparks, B. (1994) 'Communicative aspects of the service encounter', *Hospitality Research Journal*, vol. **17**, no. 2, pp. 39–50.

Spence, D. G. (1987) 'Employee voice and employee retention', *Academy of Management Journal*, vol. **29**, no. 3, pp. 488–502.

Spradley, J. P. (1979) *The Ethnographic Interview*, Holt, Rinehart, New York.

Sutton, R. I., and Louis, M. R. (1987) 'How selecting and socializing newcomers influence insiders', *Human Resource Management*, vol. **16**, no. 4, pp. 347–61.

Tidball, K. (1988) 'Creating a culture that builds your bottom line', *Cornell Hotel and Restaurant Administration Quarterly*, vol. **29**, no. 1, pp. 63–9.

Waters, J. A., and Bird, F. (1987) 'The moral dimensions of organizational culture', *Journal of Business Ethics*, vol. **6**, pp. 15–22.

Weick, K. E. (1985) 'The significance of organizational culture', in Frost, P., Moore, L. F., and Louis, M. R. (eds), *Organizational Culture*, Sage Publications, Beverly Hills, pp. 381–90.

Wilkins, A. L., and Dyer, W. G. (1988) 'Toward culturally sensitive theories of cultural change', *Academy of Management Review*, vol. **13**, no. 4, pp. 522–33.

Woods, R. H. (1989) 'More alike than different: the culture of the restaurant industry', *Cornell Hotel and Restaurant Administration Quarterly*, vol. **30**, no. 2, pp. 82–98.

Woods, R. H. (1990) 'When servers meet customers', *Hospitality Research Journal*, vol. **14**, pp. 35–42.

Zeithaml, V. A., Berry, L. L., and Parasuraman, A. (1988) 'Communication and control processes in the delivery of service quality,' *Journal of Marketing*, vol. **52**, pp. 35–48.

4

Delighting internal customers

Eberhard E. Scheuing

To become and remain a leader in a highly competitive marketplace, a hospitality organization needs competent, well-trained, highly motivated people who are dedicated to working together and supporting each other. The quality of the service rendered to external customers (guests) depends on the quality of the service rendered to internal customers (colleagues or associates). This requires that colleagues be seen as customers and their expectations understood.

This chapter provides a review of relevant concepts and a set of tools that can be used for measuring and understanding expectations and performance. It emphasizes the need to go beyond expectations to create customer delight, and points out the spillover effect such behaviour produces in the form of increased guest satisfaction.

THE DYNAMICS OF VALUE CHAINS

Customers are persons or units who depend on a supplier's performance for the success of their own efforts. Suppliers, in turn, are persons or units who enable customers to succeed in their efforts. Accordingly, suppliers and customers

- can be external or internal;
- are mutually dependent;
- need to cooperate closely;
- are links in value chains.

This situation is depicted in Figure 4.1. As this diagram shows, the chain of value creation culminates in the experience that the hospitality organization provides to the external customer or guest. But it originates far upstream with the supplier's supplier, who is also external to the organization. Returning to Figure 4.1, the production and delivery of services by a hospitality organization can thus be seen as a value chain that

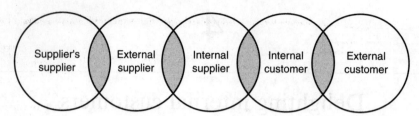

Figure 4.1   *Supplier–customer linkages in value chains*

extends from external suppliers to external customers and involves a series of internal linkages that add value to the process.

Figure 4.1 demonstrates that the value chain is also a chain of dependency. The quality of the external customer's experience with the hospitality organization vitally depends on the quality of the equipment, supplies and services it receives from external suppliers. The latter should thus be regarded and treated as crucial external resources. Top external suppliers should be brought in as partners in a strategic alliance network that enhances the capabilities and performance of the organization by leveraging its core competencies through outsourcing of peripheral services.

The core competencies of a hospitality organization are its unique strengths that differentiate it from the competition, such as multilingual staff or a renowned chef. Peripheral services, in contrast, are those that can competently be handled by outside suppliers. In fact, external suppliers may actually be better at performing these services because they specialize in them and thus possess particular expertise. Such peripheral services may include reservation and billing services, equipment repair and business services (copying, faxing, etc.), and even late-night room service.

The external customer or guest is the organization's *raison d'être*, the reason for its existence. Guest satisfaction is necessary for survival, and guest delight ensures growth. Delighting guests produces loyalty and enthusiasm, and turns customers into sales-persons (Cronin, 1993). Delighted guests return to the source of their delight, they refer friends and colleagues, and they may bring additional business, such as meetings, seminars, conferences, banquets and other business, and even private functions (Reich-held and Sasser, 1990).

Delighting guests is more a matter of attitude and commitment on the part of employees than a result of systems. Although database and operational systems are necessary and helpful, the real difference lies in the human touch at the moment of truth when a guest encounters an employee. Empathy, initiative and flexibility demon-strated by an employee at such a crucial point go a long way toward creating a difference in the guest's mind and consequent repeat business.[1] Far from being insignificant, little things matter a lot to guests because they recognize them as individuals with unique needs and offer them respect.

CREATING A QUALITY CULTURE

Some hospitality chains, such as Hampton Inns and Embassy Suites, use service guarantees to ensure guest satisfaction (Hart, 1993). Others, like Fairfield Inns, use computer terminals at check-out stations to measure guest satisfaction and link part of individual employees' compensation directly to this measure. Many use written guest

A	B	C	D
Dimension	Importance	Ratings	Weighted rating
Totals	100%		

Figure 4.3 *Supplier report card*

expectations were listed in their order of importance as reflected in their relative weights. Performance ratings in column C ranged all over the lot, from 2 on tangibles to 5 on assurance. Altogether, though, this service performer only achieved a weighted rating of 365 (out of a possible 500) and thus barely performed at the 73 per cent level in the eyes of this customer.

Using the report card periodically to elicit both input and feedback from an internal service function's customers is essential to satisfactory performance. It helps identify both relative improvement over time, and opportunities for further improvement.

A	B	C	D
Dimension	Importance	Ratings	Weighted rating
Reliability	32	3	96
Responsiveness	22	4	88
Assurance	19	5	95
Empathy	16	4	64
Tangibles	11	2	22
Totals	100%		365

Figure 4.4 *Sample report card*

EXCEEDING INTERNAL CUSTOMER EXPECTATIONS

Meeting expectations produces customer satisfaction. Measuring this internal customer satisfaction is essential (O'Reilly, 1993). But it would be dangerous to translate satisfaction into complacency. Internal customers who report being satisfied by an internal supplier's performance are merely stating that this supplier did what it was supposed to do.

Delighting internal customers requires going beyond their expectations and surprising them with an exceptional level of performance that, in turn, enables them to serve external customers in an extraordinary fashion. In other words, an internal supplier's exceptional performance allows its customer to shine and delight the guest. Such team spirit is infectious and creates a momentum of enthusiasm that not only makes it fun to work in such an organization but also spreads its fame among actual and potential external customers, thus contributing to a solid momentum of growth.

SUMMARY AND CONCLUSIONS

Service performers in hospitality organizations are vital links in value chains that extend from their external suppliers to their external customers. The patronage decisions of these external customers or guests are vitally affected by the quality of their experience during a stay which, in turn, is determined by a series of interactions with employees in 'moments of truth'.

The quality of these interactions depends on the ability of a hospitality organization's leaders to create a service culture and instill a spirit of teamwork and excellence in all of its employees. To the extent that they render exceptional service to each other, they will render exceptional service to guests. So delighting internal customers becomes a powerful force that produces exceptional results in the marketplace and ensures an organization's growth.

NOTES

1. Harvey Hotels, internal training video entitled *Exceeding Guest Expectations*.
2. This constitutes Gap 1 in the SERVQUAL model (Zeithaml *et al.*, 1990).

REFERENCES

Albrecht, K. (1990) *Service Within*, Dow Jones-Irwin, Homewood, p. 85.

Bell, C. R. and Zemke, R. (1992) *Managing Knock Your Socks Off Service*, AMACOM, New York, p. 72.

Burzon, N. J. (1993) 'Building power into quality education', in Scheuing, E. E., and Christopher, W. F. (eds) *The Service Quality Handbook*, AMACOM, New York, pp. 79–93.

Cronin, I. M., III (1993) 'Staff training delivers quality service at Tokyo's Imperial Hotel', in Scheuing, E. E., and Christopher, W. F. (eds), *The Service Quality Handbook*, AMACOM, New York, pp. 312–28.

Hart, C. (1993) 'Using service guarantees', in Scheuing, E. E., and Christopher, W. F. (eds), *The Service Quality Handbook*, AMACOM, New York, pp. 477–87.

Marriott, J. W., quoted in Albrecht, K. (1990) *Service Within*, Dow Jones-Irwin, Homewood, p. 4.

O'Reilly, P. E. (1993) 'Customer surveys: giving the customer a greater voice', in *Proceedings of the 78th International Purchasing Conference*, National Association of Purchasing Management, Tempe, pp. 53–8.

Parasuraman, A., Berry, L. L., and Zeithaml, V. A. (1991) 'Understanding customer expectations of service', *Sloan Management Review*, vol. **39**, pp. 39–48.

Reichheld, F., and Sasser, E. W. (1990) 'Zero defections: quality comes to services', *Harvard Business Review*, September–October, pp. 105–13.

Rivera, A. T. (1993) 'Selecting and developing the right people to sustain a competitive advantage', in Scheuing, E. E., and Christopher, W. F. (eds), *The Service Quality Handbook*, AMACOM, New York, pp. 233–47.

Rosenbluth, H., and Peters, D. M. (1992) *The Customer Comes Second and Other Secrets of Exceptional Service*, William Morrow, New York.

Troy, K., and Schein, L. (1993) 'Creating a service quality culture', in Scheuing, E. E., and Christopher, W. F. (eds), *The Service Quality Handbook*, AMACOM, New York, pp. 111–23.

Zeithaml, V. A., Parasuraman, A., and Berry, L. L. (1990) *Delivering Service Quality*, The Free Press, New York.

5

Communication in a multinational service organization

Svein Larsen

INTRODUCTION

This chapter reports from a study of the communication climate in an international cruise line.

The first part reviews the background to the study. An analysis of idiosyncrasies of the cruise industry is presented as well as the theoretical and practical framework for the study. It is argued that communication represents a key area concerning quality of services and levels of productivity and job satisfaction in hospitality organizations.

The second part of this chapter concerns the methodology of the study. The communication climate inventory (CCI), an instrument that measures aspects of informal communication, is described. Furthermore, this section describes the respondents and statistical procedures applied for analysing the data.

The third part presents an analysis of the data. The analysis revealed that the degree of *defensiveness* was higher and the degree of *supportiveness* was lower on board ships than in land-based operations. The second part of the analysis concentrated on the hotel departments of the two ships. Results indicate that the degree of defensiveness was higher and the degree of supportiveness was lower in the traditional hotel units (dining-room, galley, housekeeping).

In the last part of this chapter, results are interpreted from the perspective of social psychology. Suggestions are made concerning appropriate measures to be taken in order to improve on current communication practices, in this company as well as in other multinational cruise lines. Such measures include communication training, training for team-building and conflict management and a broadened perspective on organizational norms and attitudes. It is argued that development of communication skills in shipboard management is of paramount importance for the development and maintenance of high quality, in the target company as well as in other hospitality organizations.

SUPPORTIVE AND DEFENSIVE COMMUNICATION: AN OVERVIEW

Surveying recent textbooks on hospitality, hotel and general service management reveals that improved service quality is viewed as a key result area in different sectors of the hospitality industry. Gamble and Jones (1991) noted, for example, that the use of terms like 'competitive weapon', 'critical corporate priority' and 'quality as a major component of mission and competitive advantage' indicated an increased awareness of crucial employee factors for strategic quality management. Similarly, the contemporary literature tends to emphasize the importance of improving employee communication skills and abilities for achieving the 'competitive advantage' of an increased level of service quality. Jones and Lockwood (1989) argued that the communication culture of the hospitality organization constitutes an important area in developing and maintaining quality.

At the same time, the service quality literature indicates that quality control should deal with analysing gaps between actual performance and intended performance in hospitality corporations (Wyckoff, 1988). It is frequently underlined that, in order to improve service quality, hospitality organizations need to ameliorate communication skills. In line with this perspective, communication climates in the hospitality industry need to become more open. Normann (1991) maintained, for example, that training of service personnel was 'vital to the success of all service organizations'. He alleged that a psychosocial environment reflecting interpersonal trust and mutual respect between employees and between employees and management is a condition *sine qua non* in achieving the same kind of climate between front-line personnel and customers. Nevertheless, few studies have been designed to examine communication climates within the boundaries of hospitality organizations, and few studies have appeared examining the effects of various interventions.

These general reflections, along with a leadership development programme launched by the Department of Hotel Operations of an international cruise line, led to an interest in further exploring the concept of communication climate. Initially the leadership development programme had several aims. The first of these was to develop an understanding of the service idea of the target company in crew as well as in ships' management. The second was to foster an enhanced understanding of principles of managing working groups on board cruise ships in general and on board the company's vessels in particular. The third goal was to amplify an understanding of the basics of organizational communication. Related to this aim, the fourth goal of the programme was to introduce fundamental communication skills such as group management, conflict management and direct and open communication with the shipboard personnel.

A series of sessions held for managers on board the ships revealed the importance of a deeper understanding of the communication structure on board the current vessels. Supervisors attending maintained that the communication climate represented a key determinant for organizational effectiveness. It was strongly underlined that current personnel problems could be traced to a lack of supportiveness in the communication climate. Some participants maintained that they were afraid to speak out their points of view to superordinates as they feared they could lose their jobs if they were outspoken. Some supervisors were shown to be very anxious about being ascribed a role of 'nonconformist' when and if they spoke out their opinions. Such a role assignment, it was maintained, could damage the individual's career within the company, and possibly lead to a dismissal from the individual's organizational position.

The relative strength of these statements led to a decision to carry out an investigation of the communication climates in the target organization. Before presenting a short review of the theory, methodology and findings from this study, it is helpful to analyse a few idiosyncrasies of the cruise industry.

THE CRUISE SHIP AS A HOTEL

Many people seem to conceive the cruise ship as a 'boat', a 'ship' or a means of transportation. Nevertheless, according to Jones and Lockwood's (1989) definition of a hotel as 'an operation that provides accommodation and ancillary services to people away from home', the cruise ship is a hotel. This definition of 'hotel' includes all services for people who spend their time away from home for any reason, and thus it embraces services like motels, holiday camps, hospitals, prisons and cruise ships. That the cruise ship is a hotel is furthermore underlined by the fact that there is both a hotel manager and hotel staff on board cruise liners. As opposed to hospitals and other non-profit institutions that fit into Jones and Lockwood's definition, the cruise ship is a commercial operation. This implies more sophisticated means of providing the accommodation experience both in terms of the service package and in terms of business complexity.

Worsfold and Jameson (1991) and Shamir (1978) noted that the organizational model prevailing in the hotel sector seemed to be of a hierarchical and autocratic type. This model of leadership and supervision implies that there are several levels of leadership and a diversity of job titles and hierarchical levels within hotel organizations. Although research into organizational cultures in the hospitality industry is relatively scarce, this organizational pattern still prevails in many, if not most, hospitality organizations. Folgerø (1993) maintained, for example, that hierarchical organizations inevitably produce organizational climates that are counterproductive to the service delivery.

Traditionally, the cruise industry has also been hierarchically organized (Larsen and Rapp, 1993), much like the traditional ship organization (Johansen, 1978). On board cruiseliners, this hierarchy is symbolized in numerous ways, some of which are shown in Table 5.1.

This shows that on board cruise liners, highly visible boundaries between people exist. These differences concern critical factors such as status, power and competence.

Table 5.1 *Status symbols, messages conveyed and intended receivers*

Symbol	Symbol of what? (Message)	To whom? (Receiver)
Uniform	Status Power Role	Passengers and staff
Access to restricted areas	Value Equality to passengers	Passengers and staff
Cabin size	Status	Staff
Guest contact	Competence	Staff
Nationality	Value	Staff (Passengers?)
Sex	Value	Staff (Passengers?)

In addition the symbols reflect the individual employees' value in the organization. Some of these symbols are aimed at the staff, others at the passengers and some at both groups.

There are long-standing traditions for these hierarchical symbols within the cruise trade. The cruise industry is, after all, a *maritime hotel operation*. Because of this it probably carries with it obsolete norms and traditions from maritime settings. The strong belief in the absolute authority of the captain is one of these beliefs that today seems to be challenged by other groups on board. This battle for status is clearly symbolized in many of the hotel and personnel staff's rhetorical 'Have you ever heard about a hotel administered by the janitor?' Nevertheless, the belief in the captain's almost extraordinary abilities seems to prevail to a large extent, among crew members and among guests. This belief constitutes one important aspect of the cruise ship hotel, indicating a strong hierarchical structure. At the same time, of course, this aspect represents, a central area of shipboard conflicts.

In addition to the very visual and obvious symbols indicated in Table 5.1, there are numerous more subtle symbols of status, power and hierarchy in the cruise industry. Such symbols include, but are not limited to, one's knowledge of repeat clients, one's sexual orientation, one's private life and one's plans for career development in addition to one's achievements within the industry. The complexity of status indicators in the cruise industry is consequently very high.

Working on board

Typically, the cruise ship is staffed by individuals from many different nations. Some have characterized the typical cruise ship as being a miniature United Nations. Nevertheless, there is some anecdotal evidence showing that the peaceful and civilized negotiations conducted by the real UN are generally not found in the miniature UN of the cruise ship. One such story tells of a hotel manager on one of the world's largest cruise ships who once told an audience that the orientals in the crew came in very handy, inasmuch as they were small. This, he maintained, made the orientals useful for many purposes on board, e.g. providing services without being seen by the guests. In addition the orientals could be used for scrubbing areas of the boat others could not reach as easily. The racist and contemptuous attitudes behind these statements are, hopefully, not prevalent in the cruise business in general.

There are, of course, both advantages and drawbacks connected with working in such an international environment. Many consider this kind of work as an opportunity to see the world, and learn about different cultures. For some crew members, particularly the younger ones, working on board may represent an opportunity to get away from home. Since quite a few companies operate in the luxury market, many outstandingly competent tradesmen within the cooking and waiting professions get an opportunity to work in a highly competitive and technically advanced environment. Thus the cruise experience provides an opportunity to become proficient for many members of the crew.

There are, however, certain disadvantages to working on board. First and foremost, contracts in this sector are sometimes for as long as six months. This prevents the individual crew member from getting home to his or her family and friends for a long period of time. In addition, many crew members are confined to a limited area on board. These restrictions might serve as a psychosocial stressor, since there is only a limited opportunity for privacy on board. In addition, working hours in this sector are very long, and earnings are sometimes low. Crew members often have no protection against arbitrary settlements made by superordinates concerning cabin assignments, working hours, food and so forth. Thus, in spite of the many advantages of working in this industry, there also seem to be certain drawbacks related to such factors as amount of privacy, control over one's own time and low wages. Johansen (1978) furthermore underlined that the bureaucratic and authoritarian ship's organization in itself could create a number of psychological and social problems, such as various psychosomatic illnesses, interpersonal and intergroup conflicts and high turnover rates.

Why is communication important to the service company?

Analysing organizations demands that the analyst, the manager or the consultant acknowledge distinct categories for describing the particular company in focus. Maybe the most obvious aspect of the cruise line is its highly hierarchical and compartmentalized structure. Within every department of the cruise company there are highly specialized and differentiated jobs. This organizational design implies three parallel, yet distinct, departments; deck, engine and hotel on board ships, in addition to shoreside departments for passengers' and crews' air arrangements, finance, hotel operations, and departments for reservations and sales. Naturally there is also an executive department in most cruise companies. The three first-mentioned divisions (deck, engine and hotel) are on board. Together, they constitute the departments that encounter the guests after they have purchased their cruise, although the main responsibility for service delivery seems to be attributed to the hotel crew.

When studying working groups and leadership, it is possible to identify several social-psychological factors that contribute to productive or non-productive behaviours. Our first observation concerning the cruise company relates to its formal aspects – its highly hierarchical and compartmentalized structure. Social psychologists focus on group factors like norms, roles, communication and standards of decision-making within the working group. Johnson and Johnson (1991) asserted, for example, that group effectiveness depends on communication, leadership, decision-making and the practical and capable handling of intragroup and intergroup conflicts. All of these aspects of organizational life tend to have one formal and one informal side. Formal structures are imposed on people in organizations and at the same time individuals form their own norms, roles and communication patterns (Conrad, 1989).

In service operations, communication seems to be particularly important (Jones and Lockwood, 1989; Lovelock, 1988), since it is through efficient employee–guest communication that the service quality is created (Larsen and Rapp, 1993). It is also through communication that supervisors motivate, encourage, support and direct employees. An open communication climate is, furthermore, a prerequisite in order for the leadership to receive feedback on current problems, conflicts and ideas. Lack of such openness may result in higher turnover rates, increased resignation frequencies, poor timekeeping, hostility and conflict in and between working teams. Poor cooperation, absenteeism, mass resignations and strong informal groupings opposing the company's goals may be other negative results of such a communication culture, in addition to the effects of the traditional ship organization described earlier (Johansen, 1978).

Consequently, if communication in an environment like the one on the cruise ship does not function efficiently, it is to be expected that there will be fairly high turnover rates among crew members. In addition, the psychosocial environment might induce problematic structures concerning conflict management, and handling of intradepartmental and interdepartmental cooperation. In the long run these consequences are very likely to impair service quality.

DEFENSIVE AND SUPPORTIVE COMMUNICATION

Asserting that employees are under the influence of the organization's communication climate, Gibb (1961) identified characteristics of 'supportive and defensive environments'. A *defensive communication climate* tends to encourage workers to keep things to themselves and to make only guarded statements. Such behaviours will eventually lead to a feeling of being 'burned out' and alienation in the working group, the ultimate result being that employees will leave the organization after a short period. For a cruise company, it is consequently of paramount importance to be aware of the obstacles to producing excellent service inherent to the organization's communication climate.

Figures 5.1 and 5.2 describe defensive and supportive communication climates. A communication climate of the defensive nature (Figure 5.1) notably does not inspire openness. On the contrary, groups with these symptoms typically cause employees to feel insecure, scared and disrespectful in their relations with their supervisors. In the long run, the cruise line's service quality will decrease as a function of such a communication structure.

On the other hand, open and free exchange of information, constructive conflict management procedures, high degrees of worker involvement in solving organizational problems and a high degree of job-satisfaction all seem to be positively linked to a *supportive communication climate* in the organization. Gibb (1961) identified six aspects of such supportiveness, diametrically different from the defensive structure (Figure 5.2). Notably, such an environment encourages openness, in supervisors as well as in staff. It demands a particular effort from the supervisor concerning his or her willingness to allow employees openly to express opinions, feelings and ideas. The

1. **Evaluation:** The supervisor is critical and judgemental and will not accept explanations from subordinates.

2. **Control:** The supervisor constantly directs in an authoritarian manner, and attempts to change other people.

3. **Strategy:** The supervisor manipulates subordinates and often misinterprets or twists and distorts what is said.

4. **Neutrality:** The supervisor offers minimal personal support for and remains indifferent to employees' personal problems and conflicts.

5. **Superiority:** The supervisor reminds employees who is in change, closely overseas the work, and makes employees feel inadequate.

6. **Certainty:** The supervisor is dogmatic and unwilling to admit mistakes.

Figure 5.1 *Characteristics of a defensive climate*

1. **Descriptive:** The supervisor's communication is clear, describes situations fairly and presents his or her perceptions without implying the need for change.

2. **Problem orientation:** The supervisor defines problems rather than gives solutions. He or she is open to discussion about mutual problems and does not insist on employee agreement.

3. **Spontaneity:** The supervisor's communications are free of hidden motives and honest. Ideas can be expressed freely.

4. **Empathy:** The supervisor attempts to understand and listen to employee problems and respects employee feelings and values.

5. **Equality:** The supervisor does not try to make employees feel inferior, does not use status to control situations, and respects the position of others.

6. **Provisionalism:** The superisor allows flexibility, experimentation and creativity.

Figure 5.2 *Characteristics of a supportive climate*

supervisor encouraging such a climate typically knows the principles of active and passive listening, empathy and effective communication.

Since the management of the organization as well as many supervisors and crew members had expressed a desire to learn more about communication structures in the company, it was decided to carry out an investigation of current *informal* communication practices in the target company. The aim of the study was twofold. The first intention was to diagnose communication deficiencies. The second goal was that the results of the study should indicate appropriate steps the company's management in cooperation with officers and crew could take to improve communication skills, the psychosocial working environment and ultimately the service quality in the company.

METHODOLOGY

This and the next section of this chapter briefly review methodology and results. A summary of findings is presented at the beginning of the Discussion and the Conclusion.

The present study was a survey among all employees in the target organization. The questionnaire was distributed among employees by a company representative. Subjects were asked to fill in the questionnaire, put it in an envelope, close the envelope, and return it to the researcher. This was done to secure the respondents' confidentiality.

The inventory

Six introductory questions asked the subjects to identify where they worked (ashore or on board), their age, their sex, their nationality and their department (deck, engine, hotel, etc.), and whether they supervised others. In addition, for subjects working in the hotel department, a record was made of which of the hotel units they worked in (bar, dining-room, entertainment, etc.).

Costigan and Schmeidler (1987) developed the communication climate inventory (CCI). This instrument operationalized the notions of defensive and supportive communication climates (Gibb, 1961). The 36 questions of the CCI are presented in a Likert response format, and there are three questions for each of the 12 factors described in Figures 5.1 and 5.2.

The degree of defensiveness was calculated as the sum score of items concerning defensiveness, and degree of supportiveness was calculated as the sum score of items concerning supportiveness. The inventory is designed so that the lower the score, the higher the degree to which the current communication climate exists. There are three items for each of the aspects on supportiveness and defensiveness, 18 for each of the two dimensions under focus in the present study. The highest possible score on these aspects is consequently 15, and the lowest possible 3. The lowest possible score on either dimension (defensiveness or supportiveness) is 18, and the highest is 90.

On defensiveness, scores between 18 and 40 are considered to reflect a 'defensive climate', 41–55 reflect 'defensive to neutral', 56–69 reflect 'neutral to supportive' and scores above 70 indicate a 'supportive climate'. On the supportive scale, a 'supportive climate' is reflected by scores between 18 and 40, a 'supportive to neutral' climate is in the range 41–55, 'neutral to defensive' is in the range 56–69, and 'defensive' is indicated by scores above 70.

Subjects

The subjects of the study included all employees in the target company, 236 of whom had filled in the questionnaire satisfactorily; 86.87 per cent of the respondents worked on board the two ships, and the remaining 13.3 per cent worked in the offices. One hundred and seventy-eight of the respondents worked in the hotel departments of the two ships, 20 respondents worked in the deck department and six respondents worked in the engine department. The response rate was satisfactory.

There were 68 (28.8 per cent) women and 167 (70.8 per cent) men in the present study. One respondent had failed to identify his or her sex, and one respondent had failed to identify which office department he or she worked in.

A total of 139 respondents indicated that they had no supervisory responsibilities and 90 respondents indicated that they supervised others as a part of their job. Seven respondents did not indicate whether they were supervisors or not.

Mean age in the sample was 30.92 years, and standard deviation was 7.85. The median was 29.50, third quartile 34.80.

Nationalities and age in the hotel departments

Of the 178 respondents from the two hotel departments, 162 reported their nationality. Thirty-six were Asians, 20 were from the UK or Ireland, 18 were Austrians, 13 were

Norwegians and the rest were from other Western countries. In the galleys, 56 per cent (11) of the respondents were Filipino, and in the housekeeping units 31 per cent (11) of the respondents were Filipino. The crew in the hotel departments truly constitutes an international community.

Twenty-six per cent of the respondents in the hotel departments were women. Housekeeping (60 per cent), purser (78 per cent) and concession (78 per cent) had a majority of women.

There were significant age differences between the sections in the hotel departments; bar and housekeeping units, average 27 years; dining-room, average 28 years; pursers units, average 29 years; concessions and galleys, average 30 years; and entertainments and controllers, average 34 years.

Statistics

The data were analysed using the NSD-STAT + statistical programme. The T-test and one-way ANOVA was applied, with a rejection region of $p < 0.05$. The age factor was controlled for using one-way ANOVA with the statistical quartiles as a grouping factor.

RESULTS

This section firstly describes the overall defensiveness and supportiveness in the different divisions (ships and offices) and departments (deck, engine, hotel, air, executive, finance, hotel operations, reservations, sales). The second part of this section focuses on a more detailed analysis of the crew in the hotel departments of the vessels, since they obviously are the most important individuals in creating the guest's experiences.

The overall structure

Table 5.2 shows the overall communication climates (defensiveness and supportiveness) in the company's land-based operations (the offices) and on board the two ships. The higher the score, the less prevalent the current trait.

The mean defensiveness score in the sample was 58.71, which means that the degree of defensiveness leans towards being neutral. This finding implies that on average in the organization, there is a certain amount of defensiveness. Table 5.2 clearly indicates that the defensiveness score on average is lower (more defensiveness) on board the ships than in the organization's offices in Europe and in the USA. In addition, Table 5.2

Table 5.2 *Defensiveness and supportiveness in the organization*

	Defensiveness	*Supportiveness*
On the ships	57.24	41.77
In the offices	68.42	36.55
Total	58.71	41.09

indicates that the mean supportiveness score was higher (less supportiveness) on board the ships than in the offices. These differences are statistically significant tested by one-way ANOVAs (defensiveness $F(1,233) = 24.718, p = 0.000$; supportiveness $F(1,233) = 7.713, p = 0.006$). Controlling for age, there was no difference in the empirical age quartiles concerning either of the two traits (defensiveness $F(3,222) = 0.507, p = 0.6822$; supportiveness $F(3,222) = 0.033, p = 0.9869$). The differences are therefore due to a difference in communication climates between the offices and the ships, and not due to any age skewness in the two groups.

Turning to Table 5.3, the focus of interest has shifted to employees who are not leaders. Table 5.3 shows the data concerning defensiveness and supportiveness as they were reported by individuals in the organization with no supervisory responsibilities. Interestingly, these results indicate that the three ship departments obtained a lower score on defensiveness than the other departments. This indicates a higher degree of defensiveness in these departments. The finding is in accordance with the results presented in Table 5.2.

It is highly significant that the three ship departments score on the lower side of the overall mean for the total sample, whereas the land-based departments score on the higher side of this overall mean. This indicates that the crew on board the ships consider, on average, their communication climate to be 'worse' than the average communication climate in the organization concerning defensiveness. These differences are statistically significant ($p < 0.001$), thus indicating a systematic variation, not one due to coincidence.

The overall supportiveness score in the sample was 41.67, indicating that the overall climate within the organization is leaning towards being neutral. Table 5.3 demonstrates that on average shipboard personnel obtain higher scores on supportiveness than subordinates in the other departments in the target company. Again this implies a higher degree of supportiveness in land-based departments than on board. These differences are true for both sexes. It is also noteworthy that crew from the three ship departments score on the upper side of the overall mean for the total sample, whereas staff from the land-based departments typically score on the lower side of this overall mean. Again this implies that there is less supportiveness on board the floating hotel than in the offices ashore. Testing the differences statistically yields significant results ($p < 0.001$), implying that the differences are systematic and not due to coincidence.

Table 5.3 *Defensiveness and supportiveness in different departments (SD in parentheses)*

	Defensiveness	Supportiveness	N
Deck	53.20 (11.16)	46.20 (5.80)	10
Hotel	57.19 (11.58)	42.83 (9.33)	105
Engine	57.67 (6.66)	42.00 (11.53)	3
Air	61.67 (8.14)	41.00 (7.94)	3
Hotel operations	67.50 (2.12)	32.00 (5.66)	2
Executive	67.50 (6.36)	38.00 (5.66)	2
Sales	68.00 (9.63)	35.00 (2.16)	4
Finance	70.00 (2.83)	30.50 (0.71)	3
Reservations	77.50 (5.42)	30.38 (5.80)	8
Total	58.97 (12.07)	41.67 (9.34)	139

The hotel departments

From the results already presented above it is noticeable that crew in the hotel departments on average report more defensiveness and less supportiveness than the other departments in the organization. Considering the fact that our target company, and for that matter any cruise line, delivers services, and that these services are produced and delivered mainly through the crew in the hotel section, a further analysis of the communication climate in this department seems to be needed. The following analysis is based on results from both ships and from all respondents (N = 178) in the hotel departments.

Figure 5.3 shows the difference between the eight hotel units concerning defensiveness. Figure 5.3 shows that the galleys and the housekeeping units score below the hotel departments' mean score on defensiveness (i.e. higher degree of defensiveness). Concessions, entertainments, controllers, purser's unit, dining-room and bar score above the average score on this dimension (lower degree of defensiveness). Nevertheless, concessions, entertainments and controllers score significantly higher than the other groups, indicating that their communication environments are considerably better than in the rest of the hotel department. Comparing the figures behind these figures with the ones in Table 5.2 indicates that the mean score in the galley (50.09) is below the lowest score in any of the departments. On the other hand, the mean score in concessions (68.22), is significantly higher than the mean scores found in reservations and finance. The differences between the units in the hotel department are significant, tested by one-way ANOVA (p < 0.01).

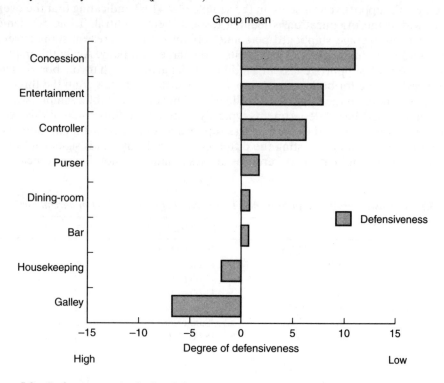

Figure 5.3 *Defensiveness in the hotel departments*

Figure 5.4 shows the difference between the eight hotel units concerning supportiveness. The impression from Table 5.2 seems reinforced, in as much as controllers, concessions, entertainments and bar staff report a higher degree of supportiveness in their sections (lower score). These groups score below the hotel departments overall mean. The purser's unit, dining-room, housekeeping and galley score above. On the extreme sides, Figure 5.4 indicates that the purser's section reported a very defensive, non-supportive communication climate, while the controllers report the highest degree of supportiveness. Comparing these figures with the figures in Table 5.2 indicates that the mean score in controllers (31.50) is about as low as the lowest score in any of the main departments of the organization. On the other hand, the mean score in the purser's unit (48.33) is higher than the highest score of any department in the whole organization. The degree of supportiveness is consequently reported to be extremely low in the purser's unit. These differences are significant, tested by one-way ANOVA ($p < 0.01$).

DISCUSSION

First and foremost, the results showed that defensiveness was higher on board ships than in the land-based divisions. In addition, a larger degree of supportive communication in the land-based operations than on board the two hotel ships was observed.

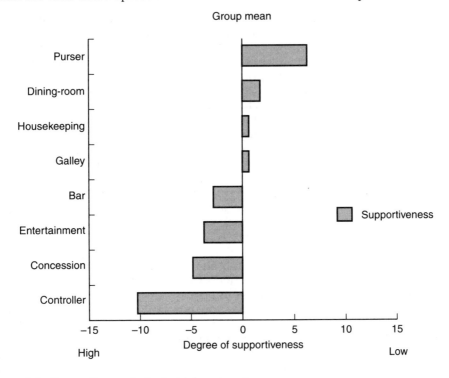

Figure 5.4 *Supportiveness in the hotel departments*

The results also indicated significant differences in defensiveness and supportiveness within the hotel departments. Concessions, entertainments and controllers reported the lowest degree of defensiveness, whereas the bar department, housekeeping and galley reported the highest degree of defensiveness. Concerning supportiveness, controllers, concessions and entertainments reported the most supportive climate, whereas the purser's unit, dining-room and housekeeping reported the lowest degree of supportiveness.

General discussion

Maritime operations tend to have a hierarchical organizational structure (Johansen, 1978; Larsen and Rapp, 1993). This structure is such that the differences between different employees' ranks is accentuated both by the mere physical elements, such as uniforms, cabin size, and access to guest areas (public areas), and by more subtle components, such as work experience and nationality. Land-based operations also have such differences, although they are not as emphasized as in their maritime counterparts. The findings illustrate that these differences in status may influence communication climates, and are therefore probably factors concerning the general level of job satisfaction, service attitudes and service quality in these departments. Larsen and Bastiansen (1992) did, for example, report data supporting the view that hierarchical organizations had significantly poorer service attitudes than less hierarchical structures.

It may very well be that the foundations and basic understanding of the personnel policies, and the application of principles of personnel management, are different in land-based and maritime operations. It might, for example, be that work in the offices is conceived of as having a more permanent nature than working on board ships, by supervisors as well as by crew. Such a conceptualization could imply an important difference in personnel management practices, since staff 'who are only here for a short while' are of less importance to the company than employees in more permanent positions. Attitudes like 'The crew is here only for a short period of time anyway', 'Why should we listen to these people, who do not depend on the work like we do?', 'Most of the crew is here just to get an opportunity to see the world', and 'These people have no experience in running cruise lines' would be likely results of such conceptualizations. Naturally, the communication climate of the ship would suffer if such attitudes were to prevail in shipboard management. In addition, such managerial attitudes might lead to a self-fulfilling prophecy: the process whereby the management's attitudes towards the crew could elicit exactly the expected behaviour from crew members (Johnson and Johnson, 1991, pp. 354–5). In other words, if crew members are treated *as if* they will leave the company after one contract only, the probability that they will do just that increases.

One central aspect of working on a cruise ship is that the individual is confined to a very restricted area, often for a long period of time. Basically this implies that the individual worker has only limited access to privacy. This mere fact may result in an experience of being 'seen' by someone else, supervisors, colleagues and guests, all the time. Such an experience would inevitably imply a subjective 'need to defend oneself', and probably lead to more defensiveness and less openness on board ships. The questions asked in the CCI concern job-related communication, and the findings *do* indicate a more defensive/less supportive climate on board ships than in the offices. This should represent an important challenge in the organization's planning and implementing of personnel strategies. It would, for example, be of importance to train managers not only to encourage openness, but also to be able to handle criticism constructively. Such training should be based on social-psychological principles of attribution theory and social perception.

The turnover rates in cruise lines are generally relatively high compared to those in land-based operations. Many employees are on board for one contract only, and some even leave before the termination of the first contract. Presumably some of the crew members are not psychologically prepared for the life and work on board a cruise ship. A strategy to influence first-time crew's expectations, and a strategy to improve on introductory training for first-time crew, consequently seems to be called for. Such strategies would imply the active administration of introductory programmes when new crew members arrive at the ship. In addition the department of hotel operations, or the personnel department when appropriate, could implement a strategy in order more carefully to influence new crew members' expectations *before* the contract is signed. If new crew members, and particularly first-time crew, are psychologically prepared for life on board, they would to a larger extent be able to handle personal and interpersonal problems during their contract. Such simple measures could in a significant way contribute to producing more supportive and less defensive communication climates on board cruise ships.

A closer look at the hotel departments

The results demonstrate that communication climates in the two hotel units of our target company were high in defensiveness and low in supportiveness. A closer analysis of the data revealed that there were significant differences between the different units within the hotel departments concerning these two aspects. The analysis showed that the more traditional hotel departments (purser, dining-room, bar, galley and housekeeping) generally showed a higher degree of defensiveness and a lower degree of supportiveness than did controllers, entertainments and concessions.

Defensiveness

The analysis of the defensiveness component revealed that *evaluation* (the supervisor is critical and judgemental and will not accept explanations from subordinates) was a prevalent trait in the galley, housekeeping, bar and dining-room units. *Control* – the supervisor constantly directs in an authoritarian manner, and attempts to change other people – seems to be a problem experienced predominantly in the same units. *Strategy* – the supervisor manipulates subordinates and often misinterprets or twists and distorts what is said – reported to be most prevalent in the galley, in the controllers' group, in the purser's section and in housekeeping. *Neutrality* – the supervisor offers minimal personal support for, and remains indifferent to, employees' personal problems and conflicts – seems to be a problem in the galley, housekeeping, entertainments and controllers' groups. *Superiority* – the supervisor reminds employees who is in charge, oversees the work, and makes employees feel incompetent – is predominantly a characteristic of the galley, housekeeping, dining-room and bar sections. *Certainty* – the supervisor is dogmatic and unwilling to admit mistakes – seems to be most prevalent in the galley, bar, housekeeping and purser units.

What might the reasons be for these findings? Why do the crew in the traditional hotel departments experience a higher degree of defensiveness in their communication climates than other groups in this study?

One explanation might be linked to the organizational culture. Some of the hierarchical structures described above may prevail in the hotel departments. The symbols of status do seem to survive in this department, and are probably made more explicit in the galley, housekeeping, bar and purser sections. The crew in these four units is, at least for three of the units, predominantly European or North American. These personnel probably expect more of their supervisors in terms of less evaluation, less control, less manipulation, more personal support and more friendliness. These crew members are used to a standard of interpersonal relations that involves treating members of the group on equal terms. Many Western crew members will simply not accept differential treatments dependent on the status symbols so common in maritime settings. They want to be judged by the standard of their performance or by the quality of their social abilities.

The personnel in these units are also younger than the crew in the other units in the hotel department. Younger people probably need more personal attention and more support than more mature crew members. This could be yet another reason why a higher degree of defensiveness was reported in these departments.

Supportiveness

Provisionalism – the supervisor allows flexibility, experimentation and creativity – was found predominantly in the controllers' group, in the bar, in concessions and in entertainments. *Empathy* – the supervisor attempts to understand and listen to employee problems and respects employees' feelings and values – was predominantly found in the same units. *Equality* – the supervisor does not try to make employees feel inferior or use status to control situations, or respects the position of others – was predominantly a trait of entertainments, controllers, concessions and galley. *Spontaneity* – the supervisors' communications are free of hidden motives and honest, and ideas can be expressed freely – was found to be more prevalent in controllers, concessions, entertainments and housekeeping. *Problem orientation* – the supervisor defines problems rather than gives solutions, is open to discussion about mutual problems and does not insist on employee agreement – was a more widespread experience in controllers, concessions, entertainments and dining-room. Finally, a *descriptive* pattern – the supervisor's communication is clear, he or she describes situations fairly and presents his or her perceptions without urging the need for change – was found predominantly in the controllers, concessions, entertainments and housekeeping.

It is difficult to interpret these findings. Nevertheless, it may well be that the traditional hotel departments (purser, dining-room, housekeeping and galley) are governed by obsolete cultural norms implying large differences between different individuals, as discussed above. Such norms imply that disagreement with a supervisor is not allowed and that conflicts are dangerous. It may further be that there is a norm stating that positive feelings, praise and support are not to be shared in these groups.

Front-line personnel in the cruise industry are in reality the people who deliver, or fail to deliver, the quality that the passengers pay for. Larsen and Rapp (1993) argued that to the extent that the cruise industry views itself as having the objective of offering high quality, these companies should also fund more and higher paid front-line personnel. This, in turn should be followed by empowering (Sternberg, 1992) front-line service workers. Such empowerment would inevitably lead to an increased status for front-line jobs, thus contributing to making the 'upside down' organizational chart manifest. It is this author's view that empowerment, higher status and better paid front-line jobs, *in addition* to an active attitude towards improving the communication environment, would have positive effects for any operator in the cruise business.

CONCLUSIONS

The main finding, that the degree of supportiveness is lower and the degree of defensiveness is higher on board ships than in the offices, implies that measures should be taken in order to improve current communication practices. There is obviously a need for more understanding of the principles of working groups, communication, norms and roles as part of the general principles of service management in the target organization and probably in most other cruise line companies. In particular, there seems to be such a demand on board the vessels.

The findings might also indicate a need for a broader understanding of the principles of modifying behaviour. Any introductory psychology text will explain the principle of positive reinforcement, and underline that positive reinforcement is a stronger factor in motivating people than negative reinforcement or punishment. Although everyone seems to be in agreement with this, it is still my impression that we have a long way to go when it comes to implementing the consequences of this knowledge in everyday management. Gibb's (1961) notion of supportiveness could prove helpful as a guideline for implementing procedures concerning positive reinforcement.

A well-known early signal of conflict is that communication skills are poor and that there is poor mutual trust between individuals and groups (Cragan and Wright, 1991; Zahl-Begnum, 1991). Such conflicts may, as indicated, sometimes have dramatic end results: mass resignations, higher turnover rates, absenteeism, poor timekeeping, excessive use of alcohol etc. This also underlines the need for a better understanding of how people function in working groups on board cruise ships. Today's employee expects a fair and humane working environment – he or she expects to be treated on his or her own terms and as an individual. In order to better manage future conflicts, the cruise company should start by developing their managers, and then their crew, concerning relevant conflict management skills.

In order to keep crew for more than one contract, and in order to improve on psychosocial working conditions, team-building skills should be developed in ship-board management. It seems necessary to actively reinforce every activity that contributes to bringing more openness and decreasing defensiveness at the managerial level of the organization. If managers could feel confident in their relations with one another on board ship, much would have been gained. If, in addition, such confidence could be built between the two ships and the offices, it would mean that managers would not have to feel insecure or alone in their handling of personnel and personal problems.

Nonetheless, it may very well be that the major problem indicated in this study is of a cultural, norm-related character. If it is true that management's basic philosophy about human nature is of a Theory X orientation (McGregor, 1960), then that is where the company should start to treat management-related problems. However difficult changing attitudes and behavioural practices might seem, it is, in this author's view, important, and economically sound, for the company to make such an investment in its leaders.

NOTE

The findings reported in this study provide some interesting insights into cruise ship inter-relationships. Nonetheless, they are exploratory in nature and further empirical work is needed to verify and elaborate the observations reported here.

REFERENCES

Conrad, C. (1989) *Strategic Organizational Communication*, Holt, Rinehart and Winston, Inc., Fort Worth/Chicago/San Francisco.

Costigan, J. I., and Schmeidler, M. A. (1988), 'Exploring supportive and defensive communication climates', in Pfeiffer, J. W. (ed.), *The University Associates Instrumentation Kit*, University Associates, Inc., San Diego, California.

Cragan, J. F., and Wright, D. W. (1991) *Communication in Small Group Discussions*, West Publishing Company, New York.

Folgerø, I. S. (1993) 'Structural shortcomings in the service industries', *Working Papers from Rogaland University Centre*, no. 174.

Gamble, P., and Jones, P. (1991) 'Quality as a strategic issue', in Teare, R., and Boer, A. (eds), *Strategic Hospitality Management*, Cassell, London, pp. 72–82.

Gibb, J. R. (1961) 'Defensive and supportive communication', *Journal of Communications*, vol. 11, pp. 141–8.

Johansen, R. (1978), 'Stress and socio-technical design: a new ship organization', in Cooper, C. L., and Payne, R. (eds), *Stress at Work*, John Wiley & Sons, Chichester/New York/Brisbane/Tokyo.

Johnson, D. W., and Johnson, F. P. (1991) *Joining Together – Group Theory and Group Skills*, Prentice-Hall International Editions, London.

Jones, P., and Lockwood, A. (1989) *The Management of Hotel Operations*, Cassell, London.

Larsen, S., and Bastiansen, T. (1992) 'Service attitudes in hotel and restaurant staff and nurses', *International Journal of Contemporary Hospitality Management*, vol. 4, no. 2, pp. 27–31.

Larsen, S., and Rapp, L. (1993) 'Creating the service driven cruiseline – competition for the 90's', *International Journal of Contemporary Hospitality Management*, vol. 5, no. 1, pp. iv–vi.

Lovelock, C. H. (ed.) (1988) *Managing Services – Marketing, Operations and Human Resources*, Prentice-Hall International Editions, New York.

McGregor, D. (1960) 'Theory X: the traditional view of direction and control' and 'Theory Y: the integration of individual and organizational goals', in McGregor, D., *The Human Side of Enterprise*, McGraw-Hill, New York, pp. 33–57.

Normann, R. (1991) *Service Management*, Wiley, Chichester.

Shamir, B. (1978) 'Between bureaucracy and hospitality – some organizational characteristics of hotels', *Journal of Management Studies*, October, pp. 285–307.

Sternberg, L. E. (1992) 'Empowerment: trust vs. control', *Cornell Hotel and Restaurant Administration Quarterly*, vol. **33**, no. 1, pp. 69–72.

Worsfold, P., and Jameson, S. (1991) 'Human resource management: a response to change in the 1990s', in Teare, R., and Boer, A. (eds), *Strategic Hospitality Management*, Cassell, London, pp. 99–119.

Wyckoff, D. D. (1988) 'New tools for achieving service quality', in Lovelock, C. H. (ed.), *Managing Services – Marketing, Operations and Human Resources*, Prentice-Hall International Editions, New York.

Zahl-Begnum, O. H. (1991) *Sosiale Konflikter*, Sigma, Bergen.

PART TWO
INTEGRATING SERVICE QUALITY

6

Quality and the role of human resources

Nicholas Horney

INTRODUCTION

As a movement which has spread into every industry and sector throughout the world, the concept of total quality is a recent and important development for international competitiveness. The search for quality has created a revolution whose momentum has been building over the past decade, and which is fundamentally altering the way in which business is conducted and customers are treated. Achieving excellence in quality has become an increasingly important element in competitive success. The vehicle by which companies will achieve that goal has come to be called total quality (TQ) or service quality (SQ).

THE CASE FOR QUALITY

During the past ten years, changes in technology, competition and economic conditions have heightened customer demand for quality. Change of this nature is not accidental. There is strategic worldwide recognition of the need for quality: witness the interest of companies in being certified to international standards for quality established by the International Organization for Standardization (ISO), known as the ISO 9000 series of standards (Burrows, 1992). Profitability is directly linked to a company's ability to provide quality to its customers (United States General Accounting Office, 1991). In fact, a recent study conducted by Tom Haller indicated that companies managed according to a total quality management (TQM) philosophy outperformed the S&P 500 Index by over 7 per cent (Haller, 1994). Moreover, if you had purchased Baldrige Award-winning company stock, you would have outperformed the S&P 500 by over 50 per cent (*Business Week*, 1993). Clearly, then, the challenge for maintaining growth and success in such a quality-conscious environment is to implement and sustain a total quality effort.

For ten years, the US balance of trade (surplus of exports over imports) has been negative, illustrating deficiency in competition with business elsewhere in the world. Lawler (1992) describes the primary source of these problems within US business organizations as the continuation of top-down organizational structure, management, and control over employees. Sadly, many hospitality organizations still reflect this top-down structure and management control culture.

SERVICE QUALITY AND HUMAN RESOURCES

A major focus in implementing quality has been the technical side of the equation. Process and product improvement often yield quality results. However, the key variable in quality improvement has been a company's human resources (HR).

Executives participating in a 1993 American Society for Quality Control/Gallup survey of perceptions on a range of competitive issues most frequently cited quality (service and product) and productivity as the key competitive issues facing them (ASCQ, 1993). The Gallup Organization interviewed 615 senior executives, 307 representing Fortune 1000 companies, the remainder from smaller firms. HR issues were the most important, as illustrated in Table 6.1.

The visibility of the TQM movement provides HR departments with a golden opportunity to move from HR management to strategic HR management. A major role in the TQM initiative puts the HR department in a position to contribute directly and visibly to the bottom line.

A number of conceptual articles have been written concerning the importance of HR practices for TQM initiatives (Brown, 1991; Hendricks and Triplett, 1989; Roth, 1989; Schuler and Harris, 1991; Yeamans, 1989). Other articles have focused on the implementation of TQM principles within the HR department (Bowen and Greiner, 1986; Carr, 1987; Kahnweiler, 1991). However, little has been written on specific HR processes and their impact on TQM programs. This chapter will address TQM, HR processes and hospitality industry examples of TQM and HR management (HRM).

Table 6.1   *1993 ASQC/Gallup survey (sponsored by the American Society for Quality Control)*

Method of improving quality	Percentage rating it highly effective
Employee motivation	85
Change in corporate culture	82
Employee education	74
Process control	53
Expenditures on capital equipment	45
More control of supplies	36
More inspections	29
Improved administrative support	28

Malcolm Baldrige National Quality Award

Although the application of TQM is unique to each company that adopts such an approach, consensus has formed around the attributes that are common to all TQM organizations. This consensus is reflected in the criteria established by the Malcolm Baldrige National Quality Award.

In 1988, the United States Department of Commerce initiated the Malcolm Baldrige National Quality Award to recognize American companies doing an exceptional job of providing high-quality products and services to their customers. In effect, the criteria outlined in the Baldrige Award application represent a set of national quality standards. Increasingly, organizations have used the criteria as diagnostic tools for their quality efforts.

Human resources development and management is one of the seven major categories of the Malcolm Baldrige National Quality Award criteria. It is allocated 150 of the total 1,000 points available. The categories and points for the Baldrige Award in 1994 are:

Leadership	95
Information and analysis	75
Strategic quality planning	60
Human resources development and management	150
Management of process quality	140
Quality and operation results	180
Customer focus and satisfaction	300
Total	1,000

The human resource development and management category examines the key elements of how the workforce is enabled to develop its full potential to pursue the company's quality and operational performance objectives. Also examined are the company's efforts to build and maintain an environment for quality excellence conductive to full participation and personal and organizational growth.

The human resource development and management category has five subcategories. The first is human resource planning and management, which addresses how the company's overall HR management plans and processes are integrated with its overall quality and operational performance plans and how HR planning and management address fully the needs and development of the entire workforce. Examples of HR plans provided in the Baldrige criteria include:

1. Mechanisms for promoting cooperation such as internal customer/supplier techniques or other internal partnerships.
2. Initiatives to promote labour–management cooperation, such as partnerships with unions.
3. Creation and/or modification of recognition systems.
4. Creation or modification of compensation systems based on building shareholder value.
5. Mechanisms for increasing or broadening employee responsibilities.
6. Creating opportunities for employees to learn and use skills that go beyond current job assignments through redesign or processes.
7. Creation of high-performance work teams.
8. Education and training initiatives.

9.   Forming partnerships with educational institutions to develop employees or to help ensure the future supply of well-prepared employees.

The second subcategory is employee involvement, which focuses on how all employees are enabled to contribute effectively to meeting the company's quality and operational performance plans. Examples of employee involvement include problem-solving teams (within work groups or cross-functional); fully integrated, self-managed work teams; and process improvement teams.

Employee education and training is the third subcategory, and addresses how the company determines quality and related education and training needs for all employees as well as how the training is evaluated. Quality and related education and training address the knowledge and skills that employees need to meet their objectives as part of the company's quality and operational performance improvement. These efforts could include quality awareness, leadership, project management, communications, team work, problem-solving, interpreting and using data, meeting customer requirements, process analysis, process simplification, waste reduction, cycle time reduction, error-proofing, and other training that affects employee effectiveness, efficiency and safety. In many cases this might include job enrichment skills and job rotation that enhance employees' career opportunities. It might include basic skills such as reading, writing, language, arithmetic and basic mathematics that are needed for quality and operational performance improvement.

The fourth subcategory is employee performance and recognition, which addresses how the company's employee performance, recognition, promotion, compensation, reward and feedback approaches support the improvement of quality and operational performance. The company might use a variety of reward and recognition approaches – monetary and non-monetary, formal and informal, and individual and group.

Employee well-being and satisfaction is the fifth subcategory. It focuses on how the company maintains a work environment conducive to the well-being and growth of its employees. Examples of specific factors for which satisfaction might be determined include: safety; employee views of leadership and management; employee development; career opportunities; employee preparation for changes in technology or work organization; work environment; team work; recognition; benefits; communications; job security; and compensation. Measures and indicators of well-being and satisfaction include safety, absenteeism, turnover, turnover rate for customer contact employees, grievances, strikes and worker compensation.

Human resources policies of Malcolm Baldrige National Quality Award winners

Blackburn and Rosen (1993) indicate that there is evidence of a paradigm shift in the HR policies adopted by those organizations having won the Baldrige Award. Traditional HR policies created in command and control cultures have given way to new HR policies supportive of cultures characterized by employee commitment, cooperation and communication. HR policies in the Baldrige Award-winning companies are mutually interdependent, congruent and directed at supporting a TQM perspective throughout the company. Blackburn and Rosen (1993) found that, collectively, the HR management policies in the Baldrige Award-winning companies work to accomplish the following:

1.   Communicate the importance of each employee's contribution to total quality.
2.   Stress quality-related synergies available through team work.

3. Empower employees to 'make a difference'.
4. Reinforce individual and team commitment to quality with a wide range of rewards and reinforcements.

What role will the human resources department play in service quality implementation?

A major challenge faces all HR executives. The challenge is the appropriate role for HR to play in the implementation of SQ. The HR department can be poised to be a contributor to the overall success of SQ or sit on the sidelines and watch as it is implemented and becomes part of a service organization's culture.

Few companies have involved the HR department as a real agent of change to help institutionalize SQ as the organization's culture. In some cases, the HR department may only be tasked with assisting in the SQ training efforts. Generally, the leadership role for quality initiatives falls to a group which 'knows the business' versus the HR 'staff support' department. The orientation of the HR department, specializing in HR policy, does not enable the department members to represent the general business orientation necessary for the comprehensive cultural initiative that SQ represents. The result is that senior management concludes that SQ is too important to allow the HR department to be in charge.

What should the role of the HR department be when implementing SQ? Although there are a number of possible roles, the most effective implementation strategy is to utilize the HR department's potential as a change agent. If this is to occur, the HR department needs to be re-engineered: (1) so that it practices SQ in the processes it creates and manages, and (2) so that it can deploy HR management practices that support SQ throughout the organization.

HR policies and procedures in a SQ company must be congruent with an organization's culture built on the shared assumptions of employee dedication to quality and customer service. Pauline Brody, chairperson of Xerox's 1990 Quality Forum, described the need for cultural transformation:

> TQM requires a change in organizational culture, a fundamental change in the way individuals and groups approach their work and their roles in the organization, that is, from an environment of distrust and fear of reprisal to one of openness and trust where creativity can flourish; from working as individuals to working as teams; from protection of organizational turfs to the breakdown of departmental barriers; from an autocratic management style of direction and control to a softer style of team leader and coach; from power concentrated at the top to power shared with employees; from a focus on results to a focus on continuous improvement of the processes that deliver the results; and finally a change from making decisions based on gut-feel to an analytic, fact-based approach to management.

RE-ENGINEERING THE HR DEPARTMENT

The HR professional must look internally at the HR function itself, and determine to what extent it is employing the same quality initiatives as the remainder of the organization. For example, can the HR department determine who its customers are and how satisfied they are with the department's products and services? To what extent have self-managed work teams been formed within HR as a way of reducing cycle time, improving responsiveness, decreasing errors, etc.? Putting the principles of SQ to work within the HR department is the first step it should make towards becoming a change agent.

Focus on the customer

Customers for the HR department are the other managers within the company who help implement the HR department's policies and procedures. Consumers are all of the employees in the company who utilize and/or are impacted by the HR department's policies and procedures. An often-used term to describe TQM is 'doing the right things right'. Much emphasis is often given in HR departments to 'doing things right'. Following the correct number of steps (i.e. being efficient) listed in the policy manual for benefits administration is an example of 'doing things right'. However, often overlooked is whether or not the steps in the manual are 'the right things'. Does the HR department ignore effectiveness ('doing the right things') by focusing only on efficiency? Is it more important to follow the steps in the Benefits Policy Manual that have been in existence for two years in order to 'do things right' or check with the department's customers to see if they are 'doing the right things'. Obviously, a good HR department would want to be both effective and efficient. Therefore, it first needs to determine what its customers' needs are. Secondly, it needs to work in partnership with its customers to design the products and services which will meet their needs. Then, and only then, should the focus turn to 'doing things right'.

A service-oriented HR department should function like a high-quality service firm which thrives on satisfying clients. They emphasize the intangibles, customize their offerings to different clients, and involve their clients in decisions that affect the services rendered. HR departments must learn to thrive on satisfying clients (e.g. line managers). In sum, HR departments embracing a SQ philosophy must get close to their customers and encourage them to help set the department agenda.

Measurement

Quantitative customer needs identification is critical to a customer-focused orientation. Line and staff managers and employees can provide feedback through surveys, focus groups and other data collection means. Hospitality firms could benchmark other companies to learn more about quantifying the needs and customer satisfaction of the HR department. The following is a sample of what one firm's HR department asks its customers when rating its work on a scale from 1 (at issue) to 5 (towering strength):

I.   Human resource professional skills and competencies
    A.   Employee communications
        1.   Sponsors two-way communication between employees and management as a way to identify and address potential issues before they become significant.
        2.   Utilizes employee surveys, focus groups, newsletters and face-to-face dialogue as business communication tools.

3. Gathers data to understand employee needs and any conflict with business objectives.
4. Influences organization managers to ensure that employees are provided with fundamental business information – who are the customers for the business, what their needs are, how competitors position themselves, etc. – and provides training so that employees understand the information and feel a sense of ownership in the business (Weyerhaeuser Corporation, personal communication).

The other subcategories under human resource professional skills and competencies which can also be measured include: worker's compensation; education, training and development; recruiting and staffing; performance management systems; affirmative action/human diversity; employee relations/labor relations; compensation; benefits; organization and succession planning. The other areas evaluated by Weyerhaeuser's HR department's customers are as follows:

II. Leadership and management skills and competencies
    A. Strategic orientation/leadership
    B. Problem-solving/decision-making
    C. Planning
    D. Communication skills
III. Change management skills and competencies
    A. Consulting and influencing skills
    B. Group and process facilitation skills
    C. Organizational development/effectiveness
IV. Business skills and competencies
    A. Company understanding
    B. Business functional understanding
V. Total quality skills and competencies
    A. Quality concepts and principles
VI. Personal values

Focus on continuous improvement

Continuous improvement of HR processes is essential for the SQ-oriented HR department. Evaluating the HR process and its results is essential to ensure that it is doing 'the right things right'. For example, a small gain of 5 per cent in customer satisfaction with training programs should be highly valued – even if it comes on top of an already high satisfaction rating (e.g. 80 per cent of the customers indicated they were 'extremely satisfied' with last year's process).

HR departmental processes

A number of areas, such as recruiting, selection, orientation, training and development, performance, review, and rewards and recognition, can have a significant impact on the integration of SQ into a company's culture. A strong case can be made for changing the way in which many HR departmental processes are designed and operated in order to accomplish this integration. A few examples follow.

Selection

For decades, selection research has focused on the validation of various selection devices (e.g. ability tests, interviews, assessment centers, etc.) as indicators of how a candidate will perform on the job. With a focus on SQ, hospitality firms will require individuals with a customer orientation, who are keen problem-solvers, and who can perform the type of mathematical work demanded by statistical process control. Techniques need to be developed to identify the candidates for all hospitality positions who have the ability to learn and apply these tools and techniques as well as the technical skills needed for their jobs.

Realistic job previews have been useful in helping produce a stable workforce that fits the organizational culture. Many hospitality firms are using probationary periods for this realistic preview while others are introducing high school students to the hospitality industry. Currently, there is an effort underway in the hospitality industry through the sponsorship of the US Department of Labor to identify core skills for job classifications. These core skills can potentially serve as building blocks for HR processes.

Due to the emphasis on group processes and the growth of self-managed work teams, selection techniques should identify people who work well in group settings. Techniques that have been introduced include assessment centers, which often utilize leaderless group discussions, and team interviews. Motorola uses videotapes of problem-solving groups in action to help determine how applicants would respond to a particular quality issue.

Career management

Career progression, under the traditional paradigm, is thought to be synonymous with preparation for upward mobility. Due to downsizing, which has occurred over the past three to five years, organizations have become much flatter, limiting promotional opportunities. In SQ organizations, promotions will be de-emphasized as a measure of corporate achievement. Career paths will increasingly become lateral to encourage a broader knowledge of the business and prepare managers for solving cross-functional issues. Strategies for this lateral movement might include job rotation, liaison assignments, and task force leadership.

Under the SQ paradigm, employees must exhibit competencies in customer service, self-direction and team development skills. Due to many of the current employment laws, the relatively narrow job descriptions currently in place in most companies must give way to broader descriptions that will include requirements for problem-solving and continuous improvement in functional and cross-functional work teams.

Employee attitude surveys

Employee attitude, opinion or satisfaction surveys represent a good application of upward communication and process assessment. Motorola, Federal Express, IBM Rochester and Stouffer and Ritz-Carlton all use comprehensive employee attitude surveys to identify employee satisfaction and identify problem areas. There surveys typically ask employees to rate a number of statements dealing with issues related to communications, leadership, support, team work, etc. Survey data and written comments are summarized and fed back to supervisors and work units. The results are used as an initial indication of overall employee morale and point out areas where process action teams might focus their attention.

Like any other tool, the attitude survey process depends on the reliability and validity of the survey, its intended use, the processing of results through problem-solving teams, and the cycle time to receive feedback from the time when the survey was administered.

Empowerment

Changes in technology, the use of teams and the way in which jobs are performed have served as the catalysts forcing changes in HR processes. Efficiency was the key to organizing work in the past. Little consideration was given to the internal customer. Supervisors compartmentalized jobs and closely monitored quality through inspection. Job design must now emphasize the role of the employee in innovation, creativity and problem-solving aimed at improving the process as well as the outcome.

This emphasis, most often referred to as empowerment, has become an underlying principle that enables employees to solve problems and satisfy customers without time-consuming, and often bureaucratic, action approvals. Where Motorola once required upper management approval for replacement of defective products, the company's sales representatives now have the authority to replace products up to six years after purchase.

Training and development

Organizations that use problem-solving teams conduct extensive training in group process and grouped decision-making. Other quality-related training topics typically include: cost of quality, statistical process control, process mapping, etc. Research done in organizations embracing an employee involvement philosophy has shown that if employees at lower levels are to be empowered to make decisions, they need team-work and problem-solving skills as well as technical skills (Lawler, 1994).

The use of teams, customer focus and technology has placed new demands on the knowledge, skills and abilities required of employees in a SQ organization. Once employees understand the organization's mission and quality plan, gained at orientation, they must have or be allowed to develop the skills and abilities necessary to achieve that plan. Stouffer, Marriott, Ritz-Carlton and many other SQ-oriented hospitality firms view training as critical to their overall success in SQ implementation. Each of these companies requires all employees to learn the fundamentals of SQ

Performance reviews

'You can manage what you can measure' is a familiar phrase in organizations. Many companies are just realizing the need to adapt their performance review process to reinforce the values and principles underlying SQ. For instance, what measures does a company use in its performance review process to indicate customer satisfaction, initiative or team work? How does a company recognize the contributions of individuals to overall team results?

Reward and recognition systems

Maintaining a culture of SQ requires recognizing and rewarding continuous quality improvement. Employee behavior is influenced and reinforced by reward and recognition. Reward is the conveyance of items of tangible value and other forms of personal

satisfaction or well-being to individuals or groups. Recognition is an ongoing communications activity by which appreciation is declared for the contributions of individuals
or groups. Team reward and recognition must become a major aspect of the reward and
recognition system.

Compensation

Job evaluation systems are used to determine how much jobs are worth (and thus how
much the incumbents are to be paid) and merit pay increases reflect how well the
individual has done the job. As with other traditional HR processes, many pay practices
conflict with the SQ emphasis on collective responsibility and horizontal relationships.

   Current job evaluation techniques suggest that an individual's accountabilities and
responsibilities are limited to the tasks that he or she regularly performs. Furthermore,
job-based pay systems tend to reward people for moving up the organization versus
lateral broadening moves. However, advocates of skill-based pay recognize individuals
for what they can do by basing increases on the acquisition of new skills and knowledge.
Individuals with this broader knowledge, it is assumed, will be more effective problem-
solvers and make greater organizational contributions.

   Merit pay systems, which place an emphasis on individual performance, often create
a competitive situation among employees. For example, since most managers have to
make decisions about percentage increases to award for merit purposes, they must take
money from one employee in the form of a low increase to give another employee a
higher increase. Lawler (1992) has emphasized pushing rewards for collective performance throughout the organization and creating a financial reason for employees to be
involved in the business and in making performance improvements.

   As with other functions, the HR department's processes must be reviewed to
determine whether they are aligned with the values of SQ or not. An example of such
as assessment is shown in Figure 6.10. Such an assessment would indicate the HR
processes which need 'realignment'.

Downsizing

The experience of 'restructuring', 'rightsizing', and 'downsizing' during much of the last
decade has spawned a significant amount of literature. What has been the impact of
downsizing on the HR department? Although we may be unable to answer that
question directly, Cascio (1993) has summarized ten key lessons for managers that have
implications for HR processes in a SQ environment:

1. Downsizing will continue as long as overhead costs remain non-competitive with
    domestic and international rivals.
2. Firms with high debt are most likely to downsize by aggressively cutting people.
3. Far too many companies are not well prepared for downsizing. They begin with
    no retraining or redeployment policies in place, and they fail to anticipate the
    kinds of human resource problems that subsequently develop.
4. Six months to a year after a downsizing, key indicators often do not improve:
    expense ratios, profits, return on investment to shareholders, and stock prices.
5. Survivors' syndrome is a common aftermath. Be prepared to manage it. Better
    yet, try to avoid it by involving employees in the planning phase of any
    downsizing effort.

6. Recognize that downsizing has exploded the myth of job security, and has accelerated employee mobility, especially among white-collar workers. It has fundamentally altered the terms of the psychological contract that binds workers to organizations.
7. Productivity and quality often suffer because there is no change in the way work is done. The same amount of work as before a downsizing is simply loaded onto the backs of fewer workers.
8. To downsize effectively, be prepared to manage apparent contradictions – for example, between the use of top-down authority and bottom-up empowerment, between short-term strategies (headcount reduction) and long-term strategies (organization redesign and systemic change in culture).
9. To bring about sustained improvements in productivity, quality and effectiveness, integrate reductions in headcount with planned changes in the way that work is designed.
10. Downsizing is not a one-tie, quick fix solution to enhance competitiveness. Rather it should be viewed as part of a process of continuous improvement.

EXAMPLE: STOUFFER HOTELS AND RESORTS

Although Stouffer had a number of elements of SQ in place, it launched its approach to SQ, called Strategy for Success, in 1990 (Figure 6.1). This program reflected the above-mentioned change in HR processes. It was founded on a philosophy of management that stressed a balance between the place to stay (i.e. guest satisfaction), the place to work (i.e. employee satisfaction) and the place to invest (i.e. profitability). In other words, Stouffer was one of the first companies to implement the concept of 'the balanced scorecard' prior to its introduction in the literature (Kaplan and Norton, 1992).

Selection

A structured interview guide was developed around the company's vision of 'stay – work – invest' in an effort to select employees based on skills as well as 'fit' with

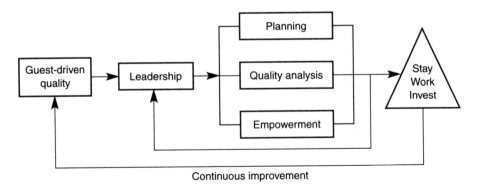

Continuous improvement

Figure 6.1 *Stouffer's Strategy for Success*

corporate culture. For example, a subcategory of 'the place to stay' dimension assessed in the interview is 'service personality'. A candidate for a job at Stouffer would receive ratings as follows:

Score	*Behavior*
5	Was exceptionally outgoing, friendly, and charming. Smiles a great deal. Provided a great deal of eye contact. Came across as sincere. Provided examples of being able to calm irate customers without patronizing them.
3	Was generally outgoing and friendly. May seem somewhat nervous or a bit reserved during the interview. Smiled most of the time. Provided eye contact most of the time; may look away occasionally when responding to difficult questions. Mentioned importance of maintaining good customer relations without significant prompting.
1	Was very reserved or tense to the point of seeming irritable. Rarely smiled. Provided no or very little eye contact. Made no mention of customer relations or their importance unless strongly prompted

A subcategory entitled 'team player' was part of the 'place to work' dimension. The following are scoring guidelines for 'team player' behavior exhibited in the interview:

Score	*Behavior*
5	Shows evidence of working well with supervisors and co-workers. Speaks well of past supervisors and co-workers. Gives specific examples of ability to accomplish things in coordination with others. Shares credit with others for accomplishments.
3	Performs well in coordination with others. Speaks generally well of past supervisors and co-workers. Mentions importance of team work without significant prompting.
1	Shows little evidence of ability to work closely with others. Speaks negatively of supervisors and co-workers. Takes credit for accomplishments, blames others for shortcomings or failures. Must be strongly prompted to recognize importance of team work.

Structured interviews using the same type of questions are also used in college recruiting. In these instances, candidates are interviewed primarily for entry into a general management training program.

Training and development

The quality skills at Stouffer are communicated through a number of custom-designed programs available for use on property and conducted through the corporate office. A brochure illustrating these programs is made available to all employees and used to assist in recruiting.

To reinforce the leadership commitment to quality at Stouffer, top management has not only participated in the training but has also conducted the training. For example, the VP of sales conducts all of the BEST (Building Effective Sales Techniques) training for all general managers, assistant general managers, sales directors and sales managers throughout Stouffer. Other examples include general managers conducting Management Training on Property (MTOP), the VP of rooms conducting Stouffer Hotels and Resorts Professional (SHARP), and the VP of food and beverages conducting sales training for the catering and sales managers at all the hotels.

Each year, the hotel director of HR would plan his or her annual training and budget allocations in concert with each hotel's senior management. New programs and seminars offered would be factored into the plan by the corporate office.

Prior to 1987, training at Stouffer Hotels and Resorts was quite fragmented, with each hotel deciding for itself how to train and develop employees. Since 1987, considerable progress has been made and a number of structured programs have emerged. Each of these programs focuses on a particular segment of the employee population and relies on a variety of delivery mechanisms.

Line employees

To train line employees, Stouffer developed their EST Programs (Employee Service Training). These programs are intended to provide line employees with the specific job knowledge and SQ orientation required to perform the day-to-day responsibilities of their positions.

The content of each of the 30 EST programs was developed by a task force of managers and line employees. The job-related information was then transferred into a consistent format for use by all of the hotels and resorts. It was based on a philosophy of structured on-the-job training.

What sets Stouffer apart from all other hotel companies is that it has also developed mini-manuals for the employees being trained. The mini-manual is in the form of a 3-inch by 5-inch book which fits in a shirt pocket. In addition to relying on text, use is make of cartoons, pictures and diagrams. In the case of a server, for example, how to set a table correctly would be illustrated, together with the correct procedures for serving and clearing the table.

The training process for line employees follows a three-step process. Step 1 is a full day of orientation. The program focuses on:

- Corporate culture – what is Stouffer Hotels and Resorts? What does it believe in as an organization and where is it going?
- A SQ video titled *Toward 2000*. This video communicates the company vision of Stouffer as a place to stay, work and invest. It serves as the introduction to quality for the new employee where he or she learns about quality concepts such as the cost of quality.
- Benefit explanation and enrollment.
- Completion of all forms and paperwork.

The second step in the training of line employees takes place in the new employee's department, when the employee is trained using the EST manuals. Responsibility for the training of a line employee rests with the employee's manager. Stouffer has expanded the concept of certified trainers to include line employees in addition to managers. All trainers/supervisors participate in a train-the-trainer course, where they are taught adult learning techniques for skills training.

The third step in the training process takes place at the completion of the introductory period, which is between 60 and 90 days after the date of hire, depending upon the hotel. At this time, the employee's manager submits to HR a one-page certification sheet signed by the manager, department head and employee, attesting that the individual has been trained completely and properly.

Management employees

The training program for management employees centers around three major programs. They are:

- MTOP – Management Training on Property
- SHARP – Stouffer Hotels and Resorts Professionals
- BEST – Building Effective Sales Techniques

MTOP   The MTOP programs are conducted locally by each hotel's management staff. They are composed of approximately twenty training modules, geared for line managers. The intent of each program is to provide line managers with specific skills necessary to effectively manage their employees on a day-to-day basis.

The different programs offered within MTOP include:

- Train-the-Trainer
- Leadership
- Communication
- Time Management
- Interviewing Skills
- Problem-solving
- Finance
- Effective Meetings
- Discipline Skills
- Fair Employment Practices

Each 3–4-hour module is designed by corporate office with input by subject matter experts from the hotels. Once designed, the program is rolled out to all hotels. The director HR at each property is responsible for managing the training system. Stouffer is unique in that these programs are designed to be conducted by experienced senior line managers, including general managers in the hotels. They participate in the company's Train-the-Trainer course before teaching a class and their facilitation skills are monitored by the director of HR. Stouffer has found this is quite effective in dealing with the attendance problems usually associated with management training in hotels. If the director of food and beverage is teaching the course, it is difficult for his managers to find an excuse not to attend.

The participation rate for this training program is tracked by individual, with a roster of all attendees sent to the corporate office for input into a database. Course evaluations are also sent to corporate office for continuous improvement of the training skills of the managers and the course content. Cycle time for improvement was dramatically improved by maintaining all program materials on a publishing system which allowed for quick turnaround of revisions.

SHARP   The SHARP program is a corporate office-driven program and was originally designed for those managers reporting directly to the hotel general manager. The program has been expanded to include additional managers who may not report directly to the general manager.

The program is intended to accomplish four goals. First, it is a quality awareness program intended to communicate the focus and vision of the company. Second, it is a training program designed to provide selected managers with a comprehensive understanding of various aspects of the business. In this regard, the sessions, which typically last five days, include the following topics:

- guest satisfaction index; how to understand and interpret it;
- cost of quality;
- importance of selecting the right individuals as employees;
- the cost of turnover and how it affects the bottom line.

The guest satisfaction index (GSI) is a composite index of guest satisfaction based on four approaches to evaluating service quality:

1. A guest satisfaction survey.
2. An operations survey report (i.e. mystery shopper).
3. Guest comment cards.
4. Unsolicited guest letters and telephone calls.

The guest satisfaction survey and the guest comment card request guests to give a fairly detailed evaluation of the hotel and hotel services. The comment card contains space for guests to elaborate on areas of satisfaction or dissatisfaction. It requests an overall rating of the hotel and asks whether the guest is likely to stay at the hotel again. Different versions of the guest satisfaction survey and guest comment card are tailored to the resort properties and the hotels. All guest comment cards are mailed to the office of guests relations. The operations survey is a detailed study of hotel operations in each property carried out by an outside research firm once a year. The assessment covers such areas as reservations, front desk, housekeeping, room service, restaurant and bar, airport pick-up, concierge, hotel courtesy, marketing, and physical plant.

Each of the four different types of feedback is given a different level of importance in the overall rating of Stouffer Hotels and Resorts. The guest satisfaction survey is given the most emphasis while unsolicited guest letters and telephone calls are only given minor emphasis. Responses to each of the four components of the GSI are given numerical values and are combined to yield a numerical rating for each property. This is totaled annually to produce an overall GSI score for each hotel or resort. In addition, GSI information is fed back to each hotel for use in problem-solving and continuous improvement.

Each property is also evaluated on meeting conventional sales and profit targets. The management and employees at each hotel and resort are able to win bonus awards based on their overall GSI score and on performance with regard to profit targets. The use of the two incentive systems ensures that the management of each property does not reduce the level of customer service to meet financial and sales goals. The incentives consist of quarterly and annual recognition awards for the superior hotel and hotel employees along with executive committee bonuses. General managers in each property are encouraged to set up employee incentive programs in order to achieve sales, profit and high GSI goals.

Third, and perhaps most interestingly, the program is intended to be an assessment center. Surveys are used to gather as much information as possible about attendees' management strengths and weakness from peers, subordinates and superiors prior to the session, so performance deficiencies can be addressed through one-on-one coaching during the five-day program. Each participant leaves with his or her individual development plan.

Finally, the program is intended to extend the approach and philosophy to be used for TQM implementation throughout all management levels. Since departmental managers in other companies implementing TQM have historically resisted due to their perceived loss of control, a great deal of emphasis was placed on the role of the manager in implementing TQM.

Stouffer has been very successful in growing and developing its general managers. For the years 1987 and 1988, 50 per cent of all new GMs were hired directly from outside the company. By 1991 and 1992, the percentage of general manager positions filled by internal candidates had grown to 80 per cent.

BEST   This is also a corporate-driven program. All sales managers are trained in the five-day program, in groups of 20. The intended purpose of the program was to provide sales managers with practical selling skills and at the same time build a network and team effort.

The program was developed by the corporate human resource development department and conducted by the VP of sales. As with almost all other training programs, Stouffer relied on internal resources for its development. This program, as with all the others, illustrates that the accountability for training resting with the functional area or immediate supervisor. HR was to act as a partner in coordinating the programs.

Career planning and performance reviews   The career planning process at Stouffer is well defined. From a philosophical point of view career development is the joint responsibility of the individual and his or her supervisor.

To assist managers in planning their own careers, Stouffer has produced a video entitled *Career Navigation*. The basic concept behind the video is that a career is somewhat like a sailing trip. It is important for the individual to have a clear goal in mind. As you navigate your way toward that goal, there will be times when you will need to make 'detours', 'avoid storms', etc.

While annual performance reviews are conducted for every manager, the career planning component or discussion is an integral part of the process. Managers are responsible for sitting with their employees to suggest possible career paths. Stouffer posts open jobs at other properties and also uses their redesigned job descriptions to assist in the process.

An example from the Stouffer performance review form is illustrated in Figure 6.2.

Salaried Performance Evaluation and Development Form
-Confidential-

Section I: Information (Print Clearly)

Employee's Name: _____   S.S. #: _____

Position Title: _____   Salary Grade: _____

Office: _____

Date Started Present Position: _____   Date of Hire with this company: _____

Evaluator's Name: _____   Position Title: _____

Year End Review: _____   Mid Year Review: _____   Other: _____   For the Year: _____

Procedures:
1. At the beginning of the appraisal period, the managers and employee meet to do the following:
    - Review the employee's Job Description, and make revisions as necessary.
    - Discuss company and hotel goals/tactics.
    - Agree upon individual objectives, and enter them in Section II, Part B.
2. Throughout the appraisal period, the manager and employee meet to review tactics and individual objectives. Changes are made as appropriate.
3. Before the Performance Evaluation and Development Interview:
    - The manager asks the employee to complete the individual objectives "Results" portion of Section II, Part B.
    - The manager completes the Performance Evaluation based on observed performance, and inputs from clients and others who have significant interaction with the employee.
    - The manager reviews the Performance Evaluation with his/her manager prior to reviewing it with employee.
4. At the Performance Evaluation and Development Interview:
    - The manager and employee meet to review this form.
    - The manager and employee complete Sections IV, Career Interests, and Section V, Development Plans.

Evaluation Ratings		
Rating	Value	Description
5	Outstanding	Performance is consistently superior.
4	Exceeds Expectations	Performance is routinely above job requirements.
3	Meets Expectations	Performance is regularly competent and dependable.
2	Below Expectations	Performance fails to meet job requirements on a frequent basis.
1	Unsatisfactory	Performance is consistently unacceptable.

| Section II: Performance Evaluation - Parts A, B, and C |
Part A - Plant, Division or Company Results (300)

Rationale:
Section II, Part A emphasizes each employee's role as part of the plant, division or company team in achieving its goals in terms of Customer Satisfaction, Employee Satisfaction, and Investor Satisfaction.
Instructions:
1. Obtain the team's Customer Satisfaction Index (CSI), Employee Satisfaction Index (ESI), and Investor Satisfaction Index (ISI) goals and results from your immediate manager. Write the goals in column "a" below and the results in column "b" below.
2. Calculate the percentage achieved ("b/a") and enter it in column "c."
3. Write the numerical value of the percent ("c") by 100, and enter that number, or a maximum point value of 100, in column "d." For example, if an objective is 90% achieved, write "90" in column "d." If it is 120% achieved, write the maximum of "100" in column "d."
4. Total the values in column "d" and write the total in Box "e." "Section II, Part A Score."

Customer Satisfaction/Employee Satisfaction/Investor Satisfaction	Goal (a)	Result (b)	Numerical Value of % Achieved (c)	Maximum Points	Final Points(d)
1. Customer Satisfaction Index (CSI)				100	
2. Employee Satisfaction Index (ESI)				100	
3. Investor Satisfaction Index (ISI)				100	
			Section II, Part A Score(e):		

Figure 6.2   *Stouffer's performance review form*

Part B - Individual Job Objectives Evaluation (500)

Rationale:
This section evaluates the employee's performance in achieving the individual objectives that were agreed upon with his or her immediate manager for this appraisal period. The objectives are organized by Customer Satisfaction, Employee Satisfaction, and Investor Satisfaction.

Instructions:

1. Write in the objectives in column ("a") below the 3-5 results-oriented, achievable, and measurable objectives that the employee agreed to meet during the review period for each category.

2. Assign each objective a percentage weight factor, ranging from 5% to 30% in increments of 5%. **The total of all assigned percentage weights for all three categories must equal 100%.** Write these in the "% Weight Factor" column ("b").

3. Copy the employee's summary of the results achieved for each objective in the "Results" column ("e").

4. Assign and Evaluation Rating (1-5) to each objective, based upon the results actually achieved. Refer to the Evaluation Ratings on page 1 of this form. Write the 1-5 ratings in the "Numerical Ratings" column ("c").

5. Multiply the % Weight Factor ("b") by the Numerical Rating ("c") and write this product ("b x "c") in the "Value" column ("d"). For example, if an objective is weighted 10%, and the rating was "4", multiply the "4" by "10," and write the result ("40") in the "Value" column.

6. Total the "Value" column for all three categories and write it in Box "1," "Section II, Part B Total Score (f)."

Objectives - Customer Satisfaction (a)	% Weight Factor (b)	Numerical Rating (c)	Value (d)	Result (e)

Objectives - Employee Satisfaction (a)	% Weight Factor (b)	Numerical Rating (c)	Value (d)	Result (e)

Objectives - Investor Satisfaction (a)	% Weight Factor (b)	Numerical Rating (c)	Value (d)	Result (e)
		Section II, Part B Score (f):		

Figure 6.2 *Stouffer's performance review form (contd)*

Part C - Interpersonal/Administrative/Technical/Management Skills (200)

Rationale:
This section evaluates the employee's use of the skills required to achieve individual and team objectives. Skills are grouped in 9 major categories (I-IX).

Instructions:
1. Rate each subcategory (a, b, c, etc.) in Column "1." Use the Evaluation Ratings (1-5) listed on the first page of this form.
2. Based on these subcategory ratings, rate each main category (I-IX) with a 1-5 rating.
3. Add the values in Column "2," and write the total in Box "a," "Total Column 2."
4. Multiply the number in Box "a" by 4.44 to convert your total to the Section II, Part C point value. Round the value to the nearest tenth, and write the total in Box "b," "Section II Part C Score."

Col.1 | Col.2

I. Business Knowledge ☐

a. Occupational/Technical Knowledge ☐
   - Is sought by others for his/her technical knowledge.
   - Is knowledgeable about the people and operations of the department and company.
   - Keeps up to date on technical developments related to his/her work.
   - Knows his/her job well.

b. Company Business Knowledge ☐
   - Can discuss business operations.
   - Can describe problems other departments face and how they impact his/her department.
   - Can state purpose of all departments.
   - Can describe Operating Plan and current performance.

c. Departmental Knowledge ☐
   - Can state his/her department's objectives.
   - Can describe the impact of company's goals and objectives to his/her job.
   - Understands impact of his/her job on the department.
   - Understands relationship between his/her function or department and other departments (e.g., Accounting, Marketing, Human Resources, etc.)

Examples:

II. Planning and Organizing ☐

a. Planning ☐
   - Makes plans that are clear and realistic.
   - Anticipates problems and develops contingency plans.
   - Develops complete, well detailed plans.
   - Actually uses plans to manage.

b. Organizing ☐
   - Effectively organizes and schedules the work of other employees.
   - Deals with higher priority problems and tasks first.
   - Maintains a balance between overall "big picture" and day-to-day needs and activities.
   - Establishes effective and efficient procedures for getting work done.

Col.1 | Col.2

c. Personal Organization/Time Management ☐
   - Makes good use of his/her time.
   - Keeps information and documentation in an orderly manner.
   - Is able to process paperwork quickly and effectively.
   - Is prompt in returning phone calls or responding to notes and written requests.

Examples:

III. Communications Skills ☐

a. Informing ☐
   - Lets those who will be affected know of his/her plans and activities.
   - Keeps others informed of upcoming changes and activities.
   - Makes sure his/her superior has no "surprises."
   - Keeps people up to date with information.

b. Oral Communications ☐
   - Facilitates communication through effective questioning.
   - Speaks effectively in front of a group.
   - Is forceful and persuasive in oral communications.
   - Is clear and understandable in oral communications.

c. Listening ☐
   - Is willing to listen to the concerns of others.
   - Listens well to others in group discussions or meetings.
   - Avoids interrupting people when they are talking.

d. Written Communications ☐
   - Writes clear, concise business memos and letters.
   - Clearly expresses ideas and concepts in writing.
   - Prepares written reports easily and quickly.
   - Uses correct grammar in written communications.

Examples:

Figure 6.2 *Stouffer's performance review form (contd)*

Col.1 | Col.2

IV. Analytical and Decision-Making Skills ☐

a. Problem Analysis and Decision Making ☐
- Considers alternative solutions before making a decision.
- Makes decisions based on adequate and accurate information.
- Gets good input before making decisions.
- Thinks through problems and analyzes issues accurately.

b. Financial and Quantitative Skills ☐
- Accurately analyzes financial information.
- Quickly understands statistical or quantitative information.
- Identifies key factors when reviewing budgets and financial statements.
- Is good with numbers.

Examples:

V. Interpersonal Skills ☐

a. Human Relations ☐
- Treats individuals fairly.
- Develops and maintains good working relationships with others.
- Gets along well with other employees at all levels.
- Shows awareness of the personal needs and motivations of others.

b. Managing Conflict and Confrontation ☐
- Does not ignore problems between individuals or groups.
- Is willing to take an unpopular stand.
- Resolves conflicting demands among employees.
- Identifies the real reasons underlying problems or conflicts.

Examples:

VI. Leadership Skills ☐

a. Leadership Style and Influence ☐
- Sets an example of personal performance which encourages excellence.
- Conveys enthusiasm about meeting department objectives and deadlines.
- When in a group, readily commands the attention and respect of others.
- Is able to convert decisions into group action.

Col.1 | Col.2

b. Motivating Others ☐
- Recognizes and acknowledges other employees' good performance.
- Creates an environment where employees work their hardest.
- Recognizes that different individuals are motivated by different things.
- Gives others a good explanation when asking them to change.

c. Delegating and Controlling ☐
- Distributes the work load evenly and fairly among the work group.
- Clearly explains the desired results when assigning tasks.
- Delegates the appropriate amount of work.
- Monitors progress on assignments and goals.

Examples:

VII. Staffing and Subordinate Development ☐

a. Staffing ☐
- Accurately analyzes and determines staffing needs.
- Effectively uses existing selection tools/processes.
- Selects the right people for the right positions.

b. Developing ☐
- Gives training and guidance to employees when needed.
- Shows interest in employees' careers by encouraging their development.
- Gives feedback which helps employees improve performance.

Examples:

VII. Adaptation Skills ☐

a. Personal Adaptability ☐
- Is able to shift priorities to accommodate changing job demands.
- Deals constructively with his/her own failures and mistakes.
- Is effective in highly stressful and pressure-laden situations.
- Avoids rigid adherence to his/her own ideas when mistaken.

b. Multi-Tracked ☐
- Can keep more than one ball in the air at one time.
- Handles several simultaneous agendas.
- Can handle multiple inputs.
- Prefers working on several projects at once.

Examples:

Figure 6.2 *Stouffer's performance review form (contd)*

Col. 1 | Col. 2

IX. Motivation and Commitment   ☐

a. Personal Motivation   ☐
    - Has the ambition to advance his/her career.
    - Is willing to work long hours when required.
    - Persists at a task despite unexpected difficulties.
    - Seeks increased responsibility on the job.

b. Results Orientation   ☐
    - Gets the most out of available resources (people, materials, equipment, etc.)
    - Can be depended on to get the job done on time.
    - Gets a lot accomplished.
    - Produces high quality work.

Examples:

Total Column 2 (a):   ☐

Section II, Part C Score (b):   ☐
(Multiply (a) by 4.44)

Section III - Overall Performance Evaluation

Instructions:
1. Enter the total scores from Section II, Parts A, B, and C below.
2. Total the point values for Section II, and write the sum in the Box marked "Total, Section II"
3. Rate the employee's performance as Outstanding, Exceeds Expectations, Meets Expectations, or Unsatisfactory based upon the point value.

Section II Total Scores:	Part A	
	Part B	
	Part C	
	Total, Section II:	

Section III: Employee's Overall Performance Rating
Check the appropriate block:

Outstanding	901-1000 pts.		
Exceeds Expectations	650-900 pts.		
Meets Expectations	350-649 pts.		
Below Expectations	150-349 pts.		
Unsatisfactory	0-149 pts.		

Section IV - Career Development

This section is to be completed by the person being reviewed. Use feedback from the reviewer when answering question #4.

1. Where do you see yourself professionally (use job title) three years from now?

2. I have geographical restrictions: ☐ yes ☐ no

   Area Preferences:

3. I will relocate: ☐ yes   ☐ no

4. What skills or knowledge will need to be developed or improved to move in your desired career direction?

Figure 6.2   *Stouffer's performance review form (contd)*

Section V - Development Plan

This section constitutes the most important part of the review. Both the person being reviewed and his/her manager should collaborate on this section.

Need Area: Identify the three highest priority needs from the earlier sections and enter a short description in the Need Area column.

Development Plan: Identify specifically what the person being reviewed will do between now and the next formal review.

Due Date: Identify an achievable date for completion of each task identified in the Development Plan.

Need Area	Development Plan	Due Date
First Priority		
Second Priority		
Third Priority		

Section VI - Comments of Person Being Reviewed

Signatures

Person Reviewed	Date
Reviewer	Date
Next Level Manager	Date
Vice President	Date

Optional-Next level Manager/Vice President's Comments

Forward the completed performance evaluation with all signatures and current Job Description to the appropriate Vice President for review and signature, then forward it to the Corporate Human Resources Department.

Figure 6.2   *Stouffer's performance review form (contd)*

The annual performance review was revised to reinforce the vision. It was organized into the dimensions of 'stay – work – invest'. Major sections of the review form are weighted to reflect the critical issues of the hotel or department. A percentage of the overall rating is assigned to the results achieved by the hotel. In addition, another percentage of the overall rating is assigned to the individual results achieved in the areas of stay, work and invest. Finally, skills used to achieve both individual and team results are assessed and form the third portion of the overall rating. Career information is included for developmental counseling and in conjunction with Stouffer's 'Career Navigation' program.

Infrastructure from TQM implementation

Although Stouffer believed that TQM would eventually become an integral part of the hotel's operations, the initial stages required a great deal of top management's time and attention. A TQM support structure was needed so that managers could give the TQM process their individual attention when it was most needed. This structure is illustrated in Figure 6.3.

Quality survey

The goal of the quality survey is to gather information and objective data that will be used by management to develop a quality plan. A sample of the quality survey customized for the HR department is illustrated in Figure 6.10 on pp. 112–14. The information obtained through the quality survey is used to identify system strengths and weaknesses. The quality survey is organized around the seven major categories of the Malcolm Baldrige criteria:

1. Leadership
2. Information and analysis
3. Strategic quality planning
4. Human resource excellence
5. Quality assurance of programs and services
6. Quality results
7. Customer satisfaction

Empowerment

The following are some examples of empowerment. An outlet manager is revising his menu. He goes to his servers to get their ideas and input. They give him a number of good suggestions as to what should be added and what should be omitted based on comments they have heard from guests. He uses many of their ideas in the new menu.

The director of reservations has an objective of developing a 'call back' program where reservations agents will be required, each day, to call two guests for whom they made reservations to ask about their stay. She delegates the tasks to the agents who design and implement the program themselves.

A small team of employees is asked to study the problem of glass breakage by the director of catering/conventions. One of the problems they find is a section of damaged floor across which servers and stewards must push carts stacked with glasses. The team members find out that a contractor in the hotel completing some renovations in another area can repair the floor quite inexpensively while he is in the building. Top management accepts the team's proposal.

A guest asks for grape jelly in one of the outlets and is told there is none. That evening the server stops by her grocery and buys a jar of grape jelly for the guest. She presents it to him the next morning. He is impressed enough to write a letter to the general manager about the incident.

These are examples of empowerment that Stouffer uses in its training. In each case, the knowledge and good judgment of the employee was used to improve service to the guest and performance of the hotel. In each case, the employees were not simply 'doing

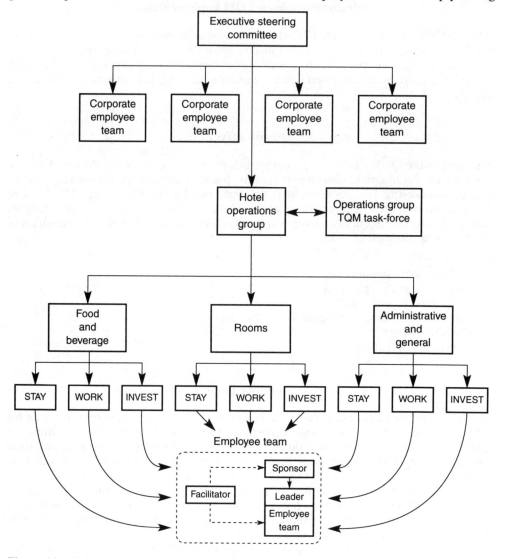

Figure 6.3 *Roles and responsibility – organization chart*

their jobs' but were empowered to use their ideas and creativity. Stouffer believes that empowerment is a business strategy aimed at providing employees at all levels with greater influence over their work. Stouffer believes that empowerment can help the performance of each hotel by:

- improved responsiveness to guest needs;
- increased ownership of guest problems by individual employees;
- increased guest satisfaction index scores;
- decreased cost of errors;
- fewer mistakes;
- less damage to equipment and loss of supplies;
- better coordination between departments;
- better control of inventories;
- quicker service response time;
- fewer guest complaints;
- fewer allowances and 'COMPS' because of guest complaints.

Stouffer believes that four forms of empowerment can exist:

1. Participative management style – employees participate in the problem-solving and decision-making that goes on in their departments and in the hotel.
2. Employee teams – employees are members of teams established to find and implement solutions to problems and to help managers accomplish their objectives.
3. Employee suggestion program – employees are able to submit ideas and suggestions and get an immediate response from management (the PAR program).
4. Self-empowerment – employees are able to take action on behalf of the guest, based upon their own judgment.

Recognition

Business strategies that include TQM define what behaviors are required for successful institutionalization of values (team work, risk-taking, etc.). Consequently, the reward and recognition process needs to support and reinforce behaviors fundamental to TQM. Fostering and rewarding team work and quality improvement team activities engages every employee in searching for the best strategies for dealing with guests, employees, material, methods, systems and processes to realize the vision of a TQM culture.

The primary focus of team recognition at Stouffer is the pyramid of quality (Figure 6.4), which is an 18-inch-tall trophy made from crystal and on a base of granite, for the hotels that represent excellence in a combination of guest satisfaction (GSI), employee relations index (ERI), and profitability. Each hotel that wins the pyramid of quality also wins a pyramid plaque. These plaques are on a decorative wood background, and are designed to be wall-mounted for display.

To further reinforce quality values throughout each hotel, a departmental plaque is awarded to the department which achieves the best balanced results of GSI, ERI and profitability. An internal customer satisfaction index as well as a cost of quality index are being developed by Stouffer to enable staff departments to be eligible for the pyramid plaque.

Individual recognition is provided through the pyramid of quality cards (Figure 6.5). Each employee who is a member of a winning hotel or department receives a laminated card with key elements of the Stouffer vision on one side and a pyramid on the other. Each hotel determines the kinds of special awards and recognition it will provide to each pyramid card holder. The card is valid for the year in which the hotel or department is recognized.

New hotel openings

The Stouffer Riviere in Chicago was the first property opened utilizing a fully integrated TQM philosophy. Results since opening in 1991 have reinforced the management decision to open The Riviere as a model TQM hotel. Results have included:

- moved to no. 1 guest satisfaction rating in the Stouffer chain;
- moved to no. 3 position in the marketplace behind Four Seasons and Four Seasons–Ritz-Carlton;
- 29 per cent improvement in occupied rooms from 1992 to 1993;
- gross operating profit improvement by 62 per cent from 1992 to 1993.

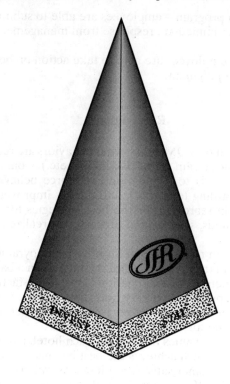

Figure 6.4   *The pyramid of quality*

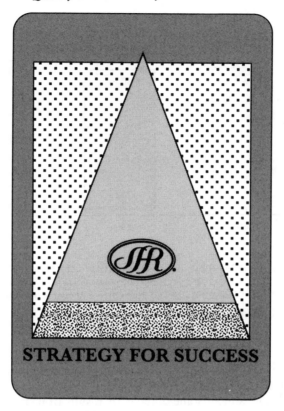

Figure 6.5 *Pyramid of quality cards*

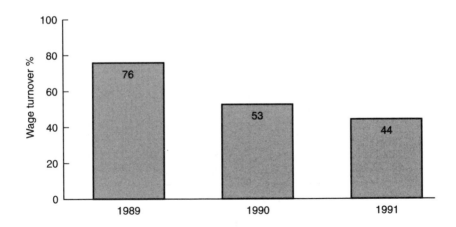

The place to work   1990–1991: 14th lowest wage turnover
                    1990–1991: 2 new hotels (Ritz Carlton and Marriott)

Figure 6.6(a) *Tower City Plaza TQM pilot (December 1989 – November 1991): wage turnover*

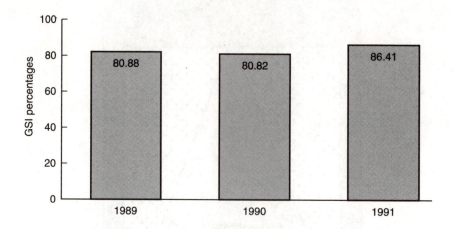

The place to stay   1990–1991: 7th best overall GSI improvement in SHR
                     1990–1991: 2nd best downtown GSI improvement
                     1990–1991: Moved from 6th to 2nd overall downtown GSI

Figure 6.6(b)   *Tower City Plaza TQM pilot: GSI percentages*

Pilot Test

Stouffer's implementation philosophy was to use Tower City Plaza in Cleveland as the location to start TQM in its operations while creating and revising corporate systems to support a company-wide launch. Some of the early results from Tower City Plaza were very encouraging, as the performance measures illustrated in Figures 6.6 (a)–(f) indicate.

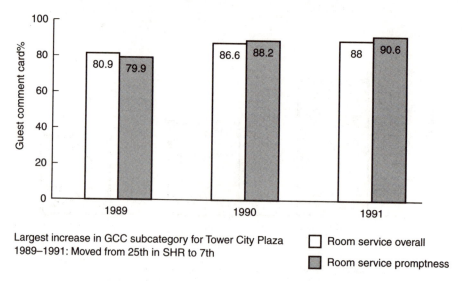

Largest increase in GCC subcategory for Tower City Plaza   ☐ Room service overall
1989–1991: Moved from 25th in SHR to 7th   ▨ Room service promptness

Figure 6.6(c)   *Tower City Plaza TQM pilot: room service (overall and promptness); employee involvement team example*

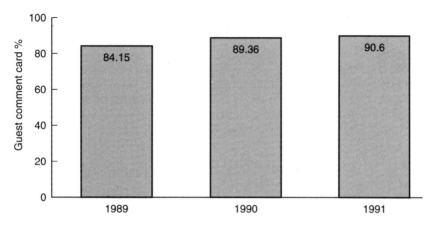

Figure 6.6(d)   *Tower City Plaza TQM pilot: guest room/bathroom*

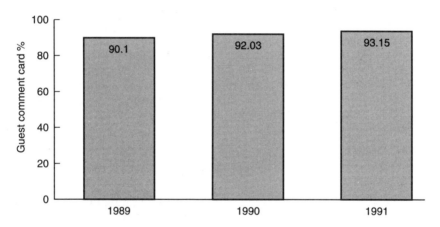

Figure 6.6(e)   *Tower City Plaza TQM pilot: front desk*

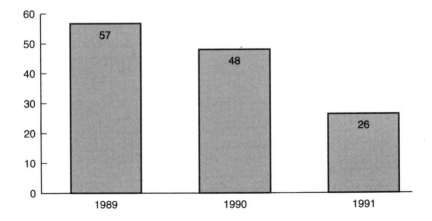

Figure 6.6(f)   *Tower City Plaza TQM pilot: medical injuries*

Significant results were achieved in guest satisfaction, employee relations, and cost of quality reduction. These early results were incorporated into Stouffer's company-wide launch entitled 'Strategy for Success'. The philosophy was communicated at a 1990 company management conference through speeches and a video entitled *Toward 2000*. Subsequent quality awareness materials were developed for use by general managers at each property. The *Toward 2000* video became a crucial element of Stouffer's orientation.

EXAMPLE: THE RITZ-CARLTON

The Atlanta-based company manages 25 luxury hotels that target primarily industry executives, meeting and corporate travel planners, and affluent travelers. In 1992, Ritz-Carlton won the Malcolm Baldrige National Quality Award. The Ritz-Carlton Hotel Company is a management company that develops and operates luxury hotels for W. B. Johnson Properties. It currently operates 23 business and resort hotels and two hotels in Australia. It also has nine international sales offices and employs 11,500 people. Two subsidiary products, restaurants and banquets, are marketed heavily to local residents.

Hallmarks of its focus on SQ include participatory executive leadership, thorough information gathering, coordinated planning and execution, and a trained workforce that is empowered to satisfy customers. All of its employees are given training in the company's 'gold standards', which set out Ritz-Carlton's service credo and basics of premium service.

Gold standards

Quality planning begins with the President and Chief Operating Officer and the other 13 senior executives who make up the corporate steering committee. This group, which doubles as the senior quality management team, meets weekly to review the quality of products and services, guest satisfaction, market growth and development, organizational indicators, profits and competitive status.

The company's business plan demonstrates the value it places on goals for quality products and services. Quality goals draw heavily on consumer requirements derived from research by the travel industry and the company's customer reaction data, focus groups and surveys. The plan relies upon a management system designed to avoid the variability of service delivery traditionally associated with hotels. The strategic planning business model in Figure 6.7 illustrates the dynamics of this model.

Key product and service requirements of the travel consumer have been translated into Ritz-Carlton gold standards, which include a credo, motto, three steps of service, and 20 'Ritz-Carlton basics'. Each employee is expected to understand and adhere to these standards, which describe processes for solving problems that guests may have as well as detailed grooming, housekeeping and safety and efficiency standards.

The corporate motto is 'ladies and gentlemen serving ladies and gentlemen'. The company trains employees with an orientation, followed by on-the-job training, the job certification. Ritz-Carlton values are reinforced continuously by daily 'line-ups', frequent recognition for extraordinary achievement, and a performance appraisal based on expectations explained during training.

To ensure problems are resolved quickly, employees are required to act at first notice – regardless of the type of problem or complaint. All employees are empowered to do whatever it takes to provide 'instant pacification'.

Detailed planning

At each level of the company, from corporate leaders to managers and employees in individual work areas, teams are charged with setting objectives and devising action plans, which are reviewed by the corporate steering committee. Each hotel has a 'quality leader', who serves as a resource and advocate as teams and workers develop and implement their quality plans.

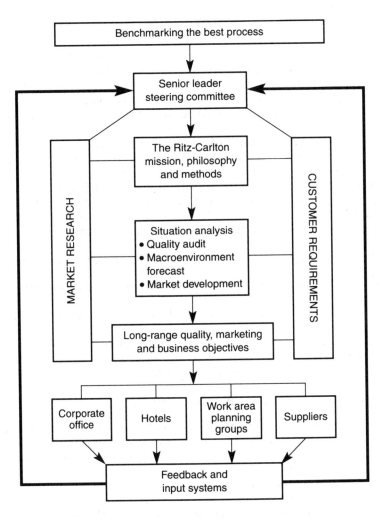

Figure 6.7 *Corporate-level planning: the Ritz-Carlton Company long-range strategic planning model*

Teams and other mechanisms are used to cultivate employee commitment. For example, each work area is covered by three teams responsible for setting quality-certification standards for each position, problem-solving and strategic planning.

The benefits of detailed planning and the hands-on involvement of executives are evident during the seven days leading up to the opening of a new hotel. Rather than opening a hotel in phases, Ritz-Carlton aims to have everything right when the doors open. A 'seven-day countdown control plan' synchronizes all steps leading to the opening. The president and other senior leaders personally conduct 'Gold Standards' training and quality management during a two-day orientation. A specially selected start-up team composed of staff from other hotels around the country ensures that all work areas, processes and equipment are ready.

Quality data

Daily production reports (Figure 6.8) derived from data submitted from each of the 720 work areas in the hotel system, serve as an early warning system for identifying problems that can impede progress toward meeting quality and customer-satisfaction goals. Coupled with quarterly summaries of guest and meeting planner reactions, the combined data are compared with predetermined customer expectations to improve services.

Among the data gathered and tracked over time are guest room preventive maintenance cycles per year, percentage of check-ins with no queuing, time spent to achieve clean room appearance, and time to service an occupied guest room.

Ritz-Carlton uses technology to assist with its automated building and safety system and computerized reservations system. Guests' likes and dislikes are entered into a computerized guest history profile (Figure 6.9) that provides information on the preferences of 240,000 repeat Ritz-Carlton guests, resulting in more personalized service.

Customer satisfaction data for Ritz-Carlton tell the results of its TQM efforts:

- Customer complaints per 100 comments decreased 27 per cent over the past three years.
- Overall customer satisfaction index for the individual traveler is 97 per cent and for the travel planner is 95 per cent.
- If given a choice between Ritz-Carlton and its competitors, 94 per cent selected the Ritz-Carlton, with the best competitor receiving 57 per cent.
- Key account retention improved from about 82 per cent in 1989 to 100 per cent in 1991.
- Received 121 travel industry awards in 1991.

Each of the Ritz-Carlton employees receives an average of 126 hours of training per year. The management staff receive even more training. The Ritz-Carlton offers continuous training; provides rewards and incentives for its employees, and promotes from within to keep turnover low.

Before an employee is permanently hired at Ritz-Carlton, he or she will complete at least three interviews. They first meet with the Human Resource Coordinator, and then the department head of the intended department. If there is an intent to hire the individual, the prospective employee is administered a test consisting of 55 questions oriented towards talents and themes.

Once a new employee is hired, he or she completes a two-day orientation before starting work. During the orientation, the new employees are thoroughly introduced to the Ritz-Carlton philosophy. The senior management team participates in the orientation.

EXAMPLE: THE WOOD COMPANY

The Wood Company is a food service firm founded in 1940. Clients of the firm include preparatory schools, colleges, universities, hospitals, nursing facilities, retirement communities and business. Customers are the students, faculty, staff, patients, residents, employees, guests and visitors of the clients.

										T	YTD
OCCUPIED ROOMS:											
PLUS COVERS:											
MINIUS FINAL ASSESSMENT AND GUEST COMPLAINTS:						TOTAL PRODUCTION:					
GUEST COMPLAINT CATEGORY	HSK	ENG	RES/COM	CIS	COS	F&B	GSVC	SEC	MISC	TOTALS	
	T YTD	T YTD	T YTD	T YTD	T YTD	T YTD	T YTD	T YTD	T YTD	T	YTD
FACILITIES RELIABILTY											
Inadequate											
Missing											
Worn											
Inoperable											
Incorrect											
SUPPLIES/F & B RELIABILITY											
Inadequate											
Missing											
Unsatisfactory											
Incorrect											
LADY/GENTLEMAN RELIABILTY											
Attitude											
Error – Timely											
Error – Other											
SERVICES MISSING											
GUEST SECURITY (i.e. Loss)											
				TOTAL SYSTEMS RELIABILITY & TIMELINESS DEFECTS							
MINUS IN PROCESS AND INTERNAL CUSTOMER COMPLAINTS:						RESOLVED SUCCESSFULLY %					
EMPLOYEE FACILITIES:	Inadequate, Inoperable or Incorrect										
EMPLOYEE SUPPLIES:	Wasteful use, Inadequate, Missing, Unsatisfactory or Incorrect										
EMPLOYEE SERVICES:	Work Done Over or Done Poorly										
EMPLOYEE SECURITY:	Mysterious Disappearance, Accident, Injury, Loss or Safety Hazard										
HOTEL PURCHASING:	Order, Shipment or Storage Defects										

KEY: HSK: HOUSEKEEPING   COS: CHECK-OUT SERVICE
      ENG: ENGINEERING   F & B: FOOD & BEVERAGE
      RES/COM: RESERVATIONS   GSVC: GUEST SERVICES
              COMMUNICATIONS   SEC: SECURITY
      CIS: CHECK IN SERVICE   MISC: MISCELLANEOUS

TOTAL INTERNAL DEFECTS:	
TOTAL QUALITY PRODUCTION:	
QUALITY PERCENTAGE:	

Figure 6.8 *Error-free service delivery: the Ritz-Carlton Company daily quality production report*

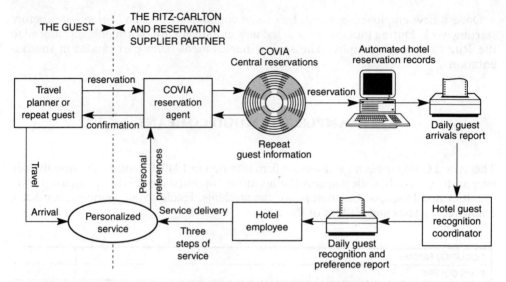

Figure 6.9   *The Ritz-Carlton repeat guest history program: an aid to highly personalized service delivery*

TQM initiatives

The Wood Company's company-wide implementation of TQM began in late 1992 after some positive experience in their early initiatives with TQM in the business dining division. The first step was the creation and communication of their 'Commitment to excellence', which included the mission, vision and values of the firm.

Mission

The Wood Company has been dedicated to providing clients and customers with excellent food service since 1940. Our clients include preparatory schools, colleges, universities, hospitals, nursing facilities, retirement communities and businesses. Our customers include students, faculty, staff, patients, residents, and employees, as well as guests and visitors of our clients. They count on us for sustenance and opportunities for socialization.

   We will continually strive to achieve excellence by staying close to and building long lasting and mutually beneficial partnerships with our clients, customers, employees and suppliers; by focusing our energies in the Mid-Atlantic market; and by treating others as they wish to be treated – with respect, fairness and honesty.

Vision

Our vision is to be the best food service management firm in our industry by partnering with clients to delight our customers through empowered employees. By the best we mean:

● the firm which provides the most value to its clients and customers;
● and the firm which is the most highly rated by clients, customers, employees and suppliers.

Values

Our culture is steeped in certain values which we believe are fundamental to our success in fulfilling our mission.

First, we will always conduct business with the highest ethical standards. Our integrity earns the trust of those we serve and of those with whom we work.

Second, we will always strive to deliver excellence in food and service as perceived by our clients and customers. To deliver excellence, we must bring foresight to their food service by anticipating and fulfilling their dynamically changing needs and expectations. To make certain that we're effective, we will constantly monitor their levels of satisfaction and perceptions through objective surveys and other forms of satisfaction measurement.

Third, we will continually improve the quality of our products and services by defining quality from our clients' and customers' perspective and making excellence in quality the responsibility of every Wood employee. Our continuous quality improvement approach gives every Wood employee the opportunity to be creative, innovative and involved in finding a better way.

Fourth, we will provide a healthy environment for Wood employees which is caring, stimulating, rewarding and personally enriching. We will provide a trusting, diverse, non-discriminating, cooperative work environment. Our communications will be honest, open, timely and widely shared. We will recognize both individual contribution and collective teamwork and provide opportunities for professional and career development. Employees who are valued, trained, motivated, respected and well informed will do the right things. They will be empowered to 'make a difference' in the lives of our clients and customers ... and in their own lives.

Fifth, we will encourage our employees to support the communities in which they live and work. The Wood Company exists by public approval and will continually strive to be an excellent, socially responsible corporate citizen.

Although the Business Dining Division had achieved early successes in its efforts, the senior management team realized that a strategic TQM effort was needed by the whole organization. This company-wide effort was aimed at sustaining the momentum of business dining and expanding the implementation throughout the other divisions and its corporate office. Although a number of the other divisions had initiated certain elements of TQM, there was no consistency of approach or systems support of the various TQM initiatives. In particular, there were no formalized human resources systems to reinforce the TQM philosophy.

The Wood Company wanted to expand its TQM efforts in order to consistently:

- increase customer and client satisfaction;
- encourage employee involvement;
- enhance the quality of work life;
- reduce the cost of delivering products and services;
- improve the effectiveness of our processes;
- ensure continuous learning;
- increase market share and operating margins.

From these objectives, it is apparent that The Wood Company's focus is on improving relationships and results with its customers, employees, suppliers and shareholders.

A framework for The Wood Company's TQM process is included in Table 6.2.

Table 6.2   *'Customer-driven service': TQM philosophy of The Wood Company*

Determine customer needs	Market research to define market segments, analyze competitors, understand client needs, expectations and buying behavior on a segment-wide basis. Example – CCRC study. Outside market researchers working with Wood teams.
	Customer perception research to determine what clients and customers (and non-customers) at a particular unit want most. Will probably be different at different points of service. Unit managers and supervisors identify customers and their needs and will continually monitor customer satisfaction. Staff/support departments will monitor their internal customers. May be done through focus groups, interviews, questionnaires.
Formulate service strategies	Based on interpretation of customer research identify what the customer values most highly. Develop strategies to win and keep customers by offering value. Select a few critical aspects the customer experience can benefit from, set specific targets that are simply expressed, observable and under the influence of employees charged with meeting them.
Empower the teams	People want to do better, and will, provided they are given the opportunity to participate meaningfully, are properly motivated and given adequate training, information and tools to be competent. Help all employees to understand what their customers expect and that they are to provide the customers with products and services that meet or exceed their expectations. Activate quality teams. Train and prepare employees to attack quality problems using teams, a disciplined step-by-step process and a set of simple process improvement tools with which they can identify problems, analyze them, develop solutions and implement. Encourage people to pay attention to the level of quality in their area and to use their ingenuity to raise it. Learn how to win and sustain employee commitment and enthusiasm to a customer-oriented spirit of service.
Improve all processes	Quality improvement can be applied to every functional area. Every activity is a process to be improved. A commitment at all levels to continuous quality improvement. Evaluate every support system in relation to contributing to the ultimate customer value. All requirements must be continuously evaluated and upgraded to reflect changing customer expectations. Realign all support systems making them more efficient, effective and customer friendly.
Measure	Measurement is to be used as a tool – not as a weapon. Manage by facts rather than relying on opinion, hearsay and conjecture. The primary focus of measurement should be on outcomes. Measure business results, client, customer and employee satisfaction and productivity improvement. Set up and measure progress on key initiatives. Estimate the cost of poor quality. Track improvements on specific quality projects. Benchmark, internally and externally.

Table 6.2 *(contd)*

Recognize and celebrate	Develop a recognition and appreciation process. Provide recognition, gratitude and celebrate individual and team successes. Seriously organize some fun. Make sure that people get feedback recognition and appreciation for the contributions they (and their teams) make to increasing customer value.

When it came time to measure results, The Wood Company identified the following dimensions of quality for measurement:

- timeliness – speed, cycle time;
- accuracy – meeting specifications, reliability, consistency;
- responsiveness – flexibility, cooperativeness, reliability;
- product;
- service – courtesy, appearance, personal touch;
- cost – economy.

However, in order for these dimensions to have any meaning, key indicators or initiatives had to be established. A key initiative was a factor that accounted for the customers' perception of quality and would help focus energies and priorities. Under each dimension, three to five initiatives were to be measured. Furthermore, since the clients and customers were different in each division, flexibility was built into the system to allow division-specific key initiatives while ensuring consistency of the same six dimensions across the divisions. Examples of these key initiatives are given in Table 6.3.

Table 6.3 *Wood Company key initiatives of customer quality effort*

Timeliness	Tray line speed, tray delivery, speed of service, catered events delivered on time.
Accuracy	Catered event delivered as specified, portion control, recipe, diet accuracy, patient charting, error-free monthly statements, no word-processing errors.
Responsiveness	Three-ring phone pick-up, return calls within same day, service recovery time, respond to special requests.
Product	Matched to product specs, temperature of food, new product introduction.
Service	Pleasant interaction with guests and internal customers, product knowledge, new service introduction.
Cost	Customer perception of value, reduction in cost of a process, reducing cost of quality.

Everyone was expected to be involved in the TQM effort. Table 6.4 illustrates the comprehensiveness of the level of employee involvement in teams.

Table 6.5 shows the implementation plan used by The Wood Company for expanding TQM throughout the company.

Table 6.4 *TQM committee structure*

Committee/team	Membership	Role	Meeting
Quality Steering Committee	Executive Management Team (EMT) including the VP of Quality	– Provide visible leadership and support to Q process – Set direction/ priorities – Review/respond to field input	2/month 2–3 hours
Division (or Home Office) Quality Councils	Divisional VP, DM's support staff Divisional Q Chairperson VP of Quality Guests (e.g. representatives of Special Interest Groups)	– Set up project team to solve division-wide problems on special issues – Review/respond to field input – Spread good ideas and best practices – Cheerleading	1/month 2–3 hours
Unit or Department Quality Improvement Teams	FSD, team leaders, managers and hourlies	– Identify customer needs – Select improvement projects – Analyze problems – Initiate change – Measure and report progress	2/month $\frac{1}{2}$–1 hour
Special Interest Groups	Cross-functional different levels, *ad hoc* or standing teams within or between divisions	– Solve specific problems – Work on common interests – Spread good ideas and best practices	1/month 2–3 hours
Quality Workshops	Cross-functional *ad hoc* teams of operations or staff management and hourlies	– Re-engineer service to improve client/customer satisfaction and/or to improve/realign internal processes	Intensive – short period until project complete

Table 6.4 *TQM committee structure (contd)*

Committee/team	Membership	Role	Meeting
Quality Process Team	VP of Quality, Divisional and HO Q Chairpersons, and Director of Training	– Provide leadership in designing, introducing and continuously upgrading the quality process – Develop guidelines – Assist in implementation and communication – Establish training modules – Track progress of quality improvement	1/month 3–4 hours

HR implications

The major HR involvement with TQM implementation at The Wood Company was through the Training Department. Quality-specific training materials were purchased primarily from outside resources. Quality Awareness Training was conducted for all management employees primarily by the division vice-presidents with the assistance of a consultant. An employee satisfaction questionnaire is being developed for use later in the TQM implementation.

Recognition and rewards

Recognition and rewards are utilized to support a number of the TQM initiatives. Some of the recognition programs include:

- 'Making a Difference' program – recognition for 'doing the right things right' and being customer-focused.
- Annual appreciation event at each unit.
- Division Appreciation Night to include 'quality achievement' or 'customer satisfaction' awards for management and hourly people.

IMPLICATIONS

Horizontal organization

Despite the 'downsizing' trends, most people still work in vertical organizations, companies where staffers look up to bosses instead of out to customers. Mere 'downsizing', in other words, does little to change the fundamental way that work gets done in a company. Recently, some of Corporate America's biggest names, from American Telephone & Telegraph and DuPont to General Electric and Motorola, are moving towards the horizontal organization (*Business Week*, 1993). Regardless of the name used, total quality management, re-engineering or business-process redesign, the trend is toward flatter organizations in which managing across has become more critical than managing up and down in a top-heavy hierarchy. In a horizontal organization, virtually everyone in the company would work together in multi-disciplinary teams that perform core processes, such as product development or sales generation. The resulting organization might only have three or four layers of management between the president and the staffers in a given process.

Lawrence Bossidy, chairman of Allied Signal, Inc., said in a recent speech, 'There's an awful lot more productivity you're going to see in the next few years as we move to horizontally organized structures with a focus on the customer'. Just as a light bulb wastes electricity to produce unwanted heat, a vertical company expends a tremendous amount of energy running its own internal machinery – managing relations among departments or providing information up and down the hierarchy. A horizontal

Table 6.5 *TQM implementation plan of The Wood Company*

	1993 Roll-out	
1.	Get input/feedback on TQM strategy and plan.	Dec. – Jan.
2.	Communicate quality awareness, vision, wins, framework, key initiatives, and their role and effort required.	Jan.
3.	Recruit VP of TQM.	ASAP
4.	Develop roll-out plan per division.	Jan.
5.	Communicate to everyone – video, handouts, newsletter, TQM manual.	Feb. – Jun.
6.	Set up quality organization structure.	Jan. – Mar.
7.	Training – educate and commit senior executives and managers at all levels – empowerment (1–2 days), team leadership/teamwork (1 day) and customer focus (1 day) and problem-solving techniques (1 day).	Jan. – Dec.
8.	Set up mostly intact teams throughout Wood.	Feb. – Dec.
9.	Market research for one segment.	Apr. – Aug.
10.	Determine baseline measures, improvement goals and reporting vehicle – Readiness to compete survey – Culture survey – managers and hourlies – Baseline key initiatives – Cost of quality – Benchmarking.	Feb. – Mar.
11.	Implement early wins – jump start TQM process with re-engineering workshops (estimated 4–6 weeks/project with consultant). For example: – Span of control – Sharing best practices – New account openings – Instant feedback from customers.	Mar. – Dec.
12.	Design and install recognition and awards package.	Sep.
13.	Create an on-going tracking and feedback system.	Dec.

Table 6.6 *Companies that have moved toward a horizontal structural model*

AT&T	Network Systems Division reorganized its entire business around processes; now sets budgets by process and awards bonuses to employees based on customer evaluations.
Eastman Chemical	Recently sold Kodak unit has over 1,000 teams; ditched senior vice-presidents of administration, manufacturing, and research and development in favor of self-directed teams.
General Electric	Lighting business scrapped vertical structure, adopting horizontal design with more than 100 processes and programs.
Lexmark International	Former IBM division axed 60 per cent of managers in manufacturing and support in favor of cross-functional teams worldwide.
Motorola	Government Electronics groups redesigned its supply management organization as a process with external customers at the end; team members are now evaluating peers.
Xerox	Develops new products through multi-disciplinary teams that work in a single process, instead of vertical functions or departments.

organization eliminates most of those tasks and focuses most of its resources on its customers. The companies shown in Table 6.6 have moved towards the horizontal model (*Business Week*, 1993).

Horizontal Organization and TQM

TQM implementation and downsizing did not produce the dramatic rises in productivity many companies hoped for. Gaining quantum leaps in performance also requires a company to rethink the way in which work and the organizational hierarchy are organized. Some organizations have adopted a new 'horizontal' organization model. Already, some of the largest United States and international organizations, from American Telephone & Telegraph and DuPont to General Electric and Motorola, are moving toward the idea (Byrne, 1993). The horizontal organization eliminates both hierarchy and departmental boundaries. In its purest state, the horizontal organization might boast a skeleton group of senior executives at the top in functions such as finance and human resources. Virtually everyone else in the organization would work together in multi-disciplinary teams that perform core processes, such as manufacturing or sales generation.

The seven key elements of the horizontal organization have much in common with total quality management (Byrne, 1993):

1. *Organize around process, not task.* Instead of creating a structure around departments, build the company around its three to five 'core processes', with specific performance goals. Assign an 'owner' to each process.
2. *Flatten hierarchy.* To reduce supervision, combine fragmented tasks, eliminate work that fails to add value, and cut the activities within each process to a minimum. Use as few teams as possible to perform an entire process.
3. *Use teams to manage everything.* Make teams the main building blocks of the company. Limit supervisory roles by making the team manage itself. Give the

team a common purpose. Hold it accountable for measurable performance goals.
4. *Let customers drive performance.* Make customer satisfaction, not stock appreciation or profitability, the primary driver and measure of performance. The profits will come and the stock will rise if the customers are satisfied.
5. *Reward team performance.* Change the appraisal and pay systems to reward team results, not just individual performance. Encourage staffers to develop multiple skills rather than specialized know-how. Reward them for it.
6. *Maximize supplier and customer contact.* Bring employees into direct, regular contact with suppliers and customers. Add supplier or customer representatives as full working members of in-house teams where they can be of service.
7. *Inform and train all employees.* Don't just spoon-feed sanitized information on a 'need to know' basis. Trust employees with raw data, but train them in how to use it to perform their own analysis and make their own decisions.

Client expectations drive function, structure, and strategy

What is important to consider with regard to a horizontal structure is that customer/client expectations must drive the function, structure and strategy of the organization. For example, the function (department) can focus on its various technical areas (e.g. compensation, benefits, recruiting, training, etc.) or it can be more client-centered and create the products and services to meet client needs. It can employ low or high technology depending upon the emphasis on cycle time. In addition, clients may demand only acceptable quality of products and services rather than top quality.

The structure of the HR department may be centralized with all of the development and delivery located in one place. An alternative is to have the function decentralized with HR generalists located nearer the clients in order to address their needs more immediately.

The strategy of the HR department may be to maintain the status quo and focus on current operations. In contrast, it could be strategic and be planning for changes that the future may bring. Many HR departments concentrate too heavily on efficiency at the expense of effectiveness. In other words, too many HR departments are interested in doing things right without considering whether they are doing the right things.

Benchmark best practices in HR

Benchmarking should be used to determine gaps in HR processes and action plans to close the gaps. A number of sources of a gap might include: size, locations, technology, service levels, outsourcing, etc. Resources for benchmarking might include the American Productivity and Quality Center. Best practices in HR processes might include:

- develop a customer-focused mission statement;
- provide SQ training to HR staff;
- establish HR Steering Committee or Advisory Board;
- establish a goal alignment process to ensure consistency of HR programs with SQ principles;
- survey internal customers;
- incorporate SQ measures into HR staff's goals and appraisals;
- conduct internal customer focus groups;

- define specific hiring criteria to serve customers effectively and complement SQ principles;
- establish an employee referral program to source new job candidates;
- subcontract portions of the employment function to reduce cost and increase effectiveness and efficiency;
- use employee teams to redesign the performance management system;
- establish specific criteria for setting team and individual performance goals;
- introduce 360-degree feedback for management development;
- conduct feedback and coaching skills training;
- select pay delivery options which support SQ principles;
- initiate a skills-based pay system;
- use training to support SQ culture change;
- deliver training in a just-in-time mode;
- involve customers and suppliers in the development of training programs.

Re-engineer to become effective as well as efficient

One of the factors that differentiates excellent service HR departments from their mediocre competition is how well they identify customer requirements, and are able to consistently deliver on those requirements. Brown (1990) suggests a modified application of Quality Function Deployment that has some use for HR departments:

Phase I – define customer requirements
Phase II – weigh importance of customer requirements
Phase III – evaluate self compared to competition
Phase IV – assess feasibility, benefits and costs
Phase V – identify impacts on each customer requirement

Few HR departments take a proactive approach to determine customer needs and wants. Often, they address the issues that pertain only to policy and not those that are strategic and add value.

Other hospitality companies should take the lead of Stouffer and identify costs of quality (Bohan and Horney, 1991). A number of the key processes in the HR department can be tracked to identify their costs (e.g. benefits claims processing, selection, training). Moreover, HR departments can make better business cases for its processes by identifying what it costs to prevent a problem from occurring (e.g. training to prevent sexual harassment) versus paying for the problem if it is not prevented or caught and corrected.

Coyle's (1991) summary of Baldrige Award winners is that the alignment of HR processes with quality initiatives is very idiosyncratic. There are few models to follow since no company has all the answers. However, the value of benchmarking other companies' HR practices cannot go overlooked. Recalling the internal customer satisfaction measures that the HR department of Weyerhaeuser uses to evaluate its products and services, hospitality companies need to look at best-in-class examples and not limit their comparisons to the hospitality industry.

HR department service quality survey

The survey items shown in Figure 6.10 can be used to assess the degree to which the HR Department is aligned with the principles of SQ.[1]

1. Leadership

1.1 *Senior Executive Leadership*

Completely	To a great extent	To some extent	To a little extent	Not at all	Unaware
5	4	3	2	1	0

Circle the point on the scale to the right of each item that most nearly describes your opinion of your HR Department's present situation. Use zero (0) to indicate that the information may be available but you are unaware of it.

1. To what extent has the HR department's management team established a clear vision or mission emphasizing quality improvement? 5 4 3 2 1 0

2. To what extent does the HR department's management team communicate its emphasis on quality to the following groups:
    a) internal customers (e.g. company employees) 5 4 3 2 1 0
    b) suppliers 5 4 3 2 1 0
    c) local community 5 4 3 2 1 0

3. To what extent is the HR department's management team visibly involved in setting improvement goals, planning, and reviewing results? 5 4 3 2 1 0

4. To what extent does the HR department's management team personally recognize staff contributions to quality improvements? 5 4 3 2 1 0

1.2 *Quality Values*

Completely	To a great extent	To some extent	To a little extent	Not at all	Unaware
5	4	3	2	1	0

---

5. To what extent does the HR department's management team focus on quality communicated in such a way that staff understand it? 5 4 3 2 1 0

6. To what extent does the HR department's management team measure the extent to which staff support the values of service quality? 5 4 3 2 1 0

1.3 *Management for Quality*

Completely	To a great extent	To some extent	To a little extent	Not at all	Unaware
5	4	3	2	1	0

---

7. To what extent are all of the staff in the HR department empowered to promote quality improvements in the programs and services it offers? 5 4 3 2 1 0

8. To what extent does the HR Department's management team encourage routine collaboration between all levels of its staff? 5 4 3 2 1 0

9. To what extent does the HR Department's management team regularly review its performance in accomplishing service Quality Initiatives? 5 4 3 2 1 0

10. To what extent does the HR Department's management team have specific standards to determine if Service Quality is practiced in the day-to-day operations of its department? 5 4 3 2 1 0

1.4 *Partnering*

Completely	To a great extent	To some extent	To a little extent	Not at all	Unaware
5	4	3	2	1	0

---

11. To what extent does the HR Department's management team work with internal customer groups and suppliers to enhance Service Quality? 5 4 3 2 1 0

12. To what extent does the HR Department's management team use attitude surveys, interviews, suggestion systems, or focus groups to evaluate its relationship with:
    a) its own staff? 5 4 3 2 1 0
    b) internal customers? 5 4 3 2 1 0
    c) suppliers 5 4 3 2 1 0

13. To what extent have evaluations of the HR Department's relationship with its staff, customers and suppliers resulted in improvements in its programs or services? 5 4 3 2 1 0

Figure 6.10 *HR quality survey*

2. Information and Analysis

2.1 *Management of Data and Information*					
Completely	To a great extent	To some extent	To a little extent	Not at all	Unaware
5	4	3	2	1	0

14. To what extent does the HR Department collect information on the needs, expectations, and satisfaction of its primary customers? 5 4 3 2 1 0

15. To what extent does the HR Department collect accurate data on customer requirements? 5 4 3 2 1 0

16. To what extent does the HR Department collect data on customer complaints? 5 4 3 2 1 0

17. To what extent does the HR Department collect accurate information on cycle times (time between a customer request and delivering the product or service)? 5 4 3 2 1 0

18. To what extent does the HR Department evaluate the accuracy of its data collection efforts? 5 4 3 2 1 0

19. To what extent have improvements in information collection resulted from the data collection process? 5 4 3 2 1 0

2.2 *Benchmarking and Comparisons*					
Completely	To a great extent	To some extent	To a little extent	Not at all	Unaware
5	4	3	2	1	0

20. To what extent does the HR Department collect information on "best practices" from other HR Departments? 5 4 3 2 1 0

21. To what extent does the HR Department collect relevant data on:
    a) benchmarked partners' service quality? 5 4 3 2 1 0
    b) benchmarked partners' customer satisfaction? 5 4 3 2 1 0
    c) benchmarked partners' supplier performance? 5 4 3 2 1 0
    d) benchmarked partners' employee-related issues? 5 4 3 2 1 0
    e) benchmarked partners' internal operations? 5 4 3 2 1 0
    f) benchmarked partners' cycle time? 5 4 3 2 1 0

22. To what extent does the HR department evaluate the sources of information about "best practices?" 5 4 3 2 1 0

2.3 *Analysis of Data and Information*					
Completely	To a great extent	To some extent	To a little extent	Not at all	Unaware
5	4	3	2	1	0

23. To what extent does the HR Department analyze the information it collects on itself to identify opportunities to improve the following:
    a) planning process? 5 4 3 2 1 0
    b) internal operations? 5 4 3 2 1 0
    c) implementing new products or services? 5 4 3 2 1 0

24. To what extent does the HR Department's management team ensure information is disseminated to those who can take corrective action? 5 4 3 2 1 0

25. To what extent has the HR Department tried to reduce the time between the collection of information and the dissemination of that information? 5 4 3 2 1 0

Other categories included in this survey are:

3. Strategic Quality Planning

    3.1 Strategic Quality Planning Process
    3.1 Quality Goals and Plans

Figure 6.10 *HR quality survey (contd)*

4   Human Resource Excellence

    4.1 Human Resource Management
    4.2 Employee Involvement
    4.3 Education and Training
    4.4 Employee Recognition and Performance Measurement
    4.5 Employee Well-Being and Morale
    4.6 Diversity
    4.7 Employee Partnering

5   Quality Assurance of Programs and Services

    5.1 Design, Development and Introduction of Programs and Services
    5.2 Quality Control of Service Processes
    5.3 Continuous Improvement of Processes
    5.4 Quality Assessment
    5.5 Documentation
    5.6 Supplier Quality

6   Quality Results

    6.1 Program and Service Quality Results
    6.2 Administrative, Operational, and Support Service Quality Results
    6.3 Supplier Quality Results

7   Customer Satisfaction

    7.1 Determining Customer Requirements and Expectations
    7.2 Customer Relationship Management
    7.3 Commitment to Customers
    7.4 Determining Customer Satisfaction
    7.5 Customer Satisfaction Results
    7.6 Customer Satisfaction Comparisons

Figure 6.10   *HR quality survey (contd)*

CONCLUSIONS

SQ and TQM programs have become prominent approaches to management. Through the increasing emphasis on the international marketplace, a series of international standards for quality have been developed and implemented throughout the industrialized world, known as the ISO 9000 series. In the United States, the creation of the Baldrige award has focused a great deal of interest by US companies in implementing a culture of quality through TQM.

A critical component of the TQM cultural initiative is the need to align human resource management systems and processes with TQM cultural values. For example, a TQM culture emphasizes customer service, team work and continuous improvement. The human resource processes of selection, performance reviews, rewards and recognition, etc. must be aligned with the TQM values in order to institutionalize them.

Company examples have been provided to illustrate how human resource processes can be developed to reinforce TQM initiatives. The bottom line from this author's research and experience on the Board of Examiners of the Malcolm Baldrige National Quality Award is that human resource processes are critical to the successful implementation of TQM. However, if the human resource systems are not aligned with the

TQM vision, mission and principles, the implementation of TQM will be perceived as another passing management fad.

NOTE

1. The complete survey can be used as the starting point for re-engineering the HR Department. For more information on the complete HR quality survey and benchmarking your results with other HR departments, contact the author at Nicholas F. Horney & Associates, P.O. Box 2126, Hudson, Ohio, USA, 44236-2345. Tel. 216-650-5024.

REFERENCES

Blackburn, R., and Rosen, B. (1993) 'Total quality and human resources management: lessons learned from Baldrige award-winning companies', *Academy of Management Executive*, vol. **7**, no. 3, pp. 49–66.

Bohan, G. P., and Horney, N. F. (1991) 'Pinpointing the real cost of quality in a service company', *National Productivity Review*, Summer, pp. 309–17.

Bowen, D., and Greiner, L. (1986) 'Moving from production to service in human resources management', *Organizational Dynamics*, Summer, pp. 35–53.

Bowen, D. E., and Lawler, E. E. (1993) 'Total quality-oriented human resources management', *Organizational Dynamics*, Summer, pp. 29–41.

Brown, D. (1991) 'HR: survival tool for the 1990s', *Management Review*, March, pp. 10–14.

Brown, M. G. (1990) 'Service quality deployment', *Journal of Quality and Participation*, March, pp. 98–104.

Burrows, P. (1992) 'Behind the facade of ISO 9000', *Electronic Business*, January, pp. 40–4.

Byrne, J. A. (1993) 'The horizontal corporation', *Business Week*, 20 December, pp. 76–81.

Carr, C. (1987) 'Injecting quality into personnel management', *Personnel Journal*, September, pp. 43–51.

Cascio, W. F. (1993) 'Downsizing: what do we know? What have we learned?' *Academy of Management Executive*, vol. **7**, no. 1, pp. 95–104.

Coyle, J. (1991) 'Aligning human resources processes with total quality', *Employee Relations Today*, Autumn, pp. 273–8.

Haller, T. (1994) 'TQM companies outperform S&P 500', *AQP Report*.

Hendricks, C. F., and Triplett, A. (1989) 'TQM: strategy for 90s management', *Personnel Administration*, December, pp. 42–8.

Kahnweiler, W. (1991) 'HRD and empowerment', *Training and Development Journal*, pp. 73–6.

Kaplan, R. S., and Norton, D. P. (1992) 'The balanced scorecard – measures that drive performance', *Harvard Business Review*, January–February, pp. 71–9.

Lawler, E. E. (1992) *The Ultimate Advantage: Creating the High-Involvement Organization*, Jossey-Bass, San Francisco.

Lawler, E. E. (1994) 'Total quality management and employee involvement: are they compatible?' *Academy of Management Executive*, vol. **8**, no. 1, pp. 68–76.

Lawler, E. E., Mohrman, S. A., and Ledford, G. E. (1992) *Employee Involvement and Total Quality Management*, Jossey-Bass, San Francisco.

Malcolm Baldrige National Quality Award Criteria (1994).

Roth, W. F. (1989) 'Quality through people: a hit for HR', *Personnel*, November, pp. 50–2.

Schuler, R. S., and Harris, D. L. (1991) 'Deming quality improvement: implications for human resource management in a small company', *Human Resource Planning*, vol. **14**, no. 3, pp. 191–207.

United States General Accounting Office (1991) *US Companies Improve Performance Through Quality Efforts*, Washington, DC.

Weyerhaeuser's Internal Customer Service Measure (1991), personal communication.

Yeamans, W. N. (1989) 'Building competitiveness through HRD renewal', *Training and Development Journal*, October, pp. 77–82.

1993 ASQC/Gallup Survey Report. ASCQ, Milwaukee, WI.

7

Operative selection techniques for service quality assurance: an exploratory investigation

Elizabeth Ineson, Anne Dickinson, and Barbara Sutton

OVERVIEW

Two selection techniques (biodata and personality assessment), which have been found to yield high predictive validities in other industries, are examined in the context of hotel employee recruitment. The aim of the research, which is reported in the chapter, is to identify characteristics which are common to hotel operatives who interact frequently with guests, who are reliable and who produce a high standard of work consistently, so that a selection tool which isolates these characteristics may be developed. Selection of applicants displaying characteristics which are the best possible match with those identified by the study should improve the service quality of the organization, particularly from the perspectives of customers, recruitment personnel and existing hotel operatives.

BACKGROUND TO THE RESEARCH

The Single European Act (Department of Trade and Industry, 1990) came into force on 31 December 1992. This enabled nationals of the 12 member states to have the right to take up work within another member state. It also permitted their families to join them, and for workers and their families to receive the same treatment in all aspects of employment as the 'host' nationals; clearly, member states offering the best quality of working life are at an advantage. Further to this, the population of 16–19-year-olds within the UK has fallen from 3.7 million in 1982 to 2.6 million in 1994, which has resulted in a demographic shift in the labour force.

Without doubt, these factors widen the opportunities for employees, but they leave employers in greater competition than ever before for a quality workforce. Additionally, spiralling costs have caused industries to re-appraise their supply of labour and re-evaluate the personnel function. The main proposals have been that industries recruit a higher proportion of females than before and that there should be a greater focus on training to overcome staff retention and motivation problems.

The hospitality industry workforce comprises male and female employees in the ratio of approximately 1:2 (Hughes, 1989). It does appear, though, that hospitality companies are attempting to widen access and training programmes. Firms such as Pizza Hut have adopted the policy of establishing well-regarded 'good training programmes' so as to retain, develop and motivate staff (Lipman, 1989).

In general the industry appears to give little attention to the selection process. Hooghiemstra (1990) wrote: 'It is often startling to see on what superficial basis, decisions about people are taken in companies.' The interview, the most commonly used selection procedure, has been found to be one of the least valid techniques (Anderson and Shackleton, 1990). The current legal environment, with the increasing emphasis upon fairness of selection procedures, such as the Race Relations and Equal Opportunity Acts, makes the use of interviews, with their susceptibility to bias, all the more remarkable.

Attributes of service employees

Normann (1984) referred to service industries as 'personality intensive', and Bowen and Schneider (1985) argued that service sector employees needed interpersonal skills, behavioural flexibility and empathy. Further to this, Poppleton (1989) identified the key feature of service occupations as the 'servicing of the customer or client needs'. It is not easy for employers to reconcile the requirement for consistency of service quality with job satisfaction. Pizam and Neumann (1988) examined roles and task characteristics, defined as the perceived attributes of jobs (Hackman and Oldham, 1975) and as determinants of job satisfaction items which can be measured using the Job Diagnostic Survey (Hackman and Oldham, 1975, 1976). Further, Hackman and Oldham found that measures of the factors dealing with customers and the skill variety required from employees to perform their job were not significant determinants of job satisfaction.

Nevertheless, Schneider (1991) concludes that employee attitudes can be related to profits via: (1) relatively low absenteeism and turnover, (2) high citizenship behaviour, (3) 'excellent customer service', (4) a driving organizational imperative. The interpersonal dimension of service has been described as conviviality, which 'involves fulfilling the customers' psychological needs'; it occurs when servers show a 'genuine personal interest in the customers' (Martin, 1991). Is it possible for hospitality recruiters to identify those applicants who are committed to displaying *genuine* interpersonal skills with consistency in their work? The findings of Ulrich *et al.* (1991) suggest that increased employee commitment leads to increased customer commitment. In an ideal world, if recruiters can find a way of measuring this sustained commitment and link it, not only to job performance, but also to job satisfaction, it is highly likely that absenteeism and job turnover will be reduced and, in turn, profit margins will increase.

THE PURPOSE OF THE SELECTION PROCESS

'A company can be dragged to its knees by the weight of ineffectual staff which decades of ineffectual selection methods have allowed to accumulate' (Smith and Robertson,

1986). The purpose of the selection process within an organization is to identify the most suitable person for a particular job requirement. As the above quote implies, failure to do so can have a crucial bearing upon the success of a company.

Prior to any selection technique being implemented, the desired characteristics for the successful candidate must be identified by creating a personnel specification; this is a detailed analysis of the job requirements so that the most appropriate selection tool can be chosen. A selection procedure must fulfil four basic requirements:

1. It should be practical and reasonable to use.
2. The selection tool should be sensitive enough to identify the desired characteristics.
3. The results should be reliable.
4. It should give a valid result. (Smith and Robertson, 1986)

In addition, Smith and Robertson (1986) identified four operational aspects that need to be considered during a selection procedure, the primary one being that a cost benefit must be involved. In other words, the advantages to be gained by the employment of any particular tool should be greater than the costs incurred. Secondly, the time involved in completing the procedure should be reasonable. The third consideration is the number of personnel and the level of training they potentially require; and fourth, the use of any special facilities necessary to carry out the selection procedure.

In order to assess the validity and reliability of a selection instrument, the method of scoring the results obtained should be examined. Two of the methods used most frequently are the *intuitive* method and *psychometrics*. The intuitive method involves the selector comparing the results of the selection process with his or her own personal experience gained through use of the selection procedure over a period of time. It is a method which deals with intangibles, i.e. both in the test results and the 'experience measure' used.

Psychometrics is the term given to the measurement of psychological characteristics. It presents psychologists with a tangible, mathematical means of assessing whether a test is valid and reliable via a scoring system based on the normal distribution curve. It assumes that in any group of people (or sample) large enough to produce a statistically significant result, a range of data values between the maximum and the minimum (following the normal distribution curve) would be obtained from the results of an assessment.

In order to check whether selection criteria are reliable, valid and effective in practice, a follow-up study of those applicants who are selected is required. Initially, information for decision-making is determined from an analysis of the requirements of a course or job and the selection criteria are evaluated subsequently as performance predictors.

The 'high significance of negative information' in the selection procedure is identified by Springbett (1958), who found that a single piece of negative information led to a 90 per cent chance of rejection and claimed that previous studies showed that selectors searched for negative criteria to reduce the numbers rather than concentrate on positive ones. Bevan and Fryatt (1988) suggest that the majority of recruiters are concerned primarily with disqualifying inappropriate candidates, whereas Dixon (1988) surmised that the prime concern of recruiters is to 'employ the right person'. Having made use of the evidence on the application form, either positively, to select those persons for further consideration, or negatively, to discard unsuitable candidates, the recent literature suggests that selectors appear to be using more varied and different ways to identify and measure selection criteria which they consider to be predictive of subsequent job performance.

Following scrutiny of the application forms, hotel operatives are selected, predominantly, on the basis of interviews and references. Many different types of interview exist. The unstructured interview permits the interviewer to decide upon the questions during the interview. In contrast, the structured interview adheres strictly to a set of pre-prepared questions. One or more interviewers may be present at either type of interview. Generally, the method of scoring is intuitive. This has produced results with low validity which are open to bias in many areas; notably sex, race, age and appearance (Asher, 1972; Anderson and Shackleton, 1986). Although it is common for employment selection to depend ultimately on assessments of candidates made during personal interviews, researchers have found interviewer decisions to be of doubtful reliability and validity (Keenan, 1975, 1977; Schmitt, 1976; Herriot and Wingrove, 1984). Recent reviews (Anderson and Shackleton, 1986, 1990) suggest that improvements could be made through the use of carefully constructed, situational interviews, and 'patterned behaviour description interviews' (a particular format of questions) hold great potential for selection purposes. Validities are generally higher for these than other types of interview. However, Schmitt and Robertson (1990) detail evidence that interviewer bias still occurs according to candidates' appearance, age and gender.

A reference is a written or verbal report concerning the candidate given by such people as previous employers. Many organizations only follow up references after a job offer has been made. Consequently, it has been recommended by Muchinsky (1986) that references should be used as a screening technique for the pre-selection process, to establish those who are clearly unsuited to the job. Little research into the evaluation of references as a selection tool could be located, but it has been reported to be of relatively low validity and low reliability (Kingston, 1971; Beason and Bolt, 1976; Reilly and Chao, 1982).

Psychometric tests have been defined as: 'a carefully chosen, systematic, and standardised procedure for evoking a sample of responses from a candidate, which can be used to assess one or more of their psychological characteristics by comparing the results with those of a representative sample of an appropriate population' (Smith and Robertson, 1986). Ghiselli (1973) wrote: 'for every job there is at least one type of (selection) test which has at least moderate validity'. Further support for this claim came from Schmitt and Hunter (1977), Hunter and Hunter (1984) and Saville & Holdsworth (1992). These tests can be divided into many subcategories; the most commonly used for recruitment purposes are cognitive, personality, motivational and special interest tests. On the whole, nationally recognized standardized tests, particularly the cognitive tests, show high validities as selection instruments (Reilly and Chao, 1982; Goodge and Griffiths, 1985; Anderson and Shackleton, 1986).

Currently, it is not uncommon for psychometric tests to be employed for selection purposes. Testing may take place at one of three stages; that is, tests may be used initially to select applicants for further investigation, which usually implies the rejection of unsuitable applicants, screening selected applicants before the final assessment, or to make or to support final selection decisions. In the latter instance, test results may be one of a number of measures which comprise an assessment centre.

Work competencies have been linked with certain personality traits (Harrison, 1979; Hollis, 1984; Willis, 1984; Schmitt and Noe, 1986). Schmitt and Noe claim that personality tests may be more valid in the management field, where the motivational and interpersonal skills which they purport to assess make a greater contribution to effective performance. Although personality tests may be more time-consuming and costly to implement for selection purposes than cognitive tests, perhaps they should be given greater consideration for operative selection in industries where personality traits are believed to be crucial to successful performance.

Swinburne (1985) notes that there is very limited research into the use of personality tests for selection purposes in the late 1970s and early 1980s. Although Sparks (1983) and Bentz (1985) offered support to the predictive validity of personality inventories in managerial selection, there is 'still little consensus about how many personality factors' could be 'measured reliably, how these should be organised or the most appropriate names for them' (Hubbard, 1985). Lord *et al.* (1986) suggest that the poor reputation of personality tests as selection instruments is due, in part, to misinterpretation of research.

Information from a person's past has been called biographical data or 'biodata' in the recent literature. Biodata (Mitchell and Klimoski, 1982; Savage, 1985) assume that personal biographical information is predictive of future behaviour and is therefore of value in selection. Some studies have shown selection techniques employing biodata to be the most consistently reliable, producing the greatest levels of validity (Reilly and Chao, 1982; Goodge and Griffiths, 1985; Mitchell, 1989; Anderson and Shackleton, 1986, 1990; Schmitt and Robertson, 1990). Despite all the evidence in their favour, however, Robertson and Makin (1986) discovered that only seven out of 108 organizations listed in the *Times 1000 Index* used biodata in any form.

At the management level, the importance of effective selection has been recognized by many companies, notably by the larger firms, and funding has been made available to explore the use of alternative methods; Allied Breweries designed a structured interview specifically for selecting pub managers. This instrument was seen to be a major contributor to the 10 per cent fall in management turnover over three years (Lunn, 1987). Compass has used other techniques such as assessment centres (Helby, 1991).

Prior to the commencement of the project reported here, there was little published evidence of research into the use of biodata for operative selection although Holiday Inn was implementing a pilot scheme, 'Score and Store' (Wolff, 1990), developed specifically for use with housekeeping and guest service personnel. Data are collected by a structured interview and processed using a specially-designed computer software package.

The selection techniques with the greatest predictive validities, i.e. psychometric tests and biodata, were more widely used in the late 1980s (Worsfold, 1989). A comparison of the key findings from two general studies (Robertson and Makin, 1986; Shackleton and Newell, 1991) suggests that during the five-year period 1984–89, the proportion of British companies surveyed who used psychometric testing for selection purposes increased from one-third to two-thirds but, quite probably because of validity generalization issues, the use of biodata remained limited. Nevertheless, the interview retained its position as a 'universal' selection technique.

THE RESEARCH PROJECT

The study reported in this chapter was designed to explore the use of biodata and Saville & Holdsworth's (1990) Customer Service Questionnaire (CSQ) as possible selection techniques for hotel operatives. One of the major advantages of using biodata and standardized tests as selection criteria is that the information is relatively easy to collect because a small group of applicants may be assessed quite quickly and simulta-neously. Although the development and testing of the final biodata measuring instrument might be somewhat time-consuming, this feature, combined with the low administration costs and savings gained through employment of the 'best' staff, should prove to be more economical in the long term.

The CSQ, which was devised originally for use with building society customer service staff, was chosen as a measuring instrument for its anticipated relevance to the needs of recruiters; it was considered that many of the qualities desirable in operatives who had customer contact within the hotel sector were synonymous with those assessed by the CSQ. Therefore, it appeared to be a potentially useful and valid technique for selection of these non-managerial staff. An additional decision-making criterion was the high validity and reliability of these selection procedures compared with alternative meth-ods and the fact that so little attention has been apparently given to the two techniques within the industry.

The nature of biodata

Biodata have been claimed to facilitate the thorough and systematic selection of applicants via the use of personal biographical information which is assumed to be predictive of future behaviour (Asher, 1972). They can be collected from application forms for current or potential employees or by evaluating additional information provided by individuals. Two types of information are used to produce biodata, i.e. things that have happened to a person in the past – verifiable information – and opinions or attitudes held as a result of previous experiences – unverifiable informa-tion. Asher (1972) defined verifiable or hard biodata items as historical, actual, memory-related, factual, specific, response-related and concerned with an event that is external to the person concerned. In contrast, unverifiable or soft items (Hammer and Kleiman, 1988; Furnham, 1990) have been defined as being future-oriented, a matter of conjecture, concerned with hypothetical behaviour and response tendencies, inter-pretive, general and dealing with an internal or personal event. One advantage of both types of data over those collected by many psychometric tests is that, because of the nature of the questions, it is very difficult for a candidate to 'guess' what response is desired.

The measurement of biodata

The main methods of collecting biodata are via either the weighted application blank (WAB) or the biographical information blank (BIB). The WAB was used originally by Goldsmith in 1922 (Mitchell and Klimoski, 1982). It is an inventory of biodata items – usually hard items – where each item is allocated a specific weighting according to an estimate of its predictive accuracy. The items having the greater weightings are those estimated to have a greater distinguishing capability (Hammer and Kleiman, 1988). The format of the WAB is a questionnaire, and candidates answer the questions by selecting an answer from the choice provided (Savage, 1985). The BIB is weighted in the same manner as the WAB. However, the range of questions is greater than for the WAB; it contains both soft and hard items. It is completed by the employer rather than the candidate, and the answers available within each question are assigned different weightings. In each case, the test consists of an inventory of biodata items with the question responses being assigned different weightings and then scored using the empirical keying method (Mitchell and Klimoski, 1982).

When constructing an instrument by which biodata might be collected, a group of employees in similar work situations (preferably identical jobs) is chosen. The group is divided into two subgroups, one of which comprises those who have the desired characteristic such as 'success in their work' and the other those who have not (Furnham, 1990). The two subgroups then complete the pilot WAB or BIB. The results are analysed to assess how accurately the instrument classified the individuals into each of the subgroups. Then, a second instrument is developed incorporating those factors which appeared to have the greatest predictive effect. The second instrument is tried out on a new group of employees to assess whether it is valid or not (Savage, 1985). Furnham (1990) recommends approximately 30 people in each of the first two subgroups and at least 150 people, in total, for the cross-validation test, to avoid any spurious results.

The use of biodata

Biodata have been researched and used in many ways and in different contexts, for example, as part of the graduate selection process (Herriot, 1985) and in America (Schneider and Schmitt, 1986); to predict rate of job turnover (Fleishman and Bass, 1974); as an accurate predictor of career success (Brush and Owens, 1979; Beatty and Schneier, 1981; Childs and Klimoski, 1986; Cook, 1988); to categorize employees (Drakeley *et al.*, 1988) and to predict test performance (Pannone, 1984).

In the hotel sector, biodata have been employed as a screening device to distinguish between potential long- and short-stay staff for a new hotel (Mitchell, 1989). Ineson and Brown (1992) conducted a pilot study of the use of biodata for selecting applicants for operational front-of-house positions, based on their interpersonal skills and their job flexibility, for a large company-owned international hotel group. Using discriminant function analysis (DFA), they found that 80 per cent of a small sample of the current employees might have been classified correctly into 'good' and 'bad' worker subgroups by the use of biodata.

There has been criticism of the use of biodata both as a research technique and on a moral basis. The temporal stability of biodata items is questionable; this was investigated by Shaffer *et al.* (1986), who found that hard items were more consistent than soft items, but both were claimed to be relatively stable. The results of previous conflicting research on transferability and validity (Hunter and Hunter, 1984) were superseded by the findings of Rothstein *et al.* (1990) who established that statistically valid biodata items for one particular organization could be transferred successfully to another organization(s) with the same level of accuracy and, thus, statistical validity. The problem of candidates faking their responses, i.e. trying to bias answers in their favour, was found to be reduced when a warning was issued that results might be checked (Cascio, 1975; Schrader and Osburn, 1977). To eliminate ethical criticisms it is suggested that biodata inventories should be screened carefully to ensure that no bias occurs in relation to gender, race, specific age groups or disabilities.

Personality assessment and the Customer Service Questionnaire

The theory of personality can be sub-divided into four broad areas: dispositional, psychodynamic, learning and social-learning theories. The majority of selection tests are based on the dispositional school of thought. This theory assumes that individuals' personalities consist of certain dispositions which cause them to behave in a particular manner. These 'dispositions' are classified in three ways – types, traits and needs. Selection tests are designed to identify particular traits or factors. These traits are then combined into groups of traits, all of which bear a close relationship to one another.

The CSQ was developed from a series of tests that Saville & Holdsworth (1990) produced known as the Occupational Personality Questionnaire (OPQ). These were founded on a systematic and detailed analysis of a series of job interests, and then categorized according to Saville & Holdsworth's categorization of the world of work (see Appendix 1). The test was developed specifically for use with non-managerial personnel, i.e. operatives, and was designed to identify those personality traits required by staff involved with a high level of customer contact. The CSQ claims to identify 11 separate personality traits which are grouped into four key areas:

1. Relationships with people
    *   need to control
    *   sociability
    *   group orientation
    *   attitude to authority
2. Thinking style
    *   understanding of people
    *   mental awareness
    *   attitude to change
    *   approach to organizing
3. Emotions and energy
    *   emotional sensitivity
    *   need for results
    *   need for social approval

The CSQ was developed to provide a valid means of assessing whether people are trustworthy, fair-minded and thorough in their work. Those persons gaining high scores are claimed to be confident, clear and sensitive communicators, whilst being reliable and consistent in their efforts. It is clear that some of these key characteristics are those sought by recruiters of hotel operatives.

The main aims of the study reported in this chapter were to:

*   Identify characteristics unique to employees considered to be reliable and who consistently maintained a high standard of work (or service);
*   Establish the basis for creating a biodata selection tool for future use in operative staff selection;
*   Isolate any factors from the CSQ which had a high predictive value in relation to their work performance;
*   Examine the feasibility of using the CSQ as part of the operative staff selection procedure.

It was apparent that previous researchers had found biodata to be valid predictors of job performance and hence they were worthy of investigation within the hospitality industry. Also, the potential relevance of the CSQ to the industry has been established. The literature provided a sound basis for this study.

METHODOLOGY

The methodology comprised defining the research population, determining the sample, designing a biodata questionnaire, conducting a pilot study, organizing the data collection, determining a method of assessing the performance of the operatives, i.e. of classifying them into subgroups, and outlining the data-processing and analytical procedures.

Research population

The research population was stipulated to be those hotel operatives who, through the course of their average working day, interacted with guests face-to-face as part of their job, or those who worked in locations where guests were likely to communicate with them, e.g. to ask for help or advice. This classification arose from the desire expressed by the personnel department to begin to train this group of staff in oral communication skills, to encourage them to promote the facilities of the hotel by bringing them to the direct attention of the guests.

Sampling and data collection

The data were collected from 51 employees, selected at random. As an incentive, three £5 gift vouchers were provided by the hotel and awarded to three randomly selected participating staff members. Staff were also given a condensed feedback of their individual test results. The sample represented each department in the hotel which employed operatives whose work was relevant to the aims of the study, over a period of two weeks. The time allowed for data collection was limited by the hotel management personnel to 30 minutes per employee.

The biodata questionnaire

Prior to the biodata questionnaire being drafted, staff at the hotel were observed so that those criteria which were judged to be related to performance might be assessed.

The biodata instrument was developed bearing in mind the key features of good questionnaire design. In particular, it needed to appear attractive and of interest to the respondents. The questions were chosen to elicit the maximum amount of information from the respondent in a non-threatening manner. The personal details were requested at the end so that the respondents would not feel intimidated by them. The questions were worded so that the respondents were not led to any particular answer and in language that could be understood easily by the least educated participant. The questions were divided into four categories to provide a clear and logical framework:

1. company information;

2. previous employment;
3. career or future work;
4. personal details.

The *company information* section was included to elicit information regarding the respondents' views about their present jobs, beginning with a series of factual questions about the conditions of work offered by the company. The answers to these questions could have been obtained from the personnel department but they were included as a means of overcoming any fears in the respondents' minds as to the nature and purpose of the research, and their ability to respond. The remainder of this section covered personal attitudes and facts relating to the work. These questions were asked to establish whether any particular views or preferences expressed were contributory factors to whether or not a member of staff was good at their job.

The questions relating to *previous employment* were designed to assess whether any prior work experiences had influenced people's performance in their current employment. Of particular interest was any service sector work experience.

The *career or future work* section comprised a filter question to determine whether the respondents wished to continue working in large hotels, followed by questions regarding their desire to stay with or to leave the company in the long or short term.

General information concerning the nature of the respondents was sought in the *personal details* section. Although the information collected in this section was useful for research purposes, it could not be used as part of a selection process, as this would contravene legal requirements such as the Sex Discrimination Act 1986 (Pannett, 1989).

The Customer Service Questionnaire

The CSQ comprises 88 questions preceded by two pages of instructions and clear illustrations relating to how the test should be answered. Respondents complete a separate answer sheet. Each question is in the form of a statement using a Likert scale. Candidates are asked to choose which one of five responses to the statement best describes them as a person. Although the CSQ questions are representative of the four specified groups of personality dimensions, this categorization is not reflected within the question sequence so that the risk of faking of responses is reduced. Within the test booklet, there is no reference to, nor can candidates make inferences from the questions regarding, the 11 factors.

Administration of the measuring instruments

The biodata questionnaire was administered before the CSQ, as it was recognized that the former could be regarded as potentially more intrusive in nature than the latter. The data were collected from small groups of three or four people simultaneously. This not only ensured a high response rate but it also permitted the researcher to check that the respondents had answered the questions and to provide help where required (though in a manner that would not influence the respondents' answer). Respondents were assured that individual answers would not be passed back to the hotel management. To gain further information they were also told that answers to the questionnaire may be queried by the researcher. This did not occur, but the point was made to reduce the risk of respondents faking their answers.

The CSQ booklets were given to the candidates together with the answer sheets, which were coded with the same identification number as the questionnaire. The test instructions were read aloud and a check was made to ensure that each respondent understood how to complete the answer sheet. It was noted that nearly every respondent queried the meaning of 'insightful' in the CSQ test. A standard reply was given to all enquirers to avoid influencing their responses.

Pilot study of the biodata questionnaire and the Customer Service Questionnaire

The pilot study was conducted on four housekeeping and four waiting staff. Problems were encountered in connection with both the administration of the instruments and the questionnaire design and content. Two candidates had no reading glasses with them, so the researcher had to read both tests, thus prolonging the test duration, and one candidate, who was colour-blind, had great difficulty in completing the CSQ answer sheet, which is printed in pale green ink. With regard to design and content, one word was underlined for greater emphasis, a typing error was identified and two questions needed additional categories in the final questionnaire. As mentioned previously, most respondents enquired as to the meaning of the word 'insightful'. Clearly, as this is a published test, this word could not be altered.

Classification of the employees into performance subgroups

Without reference to any of the data collected, the hotel management personnel were asked to classify the respondents into two subgroups. The criterion employed for this subdivision was that those persons who were reliable and produced a high standard of work consistently were given a rating of 1 ($N = 25$) and the remainder were given a rating of 2 ($N = 26$).

Data processing and analysis

The biodata questionnaire responses were coded to facilitate computer analysis of the data. For each question the answer options were assigned a code. Answers given in response to the 'Other' category were coded after all the data had been collected. The CSQ was scored manually using the two scoring keys provided; alternatively, it may be scored by computer. This resulted in each candidate having a raw score for each of the 11 factors. Prior to the data being processed using the Statistical Package for Social Sciences (PC version) (SPSSPC), it was necessary to transform the CSQ raw factor scores into sten (standard ten-point) scores to produce a standardized set of scores based upon the normal distribution curve for each factor. This process yielded a norm table for hotel operatives with customer contact.

The *statistical technique* employed to assess the abilities of the independent variables, i.e. the biodata and CSQ factors, to predict membership of one of the two performance categories, i.e. the dependent variable, was discriminant function analysis (DFA), more detail of which may be found in Appendix 2. It might be contended that the simplest scenario, i.e. to calculate the arithmetic mean of a linear combination of all the independent variables, could have sufficed for predictive purposes but this would have been a very naïve approach. It is unlikely that the criteria employed by recruiters are given equal weightings in the decision-making process.

Using stepwise DFA with minimization of Wilks' lambda, those CSQ and questionnaire variables (separate and combined) which were the best predictors of membership of the performance categories, i.e. subgroups 1 or 2, were identified, i.e. the combinations of variables giving the highest level of classification accuracy (Norusis, 1988) were obtained and compared. The method employed compares the mean scores for each of the variables included in the DFA and isolates the variable causing the greatest difference in these scores. It then removes that variable and continues in this manner until the combination of variables which gives the highest classification accuracy (Norusis, 1988) is reached.

SUMMARY OF THE RESULTS

In interpreting the results, respondents were judged to be 'identified correctly' when they were predicted by the measuring instruments to fall into the subgroup within which they had been classified by the hotel managers.[1]

Biodata as predictors of performance

From the biodata, seven combinatorial variables were created that were considered to be potential predictors of performance. These were:

1. Loyalty to the company.
2. Flexibility in work.
3. Relationship with supervisors.
4. Relationship with colleagues.
5. Pride in work performance generally.
6. Job satisfaction.
7. Previous employment in service industry work.

A stepwise DFA was performed employing the seven variables as predictors of membership of the subgroups identified by hotel management. The results are illustrated in Table 7.1, from which it may be seen that 32 (63 per cent) of the employees were classified correctly using the biodata variables, with 64 per cent of subgroup 1 and 62 per cent of subgroup 2 membership being predicted.

Prediction of performance using the Customer Service Questionnaire variables

Scores were produced for each CSQ factor based on the hotel employee sample and, as before, stepwise discriminant function analysis was employed, the results of which may be found in Table 7.2.

Table 7.1 *Predicted subgroup membership of employees using biodata (numbers in parentheses are raw percentages)*

Actual membership	Predicted membership	
	Subgroup 1	*Subgroup 2*
Subgroup 1 (*N* = 25)	16 (64%)	10 (38%)
Subgroup 2 (*N* = 26)	9 (36%)	16 (62%)

Table 7.2   *Predicted subgroup membership of employees using the CSQ*
(*numbers in parentheses are raw percentages*)

Actual membership	Predicted membership	
	Subgroup 1	Subgroup 2
Subgroup 1 (N = 25)	18 (72%)	7 (28%)
Subgroup 2 (N = 26)	7 (27%)	19 (73%)

As may be observed, this procedure identified correctly 18 (72 per cent) of the subgroup 1 respondents and 19 (73 per cent) of the subgroup 2 respondents. Overall, a higher percentage (72.5 per cent) of the respondents was classified correctly using the CSQ results than using biodata. Clearly, the CSQ variables discriminated more effectively between the two subgroups than the biodata alone.

Only three subgroup 1 respondents had linear discriminant function scores of −1.0 or less. These were traced to a management trainee and two room attendants; one of the latter was classified incorrectly by the biodata also. The two subgroup 2 respondents who scored above +0.5 were a waitress and a room attendant, neither of whom was classified incorrectly by the biodata.

It appeared that a combination of the two measures might discriminate more effectively between membership of subgroups 1 and 2.

Isolation of the factors with the highest predictive ability

To determine which of the combined CSQ and biodata variables were the best predictors of subgroup 1 and 2 membership, the seven combinatorial biodata variables and 11 CSQ variables were employed in a final stepwise discriminant function analysis. It was found that a combination of four of the CSQ variables with one of the verifiable biodata questionnaire variables produced the optimum result, shown in Table 7.3.

The classification of the employees in Table 7.3 shows that 80 per cent fell into the 'correct' subgroups following the refinement of the predictor variables. Although the overall percentage of employees classified correctly is identical to that of Ineson and Brown (1992), there is a difference in the prediction of subgroup membership. In the present study, four-fifths of each of the subgroup 1 and 2 members were classified correctly using the CSQ in combination with biodata whereas, using biodata alone, Ineson and Brown predicted 94 per cent of the employees that were classified by the management as 'not good' but only 70 per cent of the 'good' workers correctly.

The five variables isolated by DFA were as follows.
Customer Service Questionnaire variables:

- need for social approval;
- attitude to change;
- understanding of people;
- need to control.

Table 7.3   *Predicted subgroup membership of employees using biodata and the CSQ*
(*numbers in parentheses are raw percentages*)

Actual membership	Predicted membership	
	Subgroup 1	Subgroup 2
Subgroup 1 (N = 25)	20 (80%)	5 (20%)
Subgroup 2 (N = 26)	5 (19%)	21 (81%)

Questionnaire variables:

- previous employment in service industry work – experience gained elsewhere in the service sector involving regular contact with guests or customers, e.g. as a sales assistant, nursing aide or in the hospitality industry, was found to be predictive of high performance.

It can be seen from these five areas that the use of biodata does hold potential for selection within large hotels. The factor involving previous experience is an example of verifiable biodata. Questions regarding the other four areas are examples of soft, unverifiable biodata.

Clearly, these results are purely of interest; they are not comparable directly because of the small sample sizes, different locations and standards of the hotels and the exploratory nature of the studies.

Although the sample size was slightly smaller than that recommended by Furnham (1990), the results of this pilot study were encouraging. The findings appeared to support those of earlier researchers into the two techniques, particularly those of Mitchell (1989), and so the use of the CSQ together with biodata might well hold potential for selecting reliable and hard-working employees for positions involving interaction with customers in hotels.

RECOMMENDATIONS

From the results it is clear that certain identifiable and measurable factors are predictive of performance. Therefore, it is recommended that:

- Management explore further the use of the CSQ as part of their selection procedure, focusing on the factors found to have a predictive value and combines this information with verifiable biodata.

It should be noted, however, that the research was carried out with a limited sample and it is recommended that:

- A revised biodata questionnaire be devised, using work-profiling and incorporating questions to determine whether length of tenure can be predicted and what factors might be used to overcome discrimination against school leavers, who may not have any previous work experience; this constituted one of the biodata items.
- Further study involving work-profiling should be carried out, to identify additional verifiable biodata items which might be predictive of performance. This should help to reduce the possibility of faking responses.
- A standardized set of criteria for evaluating staff performance should be established. This is particularly important if the research is to be extended.
- Biodata, collected via the revised questionnaire, and the CSQ assessment are incorporated into the current selection procedure at the hotel, with the results being monitored over a period of time to determine the extent to which the 'subgroup 1' employees might be predicted using this information.
- The same procedure is adopted in other four-star hotels belonging to the company to assess the validity of the data in selecting employees across this sector. It is recognized that the working conditions at the pilot hotel are of a

very high standard relative to most other four-star hotels in the area, which might influence the quality of staff available. Also, the results might be different if the study were to be carried out in a different location, such as a small town or a rural area as opposed to a city centre.

- Further work is carried out to determine whether the results of the study can be extended to the population of operatives with customer contact in four-star hotels generally. This would enable the researcher to discover whether the research findings were specific to the company or might be valid for other comparable establishments.
- Computer programs are developed to score the tests so that potential 'subgroup 1' applicants might be identified more quickly and accurately than by manual methods, possibly at a reduced cost in the long term.

In an industry where people form an integral part of the final product, it is clear that any technique which may help to maintain good customer relations and improve the quality of the product should not be overlooked. In addition, this study points to the possibility of alleviating the problem of high operative staff turnover and hence reducing recruitment costs.

The economic environment within which the hospitality industry exists is changing rapidly. Proposed solutions to the problem of attracting a quality workforce demand an increased emphasis on training. However, the potential benefits will be realized only if a workforce of the requisite quality is recruited. Consequently, industry recruiters need to identify and use measured, reliable and valid selection criteria, and ensure that statistically valid techniques, which have been shown to be predictive of good performance, are employed to ensure selection of the 'best' staff.

Interpersonal skills are very difficult to quantify through the interview process (Samenfink, 1994; Ineson, 1993). Samenfink used a self-monitoring scale to identify the service attentiveness and job performance of employees in the hospitality industry. He concluded that the selection procedures used to indentify 'correct' employees will take on greater importance: 'the self-monitoring scale is just one way of measuring interpersonal skills. Researchers need to continue to identify and develop better measures of interpersonal skills.

IMPLICATIONS FOR FURTHER STUDY

In spite of its being developed in America, Score and Store (Wolff, 1990) appears to be working reasonably well in selecting quality housekeeping and guest service personnel in Europe. However, it was not designed, and therefore is not considered to be appropriate, for selecting food and beverage operatives who are required to interact frequently with guests, who are reliable and who produce a high standard of work consistently. Hence the need for the current phase of the research in this specific field. A further issue, raised by the hotel recruitment personnel, which needs to be borne in mind is that one can no longer expect applicants to possess the interpersonal skills and competencies necessary for these positions. Therefore, any instruments which are used for selection purposes need to be able to identify, not only whether an applicant has acquired the skills, but also whether the potential to acquire those skills is apparent. Clearly, this is not going to be an easy task.

The current project (Ineson, Papadopoulou and Wilkis, research in progress), is entitled 'Employee personal history and personality in the hospitality industry: towards the development of a conceptual framework for personnel selection'. It has four aims:

1. To determine the extent to which personality and biodata constructs are associated with employee performance in the hospitality industry.
2. To identify the unique information that personality and biodata measures contribute to the prediction of performance.
3. To evaluate concurrent and predictive research designs as approaches to establishing criterion-related validity.
4. To contribute to the generation of a theory of employee selection through the specification and testing of a causal model of performance.

ANTICIPATED OUTCOMES OF THE STUDY

It is anticipated that the outcomes of this study will contribute to knowledge in the field in addition to having practical implications.

Contribution to knowledge

The study is designed to make a contribution to the debate about the theory of personnel selection by providing a better understanding of the constructs and psychological mechanisms that underlie the hypothesized connections between predictor and criterion measures. It will give an insight into why personality and biodata measures predict job performance and what information each contributes. Finally it will contribute to the debate concerning concurrent and predictive research designs through the identification of the interpolating factors.

Practical implications of the study

The study aims to validate a cost-saving and practical selection procedure for food and beverage operatives with high customer contact. The items of both biodata and personality measures that best predict the social and personal qualities of candidates contributing to an everyday (consistent) performance of a high standard, and that contribute unique information to this prediction, will be isolated and assigned appropriate weights according to their discriminatory power. These will be used to develop an application form which includes appropriate 'hard' measures that might be assessed by the initial screening process. Hence, the quality of candidates being selected for further consideration should be enhanced. The remaining items will be incorporated into the second stage of the selection procedure, and multiple cut-off scores will be used.

One issue to be addressed is the evaluation of concurrent and predictive validity research designs. Some authors (Hesketh and Robertson, 1993) have suggested the probability that concurrent designs provide better estimates of the criterion-related validity of personality constructs. Considering that the concurrent designs are less time- and money-consuming, proof of this supposition may provide the necessary justification for the use of such designs, enabling the implementation of more useful personnel selection practices.

Having demonstrated that the system developed is effective in four- and five-star hotels within one company, the extent to which the research findings are applicable generally across equivalent hotels in other companies, less sophisticated hotels and other service organizations with similar markets might be explored.

Through the implementation of reliable, valid and tested recruitment procedures, the proportion of employees which is matched to the needs of the service positions should increase, with a corresponding decrease in employee turnover. In turn, the overall quality standards should be raised, hence boosting the morale of the employees and encouraging them to maintain or improve the quality of their performance. To stimulate the workforce to elevate the quality standards, opportunities for improvement should be offered, in particular on-the-job training at a series of levels, work incentives and bonuses and a clearly defined programme for advancement. Given the reduction in employee turnover, the benefits of training should be maximized due to longevity of employment so that training may become focused to meet the needs of the individual rather than being repetitive at the induction level. Increased professionalism amongst the staff raises the profile of a company. Not only will the customers benefit from high-quality service (which may be measured using a customer focus index on an ongoing basis) but ultimately service quality is reflected in the profit of the organization.

NOTE

1 It is important to note that the level of reliability needs to be verified by replicating the study.

APPENDIX 1   SAVILLE & HOLDSWORTH'S CATEGORIZATION OF THE WORLD OF WORK

	caring	medical
		welfare
		educational
PEOPLE	influencing	control
		commercial
		managerial
	organizational	administrative
		legal
DATA	non-verbal	financial
		data processing
	verbal	information
		media
	creative	art and design
THINGS	scientific	physical
		biological
		process
	engineering	mechanical
		electrical
		construction

APPENDIX 2   DISCRIMINANT FUNCTION ANALYSIS

Discriminant function analysis (DFA) chooses a set of independent variables which, when weighted, identifies a linear combination that yields the maximum correlation (optimal solution) with each corresponding dependent variable.

DFA allows the researcher to identify the set of independent variables which allocates cases most effectively to two categories of the dependent variable. It calculates the 'best' linear discriminating function (LDF). The contribution of the independent variables to the discriminatory procedure (i.e. between the categories) can be assessed by examining the coefficients of the selected standardized (mean = 0; SD = 1) independent variables. The LDF values should be interpreted with caution; both the magnitude and the signs of the coefficients need to be taken into account.

Based on a set of independent variables, DFA allows the researcher to distinguish between or amongst the membership of two or more mutually exclusive categories. Initially, Fisher (1936) considered the problem of obtaining the best linear combination of a set of independent variables to discriminate between members of two chosen categories. 'Better discrimination' meant specifically that 'the ratio of the between-groups sums-of-squares of this linear function to its within-groups sums of squares ... would have a larger value than that for any other linear function of the same variables'; full details of the procedure may be found in Tatsuoka and Tiedman (1963). This indicates that better discrimination occurs when the variance between the mean scores on the categories of the dependent variable and the overall mean scores is large relative to the score variances within each category. This ratio may be calculated and is referred to in mathematical parlance as an 'eigenvalue'. It is maximized by the 'best' linear discriminant function (LDF), which is of the form:

$$\text{LDF score} = \text{constant} + B_1X_1 + B_2X_2 + B_3X_3 + \ldots + B_nX_n$$

where the Xs are the independent variables and B_1 to B_n are coefficients estimated from the data, chosen to maximize the eigenvalue.

Using the above equation, i.e. with unstandardized coefficients, the LDF scores are calculated for each case and the cases are ordered according to their score values; in this study, the LDFs were calculated using SPSSPC, which sets the mean scores for all cases combined at 0 and the variance at 1. It should be noted that, because of inter-correlational effects, the magnitudes of the unstandardized coefficients are not necessarily synonymous with the relative importances of the independent variables as contributors to the LDF. However, after standardization of the LDF coefficients (mean = 0; SD = 1), variables with larger coefficients are likely to contribute more to the discriminant scores than their counterparts.

An approach by which the independent variables might be considered for inclusion in the LDF equation must be determined. Forward selection methods choose a final variable set by adding variables sequentially and testing after each addition to discover whether the addition contributes significantly to the discrimination, whilst backward selection methods include all the possible variables and then drop variables one at a time, applying this testing procedure 'in reverse'. Both of these features are combined in the chosen stepwise variable selection algorithms which re-evaluate the variables at each stage in the selection process to determine whether subsequent potential entries meet the model inclusion criterion and existing entries meet the removal criterion.

Variable selection terminates when the addition or removal of variables ceases to contribute significantly to the discrimination procedure.

As the study reported in this chapter was exploratory in nature, concern was with whether the technique might be of value and, if this were to be so, an identification of the stages, e.g. conditional or full offer stage, at which it might be able to perform most effectively in employing sets of independent variables to predict membership of the performance categories, rather than with absolute precision. Clearly, a more specific and rigorously designed study, using 'split-half' techniques, would be required if DFA were to be applied in a 'real' situation for selection purposes.

REFERENCES

Anderson, N., and Shackleton, V. (1986) 'Recruitment and selection: a review of developments in the 1980s', *Personnel Review*, vol. **15**, no. 4, pp. 19–26.

Anderson, N., and Shackleton, V. (1990) 'Staff selection decision making into the 1990s', *Management Decision (UK)*, pp. 5–8.

Asher, J. J. (1972) 'The biographical item: can it be improved?' *Personnel Psychology*, vol. **25**, pp. 251–69.

Barrick, M. R., and Mount, M. K. (1991) 'The big five personality dimensions and job performance: a meta-analysis', *Personnel Psychology*, vol. **44**, pp. 1–26.

Beason, G., and Bolt, J. A. (1976) 'Verifying applicants' backgrounds', *Personnel Journal*, vol. **55**, pp. 345–8.

Beatty, R. W., and Schneier, C. E. (1981) *Personnel Administration: An Experiential Skill-building Approach*, Addison-Wesley, Reading, MA.

Bentz, V. J. (1985) 'Research findings from personality assessment of executives', in Bernadin, H., and Bownas, D. (eds), *Personality Assessment in Organizations*, Praeger, New York.

Bevan, S., and Fryatt, J. (1988) *Employee Selection in the UK*, Institute of Manpower Studies, Falmer, Sussex.

Bitner, M., Booms, B. H., and Tetrault, M. S. (1990) 'The service encounter: diagnosing favourable and unfavourable incidents', *Journal of Marketing*, vol. **54**, pp. 71–84.

Bowen, D. E., and Schneider, B. (1985) 'Boundary-spanning role employees and the service encounter: some guidelines for management research', in Czepiel, J. A., Solomon, M. R., and Surprenant, C. F. (eds), *The Service Encounter*, Lexington Books, Boston.

Brush, H. D., and Owens, W. A. (1979) 'Implementation and evaluation of an assessment classification model for manpower utilization', *Personnel Psychology*, vol. **32**, pp. 369–83.

Campbell, J. P. (1990) 'Modelling the performance prediction problem in industrial and organizational psychology', in Dunnette, M. D., and Hough, L. M. (eds), *Handbook of Industrial and Organizational Psychology*, vol. **1**, Consulting Psychologists Press, Palo Alto, CA, pp. 687–732,

Cascio, W. F. (1975) 'Accuracy of verifiable biographical information blank responses', *Journal of Applied Psychology*, vol. **60**, no. 6, pp. 767–9.

Childs, A., and Klimoski, R. J. (1986) 'Successfully predicting career success: an application of the biographical inventory', *Journal of Applied Psychology*, vol. **71**, no. 1, pp. 3–8.

Cook, M. (1988) *Personnel Selection and Productivity*, John Wiley and Sons Ltd, New York.

Day, D. V., and Silverman, S. B. (1989) 'Personality and job performance: evidence of incremental validity', *Personnel Psychology*, vol. **42**, pp. 25–36.

Department of Trade and Industry (1990) *The Single Market – the Facts*, 6th edn, September, DTL, London.

Der Maesen, P., and Hofstee, W. K. B. (1989) 'Personality questionnaires and inventories', in Herriot, P. (ed.) *Handbook of Assessment in Organizations*, Wiley, New York, pp. 353–67.

Dickinson, A., and Ineson, E. M. (1993) 'The selection of quality operative staff in the hotel sector', *International Journal of Contemporary Hospitality Management*, vol. **5**, no. 1, pp. 16–21.

Digman, J. M. (1990) 'Personality structure: emergence of the five-factor model', *Annual Review of Psychology*, vol. **41**, pp. 417–40.

Dixon, M. (1988) 'What employers really seek in applications', *Financial Times*, 7 December.

Drakeley, R. J. (1989) 'Biographical data', in Herriot, P. (ed.) *Handbook of Assessment in Organizations*, Wiley, New York, pp. 439–53.

Drakeley, R. J., Herriot, P., and Jones, A. (1988) 'Biographical data, training success and turnover', *Journal of Occupational Psychology*, vol. **61**, pp. 145–52.

Fisher, R. A. (1936) 'The use of multiple measurements in taxonomic problems', *Annals of Eugenics*, vol. **7**, pp. 179–88.

Fleishman, E. A., and Bass, A. R. (1974) *Studies in Personnel and Industrial Psychology*, 3rd edn, The Dorsey Press, Belmont, CA, pp. 86–92.

Furnham, A. (1990) 'Back to basics: biodata', *Industrial Relations Review and Report*, January, p. 16.

Ghiselli, E. E. (1973) 'The validity of aptitude tests in personnel selection', *Personnel Psychology*, vol. **26**, pp. 461–77.

Gill, R. W. T., and Banks, J. D. H. (1978) 'Assessment of management potential in graduate recruitment', *Personnel Review*, vol. **7**, no. 3, pp. 56–61.

Goodge, P., and Griffiths, P. (1985) 'Assessment techniques: a review', *Management Education and Development*, vol. **16**, no. 3, pp. 247–57.

Guion, R. M. (1991) 'Personnel assessment, selection and placement', in Dunnette, M. D., and Hough, L. M. (eds), *Handbook of Industrial and Organizational Psychology*, vol. **2**, Consulting Psychologists Press, Palo Alto, CA. pp. 327–97.

Hackman, J. R., and Oldham, G. R. (1975) 'Development of the job diagnostic survey', *Journal of Applied Psychology*, vol. **6**, pp. 159–70.

Hackman, J. R., and Oldham, G. R. (1976) 'Motivation through the design of work: tests of a theory', *Organisational Behaviour and Human Performance*, vol. **16**, pp. 250–79.

Hammer, E. G., and Kleiman, L. S. (1988) 'Getting to know you', *Personnel Administrator*, vol. **33**, pp. 86–8, 90, 92.

Harrison, R. G. (1979) 'New personnel practice: life goals planning and interpersonal; skill development: a programme for middle managers in the British Civil Service', *Personnel Review*, vol. **8**, no. 1, pp. 40–3.

Helby, M. (1991) 'Compass points the way', *Caterer and Hotelkeeper*, 3 January, pp. 26–8.

Herriot, P. (1985) 'Graduate pre-selection: predicting the unpredictable', *Manpower Policy and Practice*, vol. **1**, no. 1, pp. 35–7.

Herriot, P., and Wingrove, J. (1984) 'Decision processes in graduate pre-selection', *Journal of Occupational Psychology*, vol. **57**, pp. 269–75.

Hesketh, B., and Robertson, I. (1993) 'Validating personnel selection; a process model for research and practice', *International Journal of Selection and Assessment*, vol. **1**, no. 1, pp. 3–17.

Heskett, J. L. (1986) *Managing the Service Economy*, Harvard Business School, Boston.

Hogan, J., Hogan, R., and Busch, C. M. (1984) 'How to measure service orientation', *Journal of Applied Psychology*, vol. **69**, pp. 167–73.

Hollis, W. P. (1984) 'Developing managers for social change', *Journal of Management Development*, vol. **3**, no. 1, pp. 16–27.

Hooghiemstra, T. (1990) 'Management of talent', *European Management Journal*, vol. **8**, no. 2, pp. 142–9.

Hubbard, G. (1985) 'How to pick the personality for the job', *New Scientist*, 31 January, pp. 12–15.

Hughes, H. L. (1989) *Economics for Hotel and Catering Students*, Stanley Thornes, Cheltenham.

Hunter, J. E., and Hunter, R. F. (1984) 'Validity and utility of alternative predictors of job performance', *Psychological Bulletin*, vol. **96**, no. 1, pp. 72–98.

Ineson, E. M. (1993) 'The predictive validity of criteria used in the selection of students for undergraduate courses and graduate training in hotel and catering management', PhD thesis, Keele University.

Ineson, E. M., and Brown, S. (1992) 'The use of biodata for hotel employee selection', *International Journal of Contemporary Hospitality Management*, vol. **4**, no. 2, pp. 8–12.

Jones, C., and DeCotiis, T. A. (1986) 'Video-assisted selection of hospitality employees', *The Cornell Hotel and Restaurant Administration Quarterly*, vol. **27**, no. 2, pp. 67–73.

Keenan, A. (1975) 'The selection interview: candidates' reactions and interviewers' judgements', *British Journal of Social and Clinical Psychology*, vol. **17**, pp. 201–9.

Keenan, A. (1977) 'Some relationships between interviewers' personal feelings about candidates and their general evaluation of them', *Journal of Occupational Psychology*, vol. **50**, pp. 275–83.

Kelly, G. A. (1955) *The Psychology of Personal Constructs*, Norton, New York.

Kingston, N. (1971) *Selecting Managers: A Survey of Current Practice in 200 Companies*, BIM, London.

Lipman, C. (1989) 'Colleges and catering', *Restaurateur*, November, pp. 77–8.

Lord, R. G., DeVader, C. L., and Alliger, G. M. (1986) 'A meta-analysis of the relation between personality traits and leadership perceptions: an application of validity generalisation procedures', *Journal of Applied Psychology*, vol. **71**, no. 3, pp. 402–10.

Lunn, T. (1987) 'A scientific approach to successful selection', *Personnel Management*, December, pp. 43–5.

McHenry, J. J., Hough, L. M., Toquam, J. L., Hanson, M. A., and Ashworth, S. (1990) 'Project A validity results: the relationship between predictor and criterion domains', *Personnel Psychology*, vol. **43**, pp. 335–67.

Martin, W. B. (1991) *Quality Service: The Restaurant Manager's Bible*, 2nd edn, Cornell University, Ithaca, NY.

Mitchell, B. (1989) 'Biodata: using employment applications to screen new hires', *Cornell Hotel and Restaurant Administration Quarterly*, vol. **29**, no. 4, pp. 56–61.

Mitchell, T. W., and Klimoski, R. J. (1982) 'Is it rational to be empirical? A test of methods for scoring biographical data', *Journal of Applied Psychology*, vol. **67**, no. 41, pp. 411–18.

Muchinsky, P. M. (1986) 'Personnel selection methods', in Cooper, C. L., and Robertson, I. (eds), *International Review of Industrial and Organisational Psychology*, John Wiley and Sons, New York, pp. 37–70.

Normann, R. (1984) *Service Management: Strategy and Leadership in Service Businesses*, John Wiley and Sons, New York.

Norusis, M. J. (1988) *SPSS/PC + Advanced Statistics V2.0 Manual for SPSS/PC system*, SPSS Inc., Chicago.

Pannett, A., (1989) *Principles of Hotel and Catering Law*, Cassell, London.

Pannone, R. D. (1984) 'Predicting test performance: a content valid approach to screening applicants', *Personnel Psychology*, vol. **37**, pp. 507–14.

Pizam, A., and Neumann, Y. (1988) 'The effect of task characteristics on hospitality employees' job satisfaction and burnout', *Hospitality Research Journal*, vol. **12**, no. 2, pp. 99–105.

Poppleton, S. E. (1989) 'Service occupations', in Herriot, P. (ed.) *Handbook of Assessment in Organizations*, John Wiley, New York, pp. 543–55.

Reilly, R. R., and Chao, G. T. (1982) 'Validity and fairness of some alternative employee selection procedures', *Personnel Psychology*, vol. **35**, no. 1, pp. 1–62.

Robertson, I. T. (1994) 'Personnel selection research: where are we now?' *The Psychologist*, vol. **7**, no. 1, pp. 17–21.

Robertson, I. T., and Kinder, A. (1993) 'Personality and job competences: the criterion-related validity of some personality variables', *Journal of Occupational and Organizational Psychology*, vol. **66**, pp. 225–44.

Robertson, I. T., and Makin, P. J. (1986) 'Management selection in Britain: a survey and critique', *Journal of Occupational Psychology*, vol. **59**, pp. 45–57.

Rothstein, H. R., Erwin, F. W., Schmidt, F., Owens, W. A., and Sparks, C. P. (1990) 'Biographical data in employment selection: can validities be made generalizable?', *Journal of Applied Psychology*, vol. **75**, no. 2, pp. 175–85.

Samenfink, W. H. (1992) 'Identifying the service potential of an employee through the use of the self-monitoring scale', *Hospitality Research Journal*, vol. **15**, no. 2, pp. 1–10.

Samenfink, W. H. (1994) 'A quantitative analysis of certain interpersonal skills required in the service encounter', *Hospitality Research Journal*, vol. **17**, no. 2, pp. 3–17.

Savage, A. (1985) 'Using past behaviour to predict performance', *Personnel Management*, August, pp. 51ff.

Saville & Holdsworth Ltd (1984) *Occupational Personality Questionnaire*, Saville & Holdsworth Ltd, Esher, Surrey.

Saville & Holdsworth Ltd (1990) *Customer Service Questionnaire: Manual and Users Guide*, February, Saville & Holdsworth Ltd, Esher, Surrey, p. 2.

Saville & Holdsworth Ltd (1992) 'Personality measures are valid predictors of job performance – it's official!', *SHL Newsline*, 11 March, Saville & Holdsworth Ltd, Esher, Surrey, p. 6.

Schmitt, F. L., and Hunter, J. E. (1977) 'Development of a general solution to the problem of validity generalisation', *Journal of Applied Psychology*, vol. **62**, pp. 529–40.

Schmitt, N. (1976) 'Social and situational determinants of interview decisions: implications for the employment interview', *Personnel Psychology*, vol. **29**, pp. 79–101.

Schmitt, N., and Noe, R. A. (1986) 'Personnel selection and equal employment opportunity', in Cooper, C. L., and Robertson, I. T. (eds), *International Review of Industrial/Organisational Psychology*, John Wiley, Chichester, pp. 71–116.

Schmitt, N., and Robertson, I. (1990) 'Personnel selection', *Annual Review of Psychology*, vol. **41**, pp. 289–319.

Schneider, B. (1991) 'Service quality and profits: can you have your cake and eat it, too?', *Human Resource Planning*, vol. **14**, no. 2, pp. 151–7.

Schneider, B., and Schmitt, N. (1986) *Staffing Organisations*, 2nd edn, Scott, Foresman and Co., London.

Schrader, A. D., and Osburn, H. G. (1977) 'Biodata faking: effects of induced subtlety and position specificity', *Personnel Psychology*, vol. **30**, no. 3, pp. 395–404.

Shackleton, V., and Newell, S. (1991) 'Management selection: a comparative survey of methods used on top British and French companies', *Journal of Occupational Psychology*, vol. **64**, pp. 23–36.

Shaffer, G. S., Saunders, V., and Owens, W. A. (1986) 'Additional evidence for the accuracy of biographical data: long term retest and observer ratings', *Personnel Psychology*, vol. **39**, no. 4, pp. 791–809.

Shannon, P. (in progress) 'Meta-analysis of personality and biographical inventories', doctoral dissertation, University of Minnesota, Wells Fargo Bank, San Francisco.

Smith, M., and Robertson, I. T. (1986) *Theory and Practice of Systematic Staff Selection*, The Macmillan Press Ltd, London.

Sparks, C. P. (1983) 'Paper and pencil measure of potential', in Dreher, G. F., and Sackett, P. R. (eds), *Perspectives on Staffing and Selection*, Irwin, Homewood, IL,

Springbett, B. M. (1958) 'Factors affecting the final decision in the employment interview', *Canadian Journal of Psychology*, vol. **12**, pp. 13–22.

Swinburne, P. (1985) 'A comparison of the OPQ and 16PF in relation to their occupational application', *Personnel Review*, vol. **14**, no. 4, pp. 29–43.

Tatsuoka, M. M., and Tiedman, D. V. (1963) 'Statistics as an aspect of scientific method in research on teaching', in Gage, N. L. (ed.), *Handbook of Research on Teaching*, Rand, McNally and Co., Chicago, pp. 142–70.

Ulrich, D., Halbrook, R., Meder, D., Stuchlik, M., and Thorpe, S. (1991) 'Employee and customer attachment: synergies for competitive advantage', *Human Resource Planning*, vol. **4**, no. 2, pp. 89–103.

Willis, Q. (1984) 'Managerial research and management development', *Journal of Management Development*, vol. **3**, no. 1, pp. 28–41.

Wolff, C. (1990) 'Software sifts out winners', *Lodging and Hospitality*, September, pp. 55–6.

Worsfold, P. (1989) 'Management selection in the hospitality industry', *Journal of Contemporary Hospitality Management*, vol. **1**, no. 1, pp. 17–21.

Zeithaml, V. A., Parasuraman, A., and Berry, L. L. (1990) *Delivering Quality Service*, The Free Press, New York.

8

Integrating quality management and customer service: the service diagnostics training system

Bonnie Farber Canziani

INTRODUCTION

Training is an essential component of service quality in hospitality organizations. This chapter describes a bi-phasal service diagnostics training system which prepares service employees as diagnosticians, problem-solvers, and designers of mini-training for their departments. Phase 1 calls for a five-step top-management-championed organizational change program that creates a service quality infrastructure upon which a process of continuous service diagnostics (Phase 2) can be conducted. The chapter reviews the literature underpinning this training system, describes how to implement the system, and discusses the implications of partial pilot tests of the system in the hotel sector.

QUALITY FRAMEWORK FOR THE SERVICE DIAGNOSTICS TRAINING SYSTEM

The service diagnostics training system offers service organizations a new look at how they train employees in customer service. This system of customer service training combines both a quality management philosophy and the belief that customer service training can be placed in the hands of customer service employees as a regular job responsibility. Many well-known quality management programs result in operational changes or suggestions for service redesign; the service diagnostics training system additionally asks employees to develop mini-training sessions when a training need results from a team-based service process improvement analysis. The overall goal of the system is to firmly integrate human resources functions such as training and perform-ance appraisal into the quality management scheme. The first part of this chapter presents an overview of quality and also discusses two traditional strategies of human resources professionals who want to improve customer service in their organizations.

Delivering quality service has become a critical strategy for hospitality firms as they recognize that enhanced customer service can differentiate their offerings from those of competitors. Many industries, including hospitality, are turning to quality management practices that focus on the needs of the customer and that support the achievement of product and service quality. Strategic initiatives and programs have been developed, e.g. total quality management and quality improvement programs, by several individuals, including Deming, Juran and Crosby. From a theoretical standpoint, service quality may be defined as translating the future needs of customers into measurable characteristics, so that products and services can be designed and delivered to give satisfaction or value at a price that the customer will pay (Deming, 1986). Management of service quality is the application of quantitative methods and human resources to control and improve materials and services supplied to a service firm, work processes or technology used to create services, and organizational focus on meeting customer needs.

Hence, quality management uses a preventive approach that requires suppliers, company managers and employees, and customers to jointly analyze inputs, e.g. machines, methods, materials and people, work processes and outcome products and services in order to continuously improve the service system. Process management tools have been developed in the manufacturing sector that are now adapted to service firms; these include process flow charts, cause and effect diagrams, histograms, pareto charts, scatter diagrams, trend charts and control charts. Although the quality revolution began in the manufacturing sector with statistical process control techniques, quality management practices have been widely incorporated into service industries. The establishment of service-sector Malcolm Baldrige awards has also inspired service companies to investigate quality management practices. The major components of quality management in service operations include: (1) collection and measurement of customer data; (2) benchmarked standards for work processes and outputs; (3) goals and action plans specifying quality outputs; (4) personnel trained in the use of teams and tools; and (5) a culture that empowers and rewards service employees.

In a total quality environment, prevention and detection of work process inefficiencies and product/service defects become key operating strategies. Employees need to be developed as service diagnosticians through training, support, and rewards that empower them to make decisions which respond to customer needs in real-time scenarios. Leaving the customer in order to track down the manager 'in charge' is not an acceptable service solution in today's competitive hospitality enterprise.

In many hospitality companies, service interactions between company representatives and customers largely determine customers' satisfaction with the service. To improve satisfaction, service personnel must both understand the significance of their role and be able to independently recognize and correct service problems. The question is, how can customer contact employees be helped to recognize and correct service problems effectively?

Generally, two basic human resources strategies have been devised to enhance employee performance in the area of customer service: (1) focus on personnel selection and motivation of customer contact employees; and (2) focus on service job script preparation and concomitant service training. We briefly review the strengths and limitations of these traditional approaches to improving service quality, and then introduce a third, integrative training approach, the service diagnostics training system, which prepares customer contact employees to diagnose and solve operational problems that affect customer service.

Selection and motivation of customer contact employees

Considerable attention is devoted within service companies to improving the selection and motivation of service managers and front-line service personnel. Leading service firms such as Disney Corporation, Federal Express and Ritz-Carlton consider the recruitment of front-line contact personnel to be critical to their success. Currently, these firms are employing simulation-based selection devices such as behavioral interviewing and role playing to provide insights into an applicant's ability to apply skills and knowledge extracted from prior experience to a given service situation. Applicants are asked to consider a situational vignette and to describe orally in their own words how they would handle the events and customers in the given scenario. Hill *et al.* (1989), Schneider and Schechter (1991) and Thompson (1989) have all tested selection devices for customer service employees, using pen and pencil tests, interviews and work simulations. Although they confirm that these selection tools enable an interviewer to gain more information about an applicant's communication style and judgment abilities under simulated job stress, they have not found any selection tool or test measuring service inclination to be strongly predictive of future service performance.

While screening for service competency and inclination has been used widely by the service industry, many companies have opted for formal script-based methods of training customer contact personnel to guide them in their service interactions with customers. This is the subject of the next section.

Training based on service scripts

Scripting is a job description activity that derives from the process of job analysis. Scripts have been developed for a multitude of hospitality service tasks, e.g. greeting hotel guests who call in for information or reservations with a standard phrase of 'Happy Hotels. How may I serve you?' or performing the table-side service of a Caesar salad in a fine dining restaurant. Training service employees to memorize and abide by standardized operating scripts continues to be a favored customer service strategy.

As a rule, creating scripts for training purposes involves consideration of five aspects of the work processes or jobs that are to be scripted:

1. How many duties or tasks can be scripted for a specific job position? How is cross-training affected?
2. How much time will any employee actually spend in scripted tasks? Will the job become too routine?
3. What is the number of different scripts any employee will need or is able to learn?
4. How complex is the script, i.e. multiple script levels, main program and invoked subprograms?
5. How intense is the wording of the script (high intensity allows for minimum variation while low intensity permits some degree of ad-libbing)?

Managers and trainers often resort to scripts when their confidence in employees is low and they want to increase their control over what the employees actually do on the job. Scripted service tasks in this scenario closely resemble the routine subtasks assembly workers perform in the factory setting; the job becomes a routine that sparks little creativity and results in maximal boredom and loss of self-esteem. Script-based job training often involves rote memorization with practice drills and tests. Employees are faced with large small-print procedural manuals that may specify exact subroutines for customer service activities, including: (a) greeting the customer; (b) using standard probing questions to test customer reactions; and (c) offering empathetic responses and positive reinforcement to customers with specific phrases and body language. Some companies even put scripted job tasks on laminated cards so employees can carry them around in their back pockets or wallets, and glance at them occasionally to remind themselves who they are and what they do on the job.

As implied by the five questions for service script design highlighted earlier, using service scripts for training employees can have some undesirable outcomes. When service organizations perceive workers as cogs in wheels that turn on one track only, they tend to opt for intense scripts that must be followed exactly as they were written. And frequently the scripts were written by managers or trainers after half-hearted attempts at surveying or observing employees on the job. When this occurs, employees are deterred from sharing in the improvement of the work they do even though they probably know more about their jobs than any one else in the organization. One also notes with the creation of service scripts a lack of attention to customer needs in that most scripts are written to an average customer. Contingencies are rarely built into service scripts. Script-based training then creates an operation where service itself becomes average – certainly not quality-driven in terms of rapid response to individual customer requests.

In contrast, organizations that seek to empower employees to think on their feet and make decisions in front of the customer will most likely discard some or all of their traditional script-based training for quality-based methods that concentrate on improving employee observation skills, diagnosing service problems and improvising quick and workable solutions. In these quality-oriented organizations the traditional supervisory role is exchanged for one of facilitation of employee decision-making at all levels. Developing managers as facilitators is a critical component of our training system that will be discussed in the second part of this chapter.

Limitations of the service script approach to training

As suggested earlier, service scripts alone cannot guarantee customer satisfaction, particularly when the service is delivered or mediated by human beings in a service encounter. The problem-solving skills of service employees are particularly tested when employees encounter situations which are not precluded or resolved through the service scripts, since it is impossible to delineate all possible variations in advance. Obvious limitations of the traditional script approach to service training include: (1) minimal employee involvement in service operation diagnostics; (2) minimal development of employee observation and attention skills; (3) overemphasis on rote memorization of limited categories of service problems and standard solutions; (4) minimal employee ownership of trainer-designed service scripts and service standards; and (5) little empowerment of employees to manage the unavoidable contingencies in service encounters.

THE SERVICE DIAGNOSTICS TRAINING SYSTEM

The service diagnostics training system is predicated on the philosophy of continuous improvement of service quality through (1) operational analysis and (2) employee-driven mini-training based on service performance data originating from customer feedback sources. The system is divided into two phases of organizational development that center on the service employee as a key provider of service quality to the hospitality customer. Figure 8.1 depicts the two phases and associated organizational development activities.

Overview of Phase 1

Phase 1 is dedicated to a set of five contiguous activities that encompass the following:

1. A statement of quality is formulated and disseminated throughout all levels of the organization.
2. Preliminary reviews of service processes are undertaken by engaging department managers and employees in team-based service blueprinting and benchmarking activities.
3. Managers are involved in a formal development session where they are encouraged to learn methods of facilitation to complement later employee training in team-based service diagnostics.
4. All customer feedback sources are reviewed by department managers and personnel, and a service log system is implemented in each department.

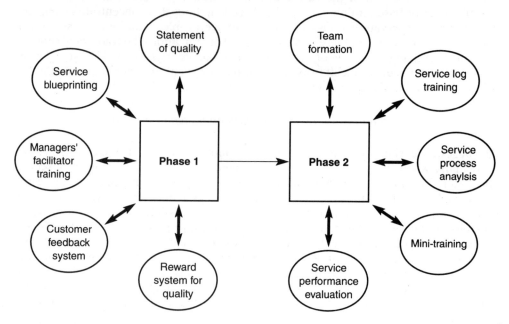

Figure 8.1   *Service diagnostics training system*

5. Managers and human resource personnel revise current compensation and incentive programs to establish linkages between reward practices and measures of employee performance in the delivery of quality service to the customer.

The goal of Phase 1 is to create an organization-wide awareness of (1) quality as a process of continuous improvement and (2) the critical role of attention to customer needs in the delivery of quality service and products. Phase 1 also commences the involvement of employees in service blueprint activities and gives them an initial indication of managerial support and potential organizational rewards for employee achievements that coincide with organizational goals for service quality and customer satisfaction.

In most organizations, it is wisest to begin any change program in those departments or with those persons who provide the most supportive climate. This decision of where to commence Phase 1 generally rests with the highest level of management that chooses to champion the goals of service quality and service diagnostics training. There is no defined time period associated with Phase 1 due to the fact that companies choosing to use this system may vary widely in terms of prior quality-based system and strategies they already have in place. However, if a company is starting from square one, it would be advised to approach the change process outlined in Phase 1 slowly and to build up management–employee relations over a period of six months to one year before attempting to implement Phase 2. This will give the organization sufficient time to disseminate value statements about quality, train managers in facilitation skills, and create preliminary department teams to engage in the service design and benchmarking activities. Special *ad hoc* teams should be developed to review the customer feedback sources, develop service log handling procedures and revise incentive/reward systems. Only when the outlined infrastructure is in place should the company proceed to Phase 2.

Overview of Phase 2

Phase 2 is the heart of the service diagnostics training system. It provides the impetus for continuous service improvement in an organization by developing specific diagnostic and delivery skills in service employees.

Service diagnostics training program format

1. Employees are invited to participate in service teams by department managers and are prepared as team members and leaders.
2. Employees are introduced to the service log and trained to monitor data from all customer feedback sources.
3. Employees are trained to continuously analyze service processes.
4. Employees are taught to develop training demonstrations and role-plays based on train-the-trainer principles.
5. Employees learn to measure service team performance and provide team-level feedback to managers regarding accomplishments.

The outlined service diagnostics training format essentially prescribes a developmental process where employees become team-mates and co-trainers in a continuous service improvement endeavor. All five activities are conducted regularly thereafter as part of the normal and essential functions of the employee teams.

Managers schedule employee hours for team meetings and service diagnostics activities on a bi-weekly basis, with monthly mini-training sessions.

Implementation of the service diagnostics training system

Detailed procedures for implementing this training system within the hotel sector are presented in this section, using examples gathered by the author in cooperation with hotel industry colleagues.

Phase 1 procedures

A statement of quality is formulated and disseminated throughout all levels of the organization   The statement of quality is developed carefully with top management input and support. Creators of the organizational statement of quality must first ascertain the organization's answers to the following ten questions, as well as define top management's vision for change in the future:

1. What level of customer satisfaction does your company want to achieve?
2. How is quality measured in your company?
3. How will your company ensure quality control?
4. How will your employees be trained to be quality aware?
5. Does your company search for the best resources and materials?
6. How do you use customer feedback to improve products and services?
7. Does your company stress team work among employees?
8. What input do employees and customers have in service design?
9. How do your employees share in the final outcome of what they do?
10. How do you reward your employees for quality-related performance?

From a compilation of the answers to the above questions, certain values and terms should emerge that may be used in writing the statement of quality. All statements of quality should use value-based language that is specific, clear, and meaningful to all key players: customers, managers, employees and suppliers. Words should be selected carefully for their ability to build self-esteem, identity and a sense of belonging, and to urge employees and customers to risk change and develop a sense of purpose. The principal goals of a statement of quality are to create a positive belief system for everyone involved with the company, to identify the company's key service strengths and to broadcast the company's willingness to take responsibility for achieving service quality. Figure 8.2 exemplifies one hotel's approach to devising a statement of quality vision.

Once the statement of quality is finalized in written form as shown, it is disseminated throughout the organization in various ways. Some sample statements follow that have appeared in one company's orientation letter to new employees:

> Our Company is committed to total quality. This means a level of service that not only satisfies but delights each and every guest. We ask that you dedicate yourself to this goal as well.

> We are always watching for signals of a non-satisfactory guest experience. When a guest has a problem, we move quickly to resolve all problems to the guest's total satisfaction. We sincerely believe that such 'moments' of truth provide us with an excellent opportunity for assuring the guest will return to our hotel on his or her next trip.

HOLIDAY INN ON-THE-BAY VISION

Each employee has the courage to change the way we
do business to consistently, over the long term,
improve the quality of service and products.
We will develop a culture in which employees:

Love their work
Are provided opportunity
Are provided education
Jobs that create challenge
Have autonomy
Feel pride
Are trusted
Have fun

Through company-wide quality control we inspire
employees, customers and the community
so that world class results and
greatness
will be achieved

Figure 8.2 *Statement of quality*

Other places where the statement of quality might appear are posters, pay envelope inserts, house newsletters, orientation materials, employee handbooks, training handouts, marketing literature, and lobby and in-room media screens.

Preliminary reviews of service processes are undertaken by engaging department managers and employees in team-based service blueprinting and benchmarking activities A second quality strategy involves standardizing the delivery of the service by developing equipment and processes that strive to ensure dependable service outcomes. Levitt (1976) coined the term 'the industrialization of service' to describe this approach. This approach was further elaborated and generalized by Shostack (1987) as a process of service 'blueprinting'. Blueprinting aims to identify likely or possible failure points in advance, in order to redesign the service and/or prepare staff to avoid or correct conditions that create service failures. All blueprints for service processes should be benchmarked against customer requirements and industry practices. Benchmarking refers to the need to continually compare a service firm's work processes with those practiced by companies perceived as the best industry-wide, and with standards dictated by the firm's customers and sales mix. A major tool used in the blueprinting process is that of service process flow charts.

Service process flowcharting deviates from traditional job analysis in that it incorporates a customer's perspective of service work, rather than relying on the employees' or managers' listings of job tasks. This is a definitive issue in the undertaking of service work design. Historically, job analysis has been used to develop comprehensive written task lists, in the style of the following hotel receptionist position:

1. Acknowledge and greet guests.
2. Perform guest check-in.
3. Provide information and messages to guests.

4. Perform guest check-out.
5. Change money and handle accounts for guests.
6. Answer and route calls at front desk.
7. Serve as liaison with other hotel departments.

Unfortunately, the job list tells the hotel employee virtually nothing about the different contact points guests have as they enter the hotel to seek a room, and even less about the potential linkages the employee has with other employees participating in the guests' total service encounter. The service flow chart, on the other hand, provides all of this information. With this in mind, we proceed with a discussion of the basic steps in flowcharting service work processes.

The first step is to identify each service encounter that a customer will have when requesting a specific type of service. Consider the core and supplementary hotel services in Figure 8.3 (Lovelock, 1992, p. 26).

A service flow chart can be drawn for any one of these hotel services. Information about individual steps comprising the service work process is elicited using a variety of data collection methods with multiple respondents: *customers, employees and managers*. Interviews and questionnaires are best used to determine lists of tasks and flow sequences of customer service activities, as well as task frequencies and importance of the activities to the customer. Direct observation of work in progress gives additional qualitative information about actual customer and employee practices and work conditions. Service logs provide detailed records of performance delays, rework and past needs for service recovery steps.

As soon as the data collection is complete enough to grant a sense of the customer's progress from initial contact points to final service delivery points, the flow chart may be designed. Generally, flow charts display inputs, i.e. *materials, equipment and personnel*, and outputs, i.e. *products or services*, and use appropriate flow chart symbols (Table 8.1) to show the service process.

Process steps that might be critical to the entire operation and also those steps that might have a high rate of failure are flagged in the flow chart. The flow chart may also

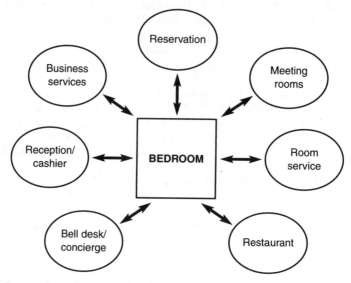

Figure 8.3 *Core and supplementary hotel services*

Table 8.1   *Common flow chart symbols*

Symbol	Meaning
	Marker. Process begins or ends
	Operation. Some expenditure of labor or machine activity
	Decision point. Leads to different processing steps
	Output. A deliverable outcome of the operation
	Direction of flow. Denotes the sequence of processing steps

indicate a dashed line separating activities that are visible to the customer from those that are conducted behind the scenes (in the back of the house). Figure 8.4 portrays a sample flow chart of a guest being checked into a hotel.

A summary checklist for creating service flow charts generally requires one to:

1. Identify the processes underlying customers' requests for service.
2. Identify the tasks that service personnel currently perform.
3. Identify critical decision points and corollary yes/no branching.
4. Evaluate processes from a layout or logistics standpoint.
5. Determine points where customer–employee interaction occurs.
6. Pinpoint existing performance delays and rework probabilities.
7. Continuously review and improve service processes.

As noted earlier, service flow charts depict the steps involved in providing a service to a customer. As a design tool they are useful to pinpoint logistical errors in the procedures built into service operation jobs. Blueprints should be created as a team effort among service firm managers and customer contact employees with additional customer input. Organizations benefit maximally by having all personnel analyze service work processes because all staff levels are then confronted with the need to (a) maximize value-added steps and (b) eliminate rework, operational delays and the need for service recovery actions.

At this point it is necessary to turn to an issue briefly alluded to earlier, that of exchanging management's traditional supervisory role for one of facilitation and empowerment of employee decision-making. The next section will outline several indispensable skills managers must gain in order to be effective facilitators of the service diagnostics training system.

Managers are involved in a formal development session where they are encouraged to learn methods of facilitation to complement later employee training in team-based service diagnostics Since business cultures are not guided by any universal value system with respect to employee participation in work, we review the four most common organizational philosophies that frame the concept of empowerment:

1. *Productivity and efficiency*: employees must be involved in strategies to improve company productivity and quality.
2. *Democratic*: employees have a basic right to be involved in decisions and to receive information.
3. *Socialistic*: employees should increase their control of processes and share in the consequences.
4. *Human growth and development*: employees are given greater influence, autonomy and responsibility in order to fulfill their needs for success and well-being.

The values expressed by these four philosophies range from stressing efficiency to emphasizing human growth and development. These may have varied appeal to managers in a hospitality operation, but the bottom line is that empowerment is yet another campaign for participative decision-making at all levels of the organization. The central objective of training managers as facilitators is not to change their value

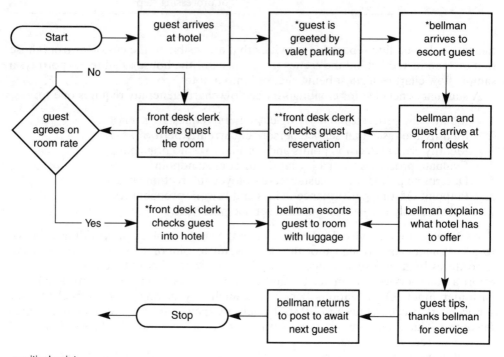

• critical point

•• high failure

Figure 8.4   *Flow chart of guest seeking a hotel room*

system, but to apprise managers of the benefits to their operations of working with employees in team-based collaboration to improve their own service processes.

The training program to develop managers as facilitators must focus on three key topics: (1) individual managers' needs for and use of power and status and how their needs might interfere with their desire to empower employees; (2) managers' styles of communicating, delegating and coaching employees on the job; and (3) managers' abilities to identify and handle self-esteem and motivation problems exhibited by employees who are faced with increased responsibility for decision-making.

One simple technique that works is to provide managers with a facilitator's vocabulary that they may use when coaching and leading employees in quality-based activities. The following list contrasts the traditional manager-speak with terms that support managers' new facilitative roles:

1. From *manager* to *facilitator*.
2. From *employee* to *associate*.
3. From *units* or *departments* to *teams*.
4. From *supervision* to *self-management*.
5. From *it's my . . . . on the line* to *it's up to us*.
6. From *it's your problem* to *we can solve it!*

Teaching managers to stay out of a project they have delegated to employee teams is a must in the quality-focused organization. Managers can still assist employee teams to think through the scope of a service analysis assignment or project at the outset by asking teams such questions as: 'How much of a priority is this problem overall? What results could we get from this project? How much background do we really need? What special skills or tools do we need? What should the feasible time frame be?'

Managers also need to isolate their own preferred styles of information handling, decision-making and control over projects and compare their styles with those styles preferred by their associates. There exists a plethora of communication and human relations training programs in the marketplace based on categorizations of personalities, e.g., Myers–Briggs workshops (McClure, 1993) or relationship awareness theory Porter (1993). These training workshops can be used effectively to impart to managers the many varied approaches that people take in solving problems and handling stress and conflict. Grasping this notion is critical for managers in the quality enterprise, who are essentially asked to work in teams with people they formerly supervised.

In simple terms, managers need to be reminded that even when employees come to them for help, they must resist the temptation to say 'I was afraid of this' or to 'pick up the pieces', and instead should respond with coaching questions, e.g. 'What do you think we should do about it? Do you need any resources to do it that way? Have you thought of this? Have you talked to so and so? What did we learn from this problem?'

Having considered the role of managers in the service diagnostics training system, we now turn to another key player in determining what service quality really is – the customer. The fourth step in Phase 1 calls for the development of customer feedback systems and service performance logs.

All customer feedback sources are reviewed by department managers and personnel, and a service log system is implemented in each department   Focus on customer satisfaction is most basic to the assessment of service quality, although historically it has been recognized that services are difficult for customers to evaluate. A major breakthrough was the identification by Parasuraman *et al.* (1988, 1991) of five service attributes that have shown to be meaningful to a cross-section of service customers: *reliability, responsiveness, tangibles, assurance* and *empathy*. Hence, in Phase 1 of the service diagnostics training system, customer feedback and service performance assessment systems are set up to evaluate customer responses about a hotel's performance on, at a minimum, these five service attributes.

Traditional marketing techniques are used to rate customer satisfaction with service operations; the principal techniques comprise communications (solicited and unsolicited calls and letters), surveys, focus groups and in-house service logs. Figure 8.5 portrays one style of service log that was developed for an independent West Coast hotel property.

A further comment is in order concerning the fact that customers generally do not take the time to give feedback on a regular basis. Several reasons have been given for why customers prefer not to complain out loud at all, including: (1) they do not believe that the benefits of complaining are worth the time or effort involved; (2) they do not want to aggrieve the service employees; (3) they withdraw from rudeness or aggressive behavior from employees, especially in a public place; and (4) they are ignorant of the proper procedures to follow. We believe that it falls upon service providers to actively encourage customers to give them feedback about how well the service delivery met the customers' expectations. We recommend a six-item 'toolkit' for proactively managing customer feedback that follows the acronym 'CATERS', as in catering to the customer:

C   for communications, e.g. '800' telephone members, in-house communiqués;
A   for advertising, e.g. service guarantees, 'we listen to you';
T   for trial programs, e.g. try out new services free of charge;
E   for evaluation systems, e.g. attribute rating devices;
R   for rewards, e.g. incentives for customers to give feedback;
S   for storage, e.g. client data storage systems for trend analysis.

The toolkit is devised along the principles of relationship marketing, which focuses on maintaining and enhancing the relationships an organization has with its customers. Benefits of increasing the bonds between customers and service organizations are

---

Department:

Date:

Time of day:

When did the incident occur?

What specific circumstances led up to this situation?

Who were the customers involved?

Exactly what did our representative say or do?

What resulted that made you feel the interaction was satisfying (dissatisfying) for the customer?

How often have you noted this type of interaction with customers in our operation?

Figure 8.5 *Service log for critical incident collection*

increased customer loyalty, word of mouth advertising, increased customer tolerance for price increases, customer-driven service design, and a clearer sense of how well service quality goals have been achieved.

The last task in Phase 1 of the service diagnostics training system is that of aligning reward and performance appraisal systems with the goals of service quality and satisfaction. We explore this further in the next section.

Managers and human resource personnel revise current compensation and incentive programs to establish linkages between reward practices and measures of employee performance in the delivery of quality service to the customer   News reports on the failure of quality management programs in the USA generally isolate people issues, e.g. team work, initiative, commitment, and existence of recognition and rewards for employee performance, as some of the more powerful determinants of the successful implementation of quality management programs and ultimately service quality. Unfortunately, many service firms have neglected to design and communicate appraisal systems that link employee service performance to organizational rewards and recognition.

In terms of performance appraisal, we are confident that human resources managers can engineer relevant appraisal systems as long as they remember to align formal appraisal goals with the goals of service quality, i.e. continuous service process improvement and meeting customer expectations. The majority of performance appraisal techniques, such as graphic scales, behavioral scales and open comments, are still appropriate, but the appraisal must increase its emphasis on employee activities related to service performance and quality. We do feel strongly, however, that the ranking technique (listing employees from most capable to least capable on specific traits or behaviors) is an undesirable appraisal format in a quality environment. Ranking employees degrades and demotivates them, labels them as average or below average, and confirms their belief that the system is set up to make at least 50 per cent of them (the bottom half) feel like losers.

And since most quality management training programs focus on increasing the frequency of use of quality problem-solving teams, measuring team performance as well as individual employee results becomes paramount as an appraisal strategy. Due to the realities of organizational power and influence, such mandated alterations (formation of quality teams) in organizational structures often carry implicit threats for incumbent managers and employees. When personnel are informed that a company requires organizational restructuring to a team-based configuration, existing power holders frequently fear losing their power and customary perquisites because they have not been informed clearly how the new quality-based organization will reward them. Both managers and employees may resort to the underlying informal political system to maintain their control over resources and rewards, creating resistance to quality practices. Hence, workers trained in quality management do not, as a result, adapt their behavior as readily as they should to achieve effective quality team structures or to implement team problem-solving practices. To avoid this outcome, organizations must design satisfactory team appraisal and reward systems to put employees in a receptive mood for team training.

A team-based organization necessitates an appraisal system that recognizes team work, as well as independent employee performance. We recommend two team appraisal strategies: (1) develop aggregate measures for team successes and performance; and (2) develop a peer and self appraisal system for individual team member contributions. The former aggregate measures look at organizationally relevant indicators such as increased reports of customer satisfaction and productivity improvements; the latter isolates specific member behaviors that advance the work of quality teams, e.g. participation in team meetings, timeliness of task fulfillment. Employees and managers can share in the appraisal process by looking at team accomplishments using the following questions: 'Do our teams clarify their goals? Listen and share information? Use problem-solving? Prioritize and allocate resources and tools? Encourage innovative ideas? Use meetings to achieve goals? Support and praise team members?' Managers should be evaluated by employees with respect to their efforts in promoting a supportive environment where team work can flourish. Specific assessment issues include: 'Do managers communicate a vision? Use empowering language? Seek solutions to service problems? Delegate and facilitate? Encourage creativity? Provide access to resources? Hold organized meetings? Give timely feedback, recognition and meaningful rewards?'

Performance appraisal and reward systems are a vital part of the service diagnostics training system because they relate to the needs of the service employees who form the backbone of service quality. In a nutshell, employees need a job (possibly a career), job security and the opportunity to make more than a passable living through incentives, pay raises and bonuses. Therefore, the service diagnostics training system incorporates a specific goal of communicating to employees the understanding that as their service skills and performance increase, so does their value to the organization, which means that they will see tangible results in their own access to recognition and rewards. Companies must search their own resources and compensation structures to find ways to tangibilize returns to their employees for superior service performance. Table 8.2 offers an aggregate overview of reward strategies offered by more than 150 US companies in a recent study undertaken by Farber and Park (1994).

Table 8.2 *Benefits, incentives and rewards associated with quality*

Benefits	Incentives	Rewards
Community relations	Career development	Cash bonuses
Decreased accidents	Discounted event tickets	Gainsharing
Decreased turnover	Equitable evaluations	Health benefits
Empowerment	Flexible scheduling	Pay tied to new skills
Improved morale	Free travel and dinners	Retirement plans
Job enrichment	Improved lounge/amenities	Salary increases
Job security	Promotions	
Reduced supervision	Quarterly award program	
Self-development	Training	

As we have indicated repeatedly throughout the section on Phase 1, an organization should attempt to enter Phase 2 of the service diagnostics training system only when all the components of Phase 1 are in place. The next section will provide detailed information about Phase 2 activities.

Phase 2 procedures

Phase 2 of the service diagnostics training system requires employees to collect service performance data from their service operation and then to identify any customer grievances, rework or needed service recovery steps in order to isolate critical incidents for analysis and training purposes. We wish to reiterate that Phase 2 provides initial employee training in the procedures outlined in the service diagnostics training program format presented earlier in this chapter. Training is critical since it is here that employee teams define for themselves real work goals or products that will be substantially different from previous job responsibilities. The work goals are quality research and evaluation ones; the work products will be specific reports to management that will be described in the next several sections. Participating in decision-making teams is likened to the challenges faced by first-time managers – employees need time to breathe in the air of empowerment and increased responsibility. Employees may also need to adjust to the visible presence of co-workers from other departments if the teams are cross-functional. We strongly recommend identifying this training period as the famous 'honeymoon' period where newly formed teams can do no wrong. Once employee teams are formed and trained, they are empowered to continually implement the service diagnostic techniques as normal operating procedures for the organization thereafter.

Employees are invited to participate in service teams by department managers and are prepared as team members and facilitators   The service diagnostics training system, founded on the principles of quality management, is team-based; employees and managers jointly work towards the solution of prioritized service problems. Teams are formed based on the insights of managers into the standing organizational culture and productive relationships already established in the workplace. Ideally, all employees would be involved in teams and teams would cut across departments to be essentially cross-functional in make-up. We are hesitant to mandate this, due to the same issues of power and organizational change that were discussed earlier in this chapter, and recommend instead that volunteer teams be formed that set the stage for positive interactions and movement towards quality. We do insist that team-building and training activities for all employees be the first step in Phase 2, since all employees will be invited in subsequent steps to perform data collection, service diagnostics and training tasks as members of service teams.

If team-building and team performance training is already a part of the hotel's basic training program and familiar to the employees, we recommend it be continued with additional insertions of specific material related to continuous quality improvement and customer satisfaction goals. As so many resources exist for the design of team-building programs, we prefer not to replicate in this chapter the bulk of information already available. However, we can direct readers to several recent authors in the arena of quality and team performance who have contributed greatly to this competency area: Aubrey and Felkins (1988); Douglass and Douglass (1992); Katzenbach and Smith (1993); Lundy (1992); and Shonk (1992).

Having confirmed the need to use teams in our service diagnostics system, we now clarify which type of teams are most useful. Katzenbach and Smith (1993, pp. 84–92) allude to a 'team-performance curve' that marks the difference between five types of teams appearing in business organizations: (1) working group; (2) pseudo-team; (3) potential team; (4) real team; and (5) high-performance team. The first two are considered the less effective of the five team types: the former lacks a common purpose while the latter lacks motivated members. The potential team is a budding team that is trying to improve its performance, and the last two types serve as models of functionally productive teams. Understandably, organizations have to build team performance up over time and should concentrate initially on creating and developing their 'potential teams' through training and by creating shared visions of service quality amongst team members; managers must also support this initial team training with time and resources. After the employees have been provided with preliminary team-building, they can be trained in the use of the service log and development of critical incidents from customer feedback data.

Employees are introduced to the service log and trained to monitor data from all customer feedback sources Employees are familiarized with the different sources of customer feedback listed in our discussion of Phase 1. Designated employee teams receive regular reports and all unsolicited and solicited customer data that relate to their functional areas of responsibility. Based on their perusal of the customer feedback data, they identify critical service incidents that become the input for future diagnostic activities; any incident which has resulted in negative customer feedback or recorded customer dissatisfaction is labelled a *critical incident*. The basic premise as per Bitner *et al.* (1990) is that the critical incident technique can be used to report actual service encounters in enough detail to understand why the customer (or employee) considered the incident significant. Our employee training system utilizes practice sessions in which employees are taught to use service logs (see Figure 8.4) in their operations to record information about service encounters. Employees are urged to be detailed while recording critical incident information in the service log, by:

1.   Making critical incident reports as detailed and accurate as possible by recording pertinent background information, e.g. time of day, day of week, weather, sale or cut-rate days, short staff, equipment problems.
2.   Reporting observed behavior factually and objectively without theorizing, explaining or judging, i.e. avoiding the use of adjectives or attributions such as 'clumsy', 'slow', 'unfriendly' or 'rotten attitude'.
3.   Comparing notes with other employee observers to reach a consensus about the reliability of the critical incident data.
4.   Noting repetitions of incidents over time or among many customers.

The service logs are then combined with other available data from alternative customer feedback sources, e.g. customer surveys, telephone interviews, complaint letters and focus groups, to be used as content material for the next step: *service process analysis*.

Employees are trained to continually analyze service processes Employees are trained to assess the critical incident data from a variety of perspectives to determine the root causes of any negative deviation in actual service from desired service benchmarks. The use of this method of service process analysis presumes: (1) that the service standards are realistic and achievable; and (2) that the employees have been informed of the company's expectations for their service performance levels during Phase 1.

The procedure known as service process analysis merges Mager and Pipe's (1970) work in goal and performance analysis with the process analysis tools offered by the quality champions. Mager and Pipe (1970) offered a basic performance diagnostic flow chart to help categorize performance problems into (1) training-solvable problems and (2) problems that require other operational interventions, e.g. redesign of facilities layout, equipment maintenance, or changes in the performance reward system. Quality management authors have provided an analysis system where organizational teams identify service problems from the customer perspective, identify work process failure points and brainstorm operational strategies that will improve these work processes.

The use of service process analysis in the hotel setting requires team meetings, i.e. specific service team problem-solving sessions. Secondly, team members need to have a recent critical incident report. Other types of performance data, including outside operational audits or budget reports, can also be provided to employees. All performance data must be reviewed from a trend analysis perspective – repeated performance discrepancies over time and among multiple customers are more reliable indicators of the need to intervene with training or operational corrections than is a one-time observation of one employee's suboptimal service encounter. Service problem priorities are set by the service employee team after considering factors such as: (1) the effect of failure to meet the customer's need; (2) the scope and location of the problem organization-wide; (3) top management's priorities; (4) the immediate need to find a solution; and (5) cost–benefit analysis (*hard costs* are money that must be spent at the time the error occurs, e.g. amenities, rebates, transportation, letters, phone charges and replacement costs; *soft costs* are costs related to events occurring as a result of an error, e.g. productivity is decreased by 15 per cent; *opportunity costs* are future sales that are lost as a direct result of the error). All identified problems with prioritization ratings clearly marked are placed on a *master organizational problem sheet* held by a service diagnostics coordinator. This list is comprehensive and also indicates when problems have been assigned to a service process analysis team. Keeping track of team projects is a necessary control issue, as the organization will want to avoid redundancy in problem-solving efforts; it also encourages teams whose projects overlap to communicate with each other.

Management facilitates the assignment of a prioritized problem to an interested employee team that then brainstorms about the problem and prepares a cause and effect diagram that organizes likely root causes of the problem into four categories: people, machines, materials, and method type. This diagram approximates the shape of a fish-bone, as depicted in Figure 8.6, which presents root causes associated with a deficient hotel telephone service. The root cause analysis aids in the identification of both training and non-training solutions to customer service problems.

When the solutions to the service problem are judged to be non-training solutions, actions are identified which may be taken to correct the identified operational flaws, e.g. replace faulty equipment, provide incentives to motivate quality employee performance. Teams then file a one-page *service problem analysis form* which recommends operational improvements to upper management. Obviously, employees who are expected to function as service diagnosticians must be empowered with delegated authority and resources to recommend (and implement) desired solutions.

When a service problem is diagnosed as training-solvable, the next step is to decide whether the solution will take the form of physical-task procedural training, training in the psychosocial aspects of service performance, or both. The diagnostic team must follow up with suggested training action steps to improve the service problem.

Employees are taught to develop training demonstrations and role-plays based on train-the-trainer principles   Service teams that have pointed to training as a solution then follow up with a *training mini action plan* (T-MAP) for training for their service unit. The T-MAP may involve any mix of physical or psychosocial skills training objectives, e.g. counting cash in a secure yet rapid manner, providing information to the customer in a friendly, efficient way, communicating a willingness to go beyond the call of duty during the encounter. Short training demonstrations or service encounter debriefings using role-plays are then carried out by designated volunteer employee trainers. The success of the latter, service encounter debriefings, usually depends on

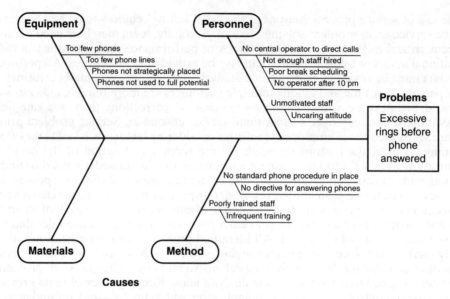

Figure 8.6   *Cause–effect diagram of slow telephone service*

how well the trainer discusses role-play scenarios in the context of social interaction
and human relations theories. Issues can range from avoiding stereotyping or ranking
customers to dealing with negative language and non-verbal behaviours.

Berger and Farber (1992) discuss important train-the-trainer concepts that employees should comprehend prior to developing the T-MAPs and training materials.
Generally, the mini-training can take place on a regular basis during general departmental meetings to continuously reinforce the organization's commitment to training
for quality customer service. At this point we move to the final step: evaluation of
service performance.

*Employees learn to measure service team performance and provide team-level feedback
to managers regarding accomplishments*   Employees are provided with regular opportunities to review their team and individual performance using assessment techniques
devised in Phase 1. Control charts and trend analysis may be performed at periodic
intervals, i.e. monthly, 3–6–9–12-month intervals, for quality and productivity measures, e.g. reduced errors, defects or complaints, reduced waste, resource usages or costs.
Employees and managers analyze these jointly to determine the effectiveness of team
solutions to service problems; records are kept about team contributions in order to
track team progress over time, noting member changes for more in-depth analysis
about team structure.

A latent variable of interest is the work environment which reportedly improves with
the implementation of quality management systems. Tangible measures of work
environment include safety, absenteeism, grievances and turnover. Organizations
should also try to capture individual measures such as employee self-efficacy, locus of
control, perceived recognition and rewards, and reduced conflict between employees
and managers. Employee surveys have been designed and validated for many of these
worklife issues and can be easily adapted to this purpose.

Several hotels we have dealt with provide opportunities for employees to nominate each other for specific service awards provided by the hotel organizations. Another hotel encourages employees to contribute their ideas and successes to a newsletter that is issued quarterly for all employees. We now review the implications arising from an invited review of the service diagnostics training system by hotel managers and trainers. At this time we are planning the first full implementation of the system with a participating hotel, but have used various portions of the system in different hotel training projects. Feedback from these projects is documented in the final part of this chapter.

IMPLICATIONS AND RECOMMENDATIONS FOR FUTURE IMPLEMENTATIONS

Highlights of manager and trainer review comments

Managers who reviewed the system felt that employees increasingly would be able to discuss service incidents from an analytical perspective, i.e. service process analysis, replacing superficial and/or emotional explanations. Both managers and trainers were impressed with the integrated problem-solving focus of the service diagnostics training system. Managers commented that they and employee teams could use the service process analysis to solve more problems early enough so that the majority of customers would not be obliged to experience a poor service incident.

However, difficulties arose in several managers' perception of the service log, due to their aim to use logs to check up on individual employees rather than for the creation of critical incidents. It became apparent that groups of managers and employees must be brought together to design the service log jointly; employees must be advised that they would not be asked to report on deficiencies of other co-workers, but rather on problems and service system bottlenecks experienced by customers during the course of a service encounter. Employees must be convinced that the log could not be used to pin blame on them and cause problems for them with their managers. In addition, the service log was extended to the purpose of collecting positive service successes as well as in order to balance the negative complaint image of the original design.

Another issue raised in the managerial reviews was that managers wanted to ensure that substantial cross-training was an outcome of this system. They thought it would be a good opportunity for employees to work on problems in other departments that linked to their own. They did, however, question the degree to which all employees could be used on teams; for example, there was some bias against involving kitchen and housekeeping staff due to perceived language difficulties. Some managers thought that only employees who had direct and usual customer contact should be involved in problem-solving.

Several trainers noted that the idea of developing training materials from the employee perspective was relatively novel and would enhance their own training design efforts. They did think that some trainers might feel territorial about having employees take on any part of the customer service training function and suggested that human resources staff or training staff be involved from the start in any decision to use the system. They were especially concerned that they be involved in both selecting designated employee trainers, and developing train-the-trainer sessions for those designated employees who would be responsible for mini-training activities. The trainers were also interested in how other training plans, e.g. accident prevention, regular skills courses, orientations and so forth, would be affected in terms of time, scheduling and resources. Lastly, the trainers who reviewed the system wanted specific information on the supposed lines of authority for service quality coordinators who would be overseeing Phase 1 and 2 activities, particularly with respect to Phase 2 training.

Results of partial implementation of the system during hotel training

In one training project that involved front desk personnel of a downtown conference hotel, the feedback was positive in terms of using the service log and learning the service process analysis. However, employees felt that not too much was going to change due to the perceived lack of resources the department had from the general manager to really change any systems. Also, they felt they were the victims of other departments who did not have any quality perspective, e.g. housekeeping, and they could not really make headway as the only department in an organization to take on the quality challenge. The same group of employees had difficulty in the initial tries at designing training solutions because senior employees who had always done the training assumed that they would be called upon to do the mini-training sessions. One last issue was the changeover in the general management position, which undoubtedly held back the progress of the system into other hotel departments. The lesson overall from this experience is that the role of top management in supporting quality strategies is crucial.

Another training program involved the training of designated team leaders from various departments of a hotel in the basic service log process analysis training method. These individuals came from four departments – restaurants, front office, house-keeping and room service – and were supervisory or senior-level hourly staff. They were to become the first cross-function team and also were to lead selected employees in their departments in team-based service analysis. The initial training was done over a three-day intensive period; feedback was gathered at a later date on how successful the trainees were in carrying the service analysis system back to their departments. A major issue that was brought up in the feedback reports was the lack of rewards for the original trained personnel. They did say that they were supported by their managers, who also had had a facilitators' training session, and that some of their ideas and mini-trainings had paid back in reduced service waiting time for customers (waiting times improved in the front office and room service areas). One department reported that its manager was very interested in the team activities, but tended to give additional assignments to the department that were not really related to the goals of service analysis. Managers in most departments preferred that the mini-training be done on a monthly basis to replace a regular departmental meeting, because it was difficult to budget for the necessary staff member training and labor costs on a more frequent basis. These managers did imply, however, that they were willing to devote more budget funds to the process as soon as they had evidence (for their general manager) of any clear money paybacks from reduced costs or improved productivity from initial employee efforts.

Another obvious issue that arose rather quickly as the original trainees returned to their departments was the need for managers to meet with these departments to formally delegate authority to team leaders; some departmental employees questioned who was going to handle any major problems they might have at work and needed to be reassured that they could still talk to the manager without having to go through the team leader. The room service and housekeeping supervisors had the most difficulty with carrying out the team sessions, since the former was short of staff and the latter had some literacy issues that had to be dealt with in terms of translating both the service log and other materials into several languages. Once this was accomplished, volunteers were asked to form two teams of six people each that represented housekeeping staff from guest rooms and public areas. The decision was made early to use a minor representation of the housekeeping staff due to managerial issues with labor and scheduling. Mini-training would be rotated amongst all employees over a period of several months.

CONCLUSION

Overall, the initial forays into applying the service diagnostics training system in hotel settings were limited in scope but served as pilot tests to check for obvious wrinkles in the assumptions upon which the system is founded. We feel that the problems and issues raised in the previous section are common with the implementation of quality management strategies and programs, and we feel positive that the benefits of the system far outweigh the initial start-up training costs and need for troubleshooting. Several recommendations can be made for the future implementation of the service diagnostics training system:

1. Service logs should involve both service problems and positive instances of employee methods in solving a service delivery problem or customer complaint.
2. Service logs should be the property of employees and not managers in order that they feel protected against reprisals based on service log information.
3. The organization's goals for cross-training employees should be assessed before implementing the service training system in order to build this into team structures.
4. Existing formal and informal lines of authority for training and customer service functions (and associated personnel) must be identified and integrated into the assignment of responsibilities for coordinating and implementing system Phases 1 and 2, in order to control political repercussions.
5. Persons with newly assigned responsibilities should be supported and visibly rewarded for their involvement.
6. Phase 1 and 2 activities must be differentiated from as well as coordinated with all other training or interventions undertaken by the organization.
7. Any major structural issues such as short staffing and impending managerial (or ownership) turnover should be identified before implementation begins.

The final conclusion is that the primordial soup into which a hotel adds substantial quantities of quality training and resources must be a nurturing, empowering, facilitative organizational culture. If top management does not devote time and resources to championing a quality-driven work culture, then their quality training or service improvement programs will turn eventually into dinosaurs and become extinct – to be ogled and remembered by hotel employees as one more managerial 'Big One' that did not make it.

In summary, we have reviewed the fundamental principles of quality management and have evaluated two traditional methods of improving customer service in hospitality companies: personnel selection systems and script-based training programs. We have introduced a bi-phasal service diagnostics training system to prepare customer service employees as diagnosticians and problem solvers. Phase 1 of this system calls for a five-step top-management-championed organizational change program to create a service quality infrastructure upon which a process of continuous service diagnostics (Phase 2) can be conducted. Finally, we have presented the results of testing assumptions and components of the service training system in hotel settings; this highlights hot spots to provide readers with additional insight into the impact that the service diagnostics training system would probably have on their organizations.

REFERENCES

Aubrey, II, C. A., and Felkins, P. K. (1988) *Teamwork: Involving People in Quality and Productivity Improvement*. American Society for Quality Control, White Plains, NY.

Berger, F., and Farber, B. (1992) *The On-Track Trainer: A Training Handbook for Hotel & Restaurant Managers*. Cornell Hotel & Restaurant Administration Quarterly, Ithaca, NY.

Bitner, M. J., Booms, B., and Tetreault, M. (1990) 'The service encounter: diagnosing favorable and unfavorable incidents', *Journal of Marketing*, vol. **54**, no. 1, pp. 71–84.

Carlzon, J. (1987) *Moments of Truth*, Ballinger, Cambridge, MA.

Crosby, P. B. (1979) *Quality is Free: The Art of Making Quality Certain*, Mentor Books, New American Library, New York, NY.

Deming, W. E. (1986) *Out of the Crisis*. MIT CAES, Cambridge, MA.

Douglass, M. E., and Douglass, D. N. (1992) *Time Management for Teams*, American Management Association, New York, NY.

Farber, B. M., and Fox, K. (1992) 'Training service employees to be service problem solvers', presented at the 2nd International Conference of Services Marketing and Management, Lelonde, France, June.

Farber, B. M., and Park, T. (1994) 'Quality and reward practices in U.S. businesses', Working Paper, San José State University, College of Business.

Hill, C. J., Garner, S. J., and Hanna, M. E. (1989) 'Selection criteria for professional service providers', *Journal of Services Marketing*, vol. 3, no. 4, pp. 61–9.

Juran, J. M. (1989) *Juran on Leadership for Quality: An Executive Handbook*, Free Press, New York, NY.

Katzenbach, J. R., and Smith, D. K. (1993) *The Wisdom of Teams: Creating the High-Performance Organization*, McKinsey & Company, Inc. (Harvard Business School Press), Boston, MA.

Levitt, T. (1976) 'The industrialization of service', *Harvard Business Review*, September–October, pp. 63–74.

Lovelock, C. (1992) 'A basic toolkit for service managers', in Lovelock, C. (ed.), *Managing Services: Marketing, Operations, and Human Resources*, Prentice Hall, Englewood Cliffs, NJ, pp. 17–30.

Lundy, J. L. (1992) *Teams: How to Develop Peak Performance for World Class Results*, The Dartnell Corp., Chicago, IL.

McClure, L. (1993) 'Personality variables in management development interventions', *Journal of Management Development*, vol. **12**, no. 3, pp. 39–47.

Mager, R. F., and Pipe, P. (1970) *Analyzing Performance Problems*, Fearon Pitman, Belmont, CA.

Maier, N. R. F., Solem, A. R., and Maier, A. A. (1975) *The Role-play Technique*, University Associates, La Jolla, CA.

Parasuraman, A., Berry, L. L., and Zeithaml, V. A. (1991) 'Refinement and reassessment of the SERVQUAL scale', *Journal of Retailing*, vol. **67**, no. 4, pp. 420–50.

Parasuraman, A., Zeithaml, V. A., and Berry, L. L. (1988) 'SERVQUAL: a multiple-item scale for measuring consumer perceptions of service quality', *Journal of Retailing*, vol. **64**, no. 1, pp. 12–40.

Porter, E. (1993) *Relationship Awareness Training Workshop*, Personal Strengths Publishing, Inc., Pacific Palisades, CA.

Schneider, B., and Schechter, D. (1991) 'Development of a personnel selection system for service jobs', in Lovelock, C. H. (ed.), *Managing Services: Marketing, Operations, and Human Resources*, Prentice Hall, Englewood Cliffs, NJ, pp. 342–54.

Shonk, J. (1992) *Team-based Organizations: Designing a Successful Team Environment*, Business One Irwin, Homewood, IL.

Shostack, G. L. (1987) 'Designing services that deliver', *Harvard Business Review*, vol. **62**, January–February, 133–9.

Solomon, M. R., Surprenant, C., Czepiel, J. A., and Gutman, E. G. (1985) 'A role theory perspective on dyadic interactions: the service encounter', *Journal of Marketing*, vol. **49**, pp. 99–111.

Thompson, A. (1989) 'Customer contact personnel: using interviewing techniques to select for adaptability in service employees', *Journal of Services Marketing*, vol. **3**, no. 1, pp. 57–65.

Wilson-Pessano, S. R. (1988) 'Defining professional competence: the critical incident technique 40 years later', Invited address, Annual Meeting of the American Educational Research Association, Division I, April 1988.

Zemke, R. (1979) 'Still trying to figure things out? Try using the critical incident method', *Training/HRD*, April, pp. 69–70, 73.

9

Training for service quality in the hospitality industry

Lyn Randall and Martin Senior

INTRODUCTION

The changes taking place in the field of vocational education and training in the UK could have significant implication for the hospitality industry in its quest for quality. There is a move towards work-based learning and assessment which opens up access for all employees to obtain a national vocational qualification for the job they do. These qualifications are expressed as national standards and they can be used by employers as operational measures in their organizations. However, it has not been sufficiently proved that they can actually help with providing a better quality of service to the customer.

This chapter considers the key findings from the literature on how service quality can be effectively delivered, why it is necessary to bother with service quality and whether current and emerging methods of staff training can contribute.

WHAT IS SERVICE QUALITY?

Quality from a marketing perspective

There are many definitions of quality but all agree that to deliver quality is to deliver what the customer requires, or believes he/she requires. This constitutes an approach to doing business that equates with the marketing concept of identifying and meeting customer requirements at a profit. The ideas being developed in services marketing see quality from a customer perspective and recognize that the only arbiter of quality is the customer.

In order to determine the importance of service quality it is perhaps necessary to define quality from a marketing perspective. Customers buy benefits, not products.

Quality is concerned with supplying superior benefits based on the opinion of the customer. The pursuit of quality is the pursuit of greater customer benefit.

However, there are a number of implications to consider:

- What constitutes a quality offering depends on the customer; in other words, what they expect, want and/or need, and what the competition can offer, affects their view of quality.
- Different customers will expect, want and/or need different things from essentially similar offerings. Where markets are segmented, different views of quality will prevail. There can be no universal standards. Products that meet customer requirements will be considered 'good' quality, those that don't 'bad'. A travel lodge, charging £32 per night for a room for up to four people, is not lower-quality than a country house hotel, charging £156 per night per person. It merely caters for the requirements of a different market segment. What will dictate whether it is of 'good' quality or not will be how well it caters for the requirements of its chosen market.
- Over time, through experience and exposure to alternatives, customer expectations will change (usually they will increase). Thus the relative benefits perceived to derive from an offer may reduce over time as competing suppliers improve their benefit offering. Quality is, therefore, a dynamic concept. While intrinsic quality may remain stable or even improve, customer perceptions of quality may very well erode.

Life would be easier if customer expectations remained static; unfortunately they do not. Rising consumer expectations constitute an economic and social phenomenon where consumers are more demanding because they are constantly being educated to be more sophisticated, and thus are able to make better judgements.

The essence of services marketing is *service*. The marketing textbooks stress the four Ps of marketing: product, place, promotion and price. In a service business the most important competitive weapon is the fifth P – *performance*. It is the performance of the service which separates one service from others; it is the performance of the service which creates true customers who buy more, are more loyal and who spread a favourable impression by word of mouth.

Competing service firms often provide similar facilities, equipment and services, but the way in which the service firm provides the service to its customers can make one firm seem very different from its competitors.

In a survey of 100 businesses, carried out in 1990, one of the most important issues was 'to create a more customer centred culture' (Coulson-Thomas, 1991). The report noted the need to go beyond traditional approaches to quality and to adopt a 'marketing-led approach'. Research in service industries has clearly identified that the only criteria to count in evaluating service quality are defined by customers. Customers judge quality and it is often the front-line staff who need to recognize what quality is in the customers' eyes so that they can deliver it effectively (Brown and Swartz, 1989; Bitner, 1990; Senior, 1992). The literature indicates that in order for firms to be successful in an increasingly competitive arena they must provide services that are of sufficient quality to meet customer requirements (Mastenbroek, 1991).

According to Grönroos (1990b), 'the perceived service quality approach still seems to form the foundation of most of the ongoing research and theory development in services marketing'. Service quality is seen as the result of comparing a customer's expectations prior to receiving the service with the customer's experiences with the service. If expectations are met or exceeded, service quality is perceived to be satisfactory. This approach can be traced back to Grönroos (1982).

Service quality is almost always defined today in terms of customer perceived quality, which in itself is a function of expected and experienced quality (Brown *et al.*, 1991; Grönroos, 1990a; Zeithaml *et al.*, 1990, 1991). Thus a service of the right quality should be adapted to the customer's needs and thereby satisfy his or her wishes/requirements. However, it must be pointed out that if customer expectations constitute what customers believe should be delivered, it would be absurd to say that if customers expected lousy service and received it they would be satisfied.

Characteristics of services

Quality has become the key to gaining the competitive advantage for firms. This emphasis on quality has made the consumers more sophisticated and demanding, and, unlike in manufacturing, the production process in most services is quite visible to the consumer, since he or she is often involved in the process.

Application of quality in service industries has been prompted by recognition that, despite much common ground, services are different from physical products in a number of ways:

- Central to the difference is the role of the customer in the production of many services. Production and consumption take place simultaneously (they are *inseparable*) and hence controls after the event may be of little value. For example, a customer organizing a large company conference would not be pleased if the service at the chosen conference venue did not conform to promised requirements, even if compensation were offered.
- Services are largely intangible – they cannot be smelled, tasted or touched. Because of their *intangibility*, precise manufacturing specifications concerning uniform quality can rarely be set as for products.
- Services, especially those with a high labour content, are *heterogeneous*; their performance can vary from producer to producer, from customer to customer and from day to day. Thus uniform quality is difficult to ensure.

The difference between satisfaction and service quality

The main difference between satisfaction and perceived service quality is that the concept of satisfaction is connected with a specific transaction while service quality is considered to be the consumers' overall evaluation of the service and resembles the attitude concept (Bitner, 1990; Bolton and Drew, 1991a, b). It is therefore possible to perceive service quality as good even though one specific transaction may have been unsatisfactory. This difference is derived from Oliver's (1981) distinction between attitude and satisfaction. According to Swan (1983) there have been doubts about the discriminate validity between satisfaction and attitude, although he himself believes that they are conceptually different. He argues that satisfaction is linked to a specific transaction while a consumer can form an attitude towards a product which he/she has not purchased or consumed. Perceived service quality, however, is always measured on services that the consumer has actually consumed. To measure perceived service quality one has to assume that the consumer has used the service at least once before.

Other views on the relationship between service quality and satisfaction have been proposed. Kasper and Lemmink (1988) and Lewis and Klein (1987) argue that perceived service quality will affect consumer satisfaction. Cronin and Taylor (1992) reported a strong correlation between satisfaction and perceived service quality, and consequently drew the conclusion that the two concepts measure the same underlying construct. Bolton and Drew (1991a) also related satisfaction to service quality.

Expectations as a standard of comparison

Disconfirmation models are based on the belief that consumers form expectations of products (goods and services) prior to purchase. Consequently, satisfaction and perceived service quality are dependent on performance compared to prior expectations.

The disconfirmation paradigm states that the consumer will feel unsatisfied if performance is below expectations (negative disconfirmation), and satisfied when expectations are confirmed or exceeded (positive disconfirmation). Satisfaction is expected to increase as positive disconfirmation increases. There is widespread agreement amongst researchers that satisfaction is a reaction to a comparison between perceived product performance and some standard of comparison, but less agreement on which standard should be used (Woodruff *et al.*, 1991). A number of different operationalizations of expectations have been proposed. Miller (1977) first suggested that there might exist different types of expectations:

- ideal;
- predicted;
- deserved;
- minimum tolerable.

Miller stressed the importance of knowing against which type of expectations the consumer compares the performance of the product. Gilly *et al.* (1983) studied these concepts and found moderate support for them as independent constructs. Research has also shown that some standards of comparison are better than others at explaining satisfaction (Woodruff *et al.*, 1991; Cadotte *et al.*, 1983a), and that the relationships between disconfirmation, performance and satisfaction change depending on the standard used. The consumer may also use several standards simultaneously (Tse and Wilton, 1988).

Ideal service

The consumer may use an ideal product as a standard (Miller, 1977; Tse and Wilton, 1988; Woodruff *et al.*, 1991). Tse and Wilton (1988) found that ideal expectations only had an indirect negative effect through performance on satisfaction.

Predicted service

Most of the studies within the disconfirmation paradigm have defined expectations as a prediction of future product performance (Day, 1977; Oliver, 1980; Swan, 1988, 1992). Predictive expectations have been found to have a direct positive effect on satisfaction (Tse and Wilton, 1988). Significant effects of expectation on perceived performance have also been found in several experiments (Anderson, 1973; Oliver, 1977, 1980).

Anderson argued that high expectations coupled with cognitive dissonance and assimilation would dominate disconfirmation in explaining consumer satisfaction with a product.

Deserved service

The deserved level is a type of equity that involves an evaluation of the consumer's inputs and outputs without any other comparison. According to Miller (1977), the deserved level ' ... reflects what the individual, in the light of his "investments", feels performance "*ought* to be" or "*should* be" '. It may be the same as, or lower or higher than, predictive expectations. Fisk and Coney (1982) and Tse and Wilton (1988) did not find any relation between this standard and the dependent variables, and drew the conclusion that 'equity' is not a good operationalization of a comparison standard. Tse and Wilton (1988) correlated overall product level ratings and average attribute ratings for 'equity', predictive and ideal expectations, and found only a very small significant correlation (0.26) between the overall ideal rating and the average attribute 'equity' rating.

Minimum tolerable/adequate service

Miller (1977) argued that this is the least acceptable level: ' ... it is "better than nothing". This level reflects the minimum level the respondent feels performance "*must be*".' The consumer will not be satisfied just because the performance is above the minimum tolerable. If, for example, performance is above the minimum tolerable level but falls below the predicted level, the consumer will feel dissatisfied. Nightingale (1986) has also suggested that consumers can be expected to have minimum requirements for certain attributes, e.g. that there has to be a parking space by the restaurant.

It is unclear which type(s) of experience-based norm(s) the authors compare the adequate service level with. Miller's minimum tolerable level is not similar to any of the experience-based norms proposed by Cadotte *et al.* (1983a, b). The best brand norm is perhaps nearest to the desired level. Cadotte *et al.* (1983b) measured the three norms and brand expectations for three different types of restaurants. The best brand norm had consistently the highest mean rating and was significantly different from the other concepts. Brand expectations had consistently a higher mean than the product norm and brand norm, but only part of these differences were significant. The positions of the brand norm and product norm varied.

According to Miller (1977) the minimum tolerable should never exceed predictive expectations. This is logical as the consumer is not likely to choose a product that is under the minimum tolerable, unless there is no alternative, or some situational variables affect the choice. The minimum tolerable level does not even have to satisfy the consumer.

Zone of tolerance

A development in the service quality discussion is to consider expectations and evaluations as zones. Poiesz and Bloemer (1991) have suggested that expectations and evaluations should be expressed as zones and not as discrete points on a scale. They argue that customers might not be capable of giving point estimates. This idea is based on Miller (1977), and Cadotte *et al.* (1983a, b), where the concept of a distribution of outcomes is introduced. This zone of indifference or *latitude of acceptance* is applied to the outcome or satisfaction and not to each component in the comparison between expectations and performance. Poiesz and Bloemer (1991) argue that subjective expectations and evaluation zones should be measured on components instead of an overall measurement. They suggest measuring an expectation zone and an evaluation zone, leading to a consideration of the overlap of the two zones.

Zeithaml *et al.* (1991) have suggested the concept *zone of tolerance* to represent the difference between what they call the adequate level of service and desired level of service. Based on focus group interviews they assume that the adequate service level is more contextually dependent than the desired level, and that this accounts for differences in the zone of tolerance. They also conclude that the zone of tolerance varies for different service attributes. The measurement of the zone of tolerance could be operationalized as the difference between measures of desired and adequate service or as a directly specified range of expectations.

Gap analysis

A frequently used approach in service quality research is to use different gap models to measure quality (Senior and Randall, 1991; Senior, 1991; Grönroos, 1990a). Data collection techniques such as in-depth personal interviews (Silvestro *et al.*, 1990), critical incident techniques (Bitner *et al.*, 1990; Bitner, 1990; Edvardsson, 1988, 1991) and focus group interviews (Randall and Senior, 1992a; Randall, 1993; Farouk and Ryan, 1991) are all able to capture certain process variables.

An experience-based measure of service quality

Research shows that services are processes, often involving customers as co-producers (Sasser *et al.*, 1978; Edvardsson, 1988; Brown *et al.*, 1991; Grönroos, 1990a, b). Therefore, the customer is really part of the service production system. As the degree and style of the participation vary (Langeard *et al.*, 1981; Lehtinen and Lehtinen, 1991), the control of service quality is more difficult than that of the quality of goods. Techniques such as service blueprinting (Shostack, 1984, 1987; George and Gibson, 1991), service mapping (Kingman-Brundage, 1989) and perceptual blueprinting (Senior and Akehurst, 1990; Senior and Randall, 1991) portray service processes as flow charts.

Furthermore, services are often intangible (Lovelock, 1983, 1988; Shostack, 1984, 1987). It is therefore difficult for the service provider to explain the actual content of the service and manage the 'evidence'. These circumstances make it hard for consumers to evaluate services before purchasing them and, consequently, contextual cues, for example, the physical environment and the appearance of employees, have turned out to be important for customers when evaluating services (Booms and Bitner, 1982; Bitner, 1990; West and Huges, 1991). Unable to experience the service in advance, the customer is really being asked to buy promises of satisfaction (Levitt, 1981). These promises are dependent on the contact with individual services providers (Crane and Clarke, 1988). Thus, the essence of the customer's service experience is people in processes, which should be seen as an organized whole. Research has indicated the need for a holistic service quality approach (Gummesson, 1990).

Quality and human resources

Given the expansion of jobs in some service industries, such as the hospitality industry, and the much-forecasted skills shortage, the challenge facing hospitality organizations in their quest for quality is the recruitment, development and retention of its human resources (Hotel and Catering Training Board, 1988). The National Council for Vocational Qualifications (NCVQ) was established in July 1988 as a result of the Government White Paper (Department of Employment, Cmnd 9823). NCVQ had been created as a result of several official reports, one of which was a major investigation of vocational education and training in West Germany, the USA and Japan (Institute of Manpower Studies, 1984).

The policies developed by NCVQ have implications for all those employed in the hospitality industry. As the industry continues to expand and consumer expectations rise, it is vital that the industry addresses the issue of training and educating its human resources if it is to meet the quality standards that customers expect. Some industries, such as the NHS, recognized the need for training for service staff in hospitals if they were to improve the quality of the service to patients (Randall and Tofts, 1991) and they attempted to make this training competence-based. More recent research in the area of support services in hospitals has indicated, that when employees are involved in service quality analysis, control and improvement, they are more likely to be able to deliver a good service (Randall and Senior, 1992a; Randall, 1993). If employees understand their customers' expectations they are likely to attempt to meet these during service encounters.

WHY BOTHER WITH SERVICE QUALITY?

There has been considerable research into the concept of service quality, with many theories being espoused and concepts being developed, yet true success in delivering service quality on a consistent basis remains frustratingly elusive for many service providers. There are several reasons for this, ranging from the difficulty of translating theories and concepts into real practice, to researchers not truly appreciating the real difficulties experienced by service organizations. Organizations which do appear to provide high levels of service quality may not have ever used academic theories, but have used simple and obvious concepts which could quite easily be labelled as 'just plain common sense'. For example, the concepts 'quality', 'value for money', 'cleanliness' and 'service' are typically cited as the foundations of success of McDonald's restaurants.

Once understood, the reason for bothering with service quality is compelling. Providing good service quality to customers on a consistent basis means that customers will be continually satisfied, will want to return and use the service again and they will want to refer the service to those around them. By retaining existing customers and gaining new customers through positive word of mouth, a service provider's customer base will continually grow without the need for expensive and unpredictable advertising. A growing customer base in line with increased turnover enables an organization to become more efficient in its activities (since it is travelling quickly down the experience curve) and buy raw products cheaper (through bulk purchases). This in turn enables the

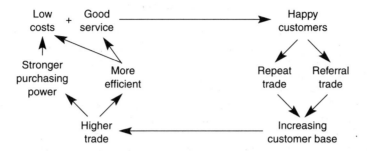

Figure 9.1   *Relationship between service quality and strong market position*

organization to increase its profits and offer the most attractive pricing structure to customers in the marketplace.

These relationships can be best illustrated in a diagram, such as the one in Figure 9.1.

The concern for service quality

Concern for quality is not new. In Britain and America it was the Second World War that gave the greatest stimulus to methods of quality control in the manufacturing industry. The need for military equipment and munitions to meet stringent standard requirements led to the further deployment of statistical quality control techniques.

During the evolution of thought and practice in service quality, the drive has come primarily from the manufacturing and operations functions. Perhaps as a consequence the drive has been largely systems- and process-based. British Standards Institute (BSI) 5750, for example, focuses on the systems and procedures in place to assure quality rather than the outcomes in terms of better products or greater customer satisfaction. However, an organization which has the BSI standard does present a certain guideline to people buying the services who may have difficulty in judging and comparing quality before purchase or use. It is often difficult to specify beforehand what one is looking for, and many services have professional aspects which it is difficult for the ordinary person (and other professionals) to assess.

Part of the difficulty faced by service firms is that the different definitions of service quality are maintained by different groups within an organization. In marketing, service quality means understanding the customers' needs and identifying ways to meet or exceed them. It is sometimes equated with customer satisfaction, or the degree to which customers' perceptions of the service meet or exceed their expectations of the service transaction. This type of service quality is evaluated using surveys, interviews and focus groups. In contrast, operations managers often view service quality as conformance to operating specifications. They use performance measures, such as waiting times, error rates in transactions, and processing times to determine whether the process is in or out of control. All too often, the two groups fail to coordinate or even communicate with each other.

The concept of value

Companies with strong service reputations are often able to charge more than their competitors because *value* is the customers' overall assessment of the experience they receive. For example, when a customer goes into a restaurant, they are buying the whole 'meal experience' not just the food. The meal experience includes the food, the decor, the location, the lighting, the noise level and the service.

The concept of value is important in that the customer has to expend more than money to use a service; he/she also bears non-monetary costs, for example, time and psychic cost. The customer may be quite willing to assume more monetary cost to reduce non-monetary cost and/or to obtain an otherwise stronger service. Service errors and complaints from customers add to the cost of the service delivery system.

In many service industries, such as the hotel industry, it is the guest experience which is sold. This is made up of the physical specification of the hotel plus service delivery. A simple technique for the guest experience could be:

$$\text{guest experience} = \text{physical specifications} + \text{service delivery}$$

It is the service which transforms the physical facility into an experience – one way or the other.

When the guest's experience of service falls short of his/her expectations, in whatever grade of hotel, it is likely that the guest is vulnerable and may be lost to a competitor. He believes that he has had a poor-value-for-money experience. However, when the service delivery is consistently equal to, or exceeds, the guest's expectations, two things are likely to happen:

- Premium pricing can be introduced.
- The occupancy of that hotel will tend to be above average.

The evidence suggests that service excellence is a major contributor to enhanced profit in hotels because it supports higher revenue achievement in respect of occupancy and room rate. The same concept can be applied to most service industries. Even though quality improvement frequently involves increased investment in marketing research, employee training, performance measurement, reward systems etc., companies with high market shares built through high quality, benefit from higher revenues due to heavy sales volume and premium prices.

Increased market share

If organizations are to maximize their profits in the 1990s they need to concentrate their efforts on retaining and developing business from their most profitable customers. They need to look beyond simply satisfying their customers. They must create plans to increase market share based on a comprehensive retention strategy which turns failpoints in the service delivery system into opportunities by uncovering dissatisfied users and changing them into long-term satisfied customers. The strategy needs to include identifying, measuring and meeting or exceeding customer expectations, then training their employees on how to develop performance improvement strategies based on customer feedback and developing a process to build stronger customer relationships through effective communication and appreciation.

In order to ensure satisfaction and retain customers in the long term, the following areas need consideration:

- Knowledge of customer requirements and expectations: there is a need to regularly and systematically study who the customers are and what they need and expect from the firm.
- Customer relationship management: listen to the customers, respond to what they say and have well-trained customer contact employees who have the authority to resolve problems promptly.
- Customer service standards: have a clearly-stated set of customer service standards governing direct contact between employees and customers.
- Commitment to customers: products and services should be backed by guarantees and warranties which are made clear to customers, and are upheld 100 per cent.
- Complaint resolution for quality improvement: customer contact employees should resolve complaints promptly and complaints should be studied to prevent the same problems from recurring.
- Customer satisfaction determination: keep track of how satisfied all types of customers are and use the information to improve the services and customer relations.
- Customer satisfaction results: collect information regularly on customer satisfaction to compare satisfaction levels with the previous year and check that complaints are down in number.
- Customer satisfaction comparison: compare customer satisfaction levels with that of other companies in similar and different industries, including those considered the best.

Quality and the employee

It is said that focusing on the employees' view is not keeping your eye on the real ball, the customers' view. This is a valid point, but identifying the employees' view as well as the customers' view may be critical to ensuring service quality is delivered consistently by those employees. If the employee shares the same values as the customer's then the employee simply provides the service that they would expect, but if the employee does not share the same values, then the employee has to provide a service different from their values. This requires a conscious effort on behalf of the employee, but since every customer is likely to vary slightly in their needs and expectations, the employee has to keep consciously reformulating the service they provide. But where are the clues for the employee? How many misses and near-hits can the employee, and organization, afford? The answer is none. Every service encounter must be seen as yet another opportunity to please a customer, to encourage them to return and pass around the good message. In most cases there are no second chances.

The gap between the employees' and customers' view

The employees' view of service quality is therefore crucial. Management must realize that employees will hold differing views from their customers, and amongst themselves, which provides the potential for service delivery to be constantly out of sync with the customers' expectations. However, if employees understand their customers' view of service quality, over time, employees will not have to keep consciously reformulating the service delivery in a vacuum, but within a broad understanding of from where customers are coming. Management therefore needs to know how closely or how differently their employees' views of the service they provide differ from the service their customers expect. Once any gaps are identified, then management can work towards closing the gaps by continuously educating the employee to think like the customer, i.e. to develop and maintain a customer-orientation.

The customer-orientation of employees

Developing customer-oriented perceptions in an organization means that there must be effective communications between customers, management and employees. Figure 9.2 illustrates an ideal communications network between these people.

If employees are found to have low empathy with their customers, then this might indicate that the organization's:

- recruitment policies are inappropriate;
- training policies are inappropriate; or
- communication channels are ineffective.

These three problems may indicate that the human resource policy in an organization is operating in isolation from the marketing and operating functions. Since human behaviour and perceptions may on occasions be related, management needs to ensure that its employees develop customer-oriented perceptions in an attempt to influence appropriate behaviour towards their customers. In all businesses, service quality is the responsibility of every individual in the organization, which means that human resources, the marketing function, and the operating function are all inextricably linked.

Although the marketing and human resources functions are often regarded as two distinct areas in an organization, for human resources to become more customer- and service-oriented, these two functions could become more coordinated. It is said that the

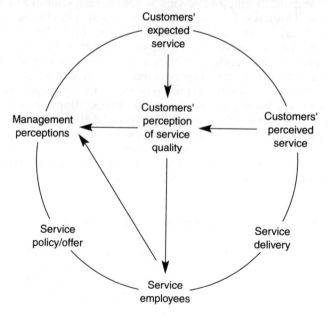

Figure 9.2 *Communication channels*

objective of customer-oriented selling is to operationalize the marketing concept at the level of the individual salesperson and the customer. If the employee workforce is either not correctly selected, not thoroughly trained, or not adequately communicated with, then management is unlikely to build a customer-oriented organization. However, if the employee workforce is correctly selected, trained and communicated with, it is possible that it may be able to contribute to the design and operation of effective service delivery systems.

TRAINING FOR SERVICE QUALITY

Training – technical or social skills?

Once the organization has recruited the most appropriate staff, there is a need to ensure that they are trained to a level that satisfies customers within organizational parameters. Appropriate training procedures are required to develop the skills of the employee to facilitate effective service delivery, and this may include developing technical skills, social skills and other skills which may improve employees' ability to perform to customer and organizational requirements. Training policies for contact-employees, though, are often designed towards developing mainly technical skills, yet since the interaction between an employee and a customer is essentially a social performance, which may in itself be a critical 'differentiating' factor in a competitive marketplace, training should focus on social skills as well as technical skills. It is likely that interactions between people skilled in a social interaction will be quite different from interactions between less socially competent individuals, and therefore employees trained in social skills may offer the competitive advantage that many organizations seek.

However, training employees in both social and technical skills requires a further consideration. Employees can suffer from 'role conflict', that is, maintaining the system as well as trying to serve the customer. To overcome role conflict, employees with strong interpersonal skills should be freed from support services to enable them to serve the customer effectively, and allow those employees with strong technical skills to provide the support function. This approach reduces the stress caused by individuals carrying out a range of jobs which can sometimes compromise each other, i.e. attempting to serve the customers' needs, which may be hindered by technical activities, or attempting to carry out technical activities, which may be hindered by the presence of customers. Training in social and technical skills may therefore have to be selective according to the orientation of the employee, but at the same time it is widely recognized that an understanding of customers' needs and satisfaction levels is a necessity for most, if not all, employees in an organization.

Staff development in the hospitality industry

For many years it had been increasingly recognized that the qualification system in place in the hospitality industry was a 'jungle', with various bodies offering numerous qualifications which had little compatibility and coherence on a national level. Furthermore, many of the qualifications that were available presented too many barriers to many people wishing to become qualified, through their strict entrance requirements and inflexible course programmes. Often the qualifications available had little relevance to industry's needs. Training and qualification provision for staff in the hospitality industry was also variable, depending on the type, size and commitment of the organization involved.

In order to reform, rationalize and improve the structure and provision of vocational qualifications in the UK, the government, in 1986, set up the National Council for Vocational Qualifications (NCVQ). The same role in Scotland was given to SCOTVEC who took responsibility for SVQs, the Scottish equivalent of NVQs.

Apart from the formation of NCVQ, the government also appointed over 160 organizations called lead bodies, to develop the new qualifications for designated industrial sectors, in line with the common criteria laid down by the NCVQ. These lead bodies are defined as employer-led organizations, such as the former Industrial Training Boards, with many of them answering to trade associations. Their three principal areas of responsibility are defined as:

1. developing national standards and the new vocational qualifications for their designated areas;
2. helping to implement the standards and qualifications;
3. maintaining their relevance.

The new types of qualifications are called National Vocational Qualifications (NVQs) for England, Wales and Northern Ireland, and Scottish Vocational Qualifications (SVQs) for Scotland. Once the NVQs/SVQs have been developed by the respective lead body, and endorsed by NCVQ and SCOTVEC, the awarding bodies make their submission to NCVQ/SCOTVEC to seek approval to offer the new qualifications.

The main lead bodies responsible for developing the national standards and the new vocational qualifications for the hospitality industry have been:

1. *Care Sector Consortium for occupations such as:*
    - Health care support workers;
    - Residential, domiciliary and day care workers;
    - Operating department staff;
    - Workers for under-sevens and their families;
    - Ambulance staff;
    - Physiological measurement technicians;
    - Medical administration staff;
    - Dental surgery assistants.
2. *Cleaning Industry Lead Body (CILB) for occupations concerned with:*
    - Building interiors;
    - Cleaning;
    - Window cleaning;
    - Care of carpets and soft furnishings
3. *Dry Cleaning and Allied Services Lead Body for occupations concerned with:*
    - Dry cleaning;
    - Laundering – washing;
    - Laundering – finishing.
4. *Hotel and Catering Training Company (HCTC) for occupations such as:*
    - Reception;
    - Housekeeping;
    - Food and drink service;

- General hospitality;
- Food preparation and cooking.
5. *MCI: Management Charter Initiative:*
   - Supervisory management;
   - Management;
   - Senior management.
6. *TDLB: Training and Development Lead Body:*
   - Trainers;
   - Assessors;
   - Verifiers.

In summary, the role of the NCVQ and SCOTVEC is therefore seen as overseeing and introducing a new framework of vocational qualifications based on a single, clear and coherent model to replace all existing vocational qualifications.

It is considered necessary that these qualifications should be:

1. Based on the needs of employment, and not be defined by the education sector;
2. Competence-based, which proves that individuals actually have the ability to perform effectively in the workplace;
3. Based on a common set of national standards, thereby facilitating wider transparency of qualifications and greater mobility amongst industrial sectors;

The implications of current and emerging training and assessment methods on quality

With the advent of NCVQ/SCOTVEC and their objectives to introducing flexibility into the education and training system, service industries, particularly the hospitality industry, have the opportunity to increase their professionalism. However, it is not clear whether this will result in a better quality of service to the customer.

There seems to be no clear indication that there is a significant link between the recommended system for training and qualifications and research findings on how to improve service quality. Research within the academic world has tended to take a customer-oriented approach to service quality, whereas research by the lead bodies for the new NVQs and SVQs has taken an employer/employee orientation.

The findings are that:

- the government has appointed lead bodies to develop occupational standards and NVQs for almost all sectors of the economy;
- the government has charged the NCVQ to control the award of occupational standards and NVQs through approved awarding bodies;
- the government intends that standards and vocational qualifications will have national currency only if they have been developed by lead bodies, accredited by the NCVQ and offered by approved awarding bodies;
- organizations wishing to develop their own standards and qualifications will be discouraged, even though they may be more relevant than the national standards and qualifications.

This final implication indicates that NVQs/SVQs may not always adequately reflect the total knowledge that an employee needs in order to provide a service which meets or exceeds the customer expectations. If, for instance, research has indicated that the customer considers specific service attributes to be particularly important in a particular organization, or if employees need to be multi-skilled, as in some support services in hospitals, it may then follow that NVQs/SVQs are inadequate and additional standards may need to be implemented.

Although each lead body determines standards for its own industrial sector through consultation with industry representatives, the delivery of service quality is likely to be defined and measured differently within each individual organization. Research has proved that, in order to deliver a constantly good service, there is a need to identify the gaps between the needs of the employee, the needs of the customer and the needs of the organization. It is not completely clear whether NVQs/SVQs help to fill these gaps.

The recommended approaches for organizations which intend to develop their staff using the national standards could be:

- encourage staff to work towards and achieve whole NVQs/SVQs which have been developed by lead bodies, even though this may require a change in their job roles, doing job swaps or collecting evidence through simulations;
- use the national standards as operational measures for their own organizations, i.e. for recruitment, job descriptions, staff development, performance indicators etc.;
- lobby the relevant lead bodies to amend or add to the national standards and qualifications to make them more appropriate to specific sectors, i.e. hospitals with multi-skilled service staff;
- lobby NCVQ/SCOTVEC and the Education and Employment Department to influence the lead bodies to become more sympathetic to the needs of under-represented groups.

Finally, the use of national standards is to be recommended for several reasons, for example:

1. They provide individuals with clear logical and progressive pathways in chosen vocational and functional areas within a national framework.
2. They provide employers with statements of competencies which are public and national and thus facilitate recruitment and development programmes.
3. They provide employers with training objectives which facilitate in-house training programmes and their integration with externally provided programmes.
4. They provide employers with broadly developed and versatile employees who should then provide a significant contribution to the delivery of an excellent service to customers.

However, as the national standards and qualifications become more prolific, researchers, industrialists and customers will form their own opinions as to whether service quality standards are improving.

CONCLUSIONS

It is becoming widely accepted that, although the standards and qualifications that have been developed by Lead Bodies may not be perfect 'fits' for people in their current jobs, the standards should be 'national' and that whole NVQs/SVQs should represent broad job roles which are not specific to individual organizations. This approach ensures that the standards are transparent within and across industries and that the qualifications enable people to develop broad competencies thus providing them with the capability to respond to market forces in employment with greater speed and efficiency. A result of this, in the hospitality industry, could be improved quality of service to the customer. However, research indicates that further standards may be needed to be implemented in order to provide a service which meets or exceeds customer expectations.

REFERENCES

Anderson, R. E. (1973) 'Consumer dissatisfaction: the effect of disconfirmed expectancy on perceived performance', *Journal of Marketing Research*, vol. **10**, pp. 38–44.

Bitner, M. J. (1990) 'Evaluating serviced encounters: the effect of physical surrounding and employee responses', *Journal of Marketing*, vol. **54**, April, pp. 69–82.

Bitner, M. J., Booms, B. H., and Terreault, M. S. (1990) 'The services encounter: diagnosing favorable and unfavourable incidents', *Journal of Marketing*, vol. **54**, January, pp. 71–84.

Bolton, R. N., and Drew, J. H. (1991a) 'A longitudinal analysis of the impact of service changes on customer attitudes', *Journal of Marketing*, vol. **55**, January, pp. 1–9.

Bolton, R. N., and Drew, J. H. (1991b) 'A multistage model of customers' assessment of service quality and value', *Journal of Consumer Research*, vol. **17**, March, pp. 375–84.

Booms, B. H., and Bitner, M. J. (1982) 'Marketing services by managing the environment', *Cornell Hotel and Restaurant Administration Quarterly*, vol. **23**, pp. 35–9.

Brown, S. W., Gummesson, E., Edvardsson, B., and Gustavsson, B. (1991) *Service Quality – Multidisciplinary and Multinational Perspectives*, Lexington Books, Lexington.

Brown, S. W., and Swartz, T. A. (1989) 'A gap analysis of professional service quality', *Journal of Marketing*, vol. **53**, pp. 92–8.

Cadotte, E. R., Woodruff, R. B., and Jenkins R. L. (1983a) 'Expectations and norms in models of consumer satisfaction', *Journal of Marketing Research*, vol. **24**, pp. 305–14.

Cadotte, E. R., Woodruff, R. B., and Jenkins, R. L. (1983b) 'Norms and expectations: how different are the measures?', in Day, R. L., and Keith Hunt, H. (eds), *International Fare in Consumer Satisfaction and Complaining Behaviour*, Indiana University, Bloomington, IN, pp. 49–56.

Coulson-Thomas, C. J. (1991) 'Managing culture change', *Managing Service Quality*, May, pp. 187–92.

Crane, F. G., and Clarke, T. K. (1988) 'The identification of evaluate criteria and cues in selecting services', *Journal of Services Marketing*, vol. **2**, no. 2, pp. 25–32.

Cronin, J. J., and Taylor, S. A. (1992) 'Measuring service quality: a reexamination and extension', *Journal of Marketing*, vol. **56**, July, pp. 55–68.

Day, R. L. (1977) 'Toward a process model of consumer satisfaction', in Keith Hunt, H. (ed.), *Conceptualization and Measurement of Consumer Satisfaction and Dissatisfaction*, Proceedings of conference conducted by Marketing Science Institute, 11–13 April 1976. Report No. NSF/RA 770003.

Department of Employment (1986) *Working Together: Education and Training*, White Paper, Cmnd 9823, HMSO, London.

Edvardsson, B. (1988) 'Service quality in customer relationships: a study of critical incidents in mechanical engineering companies', *Service Industries Journal*, vol. **8**, no. 4, pp. 427–45.

Edvardsson, B. (1991) *Service Break-downs – A Study of Critical Incidents in an Airline*, Research Report 90:10, Service Research Center, University of Karlstad, Karlstad.

Farouk, S., and Ryan, C. (1991) 'Analysing service quality in the hospitality industry using the SERVQUAL model', *Service Industry Journal*, vol. **11**, pp. 324–43.

Fisk, R. P., and Coney, K. A. (1982) 'Postchoice evaluation: an equity theory analysis of consumer satisfaction/dissatisfaction with service choices', in Keith Hunt, H., and Day, R. L. (eds), *Conceptual and Empirical Contributions to Consumer Satisfaction and Complaining Behaviour*, Indiana University, Bloomington, IN, pp. 9–16.

George, W. R., and Gibson, B. E. (1991) 'Blueprinting – a tool for managing quality in service', in Brown, S. W., Gummesson, E., Edvardsson, B., and Gustavsson, B. (eds), *Service Quality – Multidisciplinary and Multinational Perspectives*, Lexington Books, Lexington.

Gilly, M. C., Cron, W. L., Barry, T. E. (1983) 'The expectations–performance comparison process: an investigation of expectation types', in Day, R. L. and Keith Hunt, H. (eds), *International Fare in Consumer Satisfaction and Complaining Behaviour*, Indiana University, Bloomington, IN, pp. 10–16.

Grönroos, C. (1982) *Strategic Management and Marketing in the Service Sector*, Research Report No. 8, Swedish School of Economics and Business Administration, Helsinki.

Grönroos, C. (1990a) *Service Management and Marketing*, Lexington Books, Lexington.

Grönroos, C. (1990b) *Service Management Principles*, Working Paper 90:1, Service Research Center, University of Karlstad, Karlstad.

Gummesson, E. (1990) *Service Quality – a Holistic View*, Research Report 98:8, Service Research Center, University of Karlstad, Karlstad.

Hotel and Catering Training Board (HCTB) (1988) *Hotels and Catering Manpower – A Growing Force*, Research Unit Publication, HCTB, London.

Institute of Manpower Studies (1984) *Competence and Competition*, NEDO/MSC, London.

Kasper, H., and Lemmink, J. (1988) 'Perceived after-sales service quality and market segmentation'. Unpublished proceedings from the XVIIth Annual Conference of the European Marketing Academy, University of Bradford.

Kingman-Brundage, J. (1989) 'The ABC's of service system blueprinting', in Bitner, M. J., and Crosby, L. (eds), *Designing a Winning Service Strategy*, American Marketing Association, Chicago, pp. 30–3.

Langeard, E., Bateson, J., Lovelock, C. H., and Eglier, P. (1981) *Services Marketing: New Insights of Consumers and Managers*, Marketing Science Institute, Cambridge, MA.

Lehtinen, U., and Lehtinen, J. R. (1991) 'Two approaches to service quality dimensions', *Service Industries Journal*, vol. **11**, July, pp. 287–303.

Levitt, T. (1981) 'Marketing intangible products and production intangibles', *Harvard Business Review*, vol. **59**, pp. 95–102.

Lewis, R. C., and Klein, D. M. (1987) 'The measurements of gaps in service quality', in Czepiel, J. A. and Surprenant, C. (eds), *Add Value to Your Service: The Key to Success*, American Marketing Association, Chicago.

Lindqvist, L. J. (1987) 'Quality and service value in consumption of services', in Czepiel, J. A., and Surprenant, C. (eds), *Add Value to Your Service: The Key to Success*, American Marketing Association, Chicago.

Lovelock, C. H. (1983) 'Classifying services to gain strategic marketing insights', *Journal of Marketing*, vol. **47**, Summer, pp. 9–20.

Lovelock, C. H. (1988) *Managing Services, Marketing, Operations, and Human Resources*, Prentice-Hall, Englewood Cliffs.

Mastenbroek, W. (ed.) (1991) *Managing Quality in the Service Sector*, Blackwell Business, Oxford.

Miller, J. A. (1977) 'Studying satisfaction, modifying models, eliciting expectations, posing problems, and making meaningful measurements', in Keith Hunt, H. (ed.), *Conceptualization and Measurement of Consumer Satisfaction and Dissatisfaction*, Report No. 77–103 (May), Marketing Science Institute, Cambridge, MA, pp. 72–91.

Nightingale, M. (1986) 'Defining quality for a quality assurance program: a study of perceptions', in *The Practice of Hospitality Management*, AVI Publishing Co., Connecticut, pp. 37–93.

Oliver, R. L. (1977) 'Effect of expectation and disconfirmation on postexposure produce evaluations. An alternative interpretation', *Journal of Applied Psychology*, vol. **62**, pp. 480–6.

Oliver, R. L. (1980) 'A cognitive model of the antecedents and consequences of satisfaction decisions', *Journal of Marketing Research*, vol. **17**, November, pp. 460–9.

Oliver, R. L. (1981) 'Measurement and evaluation of satisfaction processes in retail settings', *Journal of Retailing*, vol. **57**, Fall, pp. 25–48.

Poiesz, T. B. C., and Bloemer, J. M. M. (1991) 'Customer (dis)satisfaction with the performance of complex products and services – the applicability of the disconfirmation paradigm', in *Marketing Thought Around the World*, EMAC 1991 Proceedings, vol. **2**, pp. 446–62.

Randall, L. (1993) 'A method for assessing and providing customer hotel service satisfaction in NHS hospitals', *Managing Service Quality – Achieving Service Excellence*, MCB University Press, pp. 7–12.

Randall, L., and Senior, M. (1992a) 'A technique for customer and employee involvement in service quality issues', in Hollier, R. H., Boarden, R. J., and New, S. J. (eds), *International Operations – Crossing Borders in Manufacturing and Service*, Elsevier Science Publishers BV, Amsterdam, the Netherlands, pp. 259–65.

Randall, L., and Senior M. (1992b) 'Measuring quality in hospitality services', *International Journal of Hospitality Management*, vol. **4**, no. 2, pp. vi–viii.

Randall, L., and Tofts, A. (1991) 'NHS support services: present and future developments in training', *International Journal of Contemporary Management*, vol. **3**, no. 1, pp. 4–9.

Sasser, E. W., Olsen, P. R., and Wyckoff, D. D. (1978) *Management of Service Operations: Text and Cases*, Allyn and Bacon, Boston.

Senior, M. (1991) 'Managing service quality: a study in the UK roadside lodge sector', PhD thesis.

Senior, M., and Akehurst, G. (1990) 'The perceptual blueprinting paradigm', presented to QUIS II Symposium, Norwalk, Connecticut, USA, 8–11 July.

Senior, M., and Randall, L. (1991) 'Control of service quality', *Managing Service Quality, Delivering Service Excellence*, vol. **1**, no. 5, July, IFS Publications.

Shostack, L. G. (1984) 'Designing services that deliver', *Harvard Business Review*, vol. **62**, January–February, pp. 133–9.

Shostack, L. G. (1987) 'Service positioning through structural change', *Journal of Marketing*, vol. **51**, pp. 34–43.

Silvestro, R., Johnston, R., Fitzgerald, L., and Voss, C. (1990) 'Quality measurement in service industries', *International Journal of Service Industry Management*, vol. **1**, no. 2, pp. 54–66.

Swan, J. E. (1983) 'Consumer satisfaction research and theory: current status and future directions', in Day, R. L., and Keith Hunt, H. (eds), *International Fare in Consumer Satisfaction and Complaining Behaviour*, Indiana University, Bloomington, IN, pp. 124–9.

Swan, J. E. (1988) 'Consumer satisfaction related to disconfirmation of expectations and product performance', *Journal of Consumer Satisfaction, Dissatisfaction and Complaining Behaviour*, vol. **1**, pp. 40–7.

Swan, J. E. (1992) 'Satisfaction work: the joint production of patient satisfaction by health care providers and patients', *Journal of Consumer Satisfaction, Dissatisfaction and Complaining Behaviour*, vol. **5**, pp. 70–80.

Tse, D. K., and Wilton, P. C. (1988) 'Models of consumer satisfaction formation: an extension', *Journal of Marketing Research*, vol. **25**, May, pp. 204–12.

West, A., and Huges, J. (1991) 'An evaluation of hotel design practice', *Service Industry Journal*, vol. **11**, July, pp. 362–80.

Woodruff, R. B., Clemons, D. S., Schumann, D. W., Gardial, S. F., and Burns, M. J. (1991) 'The standards issue in CS/D research: a historical perspective', *Journal of Consumer Satisfaction, Dissatisfaction and Complaining Behaviour*, vol. **4**, pp. 103–10.

Zeithaml, V. A., Berry, L., and Parasuraman, A. (1991) 'The nature and determinants of customer expectations of service', Working Paper, Report no. 91–113 (May), Marketing Science Institute, Cambridge, MA.

Zeithaml, V. A., Parasuraman, A., and Berry, L. L. (1990) *Delivering Quality Service: Balancing Customer Perceptions and Expectations*, Free Press, New York.

PART THREE
ORGANIZATIONAL PERSPECTIVES ON SERVICE QUALITY

10

Measuring and managing hotel guest satisfaction

Anton Meyer and Peter Westerbarkey

BENEFITS OF CUSTOMER SATISFACTION

Customer satisfaction survey results can significantly help managers and employees to focus more attention on improving service quality. It also increases satisfaction because it is a form of complaint management. This enables customers to express their opinions and experiences. The opportunities that follow these measurements are many.

Customer-oriented products and services can help customers decide their hotel of choice. With an increasing overcapacity of hotel accommodation worldwide (Dunning and McQueen, 1982; Fenelon, 1990; Litteljohn, 1985; Litteljohn and Roper, 1991; Slattery and Boer, 1991; Pannell Kerr Forster, 1990), customers realize that they can meet their basic human needs of sleep and nutrition in the economy sector (Senior and Akehurst, 1991). Yet improved customer orientation is one way for hotels to justify higher prices and build switching barriers against the competition (Anderson, 1993; Meyer and Dornach, 1992). Customer satisfaction is often defined as a major necessity for achieving customer loyalty and, hence, a prospering business. Satisfying the guests is the first step to getting more recommendations (positive word of mouth), and thus creates a favourable image, leading to rising profits. Higher customer satisfaction can increase the customer retention rate, reduce price elasticity, insulate current customers from competitor efforts, lower marketing and operational costs for existing customers, lower marketing costs for obtaining new customers, and enhance the reputation for the establishment (Anderson, 1993; Anderson and Fornell, 1994).

Listening to customer opinions is a valuable way of finding out how customers rate employee performance. Organizations can have difficulty functioning properly in the long run without some means of distinguishing between good and poor employee performance (Ilgen and Feldman, 1983). Performance appraisal systems that are based on customer feedback, support controlling functions when they are used to determine rewards and punishments. Similarly, these systems enable coaching by providing customer feedback when assessing the quality of an employee's performance. It also helps management to contribute to employee development. Although both functions are closely related, it is worthwhile separating them in order to examine the two management alternatives.

A hotel's commitment to focusing on higher customer satisfaction, i. e. delighting the customer, is a critical success factor in achieving a higher retention rate for both employees and guests, because both parties experience a positive response to their efforts. Guests could take a leadership role in developing and evaluating the different hotel attributes, whereby employees can get feedback from them on how well they have done their jobs. Results from customer satisfaction measurement can help hotel management to determine organizational shortfalls so that performance incentives can be developed at all hierarchical levels in the company. This will help to reduce the traditionally high employee turnover rate and improve the salary structure by providing merit pay, or giving recognition (e.g. employee of the month or a promotion), to help motivate the staff and improve the hotel's quality.

QUALITY DIMENSIONS

The relationship between quality and satisfaction is discussed in various ways in the literature. We will define satisfaction as being superior to quality because quality dimensions affect guests' satisfaction at the encounter-specific level. Quality perception does not require experience with the service or service provider. Many establishments (e.g. five-star hotels) are perceived as high quality by customers, or by editors of hotel guides, for example, who have never even visited them. Satisfaction, on the other hand, is purely experiential (Rust and Oliver, 1994, p. 6). Over a period of time, repeated positive or negative encounters will, as a cognitive and affective reaction, lead to an overall high or low level of satisfaction. The aim of the hotel management should be not only to meet the customers' expectations, but to exceed them a little. It is important to note, however, that 'quality overkill' – exceeding customers' expectations to a very high degree – is neither profitable nor dynamic. Not only is it costly, but customers will have even higher expectations when they come back. If these expectations are not met, and hence fall below the customers' tolerance level, it could lead to disappointed or dissatisfied customers. From a theoretical point of view, this is equally as bad as not meeting the guests' expectations from the start.

Guest satisfaction is directly connected to the level of quality which the hotel offers. Hotels have a long list of products, services and merchandising activities that are not always transparent to guests. For example, pre-prepared vegetables, and other sub-contracted work (linen service etc.), which are quite common in hospitality organizations, form part of a hotel's production performance. On the other hand, hotel rooms, or food, are characterized as typical merchandising activities which are selected, stored and sold at different quantities and various prices. The service component is often thought of as the sole business objective, yet it tends to be the most important element for the majority of guests. Furthermore, most products, or merchandising activities, are delivered to customers through human interaction. Whilst the hotel's products may appear to be nothing more than a superior form of service marketing, they clearly consist of a bundle of different attributes (products, merchandising, services). Hotels should be regarded as functional service providers (Hunt and Goolsby, 1988).

It is important to note how these attributes interact. In a restaurant, for example, physical items (food, drinks, matches, napkins etc.), sensual benefits (taste and aroma, waiter service, atmosphere, the appearance and sound of the facility, social atmosphere, the appearance and sound of people) and psychological benefits (comfort, status, sense of well-being) all influence the guests' opinions and hence their level of satisfaction (Sasser *et al.*, 1978, p. 10; Bitner, 1992). It is necessary to control not only 'what is offered', sometimes described as 'tech quality' (Grönroos, 1984; Lehtinen and Lehtinen, 1991), but also 'how it is presented' (touch quality), which also significantly influences the guests' opinions. In fact, Morris (1985, p. 53) found out in a Canadian hotel study that 44 per cent of guests' complaints were attributable to tangible aspects (tech quality) and the majority – 56 per cent – were due to intangibles (touch quality). Hence, the idea of a split structure in quality perception (Meyer and Westerbarkey, 1992) has far-reaching implications for process control and for the measurement of customer satisfaction. The model in Table 10.1 suggests that the organization's potential offerings, the service process (customers' and employees' behaviours) and the outcome affect service quality evaluations.

Tech dimensions can be observed and manipulated with statistical methods (Deming, 1991; Feigenbaum, 1983; Ishikawa, 1985) that enable management to keep track of any particular and undesired physical quality change. A quality surveillance that continuously monitors and verifies the status of procedures, methods, conditions, processes, products and services, and analysis of records in relation to predefined references is at the heart of most quality management systems in Europe (Callan, 1992). A level of error tolerance can be defined whereby unacceptable items can be changed or processes redesigned.

Ensuring quality on touch dimensions is more difficult because the dimensions vary with the type and degree of interaction between guests and employees. An excellent example is the description of two encounters from Lewis and Chambers (1989, p. 43): 'One customer says, "Wasn't the bellman nice to show us how everything worked and tell us about the restaurants?" Another says "Why can't the bellman just leave the bags instead of promoting the hotel and grubbing for a bigger tip?".' This humanistic aspect

Table 10.1 *Possible indicators of hotel quality*

Subqualities	Quality dimensions	
	Tech dimension	*Touch dimension*
Quality before delivery (quality potentials)	Hotel architecture, technical equipment, visible hotel quality gradings, etc.	Reputation, dress and behaviour of employees, etc.
Quality during delivery process (process quality)	Nutrition, room supply and amenities, business centre opportunities, etc.	Atmosphere, service orientation, helping attitude of all employees, etc.
Quality at the end and after the delivery process (outcome quality)	Recreation, transfer to airport/railway station, check-out, etc.	Satisfaction, acceptance of complaints/compliments, ex-post communication, etc.

of touch quality focuses the employees' activities and shows them opportunities to improve their performance, resulting in a higher income (Bigus, 1972, p. 153; Rafaeli and Sutton, 1988; Tidd and Lockard, 1978). At the same time this can create emotional stress (Hochschild, 1983; Terkel, 1972; Thoits, 1985; Whyte, 1948), conflict with the job role, and ambiguity for the employee.

EVALUATION APPROACHES

Critical incident technique

According to Lewis (1983a, p. 23), major incidents at hotels and restaurants are often widely communicated. The customers' increasing awareness of hotel attributes allows researchers to better understand the sometimes complex relationship between guests' experiences and their attitudes towards hotels. 'Critical incidents' is the scientific expression to describe customers' attitudes as a result of experiences which have created a lasting positive or negative impression (Fivars, 1975; Flanagan, 1954). Small 'delivery accidents', which can either delight or annoy guests, are often unforgettable and can form an irrevocable positive or negative attitude to the hotel. Management can collect these stories about critical incidents and group them in order to avoid or repeat them in the future. Empirical studies on customer satisfaction and customer incidents at work (Herzberg, 1986; Herzberg *et al.*, 1959; Latham and Wexley, 1981), in car repair shops (Hentschel, 1992; Stauss and Hentschel, 1992), in hotels, in restaurants and with airlines (Bitner *et al.*, 1990; Mohr and Bitner, 1991; Nyquist *et al.*, 1985) offer ideas on how this method can be used and where its advantages are. An example of a guest comment card using this approach is shown in Figure 10.1.

With this method, guests are not forced to fill out answers to pre-categorized problems. Hotel management will thus receive feedback on the most important quality attributes. Following the ideas from the 'House of Quality' (Hauser and Clausing, 1988), data can be analysed and used to identify solutions to problems (Behara and Lemmink, 1991; Stauss, 1992).

Thank you for residing with us; the staff and I trust your stay in Bali was enjoyable and successful. It has been a sincere pleasure to serve you. But, if we have not lived up to your expectations or you think we can do better, we would certainly like to know about it. Incidents and impressions which have surprised you in a very positive way are also interesting for us. Please use the space provided below for your comments. Wishing you a safe voyage onwards.

Positive statements   Negative statements

Figure 10.1   *Comment card using the critical incident technique*

In combination with a graphic visualization of the different processes, often called 'blueprinting' or 'service mapping', each interaction point can be analysed and redesigned. The 'blueprint' can be of great assistance for employee training and organizational process changes. The traditionally high product-oriented organization structure in hotels can be transformed into a more customer-oriented organization with interrelated work teams to assist customers before, during and after their stay. Such an approach would lead to autonomous subunits (quality profit centres) with a reduction of hierarchical levels and the demarcation of product-oriented departmental lines. For some hotels it could even be advantageous to introduce a 'hostess system', whereby a single employee or a single subunit is both the receptionist, the chambermaid and the waitress for a group of customers (Shamir, 1978). A customer-oriented organization in all hotel operations facilitates the measurement and feedback of guests' satisfaction to the employees, and this in return offers the customer a more motivated and competent interaction partner.

Attribution-based measurement

Marketing researchers argue that product and service performance exceeding some form of standard leads to satisfaction, while performance falling below this standard results in dissatisfaction (Bearden and Teel, 1983; Gronhaug and Arndt, 1979; Landon, 1977; LaTour and Peat, 1979; Liechty and Churchill, 1979; Oliver, 1989). Several studies on consumer satisfaction adopt this confirmation–disconfirmation paradigm, yet they differ in the choice of standards on how consumers form expectations (Oliver and Winer, 1987; Yi, 1990). These expectations provide a baseline or anchor for a customer's level of satisfaction.

When examining products and services according to the expectation–disconfirmation model, the 'inferred' disconfirmation approach can be used to measure expectations and performances separately. This method mathematically calculates the gap or difference between the customers' expectations and the actual performance received.

An alternative method is the 'direct' disconfirmation, which only measures the performance. Figure 10.2 shows an example of a fragmented comment card using the 'direct' disconfirmation model.

According to Bloemer and Poiesz (1989, p. 45): 'Satisfaction can be seen as the affective outcome associated with a cognitive comparison of the present situation relative to any one or a combination of several reference points, which may be inherent in the past, in the future, in other persons, or in some personal or external norm.'

Customers seem to use different standards for their comparisons depending on the product, service, situation and experience they have had (Sirgy, 1984; Wilton and Nicosia, 1986).

In Figure 10.3, 'disconfirmation paradigm type 1' describes how the customer makes evaluations based on some sort of norm as a comparison with the focal product or service. Miller (1977) and Gilly *et al.* (1982) suggested the following as norms: the ideal ('can be'), expected ('will be'), minimum tolerable ('must be') and desirable level ('should be') models. Although not discussed here, the widely cited SERVQUAL approach in its revised version seems to adopt Miller's ideal standard model for the articulation of service expectations (Teas, 1993, p. 21; Oliver, 1993, p. 71). As another example, Cadotte *et al.* (1983, 1987) view as alternative types of comparison standards the product-type norm, the best-brand norm and brand expectations. The product-type norm refers to the typical or average performance of all brands in the product category, whereas the best-brand norm measures the performance of the best brand in the product category. Cadotte and his co-authors' norms are explained with typical questions in Figure 10.4.

The other possibility, also shown in Figure 10.4, is the 'disconfirmation paradigm type 2', which uses different norms such as the value perception disparity (Westbrook and Reilly, 1983) or the comparison based on equity theory (Adams, 1963; Mowen and Grove, 1983; Swan and Mercer, 1982; Swan and Oliver, 1985). Here the content of brand expectation is not only in reference to the expectation about the focal brand. The value perception disparity theory assumes that satisfaction is an emotional response triggered by a cognitive-evaluative process in which the perceptions of an offer (product or service) are compared to one's values (needs, wants or desires). A growing disparity between the perceptions and one's values indicates an increasing level of dissatisfaction. In equity theory, satisfaction is thought to exist when persons perceive their outcome/input ratios as being fair. Individuals compare their outcome/input ratios for an offer (e.g. holiday travel package) with the net gain of some 'comparison other' (friends, other guests etc.) who has received an identical offer.

Did we measure up to your expectations?

How would you rate your
stay at this hotel overall?

Please evaluate our service in the following areas

Doorman

Luggage service

Check-in/Front desk

Concierge

Check-out/Cashier

Telephone operator

Chambermaid

Laundry

Pool attendants

Garage service

Figure 10.2   *Comment card using the 'direct' disconfirmation performance model*

Other researchers (Bolfing and Woodruff, 1988; Churchill and Surprenant, 1982; Cronin and Taylor, 1992; Liljander and Strandvik, 1993; Oliver and Bearden, 1985) doubt the validity of the disparity theories for the evaluation of consumer satisfaction and think that 'perceived performance' is the best predictor. 'Perceived performance' can be considered as being more of a straightforward measurement, more convenient, and more typical of the human cognitive processes.

The expectation–disconfirmation model is not as selective in this respect because the process experience inevitably, and perhaps unconsciously, influences guests' expectations (Kennedy and Thirkell, 1988, p. 8; Wall and Payne, 1973). Consumers could have difficulty in distinguishing between expectations and perceived performances, and hence mix both of them up when answering afterwards. Although all three concepts

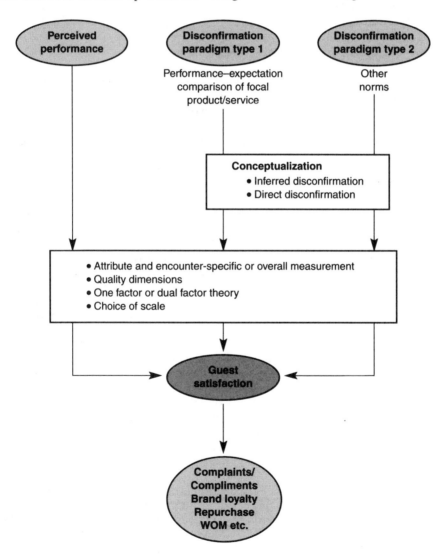

Figure 10.3 *Measurement approaches to guests' satisfaction*

Best-brand norm

'Think about the best (hotel stay) you have experienced. How would you evaluate this hotel in comparison to the attributes below?'

Product norm

'Think about a typical (four-star hotel). How would you evaluate this hotel in comparison to the attributes below?'

Predictive (brand) expectations

'What do you think (this hotel offer) will be like? Please evaluate on the attributes below.'

Figure 10.4   *Conceptualization of different comparison standards*

(inferred, direct and perceived) influence later judgement, performance ratings seem to contribute most to guests' satisfaction and the resulting consequences such as re-purchase intentions, brand loyalty and positive word of mouth (Anderson and Sullivan, 1993; Bearden and Teel, 1983; Oliver, 1980).

Other emerging perspectives in attribution-based measurement of hotel guest satisfaction include the choice of measurement scale, the composition of attribute-specific and overall evaluation, and the quest for a reliable factor structure. We will not go into detail and discuss the various measurement scales used but suggest other sources for further reference instead (Churchill and Surprenant, 1982; Hausknecht, 1990; Landy and Farr, 1980). The interrelationship between attribute-specific and overall satisfaction is often not strictly additive, leaving theoretical and empirical insights into overall satisfaction as unique characteristics which are always greater or less than the sum of their parts. At the methodological level there is a need to measure both constructs separately in order to ensure reasonable data validity.

In addition, one might encounter problems associated with aggregating across all customers to generate aggregate measures on single attributes or the overall offering. It is possible that consumers who think that an attribute is important also perceive it to be poorly supplied, while those who think that the same attribute is unimportant may perceive it to be supplied very well (Ennew *et al.*, 1993). Further work analysing the value structure of the particular importance attributed to different items and the resulting weighting factors enables detailed investigation into the determinants of guests' satisfaction. A common weakness of comment cards is their failure to measure the relative importance of different aspects of customers' experiences and to discriminate between different market segments when measuring guest satisfaction. Jones and Ioannou (1993, p. 29) refer to the results of an investigation of 15 international hotel chains operating in the UK: 'All guests were assumed to be homogeneous in terms of how their needs are satisfied, even though nearly all chains recognize that their needs are different in the first place.'

Most studies assume that customer satisfaction is one-dimensional, with satisfaction and dissatisfaction as poles of the same scale. Yet it is worthwhile considering that the two might be different constructs formed by different quality attributes (Brandt, 1987, 1988; Czepiel *et al.*, 1974; Leavitt, 1977; Mersha and Adlakha, 1992). Since both constructs are then considered to be unrelated according to the two-factor theory, the level of satisfaction could be independent of the level of dissatisfaction, allowing management to keep track of the essential satisfying factors and be able to recognize and control the dissatisfiers.

Customers tend to mark more at the positive end of scales in surveys, according to various studies (Parasuraman *et al.*, 1988, p. 26; Peterson and Wilson, 1992, p. 66; Westbrook and Newman, 1978). Yet this tendency diminishes as time goes by, resulting in a dependency on the measurement time for the evaluation (Boulding *et al.*, 1993, p. 8; Hunt, 1977; Morris, 1985, p. 28). In conclusion, Grönroos (1993) and Meyer and Westerbarkey (1995, pp. 81–103) suggest continuous measurement of satisfaction to monitor processes correctly.

MEASUREMENT LIMITATIONS

Although management tends to rely heavily on comment cards (Geller, 1984, p. 29), direct survey methods can be used to provide a link between customers and front-line employees (Pfitscher, 1992). If no feedback system exists, guests may leave without commenting, which is more likely to lead to dissatisfied customers. Satisfaction consequences such as repurchase intentions, brand loyalty, positive word of mouth and others could be used as measurement substitutes or supplements. Lewis and Chambers (1989, p. 513) assess the reply rate of comment cards to be under 1 per cent, although there are significant differences in the replies for different types of guests (Day and Bodur, 1977; Day *et al.*, 1981; Johns and Wheeler, 1991; Liefeld *et al.*, 1975; Robinson and Berl, 1980; Teare, 1991; Zaichkowsky and Liefeld, 1977). Incentives for guests can raise the response level significantly (Lewis and Pizam, 1981; Trice and Layman, 1984). Relying on research from small response is not advisable. This is because results are likely to be biased, owing to the low response rate and because guests who are either extremely satisfied or dissatisfied tend to answer comment cards.

Other alternatives to the reply card sample include video cameras (Hutchins, 1989, p. 45), silent shoppers (Lewis and Booms, 1983, p. 102), information from complaint management (Lewis and Morris, 1987; Morris, 1985; Pfitscher, 1992), focus group interviews (Jakobsson, 1992; Touzin, 1986, p. 191) and employee surveys in the form of quality circles (Momberger, 1991; Orly, 1988). Enhancing the value of comment cards with the help of statistical tools to randomize the sample and increase the rate of return would also be useful.

Giving the guests a greater role in the allocation of a hotel's activities and striving for a representative sample is behind the 'Sheraton Customer Rating Index' (Lewis and Chambers, 1989, p. 533), the 'Guest Satisfaction Tracking System' (GSTS) of Hilton International and the 'Scorecard' of Marriotts' Fairfield Inn. A similar approach to obtaining customer feedback in restaurants is described by Gamble and Jones (1991, p. 77).

The GSTS seeks guests' opinions from a randomly selected sample, measures the level of guest satisfaction on key attributes to pinpoint areas of service improvement and facilitates a worldwide benchmark survey. Once a month, sophisticated computer programs randomly sort out 600 guest addresses from all the Hilton hotels in the seven major sales regions and send them automatically to the main office, where another computer selects 50 guest records per month from every hotel. During a 12-month period nearly 75,000 customers are reached to whom a standardized questionnaire in the appropriate language is sent. With an expected response rate of 25–30 per cent, this sums up to about 22,500 sheets a year and ensures that the data on every hotel location are statistically representative. A weighting of data according to the guests' mentality (Crosby, 1992; Hofstede, 1982) and the hotel's location is not carried out.

In Marriotts' Fairfield Inns, advanced technology is being used to encourage customer participation in the evaluation of hotel quality (Heskett *et al.*, 1990, p. 196; Jones and Ioannou, 1993). At the check-out counter each guest is asked to rate the quality of their stay using a computer monitor which randomly sorts four out of six chain-wide standardized questions. Depending on the property location, a response rate between 26 and 45 per cent is reported, leading to as many as 1,000 guests in a single week.

MEASUREMENT AND MANAGEMENT SUGGESTIONS

It is not a simple task to control every quality attribute in a hotel and find out how it activates guests' impressions. Checklists from hotel cooperatives such as 'The Leading Hotels of the World' test several hundred items before a location is ranked as satisfactory. Tracking each production and service point to obtain data on customer satisfaction for each activity that a hotel offers (products, merchandise items, services) is nearly impossible. Many actions that guests never even see are performed in the background. These are mostly 'maintainer' actions. A light bulb in the bathroom, for example, is expected to be in working condition and is characterized as a 'maintainer' because it represents a basic quality requirement that must function, but it has no impressive effect on hotel guests and is generally not something that delights them. Assuring customer satisfaction requires creative management talent to find the competitive and most valued quality dimensions so that the guests' views can be easily established and are reliable. These data should be combined with regular evaluations on other items from different sources and linked to the internal process quality and the quality perceived by the customer.

Federal Express uses this method to combine arrays of internal quality data with customers' attitudes to establish a new and potentially exciting parameter for measuring customer satisfaction. We will call such combined approaches 'indicator systems' in the following. Federal Express collected all the customer complaints from previous years and grouped the data into eight problem categories (Rittersberger, 1993). This so-called 'Hierarchy of Horrors' provided the basis for the 'International Service Quality Indicators' (ISQI), with the dimensions and importance factors given in Table 10.2. This multiple indicator is quite effective because Federal Express monitors every production activity electronically and receives an up-to-the minute feedback on the mastery of the organizational service goals. Ritz-Carlton's Daily Quality Report, which analyses production and service breakages every day, communicates much the same information to the management, but in other dimensions. It is an open debate whether measured attributes should be aggregated into just one overall function, or whether the attributes should be left unaggregated and item-specific.

Analysis of the factors involved in the framing of guest satisfaction (Ananth *et al.*, 1992; Knutson, 1988; Lewis, 1983b, 1985; Lewis and Klein, 1987; Lewis and Pizam, 1981; Lutz and Ryan, 1993; McCleary and Weaver, 1992; Mehta and Vera, 1990; Moeller *et al.*, 1985; Nightingale, 1983; Pannell Kerr Forster, 1991; Saleh and Ryan, 1991; Spiegel Verlag, 1988; Teare, 1991), such as hotel surveys and restaurant guides, as well as evaluation attributes of quality prizes such as the Malcolm Baldrige, or European

Table 10.2 *International Service Quality Indicators*

Dimension	Importance factor
Delivery service failure	2
Lost packages	10
Damaged packages	10
Traces	1
Complaints reopened	5
Invoice adjustments	1
Abandoned calls	1
Missed pick-up	10
Missing proof of delivery	1
Overages/shortages	1

1 = low, 10 = high

Quality Award, can help set rules for building the factor structure of guests' opinions. Analysis of the data, combined with internal checklists (Momberger, 1991), corporate accounting figures (Johns and Wheeler, 1991; Kotas, 1977) and other data sources creates a multidimensional model of guest satisfaction measurement (Figure 10.5).

Such a combined approach with a diversity of measurement points can best monitor guests' satisfaction in every aspect of the complex, intertwined hotel offer. This approach is a broad-based valid model, providing ideal opportunity for feedback of customer desires. These multiple measurement points lead to a less volatile index and form a more solid basis for management decisions. Bundling various measurement approaches and data sources into an indicator system over a longer period of time provides a valid estimation of guest satisfaction. It is important to use the same measures and measurement approaches every time to get comparable results. Management is then enabled to redesign processes according to customer wishes and feed back the results.

The 'Bingo system' of the Accor subsidiary Ibis is an example of how this idea can work in practice. They examine the fulfilment of changing service quality indicators (Quality Bingo) by unannounced inspections from an external consulting company resulting in monthly observations of a quality standard at each hotel. If a certain amount of positive inspections result over a time period of three months, quantitative data from corporate accounting come into play. Departments that exceed sales targets are entitled to a proportional bonus for the employees. The employees of a hotel department that passes the majority of service inspections, and doubles the sales target in all three months, receive a DM 900 surplus in their quarterly bonus payment.

OUTLOOK

The concept of a broad-based indicator system to measure guest satisfaction with hotel quality goes beyond the conventional evaluation in many hotels. Although the model demands a great deal of data which are necessary for detailed planning, it is undoubtedly useful for management and employees to evaluate overall hotel quality and hence the satisfaction level of the guests. Hotel quality is what the customer says it is, and is necessary to generate high customer satisfaction.

In models other than the multifacet indicator system described, management will not receive feedback about the envisioned quality standard and will have to discover other ways of monitoring employees' performance.

The next step is the introduction of feedback and incentive systems to motivate all employees and improve quality. This relies heavily on valid evaluations of the quality standards received and, thus, measurement of indicator systems.

The motto of Ritz-Carlton hotel employees, 'We are ladies and gentlemen serving ladies and gentlemen', suggests an aspect which we have not emphasized in this chapter. It is important not only to satisfy guests as external customers, but also to care for suppliers, internal customers (fellow employees), potential future guests and other sources which communicate. Measurement and management of the more expanded definition of hotel guests' satisfaction should be embedded in the company's vision and marketing activities.

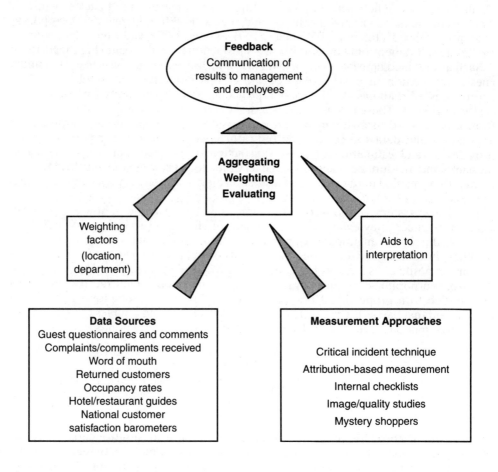

Figure 10.5 *Indicator system*

REFERENCES

Adams, J. S. (1963) 'Toward an understanding of inequity', *Journal of Abnormal and Social Psychology*, vol. **67**, no. 5, pp. 422–36.

Ananth, M., DeMicco, F. J., Moreo, P. J., and Howey, R. M. (1992) 'Marketplace lodging needs of mature travelers', *Cornell Hotel and Restaurant Administration Quarterly*, vol. **33**, no. 4, pp. 12–24.

Anderson, E. W. (1993) 'Firm, industry and national indices of customer satisfaction: implications for services', in Swartz, T. A., Bowen, D. E., and Brown, S. W. (eds), *Advances in Services Marketing and Management. Research and Practice*, vol. **2**, JAI Press, Greenwich, CT, pp. 87–108.

Anderson, E. W., and Fornell, C. (1994) 'A customer satisfaction research prospectus', in Rust, R. T., and Oliver, R. L. (eds), *Service Quality: New Directions in Theory and Practice*, Sage, Thousand Oaks, pp. 241–68.

Anderson, E. W., and Sullivan, M. (1993) 'The antecedents and consequences of customer satisfaction for firms', *Marketing Science*, vol. **12**, pp. 125–43.

Bearden, W. O., and Teel, J. E. (1983) 'Selected determinants of consumer satisfaction and complaining reports', *Journal of Marketing Research*, vol. **20**, February, pp. 21–8.

Behara, R. S., and Lemmink, J. G. A. M. (1991) 'Q-matrix: a multi-dimensional approach to using service quality measurements', Proceedings of the 1st workshop on Quality Management, EIASM, Brussels, pp. 55–65.

Bigus, O. E. (1972) 'The milkman and his customer: a cultivated relationship', *Urban Life and Culture*, vol. **1**, July, pp. 131–65.

Bitner, M. J. (1992) 'Servicescapes: the impact of physical surroundings on customers and employees', *Journal of Marketing*, vol. **56**, April, pp. 57–71.

Bitner, M. J., Booms, B. H., and Tetreault, M. S. (1990) 'The service encounter: diagnosing favorable and unfavorable incidents', *Journal of Marketing*, vol. **54**, January, pp. 71–84.

Bloemer, J. M. M., and Poiesz, T. B. C. (1989) 'The illusion of consumer satisfaction', *Journal of Consumer Satisfaction, Dissatisfaction and Complaining Behaviour*, vol. **2**, pp. 43–8.

Bolfing, C., and Woodruff, R. B. (1988) 'Effects of situational involvement on consumers' use of standards in satisfaction/dissatisfaction processes', *Journal of Consumer Satisfaction, Dissatisfaction and Complaining Behaviour*, vol. **1**, pp. 16–24.

Boulding, W., Kalra, A., Staelin, R., and Zeithaml, V. A. (1993) 'A dynamic process model of service quality: from expectations to behavioral instructions', *Journal of Marketing Research*, vol. **30**, February, pp. 7–27.

Brandt, R. D. (1987) 'A procedure for identifying value-enhancing service components using customer satisfaction survey data', in Surprenant, C. F. (ed.), *Add Value to Your Service*, American Marketing Association, Chicago, pp. 61–5.

Brandt, R. D. (1988) 'How service marketers can identify value-enhancing service elements', *Journal of Services Marketing*, vol. **2**, no. 3, pp. 35–41.

Cadotte, E. R., Woodruff, R. B., and Jenkins, R. L. (1983) 'Norms and expectations: how different are the measures?', in Day, R. L., and Keith Hunt, H. (eds), *International Fare in Consumer Satisfaction and Complaining Behavior*, Indiana University Press, Bloomington, pp. 49–56.

Cadotte, E. R., Woodruff, R. B., and Jenkins, R. L. (1987) 'Expectations and norms in models of consumer satisfaction', *Journal of Marketing Research*, vol. **24**, August, pp. 305–14.

Callan, R. J. (1992) 'Quality control at Avant Hotels – the debut of BS 5750', *Service Industries Journal*, vol. **12**, no. 1, pp. 17–33.

Churchill, G. A. Jr, and Surprenant, C. F. (1982) 'An investigation into the determinants of customer satisfaction', *Journal of Marketing Research*, vol. **19**, November, pp. 491–504.

Cronin, J. J. Jr, and Taylor, S. A. (1992) 'Measuring service quality: a reexamination and extension', *Journal of Marketing*, vol. **56**, pp. 55–68.

Crosby, L. A. (1992) 'Some factors affecting the comparability of multicountry CSM information', in Edvardsson, B., and Scheuing, E. E. (eds), Proceedings from QUIS 3 (Quality in Services), University of Karlstad, Karlstad.

Czepiel, J. A., Rosenberg, L. and Akerle, A. (1974) 'Perspectives on consumer satisfaction', AMA Winter Educators' Conference Scientific Methods in Marketing, American Marketing Association, Chicago, pp. 119–23.

Day, R. L., and Bodur, M. (1977) 'Consumer response to dissatisfaction with services and intangibles', in Keith Hunt, H. (ed.), *Advances in Consumer Research*, Proceedings of the 1977 Annual ACR Conference, vol. **V**, Association for Consumer Research, Ann Arbor, pp. 263–72.

Day, R. L., Grabicke, K., Schätzle, T., and Staubach, F. (1981) 'The hidden agenda of consumer complaining', *Journal of Retailing*, vol. **57**, no. 3, pp. 86–106.

Deming, W. E. (1991) *Out of the Crisis*, 13th edn, Doubleday, Cambridge.

Dunning, J. H., and McQueen, M. (1982) 'Multinational corporations in the international hotel industry', *Annals of Tourism Research*, vol. **9**, pp. 69–90.

Ennew, T. C., Reed, G. V., and Binks, M. R. (1993) 'Importance-performance analysis and the measurement of service quality', *European Journal of Marketing*, vol. **27**, no. 2, pp. 59–70.

Feigenbaum, A. V. (1983) *Total Quality Control*, McGraw-Hill, New York.

Fenelon, R. (1990) 'The European and international hotel industry', in Quest, M. (ed.), *Horwath Book of Tourism*, Macmillan, London, pp. 185–93.

Fivars, G. (1975) 'The critical incident technique: a bibliography', *JSAS Catalog of Selected Documents in Psychology*, vol. **5**, p. 210.

Flanagan, J. C. (1954) 'The critical incident technique', *Psychological Bulletin*, vol. **51**, July, pp. 327–58.

Gamble, P., and Jones, P. (1991) 'Quality as a strategic issue', in Teare, R., and Boer, A. (eds), *Strategic Hospitality Management: Theory and Practice for the 1990s*, Cassell, London, pp. 72–82.

Geller, A. N. (1984) *Executive Information Needs in Hotel Companies*, Peat, Marwick, Mitchell & Co., Ithaca, NY.

Gilly, M. C., Cron, W. L., and Barry, T. E. (1982) 'The expectation–performance comparison process: an investigation of expectation types', in Day, R. L., and Keith Hunt, H. (eds), *International Fare in Consumer Satisfaction and Complaining Behavior*, Association for Consumer Research, Bloomington, pp. 10–16.

Gronhaug, K., and Arndt, J. (1979) 'Consumer dissatisfaction and complaining behavior as feedback: a comparative analysis of public and private delivery systems', in Olson, J. C. (ed.), *Advances in Consumer Research*, vol. **7**, Proceedings of the 1979 Annual ACR Conference, Association for Consumer Research, Ann Arbor, pp. 324–8.

Grönroos, C. (1984) 'A service-oriented approach to marketing of services', *European Journal of Marketing*, vol. **18**, no. 4, pp. 36–44.

Grönroos, C. (1993) 'Toward a third phase in service quality research: challenges and future directions', in Swartz, T. A., Bowen, D. E., and Brown, S. W. (eds), *Advances in Services Marketing and Management. Research and Practice*, vol. **2**, JAI Press, Greenwich, CT, pp. 49–64.

Hauser, J. R., and Clausing, D. (1988) 'The House of Quality', *Harvard Business Review*, vol. **66**, no. 3, pp. 63–73.

Hauskneckt, D. R. (1990) 'Measurement scales in consumer satisfaction/dissatisfaction', *Journal of Consumer Satisfaction, Dissatisfaction and Complaining Behavior*, vol. **3**, pp. 1–11.

Hentschel, B. (1992) *Dienstleistungsqualität: Vom Merkmalsorientierten zum ereignisorientierten Ansatz*, Deutscher Universitätsverlag, Wiesbaden.

Herzberg, F. W. (1986) 'One more time: how do you motivate employees?' *Harvard Business Review*, vol. **46**, no. 1, pp. 53–62.

Herzberg, F. W., Mausner, B., and Synderman, B. B. (1959) *The Motivation to Work*, John Wiley & Sons, New York.

Heskett, J. L., Sasser, W. E., and Hart, C. W. L. (1990) *Service Breakthroughs: Changing the Rules of the Game*, The Free Press, New York.

Hochschild, A. R. (1983) *The Managed Heart: Commercialization of Human Feeling*, University of California Press, Berkeley.

Hofstede, G. (1982) *Culture's Consequences: International Differences in Work-Related Values*, Sage, Beverly Hills.

Hunt, H. K. (1977) 'CS/D: bits and pieces', in Day, R. L. (ed.) *Consumer Satisfaction, Dissatisfaction and Complaining Behavior*, Proceedings of the 2nd Annual CS/D and CB Conference, Indiana University Press, Bloomington, pp. 38–41.

Hunt, S. D., and Goolsby, J. (1988) 'The rise and fall of the functional approach to marketing: a paradigm displacement perspective', in Nevett, T., and Fullerton, R. A. (eds), *Historical Perspectives in Marketing*, Lexington Books, Lexington, pp. 35–51.

Hutchins, D. (1989) *Achieve Total Quality*, Director Books, London.

Ilgen, D. R., and Feldman, J. M. (1983) 'Performance appraisal: a process focus', in Shaw, B. M., and Cummings, L. L. (eds), *Research in Organizational Behavior*, vol. **5**, CT, JAI Press, Greenwich, pp. 141–96.

Ishikawa, K. (1985) *What is Total Quality Control? The Japanese Way*, Prentice-Hall, Englewood Cliffs, NJ.

Jakobsson, K. (1992) 'Making things easy', in Edvardsson, P., and Scheuing, E. E. (eds), Proceedings from QUIS 3 (Quality in Services), University of Karlstad, Karlstad.

Johns, N., and Wheeler, K. (1991) 'Productivity and performance measurement and monitoring', in Teare, R., and Boer, A. (eds), *Strategic Hospitality Management: Theory and Practice for the 1990s*, Cassell, London, pp. 45–71.

Jones, P., and Ioannou, A. (1993) 'Measuring guest satisfaction in UK-based international hotel chains: principles and practice', *International Journal of Contemporary Hospitality Management*, vol. **5**, no. 5, pp. 27–31.

Kennedy, J. R., and Thirkell, P. C. (1988) 'An extended perspective on the antecedents of satisfaction', *Journal of Consumer Satisfaction, Dissatisfaction and Complaining Behavior*, vol. **1**, pp. 2–9.

Knutson, B. J. (1988) 'Frequent travellers: making them happy and bringing them back', *Cornell Hotel and Restaurant Administration Quarterly*, vol. **29**, no. 1, pp. 83–7.

Kotas, R. (1977) *Management Accounting for Hotels and Restaurants*, Surrey University Press, London.

Landon, E. L. (1977) 'A model of consumer complaint behavior', in Day, R. L. (ed.), *Consumer Satisfaction, Dissatisfaction and Complaining Behavior*, Proceedings of the 2nd Annual CS/D and CB Conference, Indiana University Press, Bloomington, pp. 31–5.

Landy, F. J., and Farr, J. L. (1980) 'Performance rating', *Psychological Bulletin*, vol. **87**, no. 1, pp. 72–107.

Latham, G. P., and Wexley, K. N. (1981) *Increasing Productivity Through Performance Appraisal*, Addison-Wesley, Reading, MA.

LaTour, S. A., and Peat, N. C. (1979) 'Conceptual and methodological issues in consumer satisfaction research', in Wilkie, W. F. (ed.), *Advances in Consumer Research*, vol. 6, Association for Consumer Research, Ann Arbor, pp. 431–7.

Leavitt, C. (1977) 'Consumer satisfaction and dissatisfaction: bipolar or independent', in Keith Hunt, H. (ed.), *Conceptualization and Measurement of Consumer Satisfaction and Dissatisfaction*, Marketing Science Institute, Cambridge, MA, pp. 132–49.

Lehtinen, U., and Lehtinen, J. R. (1991) 'Two approaches to service quality dimensions', *Service Industries Journal*, vol. 11, no. 3, pp. 287–303.

Lewis, R. C. (1983a) 'Getting the most from marketing research', *Cornell Hotel and Restaurant Administration Quarterly*, vol. 24, no. 6, pp. 81–5.

Lewis, R. C. (1983b) 'When guests complain', *Cornell Hotel and Restaurant Administration Quarterly*, vol. 24, no. 4, pp. 23–31.

Lewis, R. C. (1985) 'Predicting hotel choice: the factors underlying perception', *Cornell Hotel and Restaurant Administration Quarterly*, vol. 26, no. 4, pp. 82–96.

Lewis, R. C., and Booms, B. H. (1983) 'The marketing aspects of service quality', in Berry, L. L., Shostack, G. L., and Upah, G. D. (eds), *Emerging Perspectives on Services Marketing*, American Marketing Association, Chicago, pp. 99–104.

Lewis, R. C., and Chambers, R. E. (1989) *Marketing Leadership in Hospitality: Foundations and Practices*, Van Nostrand Reinhold, New York.

Lewis, R. C., and Klein, D. M. (1987) 'The measurement of gaps in service quality', in Czepiel, J. A., Congram, C. A., and Shanahan, J. (eds), *The Service Challenge: Integrating for Competitive Advantage*, American Marketing Association, Chicago, pp. 33–8.

Lewis, R. C., and Morris, S. (1987) 'The positive side of guest complaints', *Cornell Hotel and Restaurant Administration Quarterly*, vol. 28, no. 1, pp. 13–15.

Lewis, R. C., and Pizam, A. (1981) 'Guest surveys: a missed opportunity', *Cornell Hotel and Restaurant Administration Quarterly*, vol. 22, no. 3, pp. 37–44.

Liechty, M. G., and Churchill, G. A. (1979) 'Conceptual insights into consumer satisfaction with services', in Beckwith, N. (ed.), 1979 AMA Educators' Conference Proceedings, American Marketing Association, Chicago, pp. 509–15.

Liefeld, J. P., Edgecombe, F. H. C., and Wolfe, L. (1975) 'Demographic characteristics of Canadian consumer complainers', *Journal of Consumer Affairs*, vol. 9, no. 1, pp. 73–89.

Liljander, V., and Strandvik, T. (1993) 'Different comparison standards as determinants of service quality', in Proceedings of the 2nd Workshop Dienstleistungsmarketing, University of Innsbruck, Innsbruck, pp. 1–23.

Litteljohn, D. (1985) 'Towards an economic analysis of trans/multinational hotel companies', *International Journal of Hospitality Management*, vol. 4, no. 4, pp. 157–65.

Litteljohn, D., and Roper, A. (1991) 'Changes in international hotel companies' strategies', in Teare, R., and Boer, A. (eds), *Strategic Hospitality Management: Theory and Practice for the 1990s*, Cassell, London, pp. 194–212.

Lutz, J., and Ryan, C. (1993) 'Hotels and the businesswoman: an analysis of businesswomen's perceptions of hotel services', *Tourism Management*, vol. 14, no. 5, pp. 349–56.

McCleary, K. W., and Weaver, P. A. (1992) 'Simple and safe', *Hotel and Motel Management*, vol. 207, no. 12, pp. 23–6.

Mehta, S. C., and Vera, A. (1990) 'Segmentation in Singapore', *Cornell Hotel and Restaurant Administration Quarterly*, vol. 31, no. 1, pp. 80–7.

Mersha, T., and Adlakha, V. (1992) 'Attributes of service quality: the consumers' perspective', *International Journal of Service Industry Management*, vol. 3, no. 3, pp. 34–46.

Meyer, A., and Dornach, F. (1992) 'Qualität und Kundenzufriedenheit als Basis für strategische Vorteile im Wettbewerb', *Absatzwirtschaft*, no. 10, pp. 120–35.

Meyer, A., and Westerbarkey, P. (1992) 'Feedback- and incentive-systems as a way of improving service quality', in Edvardsson, P., and Scheuing, E. E. (eds), Proceedings from QUIS 3 (Quality in Services), University of Karlstad, Karlstad.

Meyer, A., and Westerbarkey, P. (1995) 'Bedeutung der Kundenbeteiligung für die Qualitäts-politik von Dienstleistungsunternehmen', in Bruhn, M., and Stauss, E. (eds), *Dienst-leistungsqualität. Konzepte, Methoden, Erfahrungen*, 2nd edn, Gabler, Wiesbaden (in press).

Miller, J. A. (1977) 'Studying satisfaction, modifying models, eliciting expectations, posing problems and making meaningful measurements', in Keith Hunt, H. (ed.), *Conceptualization and Measurement of Consumer Satisfaction and Dissatisfaction*, Marketing Science Institute, Cambridge, MA, pp. 72–91.

Moeller, K. E. K., Lehtinen, J. R., Rosenquist, G., and Storbacka, K. (1985) 'Segmenting hotel business customers: a benefit clustering approach', in Bloch, T. M., Upah, G. D., and Zeithaml, V. A. (eds), *Services Marketing in a Changing Environment*, American Marketing Association, Chicago, pp. 72–6.

Mohr, L. A., and Bitner, M. J. (1991) 'Mutual understanding between customers and employees in service encounters', in Holman, R. N., and Solomon, M. R. (eds), *Advances in Consumer Research*, vol. **18**, Association for Consumer Research, Provo, pp. 611–17.

Momberger, W. (1991) 'Qualitätssicherung als Teil des Dienstleistungsmarketing – das Steigen-berger Qualitäts- und Beschwerdemanagement', in Bruhn, M., and Stauss, B. (eds), *Dienst-leistungsqualität. Konzepte, Methoden, Erfahrungen*, 1st edn, Gabler, Wiesbaden, pp. 366–78.

Morris, S. (1985) 'The relationship between company complaint handling and consumer behav-ior', unpublished Master's thesis, University of Massachusetts.

Mowen, J., and Grove, S. (1983) 'Search behavior, price paid, and the "comparison other": an equity theory analysis of post purchase satisfaction', in Day, R. L., and Keith Hunt, H. (eds), *International Fare in Consumer Satisfaction and Complaining Behavior*, Indiana University Press, Bloomington, pp. 17–19.

Nightingale, M. (1983) 'Determinants and control of quality standards in hospitality services', unpublished MPhil thesis, Surrey University.

Nyquist, J. D., Bitner, M. J., and Booms, B. H. (1985) 'Identifying communication difficulties in the service encounter: a critical incident approach', in Czepiel, J. A., Solomon, M. R., and Surprenant, C. F. (eds), *The Service Encounter: Managing Employee/Customer Interaction in Service Businesses*, Lexington Books, Lexington, pp. 195–212.

Oliver, R. L. (1980) 'A cognitive model of the antecedents and consequences of satisfaction decisions', *Journal of Marketing Research*, vol. **17**, November, pp. 460–9.

Oliver, R. L. (1989) 'Processing of the satisfaction response in consumption: a suggested framework and research propositions', *Journal of Consumer Satisfaction, Dissatisfaction and Complaining Behavior*, vol. **2**, pp. 1–16.

Oliver, R. L. (1993) 'A conceptual model of service quality and service satisfaction: compatible goals, different concepts', in Swartz, T. A., Bowen, D. E., and Brown, S. W. (eds), *Advances in Services Marketing and Management. Research and Practice*, vol. **2**, JAI Press, Greenwich, CT, pp. 65–85.

Oliver, R. L., and Bearden, W. O. (1985) 'Disconfirmation processes and consumer evaluations in product usage', *Journal of Business Research*, vol. **13**, pp. 235–46.

Oliver, R. L., and Winer, R. S. (1987) 'A framework for the formation and structure of consumer expectations: review and propositions', *Journal of Economic Psychology*, vol. **8**, pp. 469–99.

Orly, C. (1988) 'Quality circles in France: Accor's experience in self-management', *Cornell Hotel and Restaurant Administration Quarterly*, vol. **29**, no. 3, pp. 50–7.

Pannell Kerr Forster (1990) *Hotel Product Segmentation in Europe*, Pannell Kerr Forster Associates, London.

Pannell Kerr Forster (1991) *Corporate Hotel Users in the UK*, Pannell Kerr Forster Associates, London.

Parasuraman, A., Zeithaml, V. A., and Berry, L. L. (1988) 'SERVQUAL: a multiple-item scale for measuring consumer perceptions of service quality', *Journal of Retailing*, vol. **64**, no. 1, pp. 12–40.

Peterson, R. A., and Wilson, W. R. (1992) 'Measuring customer satisfaction: fact and artefact', *Journal of the Academy of Marketing Science*, vol. **20**, no. 1, pp. 61–71.

Pfitscher, M. (1992) 'Beschwerdemanagement in der Hotellerie', unpublished Master's thesis, University of Innsbruck, Innsbruck.

Rafaeli, A., and Sutton, R. I. (1988) 'Untangling the relationship between displayed emotions and organizational sales: the case of convenience stores', *Academy of Management Journal*, vol. **31**, no. 3, pp. 461–87.

Rittersberger, P. (1993) 'Quality measurement am Beispiel von Service-Qualitäts-Indikatoren', in *Kundennähe realisieren*, Proceedings 3. Service & Qualitäts-Forum, Gesellschaft für Managementtechniken und Technologietraining (gmft), Bonn, pp. 63–77.

Robinson, L. M., and Berl, R. L. (1980) 'What about compliments? A follow-up study on customer complaints and compliments', in Keith Hunt, H., and Day, R. L. (eds), *Refining Concepts and Measures of Consumer Satisfaction and Complaining Behavior*, Indiana University Press, Bloomington, pp. 144–8.

Rust, R. T., and Oliver, R. L. (1994) 'Service quality: insights and managerial implications from the frontier', in Rust, R. T., and Oliver, R. L. (eds), *Service Quality: New Directions in Theory and Practice*, Sage, Thousand Oaks, pp. 1–19.

Saleh, F., and Ryan, C. (1991) 'Analysing service quality in the hospitality industry using the SERVQUAL model', *Service Industries Journal*, vol. **11**, no. 3, pp. 324–43.

Sasser, W. E., Olsen, R. P., and Wyckoff, D. D. (1978) *Management of Service Operations: Text, Cases, and Readings*, Allyn and Bacon, Boston.

Senior, M., and Akehurst, G. (1991) 'The development of budget/economy hotels in the United Kingdom. The consumers' perception of quality', in Brown, S. W., Gummesson, E., Edvardsson, B., and Gustavsson, B. (eds), *Service Quality: Multidisciplinary and Multinational Perspectives*, Lexington Books, Lexington, pp. 93–107.

Shamir, B. (1978) 'Between bureaucracy and hospitality: some organizational characteristics of hotels', *Journal of Management Studies*, vol. **15**, October, pp. 285–307.

Sirgy, M. J. (1984) 'A social cognition model of CS/D: an experiment', *Psychology and Marketing*, vol. **1**, pp. 27–44.

Slattery, P., and Boer, A. (1991) 'Strategic developments for the 1990s: implications for hotel companies', in Teare, R., and Boer, A. (eds), *Strategic Hospitality Management*, Cassell, London, pp. 161–5.

Spiegel Verlag (1988) *Geschäftsreisen*, Spiegel Verlag, Hamburg.

Stauss, B. (1992) 'Customer service problems: from problem detection to problem prevention by "Service Problem Deployment" ', in Edvardsson, P., and Scheuing, E. E. (eds), Proceedings from QUIS 3 (Quality in Services), University of Karlstad, Karlstad.

Stauss, B., and Hentschel, B. (1992) 'Attribute-based versus incident-based measurement of service quality: results of an empirical study in the German car service industry', in Kunst, P., and Lemmink, J. (eds), *Quality Management in Services*, Van Gorcum, Maastricht, pp. 1–22.

Swan, J. E., and Mercer, A. A. (1982) 'Consumer satisfaction as a function of equity and disconfirmation', in Keith Hunt, H., and Day, R. L. (eds), *Conceptual and Empirical*

Contributions to Consumer Satisfaction and Complaining Behavior, Indiana University Press, Bloomington, pp. 2–8.

Swan, J. E., and Oliver, R. L. (1985) 'The factor structure of equity and disconfirmation measures within the satisfaction process', in Keith Hunt, H., and Day, R. L. (eds), *Consumer Satisfaction, Dissatisfaction and Complaining Behavior*, Indiana University Press, Bloomington, pp. 2–9.

Teare, R. (1991) 'Consumer strategies for assessing and evaluating hotels', in Teare, R., and Boer, A. (eds), *Strategic Hospitality Management: Theory and Practice for the 1990s*, Cassell, London, pp. 120–43.

Teas, R. K. (1993) 'Expectations, performance evaluation, and consumers' perceptions of quality', *Journal of Marketing*, vol. **57**, October, pp. 18–34.

Terkel, S. (1972) *Working*, Avon, New York.

Thoits, P. A. (1985) 'Self-labelling processes in mental illness: the role of emotional deviance', *American Journal of Sociology*, vol. **91**, no. 2, pp. 221–47.

Tidd, K. L., and Lockard, J. S. (1978) 'Monetary significance of the affiliative smile: a case for reciprocal altruism', *Bulletin of the Psychonomic Society*, vol. **11**, no. 6, pp. 344–6.

Touzin, M. (1986) 'The Sheraton guest experience', in Moore, B. (ed.), *Are They Being Served?* Philip Allan, Oxford, pp. 181–92.

Trice, A. D., and Layman, W. H. (1984) 'Improving guest surveys', *Cornell Hotel and Restaurant Administration Quarterly*, vol. **25**, no. 6, pp. 10–13.

Wall, T. D., and Payne, R. (1973) 'Are deficiency scores deficient?', *Journal of Applied Psychology*, vol. **58**, no. 3, pp. 322–6.

Westbrook, R. A., and Newman, J. W. (1978) 'An analysis of shopper dissatisfaction for major household appliances', *Journal of Marketing Research*, vol. **15**, August, pp. 456–66.

Westbrook, R. A., and Reilly, M. D. (1983) 'Value-percept disparity: an alternative to the disconfirmation of expectations theory of consumer satisfaction', in Bagozzi, R. P., and Tybout, A. M. (eds), *Advances in Consumer Research*, Association for Consumer Research, Ann Arbor, pp. 256–61.

Whyte, W. F. (1948) *Human Relations in the Restaurant Industry*, McGraw-Hill, New York.

Wilton, P. C., and Nicosia, F. M. (1986) 'Emerging paradigms of the study of consumer satisfaction', *European Research*, vol. **14**, pp. 4–11.

Yi, Y. (1990) 'A critical review of consumer satisfaction', in Zeithaml, V. A. (ed.), *Review of Marketing 1990*, American Marketing Association, Chicago, pp. 68–123.

Zaichkowsky, J., and Leifeld, J. (1977) 'Personality profiles of consumer complaint letter writers', in Day, R. L. (ed.), *Consumer Satisfaction, Dissatisfaction and Complaining Behavior*, Proceedings of the 2nd Annual CS/D and CB Conference, Indiana University Press, Bloomington, pp. 124–9.

11

Information systems and the quality of tourism

Bengt Sahlberg

This chapter poses the following questions: 'How can access to electronic information systems improve the tourist experience, enhance the tourist offering and reduce the consumption of resources for the customer and the producer in their search for each other? Which characteristics and qualities should an information system possess in order to fulfil its functions in the best possible way?'

Several meanings can be contained in the concept of an electronic information system, depending on its purpose and usage. Electronic *payment systems* are digital networks for the transfer of money. These systems facilitate the tourist's handling of currencies and reduce the need for banknotes and coins. Electronic *reservation systems* take care of the purchase and sale of transport services, hotel services, events, etc. *Destination information systems* electronically provide the customer with information about goods, services, events and environments. Electronic access to information about customers is available in *marketing information systems*.

Searches in literature databases for key words such as tourism, travel, services, management, destination and information systems reveal that many attempts to develop tourist information systems have been made and others are in progress. However, systematic evaluation which could illuminate the role of information systems in tourist development is lacking (Commission of the European Communities, 1991; Peroni, 1991).

This chapter begins with a quality perspective on tourism and electronic information systems, and then presents two systems: computer reservation systems (CRS) and destination information systems (DIS). This is followed by an in-depth account of Swedline, an advanced information system that is being gradually introduced during the 1990s. The chapter ends with thoughts on the future of tourism and information systems.

So far, keyboards are the most usual form of input. Soon hand movements are going to be joined by advanced voice-controlled information systems.

Computer reservation systems (CRS)

The tourists need information about services that can be booked and the providers need efficient systems for handling information about their offerings. This has led to the development of global reservation systems. They primarily emanate from airlines, but have been expanded into other sectors of the tourist industry. The dominating computer reservation systems are: Galileo and Amadeus in Europe; Sabre, Apollo, System One and Worldspan in the USA; Gemini in Canada; Abacus in Asia; and Fantasia in Australia. These systems are gradually being linked into a global network (Haynes and Truitt, 1991; Sheldon, 1993a).

Sabre was the first computerized booking system and can be used as an example of what a CRS system means in practice. The system was introduced in its first version through collaboration between American Airlines and IBM. The purpose was to keep track of seats sold on different flights. Today, Sabre is an advanced electronic booking system in use throughout the world. The system exists in 54 countries and more than 20,000 travel agencies. Almost 130,000 terminals are connected to the system. In addition to timetables for 641 airlines, the data bank contains over 165 hotel chains with 22,000 separate hotels, 57 car rental firms and over 50 tour operators. It further handles tourist services such as tickets for events, limousine services, railway tickets, weather forecasts, information about visas and passports, and additional tourist information from national tourist authorities. The number of transactions in Sabre is impressive: 2,700 per second during peak hours and 110 million transactions during peak day usage together with 750,000 new passenger files per day.

These booking systems are designed for the professional players on the market and can not be used directly by the consumer. One exception is the ticket kiosks at terminals. In most cases there is a lack of information about what can be seen and done at the destination. At present, work is being carried out to supplement the booking systems with this type of information. However, the booking systems will hardly have capacity to store comprehensive destination information. It is more probable that links to systems dedicated to destination information will be established.

Destination information systems (DIS)

In contrast to the booking systems, destination information systems (DIS) are primarily intended for non-commercial tourist services such as tourist sights. They also contain items that are subject to entrance fees, e.g. museums, or the location of shopping areas.

Existing DISs have been developed by or in cooperation with national or regional tourist authorities. Even though official evaluation and reported research about these systems are lacking, a short description will be given here (Sheldon, 1993b).

A simple way of distributing destination information is through the exploitation of existing videotext systems such as the French Minitel. In these, tourist organizations store information about their own countries, regions, etc. The actual tourist information is only a small part of all the information stored in the system. Minitel is already installed in millions of French homes, as well as in other places.

The national tourist authorities play a central role in the majority of DISs but commercial players have also appeared on the stage. One example is a German private company producing a CD-ROM called Tour Base. Among other things, it presents the names of 40,000 hotels and other forms of accommodation and 4,000 attractions. The company sells CDs to travel agencies, tour operators, conference planners and others.

The Danish system Dandata is an example of a DIS developed by a national tourist authority. It stores 15,000 domestic objects of tourist interest in Denmark as well as information from foreign countries of interest to the Danes. A central database (a prime minicomputer with connections to 100 on-line users) is kept updated by local tourist authorities. The users are the national tourist authority, the local tourist offices and offices of the Danish Tourist Authority abroad. In Switzerland, attempts were made to build a similar national tourist information system, SwissLine, but the project has been abandoned.

Examples of regional DISs are the Tyrol Information System in Austria and the Appenzellerland System in Switzerland. The Austrian system was developed in order to meet a pronounced need from the visitors for improved information and also to provide further services, such as room reservations. In Switzerland, regional businesses felt the need to make their offerings better known in the market through an information system. Similar systems have been developed, e.g. HiLine in Scotland. Sometimes the primary function of these local systems is the booking of accommodation.

Another example is taken from the USA, where the state of Minnesota has introduced an advanced information destination system. The system provides information mainly on vacation properties, activities and transportation options. Through a series of prompts on a computer screen which follow expressed vacation preferences, this expert system gathers information from a tourist until it has enough to suggest specific destinations or accommodations. Tourists at free-standing kiosks and state-level counsellors responding to telephone inquiries access the system.

A well-designed multimedia concept for 'information kiosks' has been tested in the Austrian market (Hitz and Werthner, 1993). It is aimed at locals as well as tourists. The kiosks only provide information. There is no charge for the consumers; those who provide the information pay a fee. A total of 2,000 kiosks will be established before 1997. The kiosks provide information about events, sights, restaurants, accommodation, shopping, infrastructure, sports, the cinema, transport, maps, traffic and weather information. When each item is presented, information about content, opening hours and geographic position can be included. Information about related items, such as restaurants in the vicinity of museums, is also provided. Menus are shown as pictures and signs and the system is operated through touch control. The search procedures have been developed with the customer's need for experiences and excitement in mind. The search should be fun. Tests have shown that the system has been well received by its users.

Experience shows that the environment in which the kiosk is placed is important; that the information bank and the quality of the information are of central importance; that it should be possible to vary the search procedures depending on the extent of the customer's knowledge; that the search procedure should also contain a pleasurable element to keep the customer on a high emotional level; that the user should be given the opportunity for personal interaction with the system; and that an interdisciplinary team can achieve the most attractive solutions when developing this type of self-service application.

With a few minor exceptions, successful destination information systems do not yet exist. Knowledge about how users experience the quality of the existing systems is also limited.

THE CASE OF SWEDLINE

Swedline has been chosen as a case for closer scrutiny. It has been judged to be conceptually advanced. It is gradually being established in Sweden – its country of origin – on a national level, but also internationally through the offices of the Swedish Ministry for Foreign Affairs.

The Swedline concept is based on a general consensus that the tourist industry is about to experience clearly altered consumer behaviour patterns in the coming years.

The consumer perspective

Consumers are becoming more educated, internationally experienced, articulate and demanding. They are less restricted in their preferences and prepared to choose from a wider range of alternatives. Increasing numbers of consumers are pronounced individualists who aspire to emphasize their own identity and lifestyle. One of the effects of increased competence of consumers is that that initiative, in varying degrees, will emanate from the consumers themselves. Customized solutions to personal needs and wants are preferred. This leads to a consumption that is vital for the individual's own well-being and personal development and which provides stimulation, change and excitement. It is within this sphere that travel and tourism have to find their niche.

Information technology facilitates the consumers' choice of destination and tourist offerings. Only through access to modern information technology can the consumer compare and evaluate the extensive services and products of the tourist industry prior to purchase. Consumers are given the opportunity to find those activities and experiences in culture and nature that lack marketing channels today. This, in turn, means that the activities and experiences – which are often the primary motive for travelling – will have a greater influence on the composition of the journeys. For example, a family travelling with children will more easily find leisure activities that suit each family member (Sahlberg, 1993).

The producer perspective

Production within tourism will develop towards customized mass services through the combination of modules. It will increasingly be fitted to the needs of each individual; everybody becomes his or her own market segment. Tourism is well suited to combine a large number of components into individually formed overall solutions. This process has not yet advanced particularly far.

Within the chain of service delivery, an enlarged information bank would open the way to entirely new opportunities for adjusting to customer demands. More efficient follow-up of results will provide a more secure foundation for product development and marketing, more rational delivery of services, better production control and more opportunities for collaboration between organizations. In this way it is possible to raise productivity within the tourism sector as well as the quality of the services offered. A higher standard of service for the consumer and an improved quality of services rendered should also lead to increased job satisfaction.

Over the long term, improved information systems could coordinate the range of services by means of organized cooperation of bookings, marketing, prices, discounts, product planning, etc. The establishment of cooperation and subcontractor systems in order to create a varied range of products would be considerably facilitated.

Access to efficient information technology will entail less routine work for the staff. It provides greater scope for development-oriented work assignments which will enhance the employees' knowledge and competence. At the very least, conditions for more personal and varied contacts with customers and various associates are created. The introduction of a wide-ranging information bank would thus mean that demands for professional competence will increase.

A large number of the jobs within the tourist industry are seasonal. Access to improved instruments and tools should also provide opportunities for faster learning of new staff and the capacity to quickly achieve a higher standard of service.

The ability to manage the transition to customer-oriented production and information will probably be the greatest challenge to the tourist industry in the future. The transition demands more intensive collaboration between the players in the field, where information and product development are concerned. Highly developed strong networks are needed in order to consolidate the tourist industry product and to make its parts compatible, and adaptable to the almost infinite range of varying consumer requirements. An intense exploitation of modern information technology is one of the prerequisites.

Basic organization

Swedline is an information technology architecture based on cooperative platforms for databases, data communication and work-stations. The applications are modularized with standardized application dialogues and a standardized graphical user interface. The Swedline architecture allows active cooperation between different Swedish public organizations working with tourist information (Figure 11.1).

In order to enrich the content in the system, Swedline is dependent on information collection and distribution networks, databases and primary data sources. An organization composed of central, regional and local tourist organizations has been set up to supply the system with high-quality dynamic tourist information, general information, trade information and market information. This creates tremendous opportunities for creative solutions and great advantages both on the production and distribution side.

Consumer interface

Swedline puts the human being at the heart of the development process. A great deal of work has been done to design an easy-to-use generic user interface which will stimulate the inexperienced tourist to use the system. A graphical user interface has been designed which incorporates digital maps, video, audio, pictures and text.

The work has resulted in two general programs, Map Top and TIPS. Map Top makes it possible to search for information with a coloured map as the user interface. TIPS is

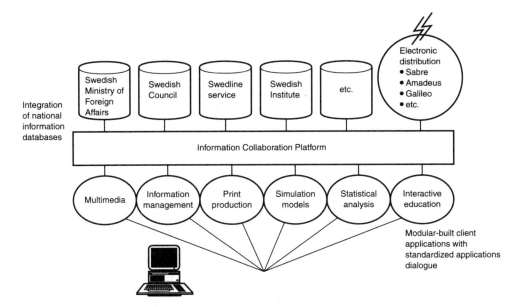

Figure 11.1   *The Swedish tourist information system*

especially suited for updating and guaranteeing the quality of information and the production of printed matter.

Map Top is a system for seeking and displaying positional information on maps. By using modern design methods adapted to the technology of today, a unique system has been created, in terms of both performance and user interface. The development of Map Top began at the national Swedish tourist board. In connection with a feasibility study, an inventory was made of all existing systems on the market. None of the systems tested fulfilled the following desired standard:

- *Simple handling.* Existing systems were mostly meant for advanced analytical work and therefore demanded of the user both experience of computers and technical competence.
- *Short response time.* The systems were all based on vector-based graphics, and were therefore slow in drawing and redrawing map images.
- *Cheap hardware.* It must be possible to run the system on an ordinary PC and Macintosh. If an acceptable performance is to be expected from a vector-based system, quick (and therefore expensive) work-stations have to be used.
- *Well-known metaphors.* A map has to look like a map; the image on the screen must be familiar to the viewer. This condition is not fulfilled by vector-based systems.

In order to fulfil the above requirements, it was decided to develop a new system characterized by the following:

- *Simple handling.* The system only contains those features that are necessary for its users; it has no fancy extras. Menus and tools function in the way that the user expects. The system uses to the greatest possible extent the same metaphors and techniques that are used in well-known programs.

- *Short response times*. The maps in Map Top are 'pixel' based (ready-made 'picture elements'). Displaying any chosen part of the map on the screen takes no more than a few seconds.
- *Cheap hardware*. The system demonstrates excellent response times in, for example, Apple's medium-priced models.
- *Well-known metaphors*. The map data used are the same as those used to print ordinary colour maps. The map displayed on the screen looks like the type of map that the viewer is accustomed to. In addition, what is known as 'anti-aliasing technology' is used to enhance the visual impression.

Map Top was implemented and proved to meet the requirements. The system was first available for Macintosh and from 1994 also for PCs.

When searching for information in Map Top, the scale and the area on the map are first selected with a magnifying glass, hand symbols or scrolls. Subsequently the desired geographic area is marked on the map with a rectangle, lasso or circle. Finally, the information that is being searched for is selected. When the search is completed, the 'hits' are shown as icons placed at those points where the sights, events or activities are located. If there are several 'hits' at the same location, a file symbol is displayed.

By marking an icon with the arrow symbol, the name of the 'hit' is given. By double clicking, detailed information about all of the 'hits' at a specific point is shown. The map picture shown on the screen can be printed with or without symbols (Figure 11.2).

A multimedia version of Map Top which integrates pictures, digital video and audio has also been developed.

Producer interface

By means of export/import functions, TIPS supports an exchange of data between local destination databases and the national destination database. If and when a regional or

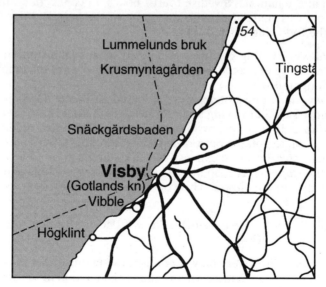

Figure 11.2   *Digital map in Map Top application*

local organization does not wish to establish its own database, an equivalent service can be obtained from Swedline. TIPS exists in both Macintosh and PC versions.

TIPS can store and make information readily available. Information can be retrieved on the screen, in simple printouts, in different types of technical and practical information sheets and directories of events, or in more advanced printed material.

Several new information services have been designed, e.g. 'touristfax', in which tourist information can be ordered by tone telephone and delivered by telefax. The service has been developed together with Swedish Telecom.

Another new telephone service concerns road traffic information. This service has been developed in collaboration with the Swedish Road Administration. A system for 24-hour service using free telephone numbers is planned for the near future.

Information systems can be used both directly for the consumer, in order to improve the qualities of the experiences, and also indirectly so that the producer can provide the customers with services tailored to their needs. The latter demands access to market information that concerns the customer's needs and behaviour and, in addition, information about those areas of the customer's journey over which the producers themselves have no direct control. In this way, the producers are able to increase the value of their own products by giving the customer increased satisfaction and by saving time during their search process.

Swedline comes integrated with additional information, offering a marketing information service based on visitor and travel experience statistics. Through this it is possible to obtain a unified picture of the Swedish tourist landscape.

Market introduction

The system is now established in Sweden and is rapidly being improved. Tests have been performed at local tourist offices and experience gained from these has been considered in the continued development. Tests within the Swedish Ministry of Foreign Affairs have been initiated.

The development began at the national Swedish tourist organization in 1987. The first stage was rationalization of internal processing of information about Swedish tourist offerings. Earlier, the processing of information had been entirely manual, using printed matter and questionnaires. In 1990, new resources were allocated to enable Swedline to develop further. This was made possible in conjunction with an extensive national programme for the application of information technology in working life, initiated by the Swedish National Board for Industrial and Technical Development (Nutek). In 1992, Swedline was transferred to a private company based in the town of Östersund in northern Sweden. The company has been granted financial support for three years. After this period, the company is expected be commercially self-supporting.

Swedline has built up information collection networks consisting of central, regional and local tourist organizations. The data contain high-quality dynamic information about events, attractions, special interest holidays, accommodation, restaurants, travel, general information and market information. Distribution takes place at tourist offices, visitor centres, Sweden's tourist promotion offices abroad, embassies, trade offices, and – via free telephone numbers – fax services, self-service terminals and computer reservation networks. The information is available on-line, on disks and on CD-ROM.

Several organizations working with various types of information about Sweden are standing in line to provide data for Swedline, among them The Swedish Sports Confederation, The Central Board of National Antiquities, and The National Environment Protection Board. New users are declaring their interest in obtaining information from Swedline, among them schools. There are plans to build a bridge between Swedline and the Swedish National Encyclopedia and the Swedish National Atlas. Stored on CD-ROM, the information can be globally distributed to universities, colleges and others at a very low cost as compared to books and atlases.

THE FUTURE

Every epoch in the history of human development has been dominated by a special system of production adjusted to satisfying the basic needs of humankind. The agricultural society produced basic products such as food and clothing. In the industrial society, whose demise in large parts of the world is beginning to be apparent, the main purpose has been to create prosperity by means of tangible products.

Now that we are entering the information and service society, a large amount of production will involve personal development through tourism, culture, entertainment and handicraft. Manufacturing and agriculture will remain important, but technical development will create a situation in which fewer people are needed to produce the goods for physical survival and to maintain standards of living.

The labour market of the future will be characterized by increased variety and flexibility. Jobs will be more tailored to the individual, and several careers during a lifetime, or even parallel careers, will be more common. Employees will have a greater influence over their working hours, and working from a distance will be more common.

The character of education will change when universities and colleges become nodes in international networks in which an exchange of information and students, researchers and professors will be a prerequisite for development. Collected digitalized knowledge of a current subject will be available no matter where or when it is sought. The EU Commission envisages that there will be 150 to 200 networks of institutions within different disciplines. For example, law schools throughout Europe can constitute a part of such a university without frontiers.

One region which had an early national strategy for the development of information technology is Singapore. In the Singapore National Information Technology Plan, the regulations stipulate that 'The information communication system is the backbone of the information economy. We must continue to have the best information communication system in the world in order to maintain an advantage in the information age.' By applying a low-price strategy to telecommunications and data communication, Singapore has attracted international traffic. Singapore exports information switching and transmission services. A range of increasingly sophisticated services is being added. The tourist industry has also accepted the challenge to take advantage of the new technology.

Much is being said about electronic highways that transmit voice, image and data simultaneously. Multimedia, in which information and electronics are combined, is a growth area of the future. The Japanese Ministry of Post and Telecommunications, MPT, estimates that the new technology in the year 2010 will have a revenue of US$500 billion in the expansion and operation of the network itself, and US$600 billion in multimedia-related industries in Japan alone.

In this light, perhaps the question of quality takes on a somewhat different dimension and the entertainment factor is going to play an increasingly larger role. The concept of 'edutainment' – which combines entertainment with the acquisition of knowledge – can become paramount when assessing quality. The sought-after quality can thus contain important ingredients consisting of spectacular and trendy elements. The commercial success can be dependent on the experiences that the information system offers to the individual and to what extent the individuals themselves can create their own personal experience in interaction with the system.

Traditional places of interest, such as museums, will offer the visitor entirely new experiences. One example is interactive time machines in which the visitors can travel on their own through history. Another example is interactive educational computer games, with which children and young people can 'compete' with each other by performing different knowledge-based tasks. In order to complete the task, the player must apply knowledge stored in the museum's digital collections.

Portable, pocket-sized work-stations – walkstations – with three-dimensional user interfaces, connected to a multi-banded fibre-based network, will revolutionize the traveller's opportunities for gaining information. Another advanced source of information will be the wristwatch working as a link between the traveller and various databases. The television set and the home computer will be the most common information source for planning a journey.

The combination of multimedia and artificial intelligence provides the opportunity to travel not only in geographic space, but also in time, e.g. by means of the history of the travel destination. With the help of one's own digital camera linked to various databases, opportunities are being created to return and experience the journey again, this time with a mass of additional information.

The digital map makes it possible to display tourist information in the form that the tourist is accustomed to from printed maps. A range of new search and presentation possibilities are available, e.g. maps showing dynamic streams of visitors on the computer screen. Specialized maps can also be put onto the screen for the tourist who is interested in finding places where the risk of bumping into another tourist is minimal.

Other services will be offered with the help of artificial intelligence. Answers to more personal and specific questions can be given, e.g. what can best be done if one has four free hours between noon and 4 p.m., has a car and is interested in local handicraft.

Despite our genuine uncertainty about the future, it is not particularly daring to declare that the front line of the process of change is going to concern efficiency and quality in handling data, information and knowledge. Knowledge management aiming towards edutainment (education by playing), science diction (user-friendly presentation of scientific knowledge) and network pedagogics (knowledge exchange in networks) will be crucially important in the future.

REFERENCES

Commission of the European Communities (1991) *Impact Information Day*, ATIS – Exchange of Tourist Data Information Between Interested Organisations, November, Information Market Observatory, D6 13, Luxemburg.

Davis, S. and Davidson, B. (1991) *2020 Vision! Transform Our Business Today to Succeed in Tomorrow's Economy*, Business Books Limited, London.

Grönroos, C. (1990) *Service Management and Marketing*, Lexington/Macmillan, New York.

Gummesson, E. (1993) *Quality Management in Service Organizations*, International Service Quality Association (ISQA), St John's University, New York.

Haynes, R. M., and Truitt, L. J. (1991) 'A model for improving productivity and quality in the travel industry', in *Tourism: Building Credibility for a Credible Industry*, Twenty-Second Annual Conference of the Travel and Tourism Research Association, Bureau of Economic and Business Research, University of Utah Salt Lake City, pp. 453–60.

Hitz, M., and Werthner, H. (1993) 'Development and analysis of a wide area multimedia information system', in Deaton, E., George, K. M., Berghel, H., and Hedrick, G., *Applied Computing: States of the Art and Practice 1993*, Proceedings of the 1993 ACM/SIGAPP Symposium on Applied Computing, ACM Press, Indianapolis.

Le Blanc, G. (1992) 'Factors affecting customer evaluation of service quality in travel agencies: an investigation of customer perceptions', *Journal of Travel Research*, vol. **XXX**, no. 4, Spring.

Norling, P., Edvardsson, B., and Gummesson, E. (1992) *Tjänsteutveckling och Tjänstekonstruktion* (Service Development and Design), Research Report 92:5, Service Research Center, University of Karlstad, Karlstad.

Peroni, G, (ed.) (1991), Proceedings of the International Conference: *Computer Networking and the Public Tourism Organisation*, Centro Italiano di Studio Superiori sul Turismo e sulla Promozione Turistica, Assisi/Perugia, Italy.

Sahlberg, B. (1993) 'The demand for new information systems in travel and tourism', AIEST – International Association of Scientific Experts in Tourism, *Tourist Review*, no. 2, pp. 20–3.

Sheldon, P. J. (1993a) 'The impact of computer reservation systems on long haul travel' *Tourist Review*, no. 4, pp. 31–3.

Sheldon, P. J. (1993b) 'Destination information systems', *Annals of Tourism Research*, vol. **20**, pp. 663–79.

Toffler, A. (1980) *The Third Wave*, William Morton and Company, Inc., New York.

12

Green service quality and its indicators: lessons from a restaurant application

Sören Bergström and Evert Gummesson

This chapter deals with environmental issues and how they affect the quality of service operations and service delivery, the *green service quality dimension*. A restaurant is used as a research laboratory in which various environmental factors are being tested. The results from this laboratory case are then transferred into general green quality indicators that are pertinent to the hospitality industry. The chapter starts with a general introduction to green service quality and continues with an account of the restaurant application and the outcomes from the research project. The chapter ends with a summary of conclusions.

GREEN SERVICE QUALITY: AN INTRODUCTION

'Green' has become a 'buzz colour' in business. It is a token of the fact that businesses can no longer avoid addressing environmental and health issues. Rather, they begin to see them as strategic opportunities. Unfortunately, this has been an exceptionally slow process; it should have happened twenty or even thirty years ago.

Environmental problems seem to be perceived as being more associated with the manufacturing sector than with services. We know, however, that the problems of pollution from the transportation and energy sectors – major components of the hospitality industry – are severe. Most of the household waste comes from products bought in the supermarket. These products result in 1,500 pounds of garbage being thrown away by every New Yorker every year; outside the USA, the amount is half or less. Legislation is now forcing manufacturers and retailers to engage in the collection and recycling of waste. Extending the manufacturing and distribution systems beyond the consumption of the finished product is a growing service area.

The hospitality industry is afflicted with environmental problems. Through acid rains and pollution from excessive car traffic, ancient cities and culturally valuable monuments erode. Beautiful scenery is subjected to littering and wearing out through too many visitors and neglected maintenance, thus losing the original attraction. Beaches close to sewers become health hazards for swimmers. The sea life of the Mediterranean is impoverished. A walk along the Seine, the Rhine or most other rivers flowing through major metropolitan areas is partly a walk along an open sewage system; the Danube is no more as beautifully blue as it was in Strauss's famous waltz.

In the hospitality industry there are also subsystems of the larger ecological system that have to be considered. The Disney theme parks are renowned for cleanliness. In Disney's terminology, an employee is not picking up litter. Instead, it is a member of the cast who is on-stage, performing; cleaning becomes naturally integrated with the entertainment. Today, hotels often have sealed windows and air conditioning systems that the guest can only marginally control if at all. The guest is forced to breathe 'air' of the wrong temperature, wrong humidity, wrong loading of negative ions, and with an unknown amount of bacteria and micro-organisms, accompanied by a disturbing noise and draught. Even worse, for the sake of saving heating costs and energy, the 'air' may be recycled several times with no clear understanding of its quality.

Few services – probably none – do not have an ecological impact. You can also look at products and services in a symbiotic relationship and on organizations as producers of offerings in order to contribute value to customers. In this value-enhancing process, the intangible service part cannot isolate itself from the tangible goods part.

The concept of *green service quality* was coined by Gummesson (1994a). A thorough study of quality dimensions used in both manufacturing and services revealed that no attention whatsoever was paid to environmental aspects. Overviews of general product quality dimensions (Garvin, 1988) and general service quality dimensions (Grönroos, 1990; Zeithaml *et al.*, 1990) make no reference to green quality. Gummesson offers an explanation:

> It may well be that in the role of individual consumers we do not perceive this as a quality dimension. Considering the environment may even be seen as lowering the individual consumer's freedom of using a certain type of product or increasing the cost of production. The environmental issues may be experienced as a societal and collective problem to be left to politicians, governments and environmental groups. The research on quality dimensions so far has directed itself to people in their role of consumers or business people and not to people in their role of citizens. (Gummesson, 1993, p. 49)

It is puzzling, not to say frightening, how late the green reaction has come. When the first global environmental United Nations conference was held in Stockholm in 1972, corporations were not present. A major international corporation wrote in its minutes from a management meeting that participation in such a conference could not be considered a serious activity. Twenty years later, when the second conference was held in Rio de Janeiro, major corporations had reconsidered the seriousness of participation.

In a book on *green marketing*, Ottman (1992) presents data from a series of attitude studies of the American consumer. In 1990, 84 per cent said that pollution is a serious problem that is getting worse. Compared to 20 years ago, 75 per cent said that the air we breathe is more polluted and 80 per cent said that lakes, rivers and streams are more polluted (Ottman, 1992, p. 3). Yesterday, minority groups of environmentalists used to protest through boycotts and rallies. Today, the consumer is 'voting' in the supermarket by leaving non-green products on the shelves (Ottman, 1992, p. 8). In 1992, 54 per cent of the US consumers studied the labels to see if products were environmentally safe and 57 per cent chose products and packaging from recycled material (Ottman, 1992, p. 8). In 1985, the number of green products introduced in the US marketplace accounted for 0.5 per cent of all new products; in 1989 the figure was 4.5 per cent and in 1991 it had jumped to 13.4 per cent, representing 810 green product introductions (Ottman, 1992, p. 13). Winter (1988, p. 18) states that a conservative estimate from the mid-1980s showed that a minimum of 6 per cent of West Germany's gross national product (GNP) was the cost for environmental destruction. For the whole of the European Union, the conservative minimum costing equals the GNP of at least Belgium. In the former Soviet Union and several third world countries, these hidden costs are considerably higher.

There are many signs that business is beginning to take a deeper interest in green issues. In *Marketing News*, a magazine published by the American Marketing Association, there have been since the early 1990s regular columns on green issues. In the treatment of *relationship marketing*, a new paradigm of marketing, Gummesson (1994bc) defines 'the green relationship' with customers as one of 30 relationships that companies have to consider in their marketing planning. The Swedish Consumer Cooperative in Stockholm has changed its logotype from blue to green and added the word 'green' to the company name. It has also introduced its own ecological product line, although this is a limited part of its assortment. The interest in health food stores, vegetarian restaurants and health spas is growing. The Body Shop, with 800 cosmetics outlets around the world in 1994, is an outstanding example of a large British company using ecology as a strategic vantage point. Ben & Jerry's Ice Cream in Vermont, USA, uses only natural ingredients in its products, and the heir to the huge ice-cream empire Baskin-Robbins has rebelled against the food industry (Robbins, 1987). Ecover, based in Belgium and selling in 20 countries, has specialized in environmentally friendly washing and cleaning products. Its new factory, built in 1992, was – in accordance with its beliefs – constructed with biodegradable and reusable material.

Environmental aspects are included in the quality awards that now exist around the world. In the criteria used by the Malcolm Baldrige National Quality Award (1992) in the US, the category 'Public Responsibility' represents 20 points out of a total of 1,000. This category encompasses 'how the company includes its public responsibilities, such as business ethics, public health and safety, environmental protection, and waste management in its quality policy and practices'. The 20 points may seem insufficient, but according to Baldrige chief executive Curt Reiman, the importance of environmental issues for the applicant is weighted against the company's potential impact on the environment. Consequently, a chemical producer is judged by harsher standards than an insurance company.

Table 12.1 shows that companies are driven by different motives in their environmental work. *Law-driven firms* only heed environmental issues when forced to by court orders. They often try to escape them through massive use of lawyers and stalling techniques. There are also those who consistently refuse to acknowledge the environmental problem. Lobbying organizations have been formed to discredit environmental efforts and to spread disinformation, demanding free use of nature for the benefit of short-term business profits. No doubt, environmental enthusiasts may sometimes have gone so far as to not accept any kind of interference with nature. For example, the planned bridge between Sweden and Denmark (15 miles) has long been the object of environmental studies and controversies. This has forced the proponents of the bridge to consider – and reconsider – its effects on the flow of water and the living conditions for fish and organisms. Any change, however, will have some effect on nature, and the question is how much is acceptable and how the harm can be reduced.

Table 12.1   *Drives of companies to deal with environmental and health issues*

Law-driven firm	Public-relations-driven firm	Value-driven firm
Defensive strategy	Utilizing an occasional opportunity	Offensive strategy
Cost to be avoided	Image enhancement	Basis for revenue
Consumers do not really care	Consumers want it to some extent	Consumers demand it
Resistance	Cosmetic add-on	Inherent in their business mission
Threat	Faddish	Opportunity for sustaining competitive advantage
Let the court decide what is a good citizen	Efforts to be perceived as a good citizen	Genuine desire to be a good citizen

Source: Gummesson (1994a). Reproduced with permission.

The *public-relations-driven firms* seem to be the most prevalent. For them, green issues are trendy and if the consumers seem to want them, firms use them in order to enhance their image. They apply a 'green-washing strategy' rather than implementing fundamental changes.

Value-driven firms – those who understand and believe – are still a minority. Few service companies have environmental and health issues in the core of their business mission and are driven by those values. Those who do are usually small businesses. The Body Shop is one of the few exceptions. It is big, grows at a rate that forces the management to hold back, and is profitable. Its values are the same as the private values of its founder, Anita Roddick (Roddick, 1991). Products should be nature friendly and not tested on animals; packaging should be minimal and recycled. Moreover, each shop franchisee, as well as headquarters, is required to actively engage in ecological programmes.

Against this background, the rest of the chapter will focus on one specific environmental project with consequences for the hospitality industry as well as for service quality in general.

THE LANTIS RESTAURANT AS AN ENVIRONMENTAL LABORATORY

Lantis is the name of the student restaurant on the campus of Stockholm University, Sweden. The Lantis Environmental Project started in 1991, and aimed to develop the restaurant into the environmental world leader in its business. It is a sizeable operation; per day (when the university is open), lunch and dinner amount to 2,400 meals and the cafés have 6,000 customers. A pub, which is open four nights a week, has 500 customers per night; in addition there is a banquet catering service. Per annum, almost half a million meals are served and more than a million customers buy drinks and snacks.

The project was intially sponsored by the Swedish Federation of Hotels and Restaurants, representatives of hospitals, schools and the military all being engaged in similar large-scale hospitality ventures. Several research councils in Sweden have given financial support both to the general project and to separate parts. The Lantis restaurant serves as an environmental laboratory.

The project is defined by means of a comprehensive checklist, covering any advance in environmental adaptation. To date, some 60 checkpoints have been scrutinized based on the notion that every operation should be commercially justified and that a superior environmental adaptation should always be preferred to an inferior. The backbone of the project is an economic principle, stating two things:

- All operations at the Lantis restaurant are commercially financed. Consequently, no environmental activity will be accepted if it is not commercially justified.
- The essence of environmental problems is the use of resources that do not provide added value to the citizen. Often too much energy is used and too much waste follows because of inefficient procedures. Too much 'violence' is used, which is synonymous with poor economy and consequently excessive costs.

INDUSTRIAL ECOLOGY AND THE ENVIRONMENTAL AUDIT

In the project, an environmental audit has been conducted. It means that most interactions between a product and the environment are monitored (Bergström and Nilsson, 1992). The environmental audit is an example of how industrial ecology may be analysed. In this section, the principles underpinning the analysis are presented.

The basic issue is to relate the business operations to their ecological foundations. This is not a simple thing to do, since one thinks differently when the object is part of the economic sphere than when it is part of the ecological sphere. Most often economic phenomena are viewed as linear while the ecological phenomena are viewed as circular.

There are several reasons for this difference in perception. Business operations constitute in practice very long processes and cycles. A production site is established, used, teared down, abolished and, eventually, forgotten. A product is 'transformed and assembled matter' (production), distributed between and from production plants, sold, used as a product and ending up somewhere in nature. In these long cycles, most participating businesses only see their own contribution and cannot view the whole chain of activities. There is lack of knowledge of the composition of the total process.

Business operations are thus not linear. They are as much involved in 'ecological cycles' as any system in nature.

A life cycle describes the history of a complex system – such as an animal or a machine – from the cradle to the grave. The life cycle model is defined by a series of transitions. In classical economic analysis, the basic production model is similar. But rather than displaying the trajectory 'from the cradle to the grave', it tells the story 'from a source to a value'. The economics approach serves to highlight certain passages of the life cycle, putting it into a context of value creation for the consumer and society.

On an even more complex level, one can recognize systems cycles. There are stable patterns building up a systems structure. System cycles consist of both explicit systems behaviour and underlying cycles of matter and life cycles. Environmental adaptation can then be defined as a process by which circulation cycles within system cycles are made as closed as possible. Matter that is regularly taken from nature should be redelivered there with the same regularity. Matter with no natural place in nature should, by the same principle, be contained in technically closed circulation. In both cases the economic principle is 'keeping leakage at a minimum'. Leakage will nearly always result in matter ending up in the wrong place.

When focusing on the cyclical aspects of the structure and operations of a social/ industrial system, the following issues are brought to the fore:

1. *Identity and discrimination.* The essence of systems analysis is the identification of a system and its subsystems, as well as the discrimination between them. How one subsystem – a process, a species, a specific type of matter – is separated from another provides the ultimate restriction on the results of the analysis.
2. *Traces of history.* Ideally, history should leave visible and identifiable traces behind. Since it does not, procedures for accounting and documentation are required. Suppose we want to identify the ecological cycles of which the food on the dinner plate is part. In practice, this analysis is dependent on available concepts, measuring procedures and measuring opportunities.
3. *Continuity and responsibility.* Ordinarily, there is a lack of continuity and responsibility for complete systems cycles. If a process is broken up into pieces and each piece is described and understood separately, no comprehensive understanding of the process as a whole is feasible. Special compensation measures are necessary to put industrial ecology into practice. In the Lantis Environmental Project close cooperation with suppliers, customers, public authorities and others, together with openness, contributes to continuity. A central project management can take on the responsibility for the whole.
4. *Communication.* If everything is happening instantly and many processes interfere with each other, the system appears to be complex. The more complex an activity is, the more important it is to have proper communication about preceding and subsequent activities. In a restaurant kitchen, declarations of ingredients in industrial food produce and instructions on machinery about installation and maintenance may serve as examples.

In the environmental audit the analysis is conducted by applying two basic metaphors. First, the Lantis system is viewed as an *ecological system*, and second, as a *classical economic system*. We will briefly comment on the former and then go into more detail on the latter.

The ecological systems view contributed to the analysis with the division into systems and subsystems. The restaurant is a subsystem within the greater Lantis system. Another important subsystem is the property owner, who is responsible for deliveries of electricity, heating and water. Some 25 different firms are involved in the day-to-day operations, including food wholesalers, transport companies, a laundry, a sewage plant and detergent suppliers. The use of the biological system metaphor is illustrated by the water cycle in Table 12.2.

The ecological metaphor emphasizes conclusions within three main areas.

First, environmental adaptation is difficult to achieve because of fragmented responsibilities. The general practice today is that a customer – with little product knowledge when buying a product – relieves the supplier of the responsibility for the product history. By the same token, the customer is given little or no responsibility for waste handling of ingredients by the supplier. A much better adaptation to the environmental

Table 12.2 *A water cycle as an example of how the Lantis system is analogous to an ecological system*

	An ecological system	The Lantis system (example: water cycle)
1. Producer	Herbs	The water cleaning plant
2. Consumer	Animals	The dishwashing department
3. Recirculator	Micro-organisms	The sewage plant
4. Inventory	Sediments	The Baltic Sea

Source: Bergström and Nilsson (1992). Reproduced with permission.

conditions could be achieved if contracts along the product cycles demanded responsibility from those who are able to take action.

Second, we have to admit poor empirical mapping of cycles, because of huge transportation distances, and very specialized agents. The processes would be much easier to trace and understand if the geographical and functional dispersion was less. It is probable that environmental strategies require a concentration on local systems.

Third, environmental adaptation is lacking a language which discriminates between favourable and unfavourable processes. The control system approach presented below provides one way to develop such a language.

By using central concepts from the sustainable development records (SDR) (Bergström, 1990, 1993), detailed outcome indicators are developed. These measure results both from an environmental and a customer service point of view. Thus, measures on effectiveness, thrift and margin are derived from a database structure similar to ordinary double-entry accounting systems. The strategy of the Lantis Environmental Project is to use these measures as indicators in a control system. They will produce valid information on which development is more sustainable than the initial state, and which is not. The control system provides a language which helps us to explain what is, in practice, meant by being adapted to the environment.

ENVIRONMENTAL ADAPTATION DEFINED BY THE CONTROL SYSTEM

In eating a meal at the Lantis restaurant, the guest uses a service delivered by the Lantis system. It consists of the restaurant and its supporting surroundings such as suppliers and public authorities. Physically, the system consists of people, capital and activities. The system can deliver the service only if it can obtain resources from nature and if it can use nature as a garbage can. This is a classical production model which can be formally described as in Figure 12.1.

The SDR approach, which is used in the model, makes it possible to integrate ecological analysis with a traditional business context. The arguments are as follows (the numbers correspond to the numbers in Figure 12.1):

1. Guests, employees and others demand a certain level and composition of service quality, including such dimensions as food, eating environment and working environment.
2. The Lantis system is an investment designed to deliver a service.

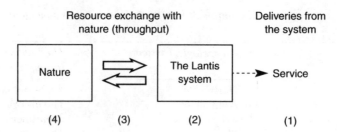

Figure 12.1 *A general SDR (sustainable development records) model of the Lantis restaurant system. The boxes represent the physical production system. 'Service' represents value for the customer*

Source: Bergström and Nilsson (1992). Reproduced with permission.

3. The Lantis system is dependent on input of matter and energy from nature. Nature must take back all matter which the system cannot consume.
4. Nature may change as a consequence of activities within the Lantis system.

After this stepwise move from the right to the left in Figure 12.1, we can develop an analysis of economic rationality (concerning such factors as *efficiency*, *profitability* or *success*) in the same four stages:

1. In the terms of *total quality management* (TQM), quality is defined as *customer-perceived quality* (Gummesson, 1993). A technically higher service level is not necessarily preferred by the customer. The Lantis Environmental Project is founded on the premise that certain service quality dimensions are required. It is part of the professional's skills to establish which these dimensions are – the right kind, the right level, the right proportions – and to do so based on knowledge about the customer perceptions of service quality. There are always limits to satisfaction (Scitovsky, 1976; Leiss, 1984). In the project, not only are the customers considered, but also the personnel and others involved in the service delivery process.
2. All structures, systems and processes carry costs. Economic rationality means keeping them as lean as possible, given the requirements of service delivery from stage 1.
3. The Lantis system must operate at a certain size. In the third stage, economic rationality is a question of minimizing input of matter and energy without putting proper functioning of the system at risk. Long depreciation periods are preferred to short, low-energy input to high, etc. For any scale of the service delivery system, the exchange with nature should be minimized.
4. Apparently some exchange with nature must occur. The service concept used at Lantis would be considered ecologically sustainable only as long as nature is not harmed by the exchange. If the result of the exchange is environmental degradation, the desirability of the system will sooner or later be disputed. The 'loss' of environmental quality may very well overrun the 'gain' from the service.

In all four steps we can recognize the basic economic *non-violence principle*: never use more force than is necessary. In the control system the non-violence principle is defined by three sets of key indicators, their general characteristics are given in Table 12.3.

These measures work as key indicators in the same way as traditional financial key indicators in business firms. This key indicator structure is, however, applicable to almost any kind of social activity since there is no conceptual restriction on monetary

Table 12.3   *General characteristics of SDR key indicators*

Effectiveness   Effectiveness will be improved when a 'smaller' cultural system can provide a certain amount of specified services. Effectiveness is a quota between a service measure and a system measure.

Thrift   Thrift will be improved if the system can provide service with a smaller exchange with nature. Technically, thrift is indicated as a quota between a system measure and a measure of the resource exchange per time unit.

Margin   The ecological margin diminishes when states of nature change as a result of the resource exchange. The margin is a quota between a resource exchange measure and a natural state (change) measure.

Source: Bergström and Nilsson (1992). Reproduced with permission.

terms of commercial institutions. Besides business enterprises, the scheme is used in the management of local governments, road network management, and housing management. An illustration of the general relationship between the basic SDR model structure (as in Figure 12.1) and the key indicators is given in Figure 12.2.

Generally one can recognize a short-term policy by intensive use of effectiveness indicators and little use of margin indicators, i.e. 'right side orientation' in Figure 12.2. Accordingly, a long-term policy will use many more margin measures. In this respect the Lantis Environmental Project has a middle-range policy and the expectation is that the range will expand as knowledge is gained from research projects. The initial key indicator scheme is given in Table 12.4.

APPLICATIONS OF THE CONTROL SYSTEM

Performance measures of the kind used in the Lantis Environmental Project provide the opportunity to treat environmental aspects as 'hard data'. The SDR key indicators are as rigorous as any financial or production plant data, at both conceptual and

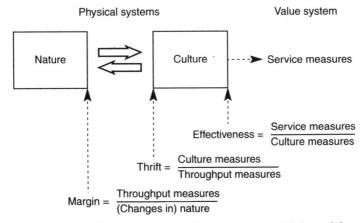

Figure 12.2   *The main key indicator categories related to the basic SDR model*
Source: Bergström and Nilsson (1992). Reproduced with permission.

operational levels. Consequently, environmental endeavours, as well as environmental obstacles, can be handled within established rationalistic action contexts. Six applications are presented below.

Environmental strategy

By means of the key indicator language it is possible to distinguish strengths, weaknesses, threats and prospects for any kind of enterprise. Since the indicators clearly describe outcome aspects, they can be used to assess design principles and other normative tools in management.

Table 12.4 *Initial key indicators and ratios in the Lantis Environmental Project*

Indicators	Definitions
Effectiveness	
Menu choice quality	Appreciation of the menu by guests, according to a questionnaire/Resources directed to menu planning
Food quality	Appreciation of the food by guests, according to a questionnaire/Resources directed to preparation of food
Delivery quality	Appreciation by guests of the delivery procedures, according to a questionnaire/Resources directed to delivery
Disposal quality	Appreciation by guests of the ways you leave used plates etc., according to a questionnaire/Resources directed to dishwashing system etc.
Site quality	Appreciation by guests of the general eating environment, according to a questionnaire
Thrift	
Food energy thrift	Number of meals/Energy use for food preparation and dishwashing
Food water thrift	Number of meals/Total water use in the restaurant
Cleanness index	Number of meals/Amount of undifferentiated garbage
Waste circulation index	Differentiated garbage/All garbage
Container ratio	Weight of delivered matter/weight of containers (certain produce)
Container recirculation index	Containers regained by suppliers/All containers
Margin	
Garbage burning/NOx	Garbage weight/NOx emissions when burned
Differentiation of phosphorus (I)	Percentage of phosphorus in solid waste which is recirculated
Differentiation of phosphorus (II)	Percentage of phosphorus in liquid waste which is recirculated
Energy input/NOx	Used MWh/NOx (kg)

MWh = megawatts per hour, NOx = nitrogen oxides.
Source: Bergström and Nilsson (1992). Reproduced with permission.

Changes in...

	Diffusion	Separation	Production	Product	Life style
...may affect... Effectiveness					
Thrift					
Margin					

Figure 12.3   *The design/assessment matrix used for the identification of strategic options. Here the matrix is illustrated with 15 cells. In practice there were 128 cells*
Source: Bergström and Nilsson (1992). Reproduced with permission.

In an early stage of the Lantis Environmental Project a matrix was elaborated, where 'ways to improve environmental adaptation' (Röpke, 1992) were listed on one axis, and key indicators as 'ways to assess performance' on the other. The design/assessment matrix considerably facilitated the search for where fruitful projects should be started. The matrix made it possible to distinguish strategic options both regarding what is perceived as possible (the horizontal axis) and regarding quality measures of the outcomes (the vertical axis). Each combination in the matrix describes a unique change in the operations and the expected contribution to the fulfillment of the strategy of the company (environmental as well as overall).

Environmental business

From the 1970s and onwards, 'ethical investments', 'environmental business' and similar concepts have shown that sound business does not have to be harmful to the environment. Between 5 per cent and 10 per cent of the turnover of the New York Stock Exchange is handled by ethical operators, funds such as Calvert and money managers such as Franklin Research. A similar pattern developed during the 1980s in the City of London, where environmental operators Bromige & Partners and Merlin Fund have been successful, and the EIRIS rating institute has gained wide acceptance.

All these operators work with 'picking the winner' concepts, where 'the winner' is a company which is well adapted to the environment as compared to its competitors. In many individual years, those companies have earned more money than their competitors. Environmentally oriented funds such as Calvert have been financially more successful than most other funds. For fund managers and rating institutes, schemes similar to the SDR key indicators are necessary tools.

For managers aiming at developing an in-house environmentally sound business, the precision in the SDR approach is even more significant. In the long run, it is of vital importance to make a clear distinction between stock and flow concepts both for avoiding the 'growth mania' and for distinguishing actual production from positional effects (Hirsch, 1975), which typically overstate the success of traditionally monitored companies.

Businesses enter into relationships with others to an increasing extent. Relationship marketing is becoming a major marketing strategy, even constituting a paradigm shift in marketing (Grönroos, 1994; Gummesson, 1994b, c). Long-term business relationships – as a supplement to competition and regulations – are essential in creating a dynamic market economy. Being part of a network of relationships requires an overview of the flow of goods and services. The SDR approach can be used in partner assessment for future alliances.

Environmental budgeting

Realistic management for sustainable development requires a capability to handle 'sub-sustainable development' systematically. If there is a long way to go, the first steps should be taken with great care. Maybe those are the most important. By using time series of key indicators, the management can scrutinize both the direction and the pace of change, and thus develop realistic goals for periods to come.

If budgets are accomplished in such a spirit, key outcome indicators can be broken down and handled as goals at lower levels within hierarchical structures. Such goals can be followed up and treated rationally. Differences in opinion about the interpretation of results can be discussed in the open.

Large enterprises have complex goals. They tend to be rigid and sluggish in an attempt to keep control of their operations and finances. Their budgeting procedures may not be susceptible to the complexity of real-world systems; the 'real' results are left to judgement calls by top management. SDR budgeting can overcome this, at least when complexity is an outcome of environmental efforts.

In the Lantis Environmental Project we have to date no accounting history for backing specific goal levels on each key indicator. The general aim is 'higher value on some, and at least the same value on all'.

Environmental accounting

When accounting is done in real terms you get a more direct picture of the economic situation than when accounting is 'filtered' through monetary measures. The theory behind SDR is in line with classical economic principles and accounting rules. Some new rules are added to make it technically possible to handle many kinds of physical measures in a single accounting framework. You get an accounting of the cycle 'from a source to a value' instead of the traditional accounting of what is sold and bought.

Environmental aspects are innate parts of such real accounting. Other aspects concern personnel, cash flow and knowledge. With the SDR scheme one uses the same principles, the same concepts and the same practical tools in the accounting of all these aspects. By emphasizing the real economics related to all resources used, management will not be forced to treat the financial part within a rational scheme and to treat other parts – such as ecological resources and human resources – intuitively.

Environmental auditing

Under the label of environmental auditing, big companies check actual and potential conflicts between company practice and environmental laws and regulations. Typically, such work is strictly internal and constitutes proprietory and confidential information. An extensive literature on the subject is available (UNEP, 1988; EPA, 1990 and later; Gray, 1993; Welford and Gouldson, 1993), but there is still little empirically based knowledge available about environmental auditing.

The SDR approach invites a closing of the gap between modern, unsystematic and subjective approaches to environmental auditing and traditional, well-documented and professional general corporate auditing. Two elements are required to make external and formal environmental auditing operational: (1) an economic structure of all kinds of problems under scrutiny, and (2) the existence of an accounting standard which includes environmental aspects.

Environmental negotiations

As when environmental budgeting was discussed, negotiations over contracts and subcontracts are dependent on 'hard data'. A strict accounting and key indicator structure facilitates settlements over claims and counter-claims. Subcontractors can be given considerable freedom to act creatively if payments are strictly regulated by environmentally relevant result measures.

The SDR control system may also be a dynamic asset in negotiations. It is much easier to present specific requirements to others when one has a clear picture of one's own position. This kind of clarity is provided by a superior control system.

SUMMARY OF CONCLUSIONS

The following conclusions summarize the messages of this chapter:

1. Service industries influence the environment just as much as manufacturing industries. Tangibles like food, waste and machinery, and intangibles like transportation, food preparation and the serving of food, have a symbiotic relationship in the hospitality industry. Service management and service quality literature so far does not deal with the green quality aspects. The Lantis Environmental Project treats green service quality as a novel dimension in quality assessment.
2. Only a few companies consider the green quality dimension unless they are forced to. It is rarely an integral part of their business mission, goals and strategies; few have been able to turn it to their favour. This is not because environmentally sound operations are inherently more costly or less profit-generating; it is because of the mental blockage, resistance to change and sluggishness of organizations. There is a difference in corporate mindsets between defensive green strategies to avoid cost and law suits, the public relations 'green-washing', and the offensive, value-driven green strategies.
3. Apart from the mindsets of companies, there are operational problems: how can a service organization turn green in practice and still make a profit? A major hurdle is the fragmentation of responsibility and knowledge among the numerous agents in a production and delivery chain. The Lantis Environmental Project represents applied research that attempts to solve such operational problems. It helps to conceptualize the environmental issues and make obvious the type and scope of ecological impact from various service activities. It is an aid to see the role of one's own activities as part of a chain of activities executed by others.
4. Using the indicators of the SDR scheme makes the environmental considerations structured and adds clarity to the assessments. The umbrella indicators – effectiveness, thrift, margin – can be broken down in some fairly

general sub-indicators and ratios. A service organization can also select its own specific sub-indicators and ratios. A number of usages have been mentioned: to select a strategy, to show that profits can be made, to provide a structured approach to budgeting, accounting and auditing, and to strengthen one's position in negotiations.

5. Finally, the need for green services is obvious. Despite the slow start and pace, companies are gradually turning greener. The principles of ecology and the health hazards of pollution are known; no more evidence is necessary to prove their existence and significance. Active resistance may seem attractive in the short term but will be lethal in the long term. Whether it is accepted in the boardrooms or not, companies will have to adjust.

REFERENCES

Bergström, S. (1990) 'Sustainable development accounting', *Development*, vol. **3**, no. 4.

Bergström, S. (1993) 'Value standards in sub-sustainable development. On limits of ecological economics', *Ecological Economics*, vol. **7**, no. 1, pp. 1–18.

Bergström, S. and Nilsson, J. (1992) *Miljörevision Lantis 92. Analys av förutsättningarna att förbättra restaurang Lantis' miljöanpassning* ('Lantis Environmental Audit 92. An Analysis to Improve the Environmental Adjustment of the *Lantis* Restaurant'), Svensk Företagsforskning AB, Stockholm.

EPA (1988) *Annotated Bibliography on Environmental Auditing*, US Environmental Protection Agency (EPA), Washington, DC.

Garvin, D. A. (1988) *Managing Quality*, The Free Press, New York.

Gray, R. (1993) *Accounting for the Environment*, Paul Chapman Publishing Ltd, London.

Grönroos, C. (1990) *Service Management and Marketing*, Lexington Books/Macmillan, Lexington, MA.

Grönroos, C. (1994) 'Quo vadis, marketing? Towards a relationship marketing paradigm', *Journal of Marketing Management*, vol. **10**, no. 4.

Gummesson, E. (1993) *Quality Management in Service Organizations*, International Service Quality Association, New York.

Gummesson, E. (1994a) 'Green service quality', in Edvardsson, B. and Scheuing, E. E. (eds), Proceedings from QUIS 3, Quality in Services Symposium, Karlstad, Sweden, June 1992, ISQA, New York.

Gummesson, E. (1994b) 'Is relationship marketing operational?' Paper presented at the 23rd EMAC Conference, Maastricht, The Netherlands, May.

Gummesson, E. (1994c) *Relationship Marketing: From 4Ps to 30Rs*, Stockholm University, Stockholm.

Hirsch, F. (1975) *Social Limits to Growth*, Harvard University Press, Boston, MA.

Leiss, W. (1984) 'Economic life as symbolic activity', in Bergström, S. (ed.), *Economic Growth and the Role of Science*. Forskningsrådens förlagstjänst, Stockholm.

Malcolm Baldrige National Quality Award (1993) *Application Guidelines*, United States Department of Commerce, Gaitherburg, MD.

Ottman, J. A., (1992) *Green Marketing*, NTC Business Books, Lincolnwood, IL.

Robbins, J. (1987) *Diet for a New America*, Stillpoint Publishing, Walpole, NH.

Roddick, A. (1991) *Body and Soul*, Crown Publishers, New York.

Röpke, I. (1992) 'Beyond clean technology: structural changes of production and everyday life', in Hansson, L. O., and Jungen, B. (ed.), *Human Responsibility and Global Change*, University of Göteborg, Section for Human Ecology, Humanekologiska Skrifter, Göteborg.

Scitovsky, T. (1976) *The Joyless Economy*, Oxford University Press, London.

UNEP Industry and Environment Quartely Bulletin (1988), vol. **4**, October–December.

Welford, R., and Gouldson, A. (1993) *Environmental Management and Business Strategy*, Pitman Publishing, London.

Winter, G. (1988) *Business and the Environment*, McGraw-Hill, Hamburg.

Zeithaml, V. A., Parasuraman, A., and Berry, L. L. (1990) *Delivering Quality Service*, The Free Press, New York.

PART FOUR
NEW DIRECTIONS FOR SERVICE QUALITY

13

The 6 Vs – a new quality circle?

Bob Brotherton and Mike Coyle

INTRODUCTION

Over recent years there has been a dramatic increase in the volume of literature concerning quality issues in general. Similarly, both academics and practitioners involved with the hospitality industry have contributed a large volume of ideas and perspectives relating to quality improvement in hospitality organizations. This process has now proceeded to such a degree that the quality debate being pursued in the literature is becoming somewhat circular. The issue of quality has been probed and explored to such an extent that an increasing number of commentators are apparently finding it difficult to develop new and original perspectives to further the debate. There is a danger that the standard perspectives and models are simply being re-hashed and applied in different contexts. Though this has proved valuable both in extending the issues to a wider range of contexts and in assisting the formulation of new perspectives, it is now perhaps approaching the point where the debate is standing still at best, and regressing at worst.

In building on our earlier work (Brotherton and Coyle, 1990a, b, 1991a, b), which explored a range of issues associated with variability, variety and variance in hospitality operations environments, we are seeking here to present new perspectives and ideas relating to the issue of quality in hospitality organizations. By extending our original work, and linking this to the issue of quality, we believe this chapter will serve to refresh the quality debate in relation to hospitality operations and thereby provide both academic and industrial parties with alternative perspectives to consider and explore. The 6 Vs model explored in this chapter is a somewhat speculative venture and, we believe, an entirely original approach to the issue of quality in hospitality organizations. We hope that this is presented in a coherent manner, and will stimulate thought and debate, and indicate a number of unanswered questions and issues requiring further research. If this chapter helps to provoke the reader into a critical evaluation of its contents it will have achieved its purpose.

THE 6 Vs: A CONCEPTUAL OVERVIEW

The 6 Vs model presented here has arisen largely as a consequence of the re-examination and development of earlier work conducted by the authors on a similar theme (Brotherton and Coyle, 1990a, b, 1991a, b). The initial formulation of the Vs model (Figure 13.1) was based upon an analysis of the relationships between the original 3 Vs – variability, variety and variance – and instability/complexity in the hospitality operations environment (HOE). Here we increase the number of Vs in the model from 3 to 6, thereby expanding the scope of its analysis, and also provide a further extension to the Vs approach through the discussion of a further dimension, quality.

The revised 6 Vs model which has emerged from this process is shown in Figure 13.2. This clearly indicates the centrality of quality in relation to the 6 Vs, with the linkage between these two dimensions provided by the issues of instability and complexity. Not only is this model wider in scope, and specifically focused upon the central issue of quality, but its formulation and presentation indicates another aspect in the development of this perspective. Whereas the original 3 Vs model was essentially linear in nature, the 6 Vs model has a different conceptual basis. The primary logic underlying the 3 Vs model was that of a linear cause–effect relationship, from variability to variety and ultimately variance. In this view external variability was seen to be as a major generator of variety within the hospitality organization's response to this issue. This

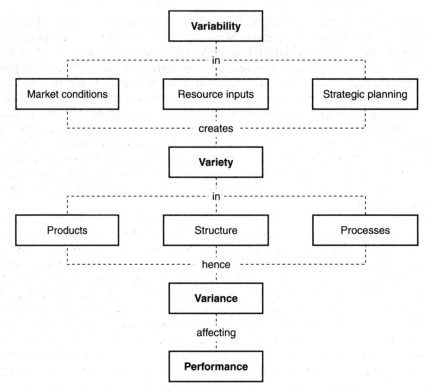

Figure 13.1   *Instability in the hospitality operations environment*

expansion of variety, particularly that of an unplanned and/or undesired nature, was then purported to have a further consequence in terms of its impact on the ability of the organization to achieve its desired performance levels, i.e. variance.

Whilst the logic of providing a closing, return loop for this progression, through the view that a greater incidence of either individual or aggregate variance within a given industry sector/market may itself impact upon the starting point of variability, may have been implicit in this original work, it was not explicitly stated or discussed in any meaningful way. The 6 Vs model differs fundamentally from this truncated logic and explicitly recognizes the circular nature of the Vs. Similarly, the dynamic two-way interrelationships between the Vs and quality are recognized and explored through the instability/complexity issues which link these two major domains.

In essence the 6 Vs model, with its speculative title as a 'new quality circle?', is a type of 'wheel' approach. The 'hub' is clearly the domain of central interest or concern, quality. The outer 'rim' is constituted by the 6 Vs, with the 'spokes' linking these two separate structures provided by the two-way channels of instability and complexity. The conceptual logic superimposed on this structure is in one sense quite simple, yet perhaps deceptively complex when applied in its totality to reality. Here we will take the simple route and return to some of the complexities later in the chapter.

The 6 Vs are seen to both reflect, and be capable of increasing or decreasing, the levels of instability and complexity faced by a hospitality organization. Therefore any individual V, or a combination of the 6 Vs may change as a result of changes in the level of instability/complexity faced by the hospitality organization, whether this arises from internal or external sources. In addition, the reverse may also be true. Any change made to one or more of the Vs will tend to affect the levels of instability and complexity experienced by the organization. Again, this can lead to these levels rising or falling. The relationship is certainly two-way in nature, but perhaps more importantly it is also

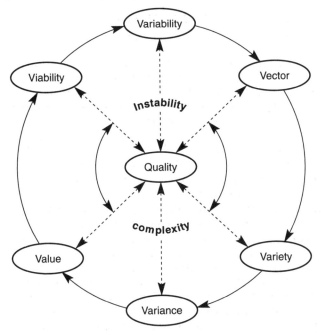

Figure 13.2   *The 6 Vs model*

iterative and therefore potentially cumulative in terms of eventual outcomes. In short, once activated, the process may accelerate into mutually reinforced spirals.

The obvious question which arises at this point is 'where does quality fit into this process?' It is our contention that instability and complexity are major factors influencing the hospitality organization's ability to create, maintain and deliver desired levels of product/service quality. This proposal is based upon the view that the greater the extent, and the faster the rate, of change in unplanned and undesirable instability/complexity faced by any organization, the more difficult it will be for that organization to both assure and control quality within its existing production and service systems. Of course this implies that the reverse must be true. If greater stability can be achieved the potential to produce and deliver higher quality should be enhanced.

At this point we must state that the 'stability = greater potential for high quality/instability = enhanced propensity for low quality' hypothesis is somewhat speculative and may or may not be empirically valid. This remains to be explored, either by ourselves or other researchers in the field. Substantiated or not, this contention should provoke an interesting debate on these issues and it also serves to provide an essential link within the 6 Vs model. In this model it is not stability *per se* which is important to the hospitality organization, but desirable stability within the 6 Vs. In contrast, undesirable instability within the Vs is seen to impact unfavourably on quality. Therefore in this perspective the main factor influencing the hospitality organization's ability to create and maintain quality is how effectively it can manage the 6 Vs. Where undesirable instability and complexity in the Vs can be reduced, controlled or eliminated, the organization will enhance its ability to create and deliver quality, and vice versa.

VARIABILITY

The incidence of favourable variability, arising from either internal or external sources, may be regarded as a potential opportunity and therefore desirable to the hospitality organization. For example, much of the government's deregulation and privatization programme over the last decade, especially in compulsory competitive tendering for catering and leisure services supply contracts, has been viewed as highly desirable compared to the previous *status quo* by many hospitality organizations. On the other hand, adverse variability is generally viewed as undesirable and a threat. In such cases variability essentially becomes a 'control' and/or 'avoidance' issue. This raises the key question; to what extent can undesirable variations be reduced, minimized, eliminated or avoided altogether by a hospitality organization?

The answer to this question is that such an ability is itself variable. The extent to which variability is controllable largely depends upon the source and nature of the variability, and the efficacy of those systems which the hospitality organization has in place for such purposes. On the issue of sources there are two fundamental options; internal or external. In general, variability arising from internal sources is easier to predict and conducive to greater degrees of control by the hospitality organization. On the other hand, externally generated variability is much harder to predict and manage due to the lack of control which the organization has in general over the external aspects of its operating environment. For example, changes in government policy, competitors' pricing strategies, customer priorities and new product developments are often extremely difficult to predict until they happen and when they do they frequently demand a response, or series of responses, from the hospitality organization.

The original 3 Vs model (see Figure 13.1) indicated that external variability is primarily generated through instability in either the product or resource markets faced by the hospitality organization. Though the genesis of such variability may lie in the wider dimensions of the macro business environment faced by the organization, e.g. government policy or demographic change, the effects of these wider changes are frequently channelled through the organization's interaction with its more immediate environment in the form of product and resource markets. Taking the view that hospitality organizations effectively operate as an 'open system' (Fitzsimmons and Sullivan, 1982; Mullins, 1993), and therefore are organisms which engage in a continual interplay of ongoing exchange with their environments (Chase and Aquilano, 1977), leads to the conclusion that variability is an inevitable issue for such organizations.

With such a variable, and inherently unstable, interface between the hospitality organization and its environment, the extent to which variability will impact upon the organization's ability to create and maintain desirable levels of product/service quality will largely be determined by the degree of instability and complexity which is reflected in this interface (Child, 1972; Duncan, 1972), and how effectively the organization manages these interactions in terms of balancing the need for flexibility/adaptation at the interface whilst maintaining internal stability. Where either product and/or resource markets are highly variable, in terms of a high frequency, extent and rate of change, and complex, in terms of a large number of variables which may change, they will be characterized by 'turbulence' (Turton, 1991).

The degree of turbulence experienced by a hospitality organization in its product market(s) will tend to be determined by a combination of 'demand' and 'structural' factors. In the case of the former, highly diverse and fragmented market patterns of customer demand, frequently evident in multi-segment markets, uncertain and rapidly changing customer quality expectations, and high levels of price sensitivity and/or fashionability, will create significant degrees of turbulence. In case of the latter, high levels of buyer power, competitive intensity, market saturation and product differentiation, vulnerability to close substitutes, susceptibility to the vagaries of economic cycles, short and unpredictable product life cycles, and operational and/or product obsolescence created by rapid technological change, will similarly generate an enormous amount of turbulence.

The implications of a given level of market turbulence for hospitality product/service quality will depend upon the extent to which the hospitality organization is able to exert control over such turbulence and therefore minimize the potentially damaging effects it may have on quality. As we have argued previously (Brotherton and Coyle, 1990a), hospitality organizations tend to have a greater potential to exert control over resource markets, through controlling input sourcing, purchase frequency and supply stability, than is possible in the case of product markets. In the latter, both customer and competitor actions introduce significant control problems (Porter, 1985).

Therefore, where such control is lost or unachievable the effects of the instability and complexity this creates will be transmitted to, and reflected in, the hospitality organization's ability to both maintain operational efficiencies and deliver the desired level of product/service quality. This is especially true in the short term, where it may be difficult, if not impossible, to change direction (vector) and move out of more turbulent markets/segments into more stable ones. In the short term it may be possible for the hospitality organization to support its quality objectives by actively seeking to manage the external turbulence it is experiencing through the process of demand management

(Rhyne, 1988; Barnett, 1988; Douglas, 1988; Armistead *et al.*, 1988; Jones, 1988). However, persistent turbulence over the longer term may require more dramatic responses on the part of the hospitality organization, e.g. a change in strategic direction and/or a fundamental revision of the organization's internal structure and processes.

The main quality issue for a hospitality organization facing this type of situation is that frequent adjustments to the organization's internal operating systems and products will introduce a significant increase in product and/or process variety, and hence detract from its attempts to pursue effective quality assurance and/or control policies and procedures. Alternatively, an attempt to simply maintain existing internal systems in the face of changing customer quality demands or competitor quality improvements will ultimately lead to a lack of long-term viability (Gale and Buzzell, 1989).

This is a type of 'Catch 22' situation, wherein the hospitality organization needs to develop a sufficiently flexible and adaptive interface between itself and its markets, whilst maintaining a relatively stable internal environment. This is the flexibility–stability dilemma we identified in the original 3 Vs work (Brotherton and Coyle, 1990a, b, 1991a, b). For the hospitality organization to simultaneously maintain the degree of internal stability required to support its quality assurance and control objectives in respect of its products and processes, and create the flexible responsiveness necessary to ensure ongoing congruence between the quality its product/service offers and the changing expectations of its customers, is undoubtedly a difficult challenge. However, it is not an impossible mission!

The solution to this dilemma may lie in the creation of what has been termed 'dynamic stability' (Boynton and Victor, 1991). Essentially this concept entails the decoupling of the organization's product and process capabilities by severing the link between the idea of synonymous product and process life cycles: in other words, the creation of more generic process capabilities which support a wider range of product variety. With less variety and variability in the organization's basic processes, stability is enhanced and 'internal' quality therefore becomes easier to both assure and control.

This implies that the wider the range of product/service variations these core processes support, the greater will be the ability of the hospitality organization to maintain the required degree of product–market fit, and hence achieve a more effective ongoing congruence between the quality expectations of its customers and its product offer. Dynamic stability is a further development from the tangible–intangible decoupling ideas proposed by a number of hospitality commentators (Voss *et al.*, 1988; Armistead *et al.*, 1988; Jones, 1988). Whilst these authors frequently take the existing process–product configuration to be a constant, the dynamic stability view would suggest a more radical approach to both process and product redesign. We shall return to this issue when considering variety later in this chapter.

VECTOR

This V is important both in its own right and as a link, particularly between the Vs of variability and variety. The concept of vector is essentially concerned with direction, and therefore is inextricably linked with strategy within the hospitality organization. Perhaps the most fundamental strategic decision taken by a hospitality organization is that of its basic direction. This will be informed by a view of what business it is in or wishes to be in, its strategic objectives, and the strategic options available to it.

The decisions made at this stage of the process will carry significant implications for the ability of the hospitality organization to create and manage quality. For example, a strategy designed to create a highly diversified corporate structure will tend to raise significant issues for the creation and maintenance of quality across the corporate entity, as it is likely to carry the consequence of high levels of variability and variety, which tend to be endemic in diversified businesses. This is particularly true in the case of unrelated diversification, where variability and variety in products, markets, structures, operational systems, processes and cultures is often considerable. The existence of such a diversified operating environment, both internally and externally, poses enormous coordination and planning problems which, in turn, are likely to be reflected in the deliverable quality of the organization's output. In short, it gives rise to higher levels of undesirable complexity and instability.

It is not surprising, therefore, that many hospitality organizations who pursued diversification strategies in the 1970s and 1980s are now seeking to reverse this process by reorienting their strategies towards a greater focus and concentration upon their 'core' businesses. For example, Grand Metropolitan went through this process in the 1980s and, more recently, it has been apparent that Forte's divestment of companies such as Gardner Merchant indicates a strategy of focusing upon its core hotel business. Similarly, a major effect of the Monopolies and Mergers Commission's (MMC) 'Supply of Beer' investigation has been to force the major, vertically integrated, brewing/licensed retail companies to re-evaluate their basic strategies towards more focused business entities in either the brewing or licensed retail sectors.

Given the choice of strategic direction, there are two important aspects of vector for a hospitality organization: the speed and magnitude of such travel along the desired path. These are both fundamental strategic change issues. Other things being equal, it is reasonable to contend that the faster a hospitality organization attempts to travel along its desired strategic path, the more difficulty it is likely to experience in maintaining the quality of its operations and products. Similarly, it is also likely that the faster the rate of travel and change experienced by the organization, the greater will be the levels of undesirable instability and complexity it has to contend with. Furthermore, where a fast rate of strategic change is combined with a radically different strategic direction, the hospitality organization will face a potential dual threat to its ability to maintain/improve the quality of its output.

As we have explored in more detail previously (Brotherton and Coyle, 1990a, b) the strategic process creates the basic framework within which operational plans and action are determined. It also tends to reflect and transmit the degree of turbulence existing in the external environment to the organization's internal environment. As the organization attempts to maintain 'market-fit', through either proactive or reactive adjustments within its strategic process, there will inevitably be changes in direction or vector. Such changes are likely to create instability within the organization as a whole and, depending upon their nature, may also tend to generate greater operational complexity. For example, where environmental uncertainty is high it has been suggested that strategic decision-making and executive information processing becomes more complex, the organization's vision more clouded, and its performance reduced (Wiersema and Bantel, 1993).

Earlier we proposed the hypothesis: 'stability = greater potential for high quality', and vice versa; now we must ask the question, is it really this simple? The answer is probably 'no' in relation to the issue of vector. Strategic and operational change is inevitable for a hospitality organization operating in a dynamic environment. Therefore, stability is a relative concept. On the one hand, stability may equate to minimal changes of direction in the short term. Alternatively, it may only be achievable in the longer term through major changes in direction.

Where the external environment is relatively stable, and continues to offer significant commercial opportunities, the hospitality organization may prosper through relatively minor strategic and operational adjustments. The basic direction or vector remains the same and only small-scale corrective action to maintain course is required. Instability and complexity are relatively low, and therefore the potential for a focus on quality improvement and strong financial performance is high. This stability should facilitate organizational learning and a type of 'continuous improvement' process in relation to current products/processes. Unfortunately these benefits are rarely achieved by organizations facing this type of situation. They tend to feel 'safe', become lazy and use such stability to simultaneously disregard the quality desires of the customer and generate excess profit. Good examples of this in the hospitality industry have been the behaviour of the major brewing companies prior to the recent MMC-inspired upheaval, and public sector catering operations prior to the introduction of 'compulsory competitive tendering'.

Very high levels of stability may therefore be counterproductive with regard to enhanced quality. Though stability *per se* does provide a strong potential for quality improvement, experience appears to suggest that organizations will not take a pro-active approach to this issue where they do not have to. In short, there has to be a 'threshold' level of motivation for organizations to move away from the 'easy route' to one where quality issues assume a greater degree of importance. This threshold will undoubtedly be reached at different levels by different managers/organizations and is therefore difficult to define precisely. Further empirical research is required to explore this issue in more detail.

At the other end of the continuum very high levels of environmental instability may paradoxically be conducive to the achievement of significant quality improvements. When major discontinuities arise in one or more of the various independent cycles constituting the external environment, the hospitality organization may be forced to re-vector its activities. New competitive conditions, technological change, government legislation and product–market shifts may pose opportunities or threats of such a magnitude that they cannot be ignored. Radical changes of direction may be demanded for survival.

These conditions may force hospitality organizations to focus upon quality improvements as a fundamental source of competitive advantage in the new environment. Where this is the case there will be major changes in strategic, organizational and operational direction to achieve the desired quality objectives. This, in turn, will create high levels of instability, and possibly complexity, in the short term as the organization attempts to make the necessary adjustments. However, in the longer term, achievement of the quality objectives will provide greater focus, stability, security and an ongoing commitment to continuous quality improvement as a source of survival/success. Unfortunately such radical re-vectoring is likely to be a painful and expensive process for all concerned, especially in the short term. Again, the brewing and public sector catering sectors provide excellent examples of such painful transitions.

To reconcile the demands of the 6 Vs, hospitality organizations should avoid both extremes of the high stability–instability continuum. High stability offers the potential for a relatively constant vector and hence quality improvement. On the other hand, high instability provides the motivational strength necessary to realize such potential.

The message, in terms of the 'vector–quality' interrelationship, would appear to be one of proactive and future-oriented management action which recognizes the need to realize the potential for quality improvement in relatively stable conditions as a means of avoiding unavoidable and forced change in the absence of such action. Planned redirection, whilst continually developing quality, will enable the organization to remain on the desired vector and improve its competitiveness at the same time. There is an alternative to atrophy and/or blind panic!

VARIETY

The relationship between variety and quality is a complex one. On the one hand, it may be argued that a reduction in variety *per se* would tend to allow the hospitality organization to concentrate its efforts and focus more effectively upon the creation and delivery of a quality product/service. However, it could equally be argued that greater variety in both product range and the delivery process may help the organization to tailor, or 'customize', its offer to the varying needs and expectations of its target customers. The central issue here is whether such variety is planned and desirable, or has merely arisen as a consequence of unplanned and unforeseen actions.

This raises the question: to what extent is quality in the hospitality organization's products/services dependent upon the elimination of undesirable variety and the promotion of desirable variety? Probably the truthful answer to this is that it is not absolutely clear. However, there may be good reasons to believe that there is value in attempts to investigate this line of thought further (Wild, 1984; Hill, 1983; Jones, 1988). In both manufacturing and service industry contexts, attempts to control such desirable/undesirable variety have long been associated with the application of the 3 Ss: simplification, standardization and specialization.

Simplification is usually primarily concerned with the elimination of unwanted or undesirable products form the product range. However, in a wider context, simplification is concerned with the reduction of complexity throughout the organization. Standardization addresses the issue of product specifications in an attempt to identify the degree of commonality existing in the components and/or processes used to create this range. Finally, specialization, operating within the rationalized environment created as a consequence of the two previous stages, is now employed to focus the organization's efforts upon those activities capable of generating the greatest added value. Therefore, the enhanced focus to an organization's operations/product range, which emanates from an application of the 3 Ss, should help to reduce operational complexity, lead to greater stability, and improve the probability that the resultant output will be of both a higher and more constant level of quality. In short, it should help to achieve a more 'streamlined' organization (Harrington, 1991).

However, whilst the progression above is undoubtedly logical, reality may not be quite as simple. In a manufacturing context, where there are both clear physical and temporal discontinuities between the production processes and final product delivery, this type of simple rationalization process may indeed provide these types of benefits. On the other hand, in a service/hospitality context, such discontinuities frequently either do not exist or are not as readily identifiable. Here the operational situation is often characterized by a need to manage the apparent paradox of a rationalized production process with a delivery process which is 'customized' to the needs of its recipients at, or near to, the point of sale/consumption.

Though a similar process may arise in certain manufactured products, it usually differs from hospitality situations in the sense that there is frequently a significant time delay between standardized production and customized delivery in manufacturing environments, and the nature of the final transaction tends not to be as individual or potentially volatile. Therefore, the successful application of the 3 Ss approach in a manufacturing context largely depends upon the physical and temporal separation of production and delivery. In addition, it is also frequently dependent upon the identification, and application, of more flexible or generic process capabilities related to higher unit production volumes.

In many hospitality environments, particularly those associated with higher quality/ price operations, it can be difficult to secure this type of separation and commonality of process. Indeed, many more 'traditional' hospitality managers would view such moves as being total anathema to their philosophy of hospitality provision, and a serious threat to their perception of what constitutes a quality product. On the other hand, the success of a number of hospitality organizations is often heavily dependent upon the application of these streamlining principles. For example, many of the branded 'chain' operations in the hotel and restaurant sectors of the industry have achieved significant levels of cost and quality control through standardization in recipes, menus, portions, suppliers, operational formats and policies.

Unfortunately, however, although these rationalization efforts tend to be focused mainly upon the input and production aspects of the hospitality operation, they also have a high propensity to be carried through to the delivery stage. This means that the customer can be faced with a rather sterile and 'faceless' interface at the point of delivery, wherein any individualization in either the product or its delivery is extremely limited at best, and non-existent at worst. Therefore, hospitality organizations face a dilemma: standardization and enhanced internal control versus customization and superior external flexibility.

A strategy which emphasizes standardization is frequently seen as one which effectively supports the internal control process within the company through the potential benefits it offers for efficiency and cost control. However, the tight control of variety created by an application of standardization principles may lead to serious competitive disadvantages in the marketplace because it tends to lead to an internal product/process focus, and an implied view that the market is either relatively homogeneous in terms of its needs/priorities or sufficiently undifferentiated to justify the provision of an 'averaged' product/service offer. In short, a standardization strategy may assist in the control of undesirable internal variety but it also tends to reduce desirable external variety.

On the other hand, a strategy which emphasizes customization suggests a customer or market orientation which will be highly flexible in meeting the diversity evident in the company's market, and its various segments. This approach should yield considerable competitive advantages in the marketplace, as the product/service offer will closely reflect the variety of customer groups, and their needs/wants. However, this can be a potentially expensive strategy for operational costs due to the large increase in the variety of product/service offers it may create through 'process proliferation' and relatively small production runs.

Both standardization and customization have a central concern with variety, even though they are diametrically opposed and focus upon variety in different domains. Standardization is concerned with the control, reduction or elimination of undesirable variety in the company's processes and product range. Customization tends to focus more upon product–market fit and delivery interface issues, and is concerned with the promotion and expansion of desirable variety in this domain. This dichotomy also reflects a central issue in the quality debate: the internal 'production' quality focus versus the external 'customer' quality focus. Therefore, there is a link between the 'standardization–customization' common denominator (variety) and quality. The product/process approach to quality emphasizes variety control/reduction, whilst the market/customer approach to quality emphasizes variety promotion.

Therefore, the question is: can the standardization–customization paradox be reconciled through the development of a coherent policy designed to achieve a simultaneous reduction in undesirable, internal variety and an increase in desirable, external variety? If either policy is adopted as a general *modus operandi* across the full range of an organization's operations, the answer to this must be no. However, if the principles of 'dynamic stability' (Boynton and Victor, 1991) are applied, the answer may be yes. Pine (1993) suggests that this is possible if organizations pursue a strategy of 'mass customization'. This he defines as 'A synthesis of the two long competing systems of management: the mass production of individually customised goods and services' (Pine, 1993, p. 48).

Dynamic stability and mass customization are inextricably linked to the issues of variety and quality, and provide an opportunity to disaggregate the simultaneous application of standardization and customization policies. This is achievable by severing the dedicated product–process link, so common in both manufacturing and service environments, by investigating the potential for a greater application of more generic processes, thereby reducing process variety, and flexible product configuration techniques, thereby increasing product offer variety. In turn, this should lead to improvements in both process/production and product/delivery quality, particularly if the principles of modularization are applied to the operation's product/process configuration.

VARIANCE

As we have argued earlier in this chapter, the response to complexity and instability in the external environment leads to an insidious potential for elaboration and inconsistency in the management of operations. The central quality management issue, therefore, is the assessment and limitation of negative effect. It is clear that variance from expected results can be positive or negative. However, merely describing variance as either positive or negative does little to explain the effects of such variance. Clearly, both positive and negative variance can be 'desirable' or 'undesirable'. Achievement in excess of expectations is one source of reward for managing operations. However, the elimination of negative effect is also an essential task for managers.

Further, the question arises concerning whether the desirable effects of instability can be planned for and managed. By their very nature variances arise because there is discrepancy between what actually happened and what was expected. If the inevitability of variance, negative or positive, planned or unplanned, is accepted then the principal concerns for hospitality organizations are to control, limit or reduce the negative effects, and encourage, promote, develop and extend the positive.

Berry *et al.* (1990) built on earlier work to recognize variance in service quality provision by identification of the gaps which occur in the transactions between customers and providers. Coyle and Dale (1993) use the earlier framework of service characteristics to establish both gaps and priorities for hospitality provision in reducing the potential for an incidence of the negative effects of variance. It is the management of such gaps, to minimize negative effect, which provides the opportunity to ensure quality in hospitality service. The quality assurance system applied to service should necessarily provide for the likelihood of mismatching between expectation and experience. Martin (1986) outlines an elegant appraisal strategy for the assessment and audit of customer service, which assists in the bridging of gaps through a checklist of 'solution criteria'. Irrespective of whether quality is 'assured in' or 'inspected in', some process must be available to recover the ground between what is expected and what is experienced.

Coyle and Dale (1993) propose a set of essentials for assuring minimal variance which may negatively affect perceptions of product or service quality. To offer a model, in visual terms, we use an analogy associated with an electrical connection. Figure 13.3 outlines the basic principles drawn from those essentials:

- Clear definition of product – designing the 'plug' to fit the socket.
- Management of culture and procedures relating to the assurance of quality – ensuring that the plug only fits one way.
- Management of the gaps in both insight and experience which are likely to occur – ensuring the continuity of supply of energy/power.

Clear definition of the product (assuring the specification does not facilitate negative variance)

The product requirements, as defined and detailed by the customer, can be seen as the 'socket' which connects the product to satisfaction or even delight! Ensuring that the product matches those requirements is a fundamental aim of hospitality provision. Validity of the service is dependent upon the plug fitting the socket as precisely as possible, i.e. with little or no variation. The scope of potential for variance to occur, of course, will depend on the situational variables relating to both customers and providers. The particular characteristics of service quality determined by Berry *et al.* (1990) may be seen to represent the connecting pins in this electrical analogy.

Managing the culture and procedures relating to quality (assuring minimal negative variance in approach)

The primary effects of culture and procedures should be to guarantee the validity and reliability of the 'product'. The pursuit of ideologies such as total quality management (TQM) and system accreditation through British Standards and/or ISO only tends to cloud the issues. As such, these outward manifestations of quality generally concern themselves with reliability and not necessarily with validity. The issue of validity of a product or service is left, and should be, with the customer alone. Closeness and listening to the customer (Peters, 1987) offers an opportunity to narrow the gap and potential for negative variance; indeed, to ensure that the plug (product) can only fit the socket (customer requirements and expectations) in one way.

Managing the gaps (recognize potential for variance in spite of our best efforts)

As we have argued in our earlier work (Brotherton and Coyle, 1990a, b, 1991a, b), managers and providers need the necessary skills and cognitive ability to accurately assess customer needs and wants. Consequently, variety in the product offering, and the likelihood of not being 100 per cent error free, demands that adequate recovery mechanisms are in place and capable of restoring complete customer satisfaction. The potential for variance, or interruptions to the flow of energy/power, are discussed in Coyle and Dale (1993). They can be summarized as follows:

- faulty perceptions of what customers want – wrong voltage;
- meeting some expectations occasionally – intermittent power;
- not keeping promises – variable voltage;
- insufficient resources – blown fuse;
- personal intervention – short circuit.

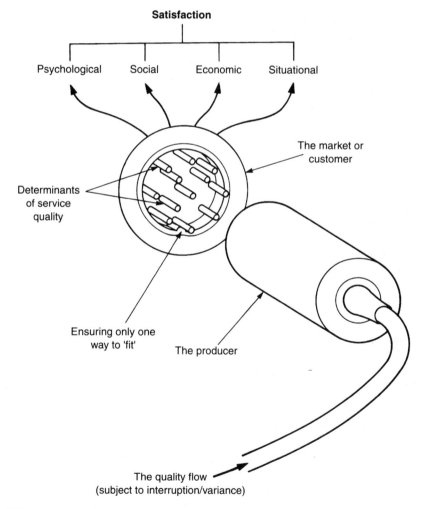

Figure 13.3 *Assuring minimal variance*

From the customer's point of view, exceeding expectation is perceived as the 'Holy Grail' of service quality. Alternatively, a failure to live up to promises, either implied or explicit, is a critical aspect of customer satisfaction. The current vogue for seeking customer 'delight' rather than the more limited goal of 'satisfaction' is a testimony to this. In this respect positive variance is seen as a desirable outcome. Production and process stability, consistency and reliability promote positive variance only when the process is geared to provide a 'valid' product. The current debate in the hospitality trade press, concerning the appropriateness of third party certification for hospitality and service providers, reveals that conformance to national standards does not guarantee customer approval (Coyle and Dale, 1993; Hutchins, 1990). If the process or delivery system is right but the product is wrong, there is no virement in customer expectation.

The economic framework of process and product management depends on variance as a control imperative. Shewhart (1931) and many others have espoused that the ultimate success of operations lies in the measurement and reduction of variance and its negative effects as the prime function of process control (Buffa and Sarin, 1987). The identification and elimination of 'common' and 'special' causes of variation has occupied writers since the end of World War II (Dale and Plunkett, 1990a). Therefore, we must accept variance as a principal component of our daily lives.

Our earlier views explored the insidiousness of variance and variety (Brotherton and Coyle, 1990a, b, 1991a, b). In building on this work it is clear that statistical process control (SPC) and variance analysis offer specific techniques for the identification, measurement and ultimate control of variation through the application of control charts which show actual performance against upper and lower control limits. The aim of such recording is to reduce variation and make the process more predictable (Garrity, 1993). Unfortunately, these methods are often construed as apportioning 'blame' to product, process or producer. However, such control is only made possible and valid with the existence of a propensity to accept tolerances and the availability of historical or extrapolated data. The ability to manage depends on the ability to interpret the signals and signs presented. Owen recognizes these weaknesses:

> Toleration and specification limits are only part of a much wider problem. Targets, quotas, grading of staff, appraisal, management by objectives all represent imposition of artificial limits on a system. It is the natural performance of people and processes within the system that lies at the heart of improvement ... (Owen, 1991, p. 35)

In our 3 Vs work we suggested that when variance arises in the form of variety, from a stable base, it may be seen as a positive advantage (Brotherton and Coyle, 1991a). This is particularly true in the hospitality environment, where, for the customer, a variation in response may be seen as a strength and positive attribute, especially of those offering individualized and custom-built contractual services. The traditional pressure to eliminate the causes and negative effects of variation, often regarded as 'errors' (Rosander, 1989), to ensure quality in products and services, whilst essential for control purposes, tends to militate against flexibility in response to market and environmental changes.

Historically, hospitality products and services have been mainly designed and delivered in specific response to individual requirements for consumption or use, e.g. provision for the family or for workers on an estate. This generated a type of 'bespoke' approach to the management of variance, with tight specification and regular progress checks against sets of likes and dislikes of the main group influencers. However, with the advent of the industrial revolution, and the consequent drive for mass production and economies of scale, the focus moved to one which sought to satisfy most of the people most of the time. This created a principle of production encouraged by the emergence of the 'brand' as a guarantee of product conformance to predetermined company standards.

It also spawned the development of the specialist/expert; the engineer, the doctor and the designer who told the customer/consumer what they wanted whilst primarily seeking to meet the requirements of the producer. In this perspective, quality variance was controlled out by 'gatekeepers' or inspectors, whose job it was to reject production, and in doing so generate waste and loss. More recent emphasis on the need to 'assure' quality by minimizing the negative effects of variance via tight specifications and attempts to eliminate non-conformance during the process is now accepted as a more effective approach.

Clearly, there are many perspectives on the notion of value. Value to whom? Value compared to what? Our emphasis, relating to the customers' perceptions of 'value' in hospitality provision, poses something of a dichotomy. On the one hand, as satisfied customers will testify, value, i.e. value for money, can be experienced regularly and reliably in any number of establishments. Customers are pleased to include 'value for money' in the criteria for judging quality in hospitality provision (Coyle and Dale, 1993). On the other, however, customers are also quick to make comparisons, say between the price of wines in supermarkets and those on the majority of restaurant lists.

What is clear is that the customer's assessment of value generally encompasses a 'package' of elements, or what has been referred to over many years as 'the meal experience' (Campbell-Smith, 1967). For example, eating away from home presents an amalgam of 'trade-offs' and compromises between a range of requirements and satisfactions in order to appraise 'value'. The interplay of situation, circumstances and availability all conspire to diffuse a clear understanding and acceptance of a standard for value. For example, scenes showing Bosnian refugees offering their contemporaries a bottle of shampoo for a price equal to one month's wages, or the pleasure derived from a meal at an award-winning restaurant for the equivalent of 20 times that amount, give an indication of the complexities of perceptions of 'value for money'.

That the consumer should experience quality at a reasonable price is at the heart of attempts to provide quality service, i.e. the return value of the service is equal to or greater than the contribution made for it. The problem arises, however, in the judgement of what is 'quality', what is 'value' and what is 'reasonable'. Gale and Buzzell (1989, p. 8) conclude that: ' ... quality (and value) is whatever the customer says it is and that he (the customer) makes his assessment on the basis of comparison: Is this offering better or worse than those of competitors.' In spite of this cost–benefit relationship, recent research (Coyle and Dale, 1993) showed that value for money was only fifth in the 'critical' priorities of customers' perception of quality in hospitality operations.

The processes used by customers to make assessments of 'value' are widely and comprehensively discussed in the literature. Amongst the interpretations of value as a concept of the human and organizational condition, discussions vary from the psychological perspectives relating to 'clarification of values' (Vroom, 1964; Porter and Lawler, 1968; Kirschenbaum, 1977), and the 'personal construct theories' of Kelly (1963) to those most closely associated with marketing (Kotler, 1984). Clearly, value provides a particularly powerful weapon in the war for competitive advantage, particularly in a congested and competitive industry. Convincing evidence to support this view is contained in the recent results of investigations into customer versus provider perceptions of quality and value (Berry *et al.*, 1990; Coyle and Dale, 1993). This work suggests that misalignment of those perceptions is a pervasive barrier to customer satisfaction in this area.

Alternative interpretation and application comes from the sphere of operations and production management (Adam and Ebert, 1989; Wild, 1984), and in financial management (Glautier and Underdown, 1976). Whilst financial imperatives look to the value issue in terms of realizable benefits and are concerned with the protection of asset values, value analysis and value engineering set an agenda which is clearly associated with the economics of production and service provision (Wild, 1984). Given the costs of inventory and the ever-present demand to reduce 'set-up' and 'changeover' costs, to have smaller 'economic order quantities' and to increase flexibility, it is not surprising that manufacturing organizations seek solace in the technologies and procedures linked with Japanese methods of Just-In-Time (JIT) (Dale and Plunkett, 1990a), all of which concentrate attention on the quality–cost–price relationship. Demand-driven supply is, of course, not new to hospitality providers. In the pursuit of value from the production system, fast-food companies such as McDonald's have long been associated with standardization and 'order-free' systems, where tills log stock uplift requirements directly from sales and orders are collated and sent automatically via modem to central suppliers.

The concept of added value also continues to be a theme of product differentiation. Efforts over the last few years have given rise to a transformation in the provision of hospitality and the search for uniqueness. Examples range from merchandising efforts, implied value by description, and sound pricing strategies to positive contributions to customers' perceptions with genuine attempts to provide real value in the product offer through portion size and variety. Jones and Lockwood (1989) report 'value for money' being evaluated according to three measurable aspects of perceived value. The operational benefits of adding value are not confined to customer perception. Strategies for the management of menus and drinks lists assume that products are subject to the rigours of the 'product life cycle'. As such, Fuller and Waller (1991) suggest that added value offers promotional possibilities, or at least alternatives to elimination for under-achieving menu items.

VIABILITY

The association between an organization's 'viability' and its external environment is clear. Viability is jointly dependent upon:

- the environment being 'sympathetic' to survival, with beneficial or at least predictable behaviour in environmental, technological, political and other domains;
- a correct assessment of the environment in which that operation works;
- the efficacy of consequential action.

Any environmental assessment must be treated as a perishable product. Late assessment and/or action could be just as fatal as inappropriate assessment and action. Similarly, precipitate action in response to environmental assessment may also store problems for later periods when conditions subtly change. As a result there are considerable pressures for adaptability, flexibility, creativity, innovation and, in the short run, nerve and conviction in the pursuit of survival. Survival is often a perquisite of appropriate performance rather than a prerequisite.

The linkage between viability and quality can be justified by the same arguments used to warrant quality on economic grounds; namely that the longer-term costs associated with the prevention of error can be more than covered by the savings available from both the reduced costs of corrective action and reductions in wasted effort. Dale and Plunkett (1990b) suggest that, conservatively, between 10 per cent and 20 per cent of an organization's revenue can be accounted for by 'quality costs'. At a time when viability cannot be assured by increasing market share or price, considerable benefit can be afforded through close scrutiny of quality costs and the shift of emphasis from inspection activity to that of prevention. Any savings from the latter source can be directly attributable to the bottom line and hence increased viability.

Dictionary definitions for 'viability' tend to emphasize this survival perspective, with references to capability for normal growth and development, independence, etc. The issue of viability is central to any assessment of the value of any effort applied to ensure the survival of hospitality operations. The origin of the term in the biological assessment of survival is apposite. A conceptual framework to understand the interdependent relationships can also be drawn from the biological sciences. On the one hand, viability in the system of provision is dependent on the effectiveness, efficiency, economy and productivity of the activities and processes comprising the system. On the other, viability is dependent on at least a state of equilibrium between investment in, and outcomes from, the system.

In the case of 'system viability', an assessment is made of the constituent parts of the operational system, whereas 'investment viability' is assessed by reference to the system as a whole. Figure 13.4 attempts to illustrate both aspects and interpretations of survivability. In the context of the 6 Vs model, it is clear that any indication of tumult or unpredictability in the external environment will impact upon the hospitality organization's ability to survive. However, this is not to say that instability is necessarily negative. As we have indicated earlier, the impact may be highly advantageous. The ability of the manager/owner to identify and seize potential is still determined by his or her ability to read the runes and interpret the signs as and when they are presented. The nature of the hospitality industry generally militates against optimizing advantage by concentrating effort and managerial competence on 'hands-on' operational issues rather than environmental scanning, creativity and innovation (Guerrier and Lockwood, 1989).

The assessment of outcomes from any hospitality provision is clearly a constant feature of management. Management activity at operational level tends to concentrate on 'incurring costs, making sales and recouping costs'. Clearly, however, the recouping of costs alone is not sufficient to ensure viability. The 'Recouping cost ... plus' box in Figure 13.4 refers to the generation of profit, surplus, contribution, etc. so as not to preclude operations which may not be oriented towards profitability as a natural outcome. The appraisal of the system's performance and its characteristic elements is generally a function of the assignation of values which are used as hard measures, e.g. costs against budget, an assessment of the acceptability of cost incurment being made according to whether the cost matches expectations or whether it can be justified, as discussed earlier in this chapter. However, whatever measures are used, ultimately customer satisfaction will dictate viability or otherwise. Table 13.1 suggests a range of possible examples for these hard measures. Clearly, each of these elements will have an associated subsystem responsible for that element's contribution to the whole provision

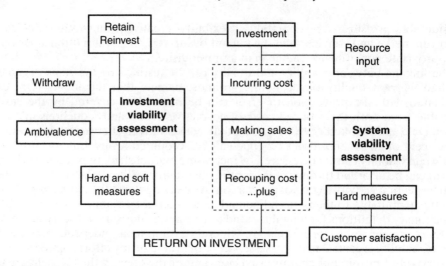

Figure 13.4 *System and investment viability assessment*

system. Consequently, each of the subsystems therefore impacts upon the ability of the whole organization to survive.

Much has been written recently about the 'soft' or 'intangible' elements of hospitality provision (King, 1989), and their particular contribution to the issue of viability. This is true in the context of their relationship to service quality. Unfortunately, there is very little reference in this literature to the survival of hospitality services on the strength of the quality of services alone. The role of quality in viability is left to that of offering a

Table 13.1 *The assessment of system performance via hard measures*

Incurring cost		Making sales		Recouping costs	
Element	Measure	Element	Measure	Element	Measure
Labour	Wages, hours	Training	Cost per trainee, additional revenue generated	Pricing	Customer comment, level of resistance
Food/drink	Food cost %, variance analysis	Promotional activity	Occupancy rates	Profit levels	Gross profit %, net profit %, stock realization
Production	Energy, standard costing	Merchandising	Customer comment, costs, additional sales	Consistency of costs	Waste, loss and fraud
Overhead	Cost allocation	Payment methods	Additional sales	Volume	Average spend, occupancy rates

differentiating feature for providers to encourage use and participation in provision and, as a result, increase revenue and hopefully profitability. Genuine attempts to match customer requirements are, however, insufficient on their own. Whilst justification can be given for the pursuit of quality on economic grounds (Hutchins, 1990), the equation that quality *per se* equals survival is fallacious. Similarly, the notion that appropriate quality attitudes amongst staff and managers will ensure profitability and subsequent survival is likewise flawed. Attitudes must be supported with appropriate, cost-efficient and effective systems which make the quality effort worthwhile.

Turning now to the issues associated with 'investment viability', it should be noted that investment, in this context, includes the combined efforts of those who might have an interest in the survival of the business (stakeholders) and those who make decisions about the application of resources on a day-by-day basis. For all, an assessment of the survivability of a given type of hospitality provision is subject to the rigours of hard measures in the same way as the system elements previously described. The difference is that the appraisal of investment, and associated assessment of viability for those investments, is subject to a greater influence from the softer characteristics of analysis. The decision to invest may be a response to a good idea rather than a specific gain in hard, measurable terms. Similarly, the decision to withdraw investment may be made in spite of economic assurances of reasonable return. It is the totality of the investment decision that occupies this further review of viability.

An additional conceptual reference point for investment viability assessment can be taken once more from the biological/clinical field: from psychology, and in particular the work of Porter and Lawler (1968). Their work on the psychology of motivation builds on earlier work conducted by Vroom (1964), which postulates that behaviour is influenced by an individual's expectations of what might happen as a result, i.e. expectancy–valence theory. This link between viability and investment is less tenuous than it may appear. A state of equilibrium in the system of operation will at best maintain the *status quo*, and at worst will lead to the establishment of further subsystems and processes affecting variety and, potentially, viability (Koontz and O'Donnell, 1976).

Any attempt to sustain a set position in revenue and profitability over the medium or longer term should be seen as suicidal. Growth is the antidote to this particular strategic fatality. The pressures faced by providers (managers and owners) to continually reduce unit and operating costs, increase revenue, increase market share, etc. will inevitably affect the return on investment. The natural consequence is for that provision to attract greater investment, thereby placing greater pressure on the system which will affect the viability of the system. An additional dimension is that relating to the organizational culture, priorities and attitudes towards viability and survival. This issue offers fruitful potential for further research.

Figure 13.5 represents the relationship of expectancy and viability. The model is adapted from Porter and Lawler (1968) and the later work of Cooper and Makin (1984). We will consider this model and assess its implications for viability:

- *Perceived value of the outcome.* Value in this context could be anything associated with the operation. It is likely to be the return on investment, but could just as easily be seen as 'doing the right thing', or the investment may have an ulterior motive. Viability will be affected if the investor is ambivalent about the survival of the company.
- *Perceived effort/outcome ratio.* The assessment of the amount of effort necessary to make the investment may be construed as the impact of any loss or gain from

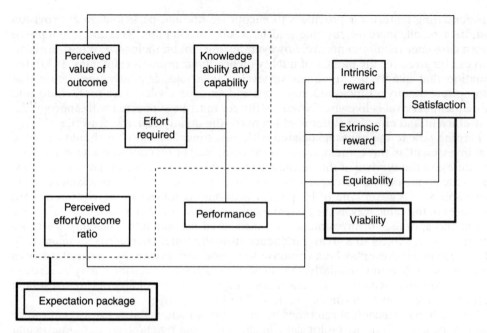

Figure 13.5 *The relationship between expectation and viability*

the investment, compared with the expected outcome. Viability may be clearly affected if actions to either increase or ensure it are perceived to be 'not worth the effort'. Also note that past success and failure will influence decisions regarding the degree of effort expended in relation to the pursuit of viability.

- *Effort required.* The model illustrates a distinction between effort and performance. That is to say that effort does not necessarily lead to achievement. Misdirected effort has clear implications for viability.
- *Knowledge, ability and capability.* This has a link with the effort required. The extent of effort will be governed by knowledge of the situation and the ability/ capability to ensure viability.
- *Performance.* Refers to the final result of effort, knowledge and abilities governed by the standards set for it to ensure viability.
- *Outcomes, extrinsic and intrinsic.* The end result of performance against which success or failure can be assessed. The extrinsic and intrinsic nature of the outcomes suggest that satisfaction is likely to be multidimensional. The strength of desire for viability, therefore, is likely to impact on viability.
- *Equitability.* On reflection, was the effort equal to, or less than, the perceived value of the outcome? Was the investment worthwhile? Either way viability is likely to be affected.
- *Satisfaction with outcomes.* On reflection, do the outcomes generate a sense of satisfaction? If satisfaction comes from the investment, then viability is assured.

The association between quality and viability is, at face value, obvious. Increased quality enhances viability, since customers are likely to prefer those operations which they perceive to match their precise requirements. That preference, if properly managed, will generate the revenue and profitability essential for survival. On the other hand, viability may not necessarily enhance quality. A concentrated effort to achieve viability, i.e. survival, would appear to do little to help the overt cause of quality. However, any attempts to consider one without the other will only serve to confuse the issue. The economic benefit derived from the implementation of a quality ethos, supported by customer orientation and sound systems, offers an enormous potential for the achievement of viability. Table 13.2 illustrates this.

The profound relationship between an organization, its people and viability is discussed at length by Beer (1991). This relationship is established through a clear understanding of the dynamics of control and communication within the organization and between the system and its environment. Beer (1991) refers to the 'cybernetic science' and 'adaptive connectivity' of the various parts and subsystems relating to the totality of the system, i.e. the often extraordinary alliances between the elements which comprise a flexible, responsive organization. Given the standard measures of performance applied in most organizations, the question arises: does satisfactory economic/financial performance assure survival? This is akin to asking whether the third party accreditation of a quality system assures customer satisfaction. Clearly, the answer is a resounding no! However, endorsing and reinforcing the adoption of system and investment viability assessment may achieve this.

CONCLUSIONS

Though there may be a feeling amongst some commentators that the quality debate is effectively over, and it is now time to move on to pastures new (i.e. business/process re-engineering/improvement), we hope that the 6 Vs approach indicates that this is far

Table 13.2 *How characteristics of quality ethos enhance viability in hospitality*

Improved design of services by building in the voice of the customer	Matching customer requirements ensures continued demand and potential for premium prices
Identification of quality costs and reduced costs of non-conformance	Elimination of waste and loss, allowing value to the customer at prices equal to those of competitors, thereby increasing market share
Reduced inventory costs	Efficient deployment of capital
Appropriate quality system	Reducing potential for fraud and concentrating effort on things that matter
Empathetic human resource management and workforce	Concentrating effort on things that matter
Training and communication	Focus on important things
Commitment of staff and management	Consistency of service and product
Reliability of service and product	Consistency and predictability, key features in influencing purchase decisions
Product specification and supplier assessment	Predictability of cost and quality
Recording and monitoring for problem-solving and continuous improvement	To cost-effectively reduce loss

from the truth. The issues associated with the 6 Vs and quality have been extensively explored, in a range of different contexts, by authors seeking to promote the debate. However, we believe there are still a number of significant questions and issues which remain unresolved within each specific area and particularly in respect of the inter-relationships between the 6 Vs and quality. Perhaps this is due to the complex dynamics this process inevitably generates.

Each of the 6 Vs requires further, detailed investigation in its own right as a significant domain of hospitality business activity. Each individual V is capable of exerting a major influence upon the success, or otherwise, of the hospitality organiza-tion, through the linkage channels of instability and complexity. Therefore, the 6 Vs in their entirety tend to have a pervasive impact on the hospitality organization. They are synergistic, in both positive and negative dimensions. Consequently, when they are linked to the crucial issue of quality, their importance becomes magnified to a greater degree.

The task of the hospitality manager is one of seeking to effectively manage the Vs, and integrate this management process with the drive for quality. This is a formidable task, and one which will not be achieved easily. Hospitality organizations will increas-ingly find that any quality 'edges' they currently have over their competitors will be eroded by all the players in the game basically playing by the same rules, and with the same deck of cards. As competition intensifies, in rapidly maturing markets, the imperative for both hospitality organizations and their managers to develop more sustainable quality advantages will intensify.

This will demand more fundamental, innovative and creative approaches to the pursuit of quality as a source of competitive advantage. Perhaps the 6 Vs approach may help to indicate why this is a crucial activity, and suggest how this may be pursued within the hospitality context. We acknowledge the fact that further work needs to be undertaken to provide a more sophisticated and systematic articulation of the dynamics of the 6 Vs/quality model but do feel that, even in its present form, it offers an interesting and valuable perspective for both academics and industry practitioners to explore further.

REFERENCES

Adam, E. E., and Ebert, R. J. (1989) *Production and Operations Management: Concepts, Models and Behaviour*, 4th edn, Prentice-Hall International, New York.

Armistead, C., Johnston, R., and Slack, N. (1988) 'The strategic determinants of service productivity', *International Journal of Operations and Production Management*, vol. **8**, no. 3, pp. 95–108.

Barnett, F. W. (1988) 'Four steps to forecast total market demand', *Harvard Business Review*, July–August, pp. 28–30, 34, 36, 38.

Beer, S. (1991) *Diagnosing the System for Organisations*, Wiley, London.

Berry, L. L. Zeithaml, V. A., and Parasuraman, A. (1990) 'Five imperatives for improving service quality', *Sloan Management Review*, Summer, pp. 29–38.

Boynton, A. C., and Victor, B. (1991) 'Beyond flexibility: building and managing the dynamically stable organisation', *California Management Review*, Fall, pp. 50–62.

Brotherton, B., and Coyle, M. (1990a) 'Managing instability in the hospitality operations environment. Part One: variability', *International Journal of Contemporary Hospitality Management*, vol. **2**, no. 3, pp. 24–32.

Brotherton, B., and Coyle, M. (1990b) 'Managing instability in the hospitality operations environment. Part Two: variety', *International Journal of Contemporary Hospitality Management*, vol. **2**, no. 4, pp. 17–24.

Brotherton, B., and Coyle, M. (1991a) 'Managing instability in the hospitality operations environment. Part Three: variance', *International Journal of Contemporary Hospitality Management*, vol. **3**, no. 1, pp. 26–31.

Brotherton, B., and Coyle, M. (1991b) 'Managing variety in the hospitality operations environment', *International Journal of Contemporary Hospitality Management*, vol. **3**, no. 2, pp. 30–2.

Buffa, E. S., and Sarin, R. K. (1987) *Modern Production/Operations Management*, 8th edn, Wiley, New York.

Campbell-Smith, G. (1967) *Marketing of the Meal Experience*, University of Surrey, Guildford.

Chase, R., and Aquilano, N. (1977) *Production and Operations Management*, Irwin Inc., Homewood, IL.

Child, J. (1972) 'Organisation structure, environment, and performance: the role of strategic choice', *Sociology*, vol. **6**, pp. 1–22.

Cooper, C. L., and Makin, P. (1984) *Psychology for Managers*, Macmillan, Basingstoke.

Coyle, M. P., and Dale, B. G. (1993) 'Quality in the hospitality industry: a study', *International Journal of Hospitality Management*, vol. **12**, no. 2, pp. 41–53.

Dale, B. G., and Plunkett, J. J. (eds) (1990a) *Managing Quality*, Philip Allen, London.

Dale, B. G., and Plunkett, J. J. (1990b) *Quality Costing*, Chapman & Hall, London.

Douglas, A. (1988) 'Build off-peak occupancy by marketing to seniors', *Hotels and Restaurants International*, September, pp. 81–2.

Duncan, R. B. (1972) 'Characteristics of organisational environments and perceived environmental uncertainty', *Administrative Science Quarterly*, vol. **17**, pp. 313–27.

Fitzsimmons, J., and Sullivan, R. (1982) *Service Operations Management*, McGraw-Hill, New York.

Fuller, J., and Waller, K. (1991) *The Menu, Food and Profit*, Stanley Thornes Ltd, London.

Gale, B. T., and Buzzell, R. D. (1989) 'Market perceived quality; key strategic concept', *The Planning Review*, March–April, pp. 6–15, 48.

Garrity, S. M. (1993) *Basic Quality Improvement*, Prentice-Hall International, New York.

Glautier, M. W., and Underdown, B. (1976) *Accounting Theory and Practice*, Pitman International, London.

Guerrier, Y., and Lockwood, A. (1989) 'Developing hotel managers – a re-appraisal', *International Journal of Hospitality Management*, vol. **8**, no. 2, pp. 82–9.

Harrington, H. J. (1991) *Business Process Improvement*, McGraw-Hill, New York.

Hill, T. (1983) *Production and Operations Management*, Prentice-Hall International, Hemel Hempstead.

Hutchins, D. (1990) *In Pursuit of Quality*, Pitman, London.

Jones, P. (1988) 'Quality, capacity and productivity in service industries', *International Journal of Hospitality Management*, vol. **7**, no. 2, pp. 104–12.

Jones, P., and Lockwood, A. (1989) *Management in Service Industries*, Pitman, London.

Kelly, G. A. (1963) *A Theory of Personality*, Norton, New York.

King, C. A. (1989) 'Service oriented quality control', *Cornell HRA Quarterly*, November, pp. 92–9.

Kirschenbaum, H. (1977) *Advanced Value Clarification*, University Associates, La Jolla, CA.

Koontz, H., and O'Donnell, C. (1976) *Management: A Systems and Contingency Analysis of Managerial Functions*, 6th edn, McGraw-Hill/Kogakusha.

Kotler, P. (1984) *Marketing Management: Analysis, Planning and Control*, 5th edn, Prentice-Hall International, New York.

Martin, W. B. (1986) 'Measuring and improving your service quality', *Cornell HRA Quarterly*, May, pp. 80–7.

Mullins, L. J. (1993) 'The hotel and the open systems model of organisational analysis', *Service Industries Journal*, vol. **13**, no. 1, pp. 1–16.

Owen, M. (1991) 'Understanding variance', *Proceedings of 4th International Conference on TQM*, Bedford, England, 3–5 June, IFS.

Peters, T. (1987), *Thriving on Chaos*, Gruid Publishing, London.

Pine, B. J. (1993) *Mass Customisation: The New Frontier in Business Competition*, Harvard Business School Press, Boston, MA.

Porter, M. (1985) *Competitive Advantage*, The Free Press, New York.

Porter, L. W., and Lawler, E. E. (1968) *Managerial Attitudes and Performance*, Irwin-Dorsey, Homewood, IL.

Rhyne, D. (1988) 'The impact of demand management on service system performance', *Service Industries Journal*, vol. **8**, no. 4, pp. 446–58.

Rosander, A. C. (1989) *The Quest for Quality in Services*, ASC Quality Press, Milwaukee.

Shewhart, W. A. (1931) *Economic Control of the Quality of the Manufactured Product*, Van Nostrand Reinhold, New York.

Turton, R. (1991) *Behaviour in a Business Context*, Chapman and Hall, London.

Voss, C., Armistead, C., Johnston, B. and Morris, B., (1988) *Operations Management in Service Industries and the Public Sector*, Wiley, New York.

Vroom, V. H. (1964) *Work and Motivation*, Wiley, New York.

Wiersema, M. F., and Bantel, K. A. (1993) 'Top management team turnover as an adaptive mechanism', *Strategic Management Journal*, vol. **14**, no. 7, pp. 485–504.

Wild, R. (1984) *Production and Operations Management*, 3rd edn, Holt, Rinehart and Winston, London.

14

Marketing quality in the hotel sector

Gail Ayala, Edward V. Staros and Joseph J. West

INTRODUCTION

This chapter explores the manner in which managers of hotel companies can utilize quality service as an effective strategic marketing tactic. The chapter begins with an overview of the service quality literature which provides a background as to the manner in which quality perceptions affect the hotel guests' decision-making processes. A discussion of the importance of the strategic quality plan to the success of individual lodging properties follows the review of the literature. Then the authors present a dynamic model to illustrate the lodging guest decision-making process, including the role played by service quality. The Ritz-Carlton Hotel Company is used as a case study to test the fit of the model on a currently successful chain in the luxury hotel market. As the first and only travel and tourism firm to win the Malcolm Baldrige National Quality Award, Ritz-Carlton has demonstrated a single-minded commitment to quality. Its experience is used to explore the role played by quality in the decision-making processes of consumers in the luxury segment of the hotel sector. They will also provide an example of the manner in which a strategic marketing plan can be used to guide quality service delivery.

REVIEW OF THE QUALITY SERVICE LITERATURE

The importance of effective delivery of quality service is becoming more evident throughout all aspects of business. Quality management is essential in that it directs an organization's goals and has a profound influence on the functions and operations of individual employees (Krishan *et al.*, 1993). Researchers have concluded that quality has become the key to competitive success and long-term survival (Gourdin and Kloppenborg, 1991). Empirical research has demonstrated a positive relationship between service quality and organizational performance (Parasuraman *et al.*, 1991). In an article in *USA Today* (10 February 1994) Joel Marvil, chief executive officer of Ames Rubber, a 1993 Baldrige Award winner, stated that companies who were previously unaware of his firm were now doing business with it as a result of the award. Further, quality can be used as an effective strategy for raising return on investment, increasing market share, improving productivity, lowering costs, and achieving customer satisfaction (Mohr, 1991; Tse and Wilton, 1988; Anderson and Zeithaml, 1984). In order to turn service quality into a powerful competitive weapon, hospitality managers must diligently strive for service superiority by consistently performing above adequate guest service levels while constantly striving for continuous improvement (Juran, 1992).

The increased importance of service quality to consumers is especially critical in the management of lodging establishments. Research has suggested that the long-term success of marketing efforts should not be determined solely by the number of initial visits to a lodging establishment. A more important measure of success should be the number of first-time visitors who are converted to repeat visitors (Saleh and Ryan, 1991). These researchers also suggest that when considering the determinants of success in attracting repeat visitors to a hotel, service quality is paramount. With this in mind, an understanding of the determinants of service quality as well as the role of quality in consumer decision-making processes is needed if hotel managers are to successfully compete in a sophisticated, mature marketplace.

What is quality?

There have been varied definitions of quality in research relating to products, with no clear consensual agreement. Quality has been defined as: conformance to standards (Hall, 1990), conformance to requirements (Crosby, 1979), fitness for use (Juran, 1980) and 'what consumers say it is' (Feigenbaum, 1990). Recently, Juran (1992), in examining quality as it relates to goods and services, has bisected quality into two definitions:

1. product/service features – what the customer desires;
2. freedom from deficiencies.

Since services are different from products in that they are intangible and heterogeneous, and production and consumption occur simultaneously (Zeithaml *et al.*, 1985), they require a different definition of quality than products. Barrington and Olsen (1987) found that the uniqueness of the hospitality industry in part is due to the fact that the customers must be provided with the correct service when and where they want, consistently. Therefore, service quality is evaluated in thousands of temporary relationships between service providers and customers (Turley, 1990). In an effort to recognize these differences, an early definition of quality in the services literature was provided by Parasuraman *et al.* (1985) and applied to the lodging industry by Saleh and Ryan (1991). They used gap analysis to define service quality as the gap or difference between expectation and perception. However, this definition has been challenged recently by a number of researchers (Cronin and Taylor, 1992; Teas, 1993) who question the perception minus expectation framework.

Calling upon the work of Juran (1992), who found that the definition of quality was too rich to be defined along one dimension, and Grönroos (1991), who partitioned service into three components, technical, functional and image, we define quality service in the lodging industry along three dimensions: (1) doing the right thing (guest driven), (2) doing it right (technically correct), and (3) doing it consistently. This definition of service quality captures the richness of the construct in that it recognizes the guest-driven aspect of quality as well as the technical considerations of correctness and consistency. Additionally, there are two aspects of being technically correct: (1) being correct the first time a service is performed; and (2) immediately correcting a service delivered incorrectly the first time. Lewis and Chambers (1989) have found that service breakdown and guest complaints can positively alter perceptions of quality if they are resolved promptly and correctly.

Perception, expectation and evaluation of service quality

Understanding consumers' perceptions and expectations of quality is increasingly important to service firms. Research has indicated that assessments of quality and satisfaction are critical in the process by which a consumer develops a positive attitude towards a particular experience, makes a repeat purchase, and develops brand loyalty (Webster, 1991), which are all primary goals of marketing in hotel properties. Parasuraman *et al.* (1985) suggest three underlying themes relating to the evaluation and perception of service quality. First, service quality is more difficult for consumers to evaluate than product quality. Second, service quality perceptions result from a comparison of consumer expectations with actual service performance. Finally, quality evaluations are not solely made on the outcome of a service; they also involve evaluations of the process of service delivery. They have also hypothesized that there is a gap which exists between management perceptions of consumer expectations and what consumers actually expect.

There have been a number of empirical examinations in the hotel industry of this gap between managers' perceptions of guests' expectations and hotel guests' actual expectations. Lewis and Klein (1987) and Saleh and Ryan (1991) are two studies that seemed to indicate that there is not complete agreement between management and guests as to what the guests actually desired. Lewis and Klein (1987) examined 44 attributes of hotel service and discovered agreement by management and guests in only 17, while Saleh and Ryan (1991) found agreement on 19 of 33 items measured by a modified SERVQUAL instrument. Another study reported by Nightingale (1986) also discovered that management perceptions of guests' expectations did not correspond to the guests' actual expectations. These studies seem to imply that the first component of our service quality definition (doing the right thing) is not being successfully accomplished in the hotel industry.

Boulding *et al.* (1993) conclude that the delivery of service quality is a dynamic as opposed to a static process. They provide a model which shows that individuals enter a service encounter with two types of expectations of service quality: (1) what will happen; and (2) what should happen. After the service encounter, individuals develop a cumulative perception of the delivered service on each dimension based upon initial expectations and the actual service delivered. Perceptions on each dimension of service contribute to an overall assessment of the level of service quality, which in turn leads to behavioral outcomes. This model suggests that expectations lead to perceptions which in turn lead to behavioral intentions. It also indicates that perceptions from one service encounter will contribute towards the expectations in the next service encounter with the same service provider.

New directions for service quality

The Malcolm Baldrige National Quality Award

The Malcolm Baldrige National Quality Award (MBNQA) was established by the United States Congress to promote national awareness of the need for improved quality management in business and industry throughout the USA. The award is the highest recognition for quality that US company can receive (DeCarlo and Sterett, 1990). The award, a part of the Malcolm Baldrige National Quality Improvement Act signed into law by President Ronald Reagan on 20 August 1987, is named for Malcolm Baldrige, the late Secretary of Commerce who served from 1980 to 1987. Over the past few years, the award has gained both national and international prestige. Table 14.1 provides a chronological history of the events leading to the establishment of the award.

The 1993 MBNQA Application Guidelines state that the Baldrige Award promotes: '(1) awareness of quality as an increasingly important element in competitiveness; (2) understanding of the requirements for quality excellence; and (3) sharing of information on successful quality strategies and the benefits derived from implementation of these strategies' (National Institute of Standards and Technology, 1993). Up to two awards are given annually to companies in each of three categories: manufacturing, service, and small business. Applicants for the MBNQA are evaluated in seven principal categories – leadership, information and analysis, strategic quality planning, human resource development and management, management of process quality, quality and operational results, and customer focus and satisfaction (Partlow, 1993). A 1,000-point scale is used to evaluate applicants. Table 14.2 explains the point allocations for each category and subcategory for the 1993 award competition.

The MBNQA continues to provide a benchmark for the best leadership quality system as well as quality results for companies operating in the USA. Not only has the award proven to be a benefit to the past winners, but it has also been quite valuable to

Table 14.1 *Time line of the establishment of MBNQA*

Early 1980s – Councils formed to study the ability of the USA to compete in the global marketplace, with the improvement of quality in goods and services as the main objective.

1983 – The American Productivity and Quality Center recommends the establishment of a national quality award.

1984 – The White House Conference on Productivity called for a national medal for productivity.

1985 – The Committee to Establish a National Quality Award was formed.

1986 – Congressman Don Fuqua (D-FL) introduced House Bill 5321. Designed to establish a national quality improvement award. The bill was never acted upon.

1987 – Congressman Doug Walgreen (D-PA) reintroduced the legislation while Senator Bob Graham (D-FL) sponsored a version of the bill to the Senate. The measure passed the House on 8 June and was sent to the Senate. 25 July 1987 – Secretary of Commerce, Malcolm Baldrige, was killed in a rodeo accident. Three days after the death of Baldrige, the legislation was renamed in his honor. The bill was passed in the Senate and the House agreed to the name change. 20 August 1987 – President Reagan signed the Malcolm Baldrige National Quality Improvement Act of 1987 into law, establishing the Malcolm Baldrige Award Program for the United States.

Source: George (1992).

those who have gone through the application process as well as those who use the award criteria as a guideline for establishing quality standards within their operations.

Table 14.3 provides a listing of companies that have been recognized as quality leaders in the USA by winning the MBNQA. The list contains only one firm from the travel and tourism industry – The Ritz-Carlton Hotel Company. An unwavering

Table 14.2 *1993 Malcolm Baldrige National Quality Award criteria*

Categories and item	Maximum points
1.0 Leadership	**90**
1.1 Senior executive leadership	40
1.2 Management of quality	40
1.3 Public responsibility and corporate citizenship	25
2.0 Information and analysis	**80**
2.1 Scope and management of quality and performance data and information	20
2.2 Competitive comparisons and benchmarking	20
2.3 Analysis of uses of company-level data	40
3.0 Strategic quality planning	**60**
3.1 Strategic quality and company performance planning process	35
3.2 Quality and performance plans	25
4.0 Human resource development and management	**150**
4.1 Human resource planning and management	20
4.2 Employee involvement	40
4.3 Employee education and training	40
4.4 Employee performance and recognition	25
4.5 Employee well-being and satisfaction	25
5.0 Management of process quality	**140**
5.1 Design and introduction of quality products and services	40
5.2 Process management: product and service production and delivery processes	35
5.3 Process management: business processes and support services	30
5.4 Supplier quality	20
5.5 Quality assessment	15
6.0 Quality and operational results	**180**
6.1 Product and service quality results	70
6.2 Company and operational results	50
6.3 Business process and support service results	25
6.4 Supplier quality results	35
7.0 Customer focus and satisfaction	**300**
7.1 Customer expectations: current and future	35
7.2 Customer relationship management	65
7.3 Commitment to customers	15
7.4 Customer satisfaction determination	30
7.5 Customer satisfaction results	85
7.6 Customer satisfaction comparisons	70

Source: National Institute of Standards and Technology (1993).

commitment to the delivery of a quality lodging experience for its guests has long been the focus of its operations.

The Ritz-Carlton Hotel Company

In 1993, W. B. Johnson Properties acquired the Ritz-Carlton Boston as well as exclusive rights to the Ritz-Carlton name in North America. With the acquistion of the Ritz-Carlton name, the top management team made a commitment to develop the highest-quality service hotel company in the USA. At the time, there was no clear leader in the US luxury hotel market. The market was fragmented, with mainly independent properties, whose levels of service varied greatly. There was a need for a hotel company with a guest service delivery system designed to provide premium service with an emphasis on reliability and timely delivery of service. As a result of the need for that hotel product in the market, Ritz-Carlton is currently under management contract with 30 hotel properties throughout the USA, Spain, Australia, Hong Kong and Mexico after only ten years in business. With a primary target market roughly divided in half between affluent pleasure/business travelers and corporate incentive/meetings groups, quality service has always been the primary focus of operations. That Ritz-Carlton has been successful in its quest is attested by the fact that, in addition to winning the MBNQA 1992, Ritz-Carlton was a finalist in the 1991 competition. Additionally, it has won over 121 quality-related awards, establishing it as a quality leader in the hotel industry.

Table 14.3 *Malcolm Baldrige National Quality Award winners*

1992
AT&T Network Systems Group/Transmission Systems Business Unit
Texas Instruments Defense Systems & Electronics Group
AT&T Universal Card Services
The Ritz-Carlton Hotel Company

1991
Marlowe Industries
Solectron Corporation
Zytec Corporation

1990
Cadillac Motor Car Division
IBM Rochester
Federal Express Corporation
Wallace Company Inc.

1989
Milliken & Company
Xerox Business Products and Systems

1988
Globe Metallurgical Inc.
Motorola Inc.
Westinghouse Commercial Nuclear Fuel Division

Much of the success of the Ritz-Carlton management team can be attributed to the fact that quality service has been inculcated in the company philosophy and corporate culture. This is evidenced by their Gold Standards, which include their credo, motto and the Ritz-Carlton Basics (Figure 14.1). At The Ritz-Carlton, quality products,

---

THREE STEPS OF SERVICE

1
A warm and sincere greeting. Use the guest name, if and when possible.

2
Anticipation and compliance with guest needs.

3
Fond farewell. Give them a warm good-bye and use their names, if and when possible.

"We Are Ladies and Gentlemen Serving Ladies and Gentlemen"

THE RITZ-CARLTON

CREDO

The Ritz-Carlton Hotel is a place where the genuine care and comfort of our guests is our highest mission.

We pledge to provide the finest personal service and facilities for our guests who will always enjoy a warm, relaxed yet refined ambience.

The Ritz-Carlton experience enlivens the senses, instills well-being, and fulfills even the unexpressed wishes and needs of our guests.

THE RITZ-CARLTON BASICS

1 The Credo will be known, owned and energized by all employees.

2 Our motto is: "We are Ladies and Gentlemen serving Ladies and Gentlemen". Practice teamwork and "lateral service" to create a positive work environment.

3 The three steps of service shall be practiced by all employees.

4 All employees will successfully complete Training Certification to ensure they understand how to perform to The Ritz-Carlton standards in their position.

5 Each employee will understand their work area and Hotel goals as established in each strategic plan.

6 All employees will know the needs of their internal and external customers (guests and employees) so that we may deliver the products and services they expect. Use guest preference pads to record specific needs.

7 Each employee will continuously identify defects (Mr. BIV) throughout the Hotel.

8 Any employee who receives a customer complaint "owns" the complaint.

9 Instant guest pacification will be ensured by all. React quickly to correct the problem immediately. Follow-up with a telephone call within twenty minutes to verify the problem has been resolved to the customer's satisfaction. Do everything you possibly can to never lose a guest.

10 Guest incident action forms are used to record and communicate every incident of guest dissatisfaction. Every employee is empowered to resolve the problem and to prevent a repeat occurrence.

11 Uncompromising levels of cleanliness are the responsibility of every employee.

12 "Smile – We are on stage." Always maintain positive eye contact. Use the proper vocabulary with our guests. (Use words like – "Good Morning," "Certainly," "I'll be happy to" and "My pleasure").

13 Be an ambassador of your Hotel in and outside of the work place. Always talk positively. No negative comments.

14 Escort guests rather than pointing out directions to another area of the Hotel.

15 Be knowledgeable of Hotel information (hours of operation, etc.) to answer guest

inquiries. Always recommend the Hotel's retail and food and beverage outlets prior to outside facilities.

16 Use proper telephone etiquette. Answer within three rings and with a "smile." When necessary, ask the caller, "May I place you on hold." Do not screen calls. Eliminate call transfers when possible.

17 Uniforms are to be immaculate; Wear proper and safe footwear (clean and polished), and your correct name tag. Take pride and care in your personal appearance (adhering to all grooming standards).

18 Ensure all employees know their roles during emergency situations and are aware of fire and life safety response processes.

19 Notify your supervisor immediately of hazards, injuries, equipment or assistance that you need. Practice energy conservation and proper maintenance and repair of Hotel property and equipment.

20 Protecting the assets of a Ritz-Carlton Hotel is the responsibility of every employee.

Figure 14.1 *Ritz-Carlton Gold Standards*

services and solutions are the dynamic processes that guide every action of management and employees.

STRATEGIC QUALITY PLANNING PROCESS IN THE LODGING INDUSTRY

Considering the factors contributing to guest perceptions of quality reported in the literature and the criteria of the Malcolm Baldrige Award, the authors have developed a model to assist hotel managers in the development of specific strategic quality planning processes in their properties. This model may be utilized by managers in any segment of the industry, since price alone is not an indicator of quality. However, we will use this model to examine the quality planning process at The Ritz-Carlton Hotel Company, since it is internationally recognized as a leader in the field of quality in the lodging industry. The components of the model will be examined and then Ritz-Carlton's philosophies and operations will be used to illustrate how the model can effectively guide management in its quest to use quality as an effective competitive tactic. Of course, this model is applicable to other hospitality establishments in addition to lodging operations. Before introducing the model it is necessary to discuss the important preconditions which must exist in a lodging firm. The principles will be stated and then Ritz-Carlton's experiences and lessons learned will be presented.

Commitment to quality

Any successful quality hospitality program begins with the strong commitment of the top management team, which must permeate the organization. This commitment to quality is evident in the company's philosophy, motto, and corporate culture that posits the total satisfaction of the guests' wants, needs and desires as the first priority for the company. As was demonstrated in Figure 14.1, this top-down commitment is clearly communicated in The Ritz-Carlton Hotel Company. In a recent company-wide survey, 96 per cent of the employees stated that 'excellence in guest services' is a top priority. This is extraordinary when you consider that the company has added 3,000 new employees in the past three years! '*Lessons learned*: when senior leaders personally instill a strong vision and a set of principles in their employees and then give them the confidence, freedom and authority to act, people take responsibility for their jobs and do whatever is necessary to satisfy their customers' (Ritz-Carlton, 1993).

Selection process

This total commitment to quality begins in the selection process of new employees and continues throughout the employee training and empowerment process. At Ritz-Carlton a highly predictive instrument is employed to determine each job candidate's ability. Known as 'character trait recruiting', it helps reduce that portion of service variability attributable to the service employee and ensures that the right people are in the right position. This testing has enabled Ritz-Carlton to reduce turnover by 50 per cent in the past three years (Ritz-Carlton, 1993).

Training process

After selection of the most highly competent individuals for the position, it is necessary for the lodging firm to provide the employee with a complete set of tools to accomplish their jobs. At Ritz-Carlton this is the responsibility of the work area leader and the department trainer. New employees undergo a comprehensive training period which provides them with the necessary skills to carry out their assignments according to the gold standards. Upon completion of the formal training period the employee must pass a written test as well as a skill demonstration in order to be certified. The standards for certification are not set at corporate level; rather, they are set by the work area team, thus giving local ownership to the employees. Training does not stop with certification, but continues during the entire career of the employee. Each year employees receive over 100 hours of quality training. To reinforce the principles taught during training there are 39 awards given annually to recognize outstanding service, and performance appraisals are based upon the expectations developed during initial training, orientation and certification. *Lessons learned*: a collective quality commitment must be gained from the entire workforce. There is no substitute for selecting employees who believe in the organization's values.

Strategic quality plan

This strong company commitment to providing a quality experience for guests leads to the development of a strategic quality plan that takes into account the needs of the guests and employees, as well as the well-designed process which enables satisfied employees to fulfill identified guests' needs.

The strategic quality plan is a continuously updated blueprint for the delivery of a quality lodging product. It takes into account guest feedback of the service experience as well as employee and management input on the ease of delivery of the quality service product. At Ritz-Carlton the quality plan is the business plan, whose primary objectives are to improve the quality of the hotel product and service, reduce cycle time and improve price value as well as guest retention.

It is important to have only one overall quality plan in order to avoid the confusion which might result from many different quality improvement programs operating in the property simultaneously. The goals of an effective quality plan are to develop a program that stresses consistency throughout the company, performance standards for employees, timeliness of service delivery, focus on detail, and emphasis on fulfilling guests' needs. At Ritz-Carlton, each level of the company is involved in the development of the plan. Objectives and action plans are developed and reviewed by the corporate steering committee. These action plans proceed through a screening process that ensures that they have been adequately researched; and they are not undertaken unless there are adequate resources to support them. All plans center on directing the resources (time, money and people) of the Ritz-Carlton to the needs and wishes of guests and employees. *Lessons learned*: action plans developed by each level of the organization must be screened to ensure they: (1) have been adequately researched; (2) have been adequately resourced; and (3) contain no complexity before they are undertaken (Ritz-Carlton, 1993).

In a hotel stay, there are three critical factors instrumental in the determination of a quality service product; (1) identification of the hotel product desired by the guest; (2) development of the process by which the hotel product is delivered to the guest; and (3) freedom from defects of the goods and services associated with the guest's stay. The strategic quality plan takes these three factors into consideration and then determines the process of service delivery appropriate for the property.

Service product features

The first factor, service product features, includes all of the tangible and intangible benefits associated with the delivery of the lodging experience. This component corresponds to the product features that are a concrete part of the guest experience. These factors contribute to guests' interpretation of quality during their stay. The strategic quality plan identifies those product features desired by the guest and then ensures that all tangible product features, psychological experiences and sensory perceptions desired by the guest are anticipated and in place prior to the service encounter. Guidelines for handling guest special requests are established, and identification of amenities and decor packages to enhance the guest's stay, etc., are all components of the strategic quality plan.

Periodic feedback is required from guests to ensure that their wants, desires and needs are being met. This information should be obtained with formal survey methods using the data available at the property, but more often it is obtained from employees or managers who interface directly with guests. While anecdotal information is important and should be used by the management team, the more formal survey methods provide the best feedback. At Ritz-Carlton, focus groups are utilized to identify: (1) critical product and service features that will satisfy and motivate guests; and (2) critical product and service errors and omissions. In addition, Ritz-Carlton employs a guest satisfaction measurement system to evaluate guest satisfaction after the completion of the stay. This will be discussed in detail later in the chapter.

Service delivery process

When the guest comes in contact with the first employee of the lodging establishment the service encounter begins. This first encounter may be the making of the reservation or the instant the guest arrives at the property. The strategic quality plan ensures that all employees are not only well trained in their specific job requirements but also possess a general knowledge of the hotel and its services. Here the plan is instrumental in developing a service delivery process where fulfilling the wants and needs of the guest are paramount for each member of the service team. Employees should have the knowledge and ability to correct any problem encountered by the guest during their stay in order to enhance the guest's perception of quality and satisfaction.

Service product freedom from defects

This component corresponds to the intangible or process-oriented component of the service encounter. Juran (1992) states that freedom from deficiency is a major component in determining the quality of an establishment because, in the eyes of the customer, the fewer the deficiencies, the better the quality. In a hotel establishment, the strategic quality plan governs the manner in which management ensures a defect-free environment as well as outlining procedures for handling service breakdowns or defects which arise during the service delivery process. Actions such as establishment of preventative maintenance programs, scheduling of adequate staffing levels, and use of quality suppliers, aid management in its quest for zero-defect service delivery.

THE QUALITY SERVICE MODEL

We are now ready to examine the role of quality in strategic marketing. The model presented in Figure 14.2 examines the role of quality in lodging guest decision-making. It is a dynamic model in that it not only illustrates how the initial decision to choose a lodging property is made, but also examines how the guest's previous visit contributes to their decision to return to a lodging property. The model is divided into three segments:

1. Pre-visit – where the guest begins the process of choosing a lodging property.
2. Actual visit – where the guest evaluates actual performance based upon expectations.
3. Post-visit – where the guest's overall perception of the lodging experience is developed.

Pre-visit

When guests make an initial decision to stay at a lodging establishment there are generally several factors that are taken into consideration. Of primary importance in the selection of a hotel establishment is the need for the service. The purpose of the visit is important, since if the need for lodging is business based as opposed to vacation/pleasure based, the services desired and the location of the property will impact greatly on the selection process.

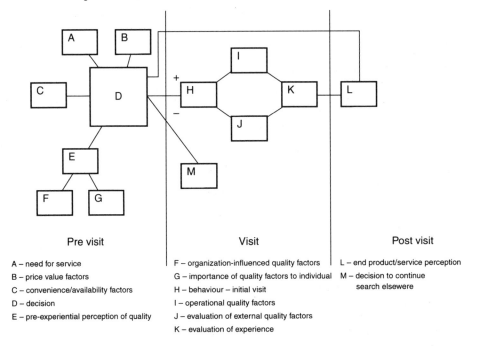

Pre visit	Visit	Post visit
A – need for service	F – organization-influenced quality factors	L – end product/service perception
B – price value factors	G – importance of quality factors to individual	M – decision to continue search elsewere
C – convenience/availability factors	H – behaviour – initial visit	
D – decision	I – operational quality factors	
E – pre-experiential perception of quality	J – evaluation of external quality factors	
	K – evaluation of experience	

Figure 14.2 *The role of quality in guest decision-making*

The guest's perception of the price–value relationship projected by the property will also influence the selection or decision process. Other factors such as availability, location, convenience, competitive environment etc. also play a primary role in the selection of a lodging establishment. The perceived quality level associated with an establishment can also play an instrumental role in how consumers go about deciding between lodging establishments.

Organizational influenced quality factors along with their importance weights contribute to the development of a pre-experiential perception of quality. Organizational influenced quality factors are those factors which are a result of the messages consumers receive regarding the quality of an establishment prior to a stay. Consumers receive varied messages from various sources. In a study of consumer expectations of services, Webster (1991) found that information sources have a significant effect on quality expectations of service. The study revealed that the effects of past personal experience and word of mouth communications appear to have the greatest effect on quality expectations, followed by advertising and sales promotions. These conclusions are also supported by the research of Parasuraman *et al.* (1988), which found that past experience is important in forming informed perceptions of a service offering. The Ritz-Carlton conveys a quality image to consumers through promotional and advertising messages which strive to instill confidence in the Ritz-Carlton reputation with the message 'expect the best'. As may be seen in the following three marketing strategies utilized by Ritz-Carlton, the company pays attention to both local word of mouth communication and advertising/sales efforts.

1. *The Ritz-Carlton promotional strategies:*
    - Promote the enduring quality reputation of the Ritz-Carlton.
    - All promotional communications project a sensory image of warm, gracious, personal service.
    - Recruit, select and train sales personnel who desire to serve in a warm, gracious manner.
    - Most of the marketing promotional resources are dedicated direct sales efforts, translating into warm, gracious, personal service.
    - Use the National Quality Award logo on all promotional literature to provide added credence to the quality leadership image.
    - Provide obvious quality products and services to local residents.
2. *The Ritz-Carlton pricing strategy:*
    - The Ritz-Carlton charges premium prices in order to give greater weight to its service quality leadership position.
3. *External factors used to convey a quality image:*
    - quality superiority obvious to local residents;
    - quality superiority obvious to travelers;
    - quality superiority obvious to the travel industry;
    - quality superiority claims made by the Ritz-Carlton.

This quality superiority is based upon four features and one ultimate expectation (a memorable experience):

1. Highly personalized and timely service from a genuinely caring staff.
2. Comfort.
3. Beauty.
4. Timely problem resolution.

The Ritz-Carlton approach is that their logo and direct sales efforts provide evidence of the level of quality service, while the Malcolm Baldrige National Quality Award and local resident referrals are a warranty of reliability.

These messages and the corresponding importance that each individual places on these factors develop a guest's perception of the desired quality level of a particular establishment. Through the process of evaluating the firm's external quality factors against their quality needs, guests develop pre-experiential quality perceptions, and when they analyze these with the other decision factors, they arrive at an internal ranking of all establishments in their choice set. Only one establishment will be selected per lodging experience. Consumers will continue their search until they find an establishment that provides an acceptable ranking. They will evaluate each known hotel product that is available in the market and either choose to continue the search or make the initial visit to the property.

Visit

At the commencement of the visit phase, the guest has selected the lodging property and developed a set of expectations based upon the decision factors utilized in the selection process. Expectations have been defined as 'pretrial beliefs about a product that serve as standards or reference points against which product performance is judged' (Zeithaml *et al.*, 1993). A successful service encounter begins with the ability of management to correctly assess the guest's expectations (Saleh and Ryan, 1991). This is difficult to accomplish since expectations are not standard across individuals, but are based upon a broad range of factors such as the guest's psychological state at the time of the service delivery to their experiences with the firm's competitors (Zeithaml *et al.*, 1993). In their research on expectations of service, Parasuraman *et al.* (1991b) found that the principal expectations of hotel consumers are for the establishment to provide a clean room, provide a secure environment, treat the guest as a guest, and keep the promises it made.

During the visit, guests experience and make assessments of the property's operational quality factors. In this phase guests evaluate whether the firm is doing the right things right. Past research has indicated that there are five primary dimensions for the categorization of customer service expectations: reliability, tangibles, responsiveness, assurance and empathy (Parasuraman *et al.*, 1988). When evaluating the service delivery process, reliability is seen as a service outcome by the guest based upon their evaluation of the other four factors which basically comprise service delivery process. During the visit, guests constantly evaluate service delivery performance on these four factors.

Additionally, Grönroos (1990) identified three components which are useful in assessing the quality of the service delivery process: technical, functional and image qualities. Technical qualities pertain to the actual physical components of the hotel, its rooms, reception area, grounds, etc. The functional component is made up of the performance of the service such as the nature of the greeting, the care and attention given to the guests etc., while the image component is the corporate perception.

The evaluation of the service quality component of the model addresses the question: is the establishment doing the right things right? This component directly addresses the service delivery segment of the process. Is there a significant gap between guest expectations and firm performance? If there is a service gap or breakdown, how quickly does the firm recognize it and begin the recovery process? Brandt and Reffett

(1989) report that consumer's attention to service quality may be magnified in problem situations; in fact, this effect is so pronounced that in many cases it is only when consumers experience problems that they actually notice the level of service quality.

In addition to focus groups, Ritz-Carlton uses a very sophisticated program to track repeat guest special requests and needs, which helps ensure that the service delivery process matches guest expectations. Utilizing technology available today, the Ritz-Carlton Repeat guest history program, illustrated in Figure 14.3, has proved to be an effective component of the delivery system, allowing the company to attain its goal of providing highly personalized guest service. When a repeat guest visits any Ritz-Carlton property, this information is retrieved prior to the guest's arrival.

In the case of first-time guests as well as repeat visitors, Ritz-Carlton attempts to ensure that service matches expectations through a number of management and employee actions. Adherence to the gold standards provides the staff with guidance for most routine service encounters. Sensory inspection of these standards is performed by hotel staff at all levels, with attention paid to 'The Three Steps of Service' (Figure 14.4).

In the event of a service breakdown, Ritz-Carlton requires employees to leave their routine duties and immediately attempt to provide the guest with instant pacification. Each employee is authorized to apply immediate positive action with a $2,000 spending authority. Each problem occurrence is documented in order to provide an early warning system which allows management to analyze the situation and take the necessary action to adjust the service delivery system. Upon resolution of the problem, the service employee is expected to 'snap back' into their routine.

Post-visit

Evaluation of the service begins immediately following the completion of the service encounter. In this phase consumers combine their perceptions of the effectiveness of all

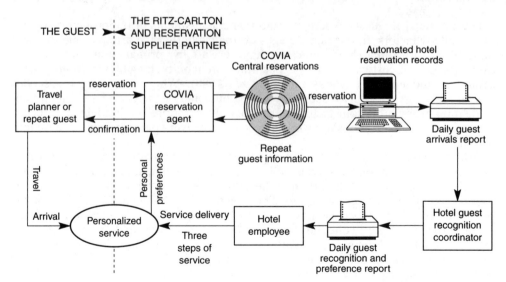

Figure 14.3 *The Ritz-Carlton repeat guest history program: an aid to highly personalized service delivery*

of the individual service encounters which have taken place during their stay to attain an overall perception of the property's service quality performance. This theory is supported by Grönroos (1984), who suggests that the service provided is subjected to an evaluation phase in which consumers compare firm performance during the service delivery process with predetermined expectations. Therefore, quality is dependent not only on the actual service provided but also on the nature of the pre-visit expectations. Guests develop an overall perception of quality utilizing the entire decision process, and service quality perceptions are the result of comparing expectations with actual service performance (Grönroos, 1982; Lehtinen and Lehtinen, 1982).

The Ritz-Carlton Hotel Company attempts to track guest satisfaction after the visit through 'The Ritz-Carlton Guest and Planner Satisfaction Measurement System' (Figure 14.5).

Begun in 1983, revised in 1990 and again in 1993, the Ritz-Carlton satisfaction survey includes three primary metrics of customer satisfaction and 22 questions covering: market image, important product/service features, problem significance and competitive standing. The customer satisfaction metrics are: the percentage satisfied, the sum of significant problems, and the percentage of guests reporting dissatisfaction with the resolution of their problem. Each quarter, Customer Service Marketing (a research firm) randomly selects 30 guests from each property and conducts a 3–5-minute telephone survey. The surveys are processed daily and result in weekly reports

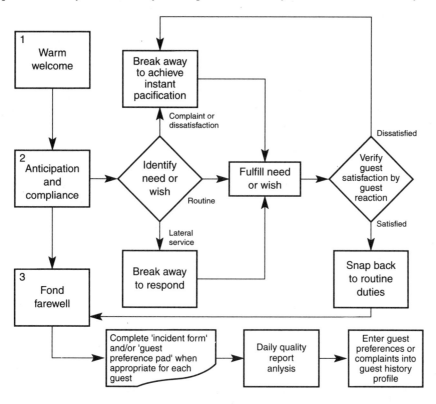

Figure 14.4 *The Ritz-Carlton Hotel Company: Three Steps of Service*

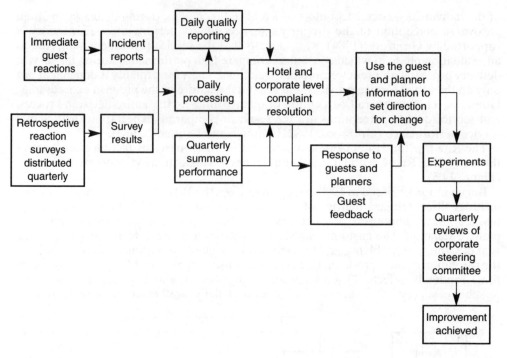

Figure 14.5 *The Ritz-Carlton Guest and Planner Satisfaction Measurement System*

submitted to the corporate office for immediate response to guest concerns. Comprehensive reviews are an integral part of their approach, with plans to segment responses according to hotel and functional area of responsibility.

The Ritz-Carlton meeting planner questionnaire includes the same three customer satisfaction metrics and also 75 questions covering: the sales phase of the meeting, the pre-event phase, the event phase, and the post-event phase of the meeting. Each month J. D. Powers ensures that 40 per cent of the meeting planners who held a meeting during the past month at a Ritz-Carlton hotel respond to the survey. Once again the information is reported to the corporate office for action, with plans to develop a comprehensive report by hotel and functional department. Through this sophisticated, statistically accurate survey program, The Ritz-Carlton Hotel Company is able to track the post-visit perceptions of its guests.

SUMMARY

Results of focus group studies have shown that perception development can take place before or after the delivery of a service. The model presented in this chapter has incorporated both of these facets by beginning with a guest's perception of quality based on their search process and exposure to messages regarding the quality of an establishment, and concluding with an overall perception of quality resulting from the delivery of the service. Consistent with Boulding *et al.* (1993), the ramifications of service quality perceptions are continuous. The overall perceptions achieved at the conclusion of a service arrangement feed back into the decision process when a guest is deciding to make a repeat visit. The overall perception of quality resulting from the initial visit now becomes one of the messages (incidently a very strong message) used in determining the pre-experiential perception of the second visit. Based upon what has happened in the first visit coupled with the existing decision factors at the time, consumers decide to make a repeat visit or to continue the search elsewhere. In addition, the experience of The Ritz-Carlton Hotel Company has been used as a case study to demonstrate the effectiveness of the model presented.

REFERENCES

Anderson, C., and Zeithaml, C. P. (1984) 'Stage of the product life cycle; business strategy and business performance', *Academy of Management Journal*, vol. **27**, March, pp. 5–24.

Barrington, M. N., and Olsen M. D. (1987) 'Concept of service in the hospitality industry', *International Journal of Hospitality Management*, vol. **6**, no. 3, pp. 131–8.

Bemowski, K. (1992) 'Inside the Baldrige Award Guidelines', *Quality Progress*, vol. **26**, p. 24.

Boulding, W., Kalra, A., Staelin, R., and Zeithaml, V. (1993) 'A dynamic model of service quality: from expectations to behavioural intentions', *Journal of Marketing Research*, vol. **30**, February, pp. 7–27.

Brandt, D. R., and Reffett, K. L. (1989) 'Focusing on customer problems to improve service quality', *Journal of Services Marketing*, vol. **3**, no. 4, pp. 5–14.

Cronin, J. J. Jr, and Taylor, S. A. (1992) 'Measuring service quality: a reexamination and extension', *Journal of Marketing*, vol. **56**, no. 3, pp. 55–68.

Crosby, P. B. (1979), *Quality Is Free*, McGraw-Hill, New York.

DeCarlo, N. J., and Sterett, W. K. (1990) 'History of the Malcolm Baldrige Quality Award', *Quality Progress*, vol. **23**, pp. 21–7.

Feigenbaum, A. V. (1990) 'Why total quality is a tall order for U.S. managers', *Electronic Business*, vol. **16**, no. 19, p. 119.

George, S. (1992) *The Baldrige Quality System – The Do-It-Yourself Way to Transform Your Business*, John Wiley & Sons, Inc., New York.

Gourdin, K. T., and Kloppenborg, T. J. (1991) 'Identifying service quality gaps in commercial air travel: the first step toward quality improvement', *Transportation Journal*, vol. **31**, pp. 22–30.

Grönroos, C. (1982) *Strategic Management and Marketing in the Service Sector*, Swedish School of Economics and Business Administrations, Helsingfors.

Grönroos, C. (1984) 'A service quality model and its marketing implications', *European Journal of Marketing*, vol. **18**, pp. 36–44.

Grönroos, C. (1990) *Service Management and Marketing: Managing the Moment of Truth in Service Competition*, Lexington Books, Toronto.

Haavind, R. (1992) *The Road to the Baldrige Award – Quest for Total Quality*, Butterworth-Heinemann, Boston.

Hall, S. S. J. (1990) *Quality Assurance in the Hospitality Industry*, ASQC Quality Press, Milwaukee, WI.

Juran, J. M. (1980) *Quality Planning and Analysis: From Product Development Through Use*, McGraw-Hill, New York.

Juran, J. M. (1992) *Juran on Quality By Design: The New Steps for Planning Quality into Goods and Services*, The Free Press, New York.

Krishnan, R., Shani, A. B., Grant, R. M., and Baer, R. (1993) 'In search of quality: problems of design and implementation', *Academy of Management Executive*, vol. **7**, no. 4, pp. 7–20.

Lehtinen, U., and Lehtinen J. R. (1982) 'Service quality: a study of quality dimensions', Unpublished working paper, Service Management Institute, Helsinki, Finland.

Lewis, R. C., and Chambers, R. E. (1989) *Marketing Leadership in Hospitality: Foundations and Practices*, Van Nostrand Reinhold, New York.

Lewis, R. C., and Klein, D. M. (1987) 'The measurements of gaps in service quality', in Czepiel, J. A., Congram, C. A., and Shanahan, J. (eds) *The Services Challenge: Integrating for Competitive Advantage*. American Marketing Association, Chicago.

Mohr, I. (1991) 'The change to total quality: phenomenological insights from corporate quality executives', doctoral dissertation, City University of New York, Ann Arbor.

National Institute of Standards and Technology (1993) *Malcolm Baldrige National Quality Award 1993 Application Guidelines*, National Institute of Standards and Technology, United States Department of Commerce, MD: Washington, DC.

Nightingale, M., (1986) 'Defining quality for a quality assurance program: a study of perceptions', in Lewis, R. C., Beggs, T. J., Shaw, M., and Groffoot, S. (eds), *The Practice of Hospitality Management*, **II**, AVI, Westport, CT, pp. 35–59.

Olson, J. C., and Dover, P. (1979) 'Disconfirmation of consumer expectations through product trial', *Journal of Applied Psychology*, vol. **64**, pp. 179–89.

Parasuraman, A., Berry, L. L., and Zeithaml, V. A. (1991a) 'Perceived service quality as a customer-based, performance measure: an empirical examination of organizational barriers using an extended service quality model', *Human Resource Management*, Fall, pp. 337–61.

Parasuraman, A., Berry, L. L., and Zeithaml, V. A. (1991b) 'Understanding customer expectations of service', *Sloan Management Review*, Spring, pp. 39–48.

Parasuraman, A., Zeithaml, V. A., and Berry, L. L. (1985) 'A conceptual model of service quality and its implications for future research', *Journal of Marketing*, Fall, pp. 41–50.

Parasuraman, A., Zeithaml, V. A., and Berry, L. L. (1988), 'SERVQUAL: a multiple-item scale for measuring consumer perceptions of service quality', *Journal of Retailing*, vol. **64**, Spring, pp. 41–50.

Partlow, C. G. (1993) 'How Ritz-Carlton applies "TQM"', *Cornell HRA Quarterly*, August, pp. 16–24.

Reimann, C. W. (1990) 'America unites behind the Baldrige quality crusade', *Electronic Business*, vol. **16**, p. 63.

Ritz-Carlton (1993) 'Application Summary: The Ritz-Carlton Hotel Company, Malcolm Baldrige National Quality Award 1992 Winners', Brochure distributed by The Ritz-Carlton Hotel Company, Atlanta, Georgia.

Saleh, F., and Ryan, C. (1991) 'Analyzing service quality in the hospitality industry using the SERVQUAL model', *Service Industries Journal*, vol. **11**, no. 3, pp. 324–45.

Teas, R. K. (1993) 'Expectations, performance evaluation and consumers' perceptions of quality', *Journal of Marketing*, vol. **57**, October, pp. 18–34.

Tse, D. K., and Wilton, P. C. (1988) 'Models of consumer satisfaction formation: an extension', *Journal of Marketing Research*, vol. **25**, May, pp. 204–12.

Turley, L. W. (1990) 'Strategies for reducing perceptions of quality risk in services', *Journal of Services Marketing*, vol. **4**, no. 3, pp. 5–12.

USA Today (1994) 'Baldrige winners: quality starts with CEOs', 10 February, 4B.

Webster, C. (1991) 'Influences upon consumer expectations of services', *Journal of Services Marketing*, vol. **5**, no. 1, pp. 5–17.

Zeithaml, V. A., Berry, L. L. and Parasuraman, A. (1993) 'The nature and determinants of customer expectations of service', *Journal of the Academy of Marketing Science*, vol. **21**, no. 1, pp. 1–12.

Zeithaml, V. A., Parasuraman, A., and Berry, L. L. (1985) 'Problems and strategies in services marketing', *Journal of Marketing*, vol. **49**, Spring, pp. 33–46.

15

Implementing the intangibles: a total quality approach for hospitality service providers

Cherylynn Becker

As we enter the twenty-first century there is consensus between management experts and today's sophisticated consumers that quality in services continues to lag behind the quality attained in product markets. Hospitality firms are no exception. Many attribute the low level of quality in services to the population boom which followed World War II. They suggest that during the 1950s and 1960s the rapidly increasing size of the consumer market enabled service providers to skimp on quality without the threat of losing customers (Power and Zinn, 1991). This is an optimistic perspective for service firms pursuing quality objectives, since it implies that although the attainment of service quality has been delayed, with proper attention it can still be achieved. On a more pessimistic note, there is also a widespread belief that the pursuit of quality in services is severely handicapped by the elusive, fleeting nature of the service process. As a top executive for one service corporation explained, 'You can't use traditional manufacturing tools to measure it (quality) or inspect it before you deliver it. ... Our employees create it, and then it just disappears' (Armstrong and Symonds, 1991, p. 100). The opinion expressed by this executive seems to be shared by many service providers. Yet a review of the various perspectives on quality suggests that this popular belief is fostered by an inadequate understanding of the different approaches to quality and how these can be successfully integrated to meet the needs of service providers for the future.

Hand in hand with the quality issue is the equally compelling challenge associated with managing service sector productivity. Like the attainment of quality, productivity gains in services have continued to decline relative to those achieved in manufacturing and product markets (Drucker, 1991). The culprit most often cited for this state of affairs is, once again, the abstract, intangible nature of service output, which defies measurement and cannot be effectively subjected to the same management controls which have been successful at increasing productivity in product manufacturing.

There are different perspectives on the expected relationship between quality and productivity. Some assert that when quality goes up, productivity, which is measured by the ratio of input and output, must decline. Others suggest that the correlation between quality and productivity is positive, so that any improvement in quality will also result in a corresponding improvement in productivity. A closer examination of the service sector suggests that the correlation between quality and productivity is a positive one, but unfortunately the direction for both is negative, since both quality and productivity in the vast majority of services continues to decline. The information presented in this chapter explains this relationship by providing an in-depth look at the various approaches to defining quality and examining how each of these interacts with the characteristics inherent in services. Finally, a method for the effective management of service firms is suggested which has the potential to impact positively on both service productivity and service quality.

WHAT IS QUALITY? A HISTORICAL PERSPECTIVE

Over the years and depending upon the perspective, the concept of quality has meant different things to different people. A recent review of the quality literature suggests that divergent approaches to how quality is defined and how it is understood are still prevalent today. These divergent views on what quality is and how it can be achieved appear to have hindered our progress toward achieving total quality, particularly as it relates to the service sector. A holistic approach to managing quality for the twenty-first century requires an understanding of how each of the multiple approaches to quality management have evolved over time. It requires, first, the ability to recognize and discard archaic components of quality which are not relevant to services, and second, an ability to integrate the relevant but divergent perspectives into an operational plan for the future.

The most traditional view of quality is philosophical in nature. It corresponds closely with the definition of quality which we find in the dictionary. This perspective views quality as synonymous with the idea of innate excellence (Pirsig, 1974). The concept is similar to the philosophical concept of beauty: quality is considered to be an unanalyzable characteristic which can only be recognized through experience (Garvin, 1984). This definition implies that, from its earliest conceptualization, the perception of quality has been contingent upon the existence of previously established standards.

The product approach to quality

The product-based view of quality takes a more pragmatic approach. Here quality is viewed 'as a precise and measurable variable' which facilitates the ranking of products based upon the amount of some desired attribute or characteristic which a product possesses (Garvin, 1984, p. 25). Traditionally, the product approach to quality made the assumption that higher quality is always correlated with higher purchase prices and higher input costs, particularly those costs associated with materials. This definition, adopted by early economists, primarily focused on the issue of durability. Economists equated quality with how long a given product held up over time. Some residue from this perspective can still be identified in the writings of economists, who continue to cast the non-durable output of the service sector in a less than favourable light. Other evidence of this residue is exhibited by those who continue to subscribe to the assertion that there is a negative relationship between cost and quality. Conceptually, the product approach to defining quality is less applicable to the service sector than other models because it focuses entirely on the physical attributes associated with materials input. Yet it is still frequently emphasized by hospitality managers, who stress the importance of the tangible atmospheric elements associated with services. This approach is deficient because an accurate assessment of service should include an evaluation of the activities associated with delivery in addition to the product components. The product approach to quality provides no means to evaluate many of the components important to the service delivery process.

The manufacturing approach to quality

The manufacturing approach to defining quality utilizes a technological process perspective. This approach embodies the concept of total quality management (TQM) as espoused by the movement's founder, W. Edward Deming. Deming's view of the relationship between quality and costs stands in direct opposition to that taken in a product approach to defining quality. Deming (1982) maintains that, contrary to the product perspective on the relationship between costs and quality, true quality actually reduces costs. Deming asserts that a process control approach which facilitates consistent and uniform output is really less costly because it reduces mistakes and the resulting waste associated with misused materials and ineffectively utilized labor. In the long run, it costs less to do things correctly the first time around. The process approach to quality relies heavily on statistical controls to monitor production during the process stage rather than using specifications to evaluate the finished product. The focus is not on catching defects and correcting them, but rather on monitoring the process so that defects do not occur. The standards applied from a manufacturing perspective are internally generated and controlled. A major difference between the manufacturing perspective on quality and the product perspective is the focus on the process rather than the product. Since a large component of the service output is related to the process of service delivery, the evaluation of service quality should be more amenable to a manufacturing approach to quality than to a product approach.

The user-based approach to quality

Another approach to defining quality is generated from a user perspective. This is commonly the approach used to define quality in the marketing discipline, especially with regard to service quality. This approach is based upon the premise that quality is a subjective perception which is best evaluated by the consumer. Using this perspective, quality is judged to be highest for those products that best meet the customers' wants or needs. This perspective equates customer satisfaction very closely with quality. The objective, physical attributes related to product characteristics are of secondary importance. A popular variation on the user-based definition of quality was introduced during the latter half of the 1980s to specifically address the issue of quality in the service sector. This variation focuses on the concept that quality in services output is primarily a function of meeting customer expectations. Quite simply, quality is perceived when there are no gaps between what the customer expects and what the customer gets (Parasuraman *et al.*, 1985, 1988; Zeithaml *et al.*, 1988). Although this is by far the most popular approach to quality used by service firms, there is an inherent weakness in this approach which should be recognized. Customer expectations may not be realistically defined. One exceptional experience rendered under unusual circumstances may create expectations that cannot be duplicated on a day-to-day basis or under normal operating conditions. When too great an emphasis is placed on the externally generated standards associated with customer expectations, opportunistic behaviors may be pursued by customers who seek unequitable personal advantage. This approach can be dysfunctional to a business organization which requires bottom-line profitability to ensure its long-term survival.

The value-based approach to quality

A final approach to defining quality relies on the relationship between costs and customer-perceived performance. This is called a value-based approach. This view of quality integrates some of the elements from the manufacturing perspective with some of the elements from a user-based perspective. The value-based approach to defining quality implies that the standards set by customer expectations vary according to the purchase price associated with a given product or service. From this perspective, standards for judging quality are moderated by associated costs. Thus, one would not expect the same attributes or embellishments to be associated with a hamburger purchased for 99 cents at a quick service restaurant that one would expect to receive when purchasing an eight dollar burger from a full service restaurant. Along the same lines, when evaluating quality between two products or services that are largely undifferentiated, the one with the lowest price tag attached would be considered of higher relative quality. The value-based perspective is becoming increasingly more prevalent in contemporary consumer markets (Garvin, 1984). Successful implementation of quality from the value-based perspective requires that one apply the manufacturing standards necessary to minimize costs while simultaneously keeping in mind a user-based perspective that focuses on quality as a measure of meeting customer expectations.

A summary of perspectives on quality

In spite of the fact that the approaches to defining quality are quite diverse, there is one compelling similarity shared by all perspectives: each approach requires some standard for evaluation. In the product approach, standards are based upon the inherent characteristics of the material components and the degree to which the final output compares favorably with established specifications. The manufacturing approach uses standards associated with the process used to create the final output. The user-based approach incorporates standards that are set based upon the customer's perception of satisfaction and met expectations. And finally the value-based approach looks at pricing levels and associated cost factors to establish the standards for determining quality.

   In practice, the actual approach used for quality attainment is usually an integration of more than one approach. Most frequently, the user-based approach is combined with the product approach and consumer research is incorporated into the specifications used to establish product standards. When these two approaches are combined, market share is emphasized as a confirmation of quality achievement. And finally, any operation competing as a low-cost provider must by necessity incorporate the ideas of process control into their quality efforts in order to maintain both a competitive position and level of profitability adequate enough to stay in business. This is the approach which has worked so successfully for McDonald's. The process approach has enabled this chain to provide a consistent, reliable product. Because the output is consistent, customers do not experience much variation in the McDonald's experience from one visit to the next. Expectations remain constant and, because the cost is kept to a minimum, the standards for evaluating the output are adjusted accordingly. Many would argue that quick service operations such as McDonald's are not representative of the majority of hospitality services. McDonald's and its quick service competitors are highly standardized operations, and many would say they are more like a factory assembly line than like the typical restaurant. Yet this was not always the case. At one time, quick service, low-cost burger operations were just as unpredictable and unstandardized as any other restaurant (Levitt, 1972). Both quality standards and output varied depending upon who was doing the cooking and who was doing the serving. At one time these operations were also services that fluctuated depending upon the human factors that make the labor-intensive service industry so unique. Could the same concepts that revolutionized the burger industry be extended to other hospitality services or are these services just too different?

HOW DIFFERENT ARE SERVICES?

One recurring theme that has dominated the services literature in the past has been how services differ from manufacturing and why the techniques that work in manufacturing cannot be effectively applied within the service sector. Yet the more research and attention that is devoted to the topic, the less the traditional perspective and the traditional arguments seem to apply. While certainly there are aspects of services that cannot be reconciled with the manufacturing perspective, there are aspects that can be applied which have the potential to benefit the service sector immensely in terms of enhancing productivity, efficiency and effectiveness, and ultimately in achieving quality objectives. A review of the characteristics inherent in services which provides a fresh perspective provides an ideal starting point to clarify this position.

If the idea of quality can be called nebulous due to the multiple concepts and definitions that surround it, it is fair to say that the idea of service is even more nebulous. One well-known authority on the English language provides over 33 separate definitions for service.[1] In essence, services are performances rendered by one party for another. While it is true that services often have a physical product component, this physical output is secondary to the delivery process that makes services unique. It is the performance side of service that has presented the greatest challenge to management. And rightly so, as it is the performance side of service that is responsible for the characteristics which have made the measurement of services so difficult. But to say that the measurement of services is elusive is not to say that the measurement of services is impossible, only to say that the accomplishment of such objectives will involve difficult, arduous work. The section which follows examines each of the traditional characteristics associated with services and presents a counterpoint which argues an alternative perspective.

Intangibility

First and foremost among the characteristics used to define service is intangibility. Intangibility is considered the most problematic characteristic of services and the characteristic at the root of all other characteristics which distinguish services from products. The traditional perspective is that because services are performances that are largely intangible they cannot be physically felt, seen, tasted, smelled or heard in the same concrete manner which can be applied to the manufacture and evaluation of products. This has led to the generally accepted assumption that the nature of service is too elusive to be amenable to measurement. A counterpoint to this argument is made on the basis that while services may not be experienced in the same concrete manner which applies to products, the intangible attributes associated with services are experienced in a psychological manner. And while psychological aspects associated with services are more difficult to measure than traditional product attributes such as material durability, fabric softness or dye lots, they are not impossible to measure. If this were so, the whole disciplinary area of psychology would not exist. Certainly it is true that such measurements may be more variable and less precise than the measurement of physical properties, but, as any social scientist would testify, measurement need not be perfect to be useful.

Heterogeneity

A second characteristic considered to be inherent in the performance of services focuses on heterogeneity. Heterogeneity refers to the state of being different or dissimilar. It is used to describe the fact that no two service performances are ever exactly alike. Because services are performed by people for people, it is generally accepted that service performances cannot really be controlled since some variation in the service experience will always occur. Often this is because the same service tends to be performed with some variability when executed by different individuals. At other times services vary just because someone, an employee or a customer, had a bad day. This perspective on heterogeneity emphasizes the spontaneous aspect associated with service performances, especially the psychological elements. Like intangibility, this type of heterogeneity is not considered amenable to measurement. It appears that service providers have largely subscribed to the belief that service excellence is more highly dependent upon the fluctuating mood and disposition of the service performer than the service task itself. Yet an in-depth analysis of the service task should be able to identify both physical and emotional aspects of labor that are integral parts of delivering excellent service.

To date, the management of emotional labor has focused largely on internal marketing (the idea that employees should be treated with the same care and consideration that is extended to the customer). The internal marketing movement is based upon the premise that happy, satisfied employees are more effective and more efficient at performing their jobs. But years of research into the relationship between job satisfaction and job performance does not provide much support for the hypothesized outcome. Happy, satisfied workers may be more likely to remain in their present jobs with their present employers, but there is little support for the idea that they perform better. Internal marketing is certainly a good idea from a human resource management perspective but it is not likely to impact on the personal factors which are equally important in influencing contact employees' dispositions. A conflict with a friend, or an unexpected car repair bill, can dampen employee dispositions, and there is little chance that internal marketing can reverse the effects of these external factors. What will be more likely to impact on performance is related to the concept of identifying the intangible characteristics which are prerequisites for successful job performance and communicating these to employees. Since large components of the service task may involve psychological, emotional labor, as well as physical labor, these components should figure equally in determining the standards for a job well done. If statistical analysis has provided any insight into the relationship between successful job perform-ance and the prerequisites needed to achieve it, it lies more in the identification of the essential tasks associated with a job and the subsequent communication of specific job expectations rather than in a general perception of job satisfaction. An in-depth examination of the emotional labor associated with many service tasks suggests that appropriate levels of emotional display can be achieved by surface acting alone. Thus, service performers need not 'feel' an emotion at a personal level in order to express it at a professional one (Ashford and Humphrey, 1993).

There is also a second side to service heterogeneity which is equally relevant. This aspect of heterogeneity is not spontaneous. Neither is it uncontrollable or unplanned. It is likely to represent the greatest source of heterogeneity associated with services. Yet, in spite of these facts, it is frequently overlooked in both the conceptualization of services and the application of operational strategies. Often heterogeneity in service performance occurs as a conscious organizational effort to differentiate service ele-ments of one provider from those of another. In essence, it is the result of a differentiation strategy applied to the performance component of service. Since this type of heterogeneity is intentional, it should be identifiable, and once identified it should be reflected in attempts to generate appropriate standards for measuring and evaluating the service performance process.

Inseparability

A third factor which has often been used to describe the unique attributes associated with services focuses on the inseparability of production and consumption. The inseparable nature of the production and consumption of services requires that consumers and providers of services engage in direct interaction. This attribute of services has received a considerable amount of attention because it is consistently recognized as facilitating a higher degree of tangibility. The customer's entry into the service facility provides an opportunity for service providers to overcome some of the ambiguity associated with the actual service performance process. For example, the atmosphere of the service establishment can incorporate decor, sound systems and other tangible evidence to embellish and support the desired service image.

Although some view customer participation as a fourth and separate attribute of service provision, from a practical perspective it is difficult to separate the two concepts. Both involve the customer's presence in the physical facility where services are produced. Typically, customers may participate by providing service providers with the information needed to initiate and perform the desired service, or customers may actually perform some of the tasks associated with the service. In cafeterias, for example, customers select their own menu choices and seat themselves. This aspect of service has engendered the concept of customers as partial employees.

To date, the management of quality in services has largely focused on customer involvement. In the absence of internally generated controls for managing and evaluat-ing intangible service behaviors, customers have been delegated as the quality control experts for service firms. In spite of the fact that services are considered to be more intangible than tangible, much of the quality control has been delegated to the evaluation of the tangible components associated with service output. This is especially true of hospitality organizations, where effective strategies for quality control have focused largely on the evaluation of atmospheric attributes associated with service facilities or product standards associated with menu items rather than on the characteristics associated with the actual service performance. That customers, and not employees, are responsible for monitoring these aspects of quality appears problematic. When the tangible factors associated with services assume the primary role in the evaluation process, the responsibility for setting standards and determining whether or not these are met should be no different in services than in traditional manufacturing firms. These evaluations focus on physical attributes. Quality specifications can be established and monitored. It should not require customer input to establish that a hotel room is unclean, the air conditioning system is on the blink, or a rib roast is underdone. Evaluation of such attributes should proceed internally based upon physical properties alone. The fact that services are in large part intangible provides no excuse for skimping on the internal controls necessary for monitoring the tangible factors associated with service output.

A summary of service attributes and their implications

A summary of this section isolates some pertinent facts. Services are differentiated from products primarily because of the intangibility factor. Because it is difficult to measure intangible attributes associated with service delivery, attempts to integrate intangible factors into the evaluation of service output have not been pursued at an operational level. Further, it is assumed that the heterogeneity associated with services is largely spontaneous and uncontrolled, thus providing a second factor to discourage any implementation of measurement attempts or control devices. Finally, because of the difficulties associated with the factors identified above and because of the integral role which customers assume in the service production process, it has been typical to delegate control responsibilities to the customers of service firms. In some ways this is easier for managers of services because it reduces their responsibilities. In this regard customers have been given the role of quality control expert for both the highly visible and tangible aspects of service as well as the less tangible and more ambiguous factors. This is disturbing since it suggests that the failure to secure quality objectives in hospitality can be blamed only partially on the intangible attributes associated with service delivery. When the physically measurable components associated with services are also delegated to customers for evaluation, this suggests that the essence of the problem is not inherent in the intangible components of the service process but rather that it is associated with a failure to develop adequate internal controls.

There is a plausible explanation of why the development of internal controls has not been put in place in many hospitality operations. Competition has increased while both productivity and profitability have continued to decline. A reduction in staffing has generally provided one of the primary means to offset the increasing costs of staying in business. With a smaller workforce, existing responsibilities have been reallocated among a smaller number of employees. Ultimately the customer bears some of the burden which was once a management function. In the process the system becomes increasingly inefficient. It is feasible that in large part the decreasing profitability and productivity associated with service firms has been accelerated by an investment in TQM programs that have nothing to do with real quality management at all.

IS IT REALLY QUALITY?

In consideration of quality control

Increasingly we are hearing about hospitality firms where quality comes first. To meet that objective, rooms are comped, rebates are issued, and discounts abound. Such practices provide excellent examples of current trends toward empowerment and recovery strategies which are often integral parts of the TQM efforts pursued by hospitality firms. Yet are such practices really examples of quality management? Quality experts would say no, explaining that such strategies are more accurately defined as defect management, for two reasons (Deming, 1982). First, they divert the organization's focus away from doing things right the first time, and second, they simultaneously incur higher costs in the process. Deming sums up the cost inefficiency inherent in such approaches quite effectively: they require paying out good money to create defective output, and then paying out good money again to correct the defects. Deming (1982) maintains that this approach usually more than doubles organizational costs, since the expense associated with the correction of defects is generally higher than any original costs involved.

From this perspective it is clear that the service recovery approach which is being widely utilized in hospitality organizations is exactly the opposite from true quality management. The foundation for effective quality management lies in internally generated and monitored controls; the recovery approach to quality is curiously lacking in either. Furthermore, research indicates that user-based perceptions of quality align closely with those espoused by Deming and 'that customers perceive reliability – "doing it right the first time" – as the most important dimension of service quality' (Bowen and Lawler, 1992, p. 34).

In consideration of quality standards

A second example of misdirected efforts to implement TQM is an overreliance on inappropriate copy-cat strategies. All too often management decision-makers overlook the unique, critical factors associated with their own service objectives, and emulate strategies reported to be successful for firms with very different objectives. In sum, they ignore the intentional heterogeneity which may dictate highly differentiated standards. The standards which are synonymous with quality in a Four Seasons Resort Hotel would be largely inappropriate for a Holiday Inn. If Holiday Inn ignored this fact and adopted those standards anyway, it would be investing unnecessary money, energy and efforts on embellishments that customers were not really expecting when making purchase decisions. The only empirical study to date which addresses this issue involves not a hospitality organization but a convenience store chain (Sutton and Rafaeli, 1988). The implications of the research are applicable, since hospitality executives, like those of the convenience store chain, have also been swayed by the popular business press and the idea that quality for all can be obtained by applying a universal set of standards. The story recounted below provides a most effective illustration of how misplaced strategies for obtaining quality objectives can involve costly mistakes.

Influenced by the ideas promoted in *In Search of Excellence* (Peters and Waterman, 1982), a group of convenience store corporate executives embarked on a chain-wide effort to enhance quality service through increased courtesy. The implementation phase of the strategy included the development and execution of numerous training programs which emphasized courtesy by stressing the need for displaying friendliness to customers through smiling, eye contact, verbal greetings and saying 'thank you' to each and every customer. Employee behavior was monitored and bonus prizes distributed to employees who were 'displaying the required good cheer to customers' (Sutton and Rafaeli, 1988, p. 465). Rewards for conforming to the new standards included cash prizes in some regions, and new cars in others. Management personnel were eligible for bonuses of more than 25 per cent of their base pay. Together the training and incentive rewards cost the corporation over ten million dollars. In spite of the large financial investment, the executives were satisfied with the results and most believed that their new commitment to quality had payed off by increasing sales. To secure quantitative evidence to support their beliefs, researchers were engaged and a major study was undertaken. The study was well designed and used a sample of 576 stores distributed across all 18 corporate divisions in the USA and Canada. The research hypothesis stated that store sales would be greater to the extent that contact employees displayed pleasant emotions to customers. An unexpected negative relationship between the variables of interest was observed. The most successful stores were also those demonstrating the lowest levels of friendliness. In sum, the research provided no support for a ten million dollar investment in the 'service obsession' strategy.

A simple analysis of this case suggests that in convenience stores customers are paying a premium for fast, convenient service. Friendly interactions that slow down transactions are not likely to be highly valued by customers. In spite of their intuitive appeal, psychological embellishments such as friendliness, caring and individualized attention may not be necessary, or even desirable, in all types of service transactions. When service employees unnecessarily engage in activities which are neither desired nor appreciated, it is not quality; it is overcapacity and it is inefficient. Yet until service providers take a task-oriented approach to identify the intangible emotional attributes best suited to their operations, inappropriate allocations of organizational investments are likely to continue.

Total quality: standards plus controls

There are two vital elements in quality management: first, the identification of applicable standards, and second, the use of internally generated controls to objectively measure performance in accordance with those standards. In the service recovery and empowerment example, standards are implied by the very fact that the failure to meet them is compensated, but internal controls needed to ensure that standards are met appear to be lacking. In the pursuit of generic strategies for quality, there seems to be a lack of awareness regarding the choice of appropriate standards for a given organization. The use of internally generated controls does not suggest that a user-based perspective on establishing quality standards should be abandoned, but merely that the more effective time to solicit user input is prior to defining these standards, not after the service has been rendered. This is the only approach that can lead to reliability in service delivery – the most important indicator of quality from a user-based perspective.

In sum, the tradition in the service sector has been to dwell on the elements of service that make it difficult to measure and not amenable to internal control. It is a negative approach. In the words of Levitt (1972), it represents a 'paralyzing legacy' of inherited attitudes which has diverted our attention away from seeking the new solutions necessary to improve services. As a result service managers have been severely handicapped in their pursuits of both quality and productivity. Until an effective approach to identifying measurable standards and developing related controls can be achieved, there can be little hope for enduring improvement in service quality.

THE RESEARCH

The research reported here was not undertaken with the objective of furthering the TQM movement in hospitality firms, but the results have implications for quality management which should not be ignored. The research methodology which was utilized provides a foundation for establishing quality control standards for services that incorporate the intangible emotional side of service labor, which has long eluded measurement. The primary objective sought in the study reported was the development of a classification system for services which focused on identifying the intangible attributes associated with service activities. It was based upon two assumptions: first, that observable behaviors provide a primary mechanism for communicating the intangible, psychological and emotional components integral to service performances, and second, that customer expectations for intangible, psychological embellishments would differ depending upon the service being performed.

Initial research efforts utilized customer focus groups and extensive literature reviews to isolate those behavioral dimensions which were deemed relevant and important in face-to-face encounters between customers and service providers. This information was then utilized in the development of behaviorally anchored rating scales.[2] This measurement approach gave respondents an opportunity to choose among descriptions of alternative service employee behaviors and identify the behavior which demonstrated the most desirable level of each intangible attribute being considered. The use of behavioral descriptions as anchors for the responses provides information that can be directly applied to the establishment of operational standards. The methodology is amenable to the manufacturing approach to quality because it views intangible service behaviors as a set of activities that can be broken down into observable units. It is amenable to a user-based approach to quality because service customers provided the input used to differentiate among appropriate and inappropriate behaviors, depending upon which type of service organization was being considered. Finally, because the measurement instrument also provided information on the respondents' willingness to purchase the services of each specified provider based upon relative price levels, it also incorporates elements from the value-based perspective on quality.

Five of the 15 service organization types examined in the original research were hospitality service providers: quick service restaurants, casual restaurants, tablecloth restaurants, chain motels and luxury hotels. Yet, when all 15 organizational types (hospitality and non-hospitality) were grouped based upon the similarity in scores on each of the behavioral dimensions, the results indicated that hospitality providers are not a homogeneous subset of the service sector (Becker, 1992; Becker and Olsen, 1995). In fact, the results of the grouping procedure, which are shown in Table 15.1, indicate

Table 15.1 *The service typology*

Group I	Group II
Family physicians	Tablecloth restaurants
Medical specialists	Luxury hotels
Life insurance services	Medical clinics
Beauty shops	Barbers
	Speciality shops
	Car repair
Group III	Group IV
Full service department stores	Fast-food restaurants
Chain motels	Discount department stores
Casual restaurants	

that in many instances hospitality providers might more effectively build on operational strategies developed for and from service organizations outside the hospitality field than from those within it.

To get a closer look at how hospitality organizations compared with each other, an in-depth examination of the five types of hospitality firms included in the original study was undertaken. Because the survey instrument was developed for the purpose of evaluating a wide range of services, the focus is on generic aspects of all services rather than the specifics associated with hospitality providers alone. In spite of this limitation, the format proved effective at differentiating among the intangible attributes associated with hospitality services, and the results secured provide information which should serve hospitality providers in the identification and establishment of standards for quality management objectives. The section which follows briefly identifies the methodological considerations pertinent to the research. The behavioral dimensions most relevant to the development of quality standards are then individually explored with reference to each of the five types of hospitality firms examined.

Research methods and results

During the scale development process, ten intangible attributes were isolated to identify the specific employee, organizational and customer behaviors that conveyed the intangible attributes of service which customers felt were most important. These included: friendliness, caring, customer recognition, provider expertise, special treatment, trust, decision responsibility, customer–employee attachment, informational needs, and relative cost factors. A five-level behaviorally anchored rating scale was developed for each. The survey instrument was pilot tested on 108 respondents. After minimal refinements the instrument was pretested and then administered to 128 service customers. The sampling strategy employed three demographically diverse convenience samples which included residents from over 18 different states. When this sampling procedure is used and the scores secured from separate samples do not exhibit statistically significant differences, the data can then be aggregated to generate results with greater external validity and generalizability then could be secured with a single, homogeneous convenience sample (Webb *et al.*, 1966).

A repeated measures multivariate analysis of variance was used to compare the scores for the five hospitality service providers on each of the behavioral attributes examined. Results indicated that the scores for each attribute differed among the five types of hospitality services being evaluated ($p < 0.001$). Contrast analyses were used to examine the differences between the hospitality firms on a one-to-one basis. The following contrasts were evaluated: quick service operations were compared to casual restaurants, casual restaurants were compared to full service restaurants, full service restaurants were compared to luxury hotels, and chain motels were compared to luxury hotels. Except where noted in the report of research results, all contrasts indicated significant differences for each pair of hospitality service providers which was examined ($p < 0.01$).

The section which follows provides a limited description of seven of the ten attributes which were evaluated in the research. Each description is supplemented with an illustration of the five-level rating scale used for measurement, and the scores secured for each hospitality service provider are reported. Although the analyses of customer–employee attachment, informational needs and decision responsibility were significantly different among the five hospitality service providers, these three dimensions have limited application for the development of behavioral standards which directly address service employees. Thus, they have been omitted from continued discussion.

Friendliness

The idea that service employees should be friendly to customers is intuitively appealing. Both the review of literature and the consumer focus groups provided support for this assumption. The results of the convenience store study cited earlier suggested that the appropriate level of friendliness might differ depending upon the context and type of service exchange taking place. The data displayed in Table 15.2 provide additional support for the correctness of this assumption.

The contrast analyses indicated that the desired level of friendliness was significantly different for each of the food service operations and between the two types of lodging firms ($p < 0.01$). The differences between desired level of friendliness in tablecloth restaurants and luxury hotels were not statistically significant.

Table 15.2

When I consider the 'friendliness' appropriate for employees providing this service, I think employees should . . .
5 = take time to talk with me about personal interests, family, etc.
4 = chat with me about non-personal topics
3 = exchange a few social pleasantries
2 = give a smile or a nod and leave it at that
1 = friendliness gets in the way of work efficiency

Organization type	Mean score	SD
Quick service	2.19	0.71
Casual restaurants	2.99	0.68
Tablecloth restaurants	3.41	0.87
Chain motels	2.84	0.71
Luxury hotels	3.30	0.80

Table 15.3

In this type of service, when I think about 'caring for the customer' I really feel the employees should ...
1 = focus on the physical requirements of their jobs
2 = briefly acknowledge customers' feelings
3 = make an extra effort to acknowledge customers' feelings
4 = anticipate customers' feelings and demonstrate concern/support
5 = care for customers like friends

Organization type	Mean score	SD
Quick service	2.15	1.10
Casual restaurants	3.17	1.00
Tablecloth restaurants	3.94	0.98
Chain motels	2.65	0.92
Luxury hotels	3.49	0.94

Caring

Like friendliness, caring for customers is another intangible attribute of service exchanges which has strong intuitive appeal and high surface validity. This attribute corresponds closely to the idea of empathy which was identified by Zeithaml *et al.* (1990) as an important dimension of the service exchange. The research results (Table 15.3) indicate that standards for demonstrating care to customers vary from one hospitality service provider to the next.

All contrast analyses were significant ($p < 0.01$).

Customer recognition

The idea that being 'recognized' provides customers with ego gratification is not new to the hospitality literature (Kotschevar, 1975). Yet the increasing number of self-service facilities and food service operations that focus primarily on convenience provided reason to believe that this intangible attribute would not be equally important in all service exchanges between customers and hospitality contact employees. This assumption was supported (Table 15.4).

All contrast analyses were significant ($p < 0.01$).

Provider expertise

Provider expertise represents another intangible characteristic of service production where pre-existing customer standards were expected to vary depending upon the type of hospitality service being performed. Since expertise is most often achieved through costly investments in training and selection strategies, an *a priori* knowledge of customer standards should indicate which types of hospitality services are likely to benefit most from such investments. The research results indicated that the expected level of expertise for hospitality employees varied significantly across the five organizational types examined in the study (Table 15.5).

All contrast analyses were significant ($p < 0.01$).

Table 15.4

When I'm a customer in this type of service, I prefer it when the firm's employees ...
1 = let me service myself without being acknowledged
2 = acknowledge me as a customer, not as an individual
3 = remember my face
4 = remember my name and face
5 = remember who I am and details about my special needs

Organization type	Mean score	SD
Quick service	2.10	0.82
Casual restaurants	2.84	0.94
Tablecloth restaurants	3.85	1.09
Chain motels	2.41	0.86
Luxury hotels	3.02	1.09

Table 15.5

The employees in this service should have expertise to ...
1 = know a little bit more than I do
2 = answer questions about product availability, prices, etc.
3 = make general recommendations about a few alternatives
4 = provide detailed professional advice about many alternatives
5 = assume legal responsibility for advice and service

Organization type	Mean score	SD
Quick service	1.82	0.80
Casual restaurants	2.96	0.56
Tablecloth restaurants	3.83	0.65
Chain motels	2.48	0.93
Luxury hotels	3.25	0.85

Special treatment

The importance of treating customers to specialized service is extended by the works of both academic researchers and writers in the popular press (Bitner *et al.*, 1990; Zeithaml *et al.*, 1990; Hinton, 1991). From an operational perspective the willingness to individualize service is often viewed as a means for service providers to maintain a competitive advantage in their respective markets. The concept is important because the more individualized are the services provided, the less amenable the operation will be to cost-efficient standardization. Any attempts to specialize services beyond the level expected by customers may ultimately be dysfunctional to the organization's bottom line and its long-term survival. Research results (Table 15.6) indicate that customers set different standards for the degree of specialized service they expect to receive when using different types of hospitality services.

All contrast analyses were significant ($p < 0.01$).

Trust

The concept of trust, in spite of its intuitive importance, has received little direct attention in the services literature. The idea of credence in the evaluation of services (Zeithaml, 1981) and the security factors isolated in the SERVQUAL study (Parasuraman *et al.*, 1988) represent two limited applications of the trust dimension. The consumer focus group that participated in the development of the survey instrument identified trust as a major factor in decisions regarding which service organizations to patronize. There was reason to believe that the organizational and provider behaviors which symbolized an acceptable level of trust would vary depending upon which type of service was being used. The research results confirmed this expectation (Table 15.7), suggesting that the standards which symbolize trustworthiness to customers do differ among hospitality service providers.

Contrast analyses were significant ($p < 0.01$) for all comparisons except tablecloth restaurants and luxury hotels, where the differences were not significant.

Table 15.7

When I think about the importance of trust in this type of service firm, I really feel ...
1 = trusting the provider is not an issue
2 = a neatly organized firm is not an issue
3 = recommendations by others are good indicators of trustworthiness
4 = legal certification is needed before I can trust this firm
5 = trust requires more than legality; the provider must understand me and put my best interest first

Organization type	Mean score	SD
Quick service	1.90	0.89
Casual restaurants	2.55	0.82
Tablecloth restaurants	3.00	0.95
Chain motels	2.42	0.85
Luxury hotels	2.87	0.97

Cost

While it can be argued that cost is not, strictly speaking, an intangible aspect of service, pricing strategies can be viewed as an organizational behavior which impacts upon how an organization can be profitably managed. The inclusion of the variable in this study was largely due to the input of consumer focus group participants, who felt that prices provided critical information about service expectations. The cost factors associated with services set parameters which affect the overall standards which customers use to evaluate service quality. Although today's consumers have become increasingly cost-conscious when making many purchase decisions, the results secured here (Table 15.8) indicate that cost factors are not equally considered when making purchase decisions regarding different types of hospitality services.

All contrast analyses were significant ($p < 0.01$).

Table 15.8

I am willing to purchase the services provided by this firm ...
1 = only if I can get them at a bargain
2 = if prices are lower than those of competing services
3 = when prices are set at the normal rate
4 = even though prices are higher than those of competing services
5 = regardless of how high prices are

Organization type	Mean score	SD
Quick service	2.69	0.83
Casual restaurants	3.09	0.49
Tablecloth restaurants	3.87	0.71
Chain motels	2.49	0.72
Luxury hotels	3.39	0.85

Research implications

Taken as a whole, the research results reported here support the contention that the intangible elements associated with hospitality services can be observed and measured, and further that customers do not apply uniform expectations across all hospitality organizations. Consumers of hospitality services appear to have preconceived ideas about how much intangible embellishment is appropriate, depending upon the type of service that is being performed. Embellishing service performances beyond the expectations of customers equates to the addition of unnecessary costs. Ultimately such costs must be absorbed either by the organization, through reduced profitability, or by the customer, through increased prices. The value-based perspective on quality indicates that customers moderate their standards for evaluating quality in both products and services based upon prices. Thus, it is important that hospitality service providers remain cognizant of this relationship and how operational strategies for pursuing quality may impact upon it. Since customer expectations vary from one type of hospitality organization to the next, it follows that the strategies that work effectively to attain service quality in one type of hospitality operation may not be equated with quality in another. The appropriate approach for managing quality will be dictated by the identification and application of those standards relevant to the specific operation under consideration.

Standards are, after all, the essence of quality. Regardless of what perspective we use to define it, quality is a relative concept. As expectations and standards change, the effective management of quality will likewise change. To date, many of the attempts made by hospitality organizations to secure quality objectives have been hindered by the assumption that behavioral standards associated with service delivery tasks are relatively homogeneous across the wide range of hospitality services which they provide. As a result, hospitality executives, like those associated with the convenience store chain referred to earlier, have often embraced quality service objectives from a generic perspective. The results of the research reported here suggest that customer expectations of hospitality services are neither generic nor homogeneous. Thus organizations pursuing quality objectives should realize success to the extent that they have analyzed their own operations and identified the applicable standards.

A second obstacle to quality attainment resides in the traditional belief that the intangible, emotional aspects associated with service performances are too elusive for measurement and thus not amenable to control. Rather than analyzing the emotional labor component associated with service delivery, hospitality managers have placed undue emphasis on the dispositional characteristics of service employees. Typically they ascribe to the belief that hiring people with the 'right' personality and implementing a 'customer-focused' organizational climate will ensure that employees do the right thing, in spite of the fact that the ideal behavioral response has never been clearly identified. This approach can, and does, work for the few financially advantaged firms that can afford the luxury. Yet, in an era marked by increased competition and lower profitability, this is no solution for the vast majority of hospitality providers. Ultimately this is the very approach that is responsible for the downward trend in both quality and productivity which is currently associated with the aggregate of service sector organizations. The results generated by this research suggest that acceptable levels for the intangible attributes associated with service delivery can be differentiated at an organization-specific level. The procedures implemented in this research provide the means to identify the relevant organizational and behavioral standards necessary to implement quality objectives that can be monitored and controlled. Only with well-defined standards and the associated controls will consistent product delivery ever become more than a hit or miss affair. In the absence of either, 'doing it right the first time' will remain an elusive goal.

The attainment of total quality in any organization is never a simple one-step process. It begins with the identification of acceptable standards and follows through with strategies for meeting and maintaining those standards over time and in a manner which ensures that organizational profit objectives can be realized. In the hospitality service industry, true quality management should begin, not end, with customer input. The use of behaviorally anchored rating scales enhances the specificity of customer input beyond that secured by scales which typically rank ambiguous service attributes in terms of importance. Friendliness may be equally important in two different service settings, yet, at the same time, what is perceived as an appropriate expression of friendliness in one setting may not be deemed appropriate in another. A measurement approach which identifies customer expectations in behavioral terms provides hospitality managers with actionable standards that can serve as a basis for implementing controls. When standards rely heavily on tangible embellishments, mechanisms for monitoring and controlling can be effectively borrowed from the traditional manufacturing models for quality control. When standards emphasize the less tangible behavioral elements, controls are more likely to reside in the traditional human resource functions. At the individual level, job descriptions may need to be expanded to accurately reflect the total job. This is particularly true when emotional tasks are considered essential to meeting customer expectations. Less essential tasks may need to be reallocated in order to facilitate the employees' ability to perform up to quality standards. Incorporating behavioral standards for emotional labor will provide internal controls for monitoring employee performance as it occurs. As in the manufacturing model, this process approach to quality should help to prevent serious service *faux pas* before they can impact upon customer perceptions.

Limitations

Because the research goals pursued by this project were broad in scope, the primary contribution of the research toward quality management objectives lies not in the specific scores reported here, but in the development of a process which promises to be effective in identifying the standards associated with the intangible components inherent in the performance of service. The standard deviations exhibited by the behavioral measures reported in this research project indicate a high degree of variance, higher than would be exhibited if the research objectives had focused on securing the measurement precision necessary for the establishment of quality standards for any specific organization. In large part, the variance demonstrated in the results shown here is a reflection of a research objective which required the sacrifice of specificity to achieve a higher level of generalizability. To secure the information necessary to establish more precise standards for the evaluation of quality, the process used here could be replicated and the trade-off between specificity and generalizability reversed. This reversal can be accomplished by first adjusting the measures to include only those anchoring behaviors that describe situations relevant to the organization being evaluated, and second, through the use of a sample composed of the specific consumer market for the service being evaluated. With regard to both adjustments, the consideration of cultural factors cannot be overlooked. Such factors heavily influence the determination of what standards customers consider appropriate. For organizations that operate in locations dispersed over wide geographic regions, consumer input should be solicited at a regional level to capture any differences which may be present depending upon the cultural inclinations of local markets. Even in the USA, cultural norms may dictate different standards for operations located in different geographic regions.

Considering the international expansion taking place in many hospitality firms, the need for local-level consumer research is even greater. The recent opening of McDonald's in Moscow illustrates the point. In this example, the concept of a universal standard was applied in training staff members to smile at customers and display the Western norms associated with service excellence. Soviet customers were not favorably impressed; to the contrary, they thought that employees were mocking them (Ashford and Humphrey, 1993).

Herein lies the major functional difference between the customer contact service provider and the traditional manufacturing firm. Because it is necessary for service providers to disperse into unit-level operations convenient for customer usage, the need for local research cannot be overemphasized. Beyond this differentiating factor, it would appear more beneficial to visualize service performances using the same analytical approach that has worked so well at increasing both the quality and productivity associated with the manufacture of products. Although service performances may be more difficult to measure, they are processes that can be broken down into both physical and emotional components. In this way both the relevant behaviors and the standards to evaluate them can be identified. This suggests that services are amenable to the manufacturing approach for quality control. Further, since this approach appears to be effectively facilitated through customer-generated input, it is equally responsive to the user-based approach to quality. In the final analysis, quality management, from any perspective, is contingent on the existence of clearly defined and measurable standards. The approach outlined here provides both the method and the means for establishing these standards.

NOTES

1. *The Random House Dictionary of the English Language* (1970), New York, p. 1304.
2. The author would like to acknowledge the assistance and participation of Dr Suzanne Murrmann of Virginia Polytechnic Institute and State University. Her input was vital to the development of the measurement scales used in this study.

REFERENCES

Armstrong, L., and Symonds, W. (1991) 'Services: beyond "May I help you" ', *Business Week*, 25 October, pp. 100–03.

Ashford, B. E., and Humphrey, R. H. (1993) 'Emotional labor in service roles: the influence of identity', *The Academy of Management Review*, vol. **18**, no. 1, pp. 88–115.

Becker, C. F. (1992) 'A middle range approach to theory development for service organizations', doctoral dissertation, Virginia Polytechnic Institute and State University, Blacksburg, VA.

Becker, C., and Olsen, M. D. (1995, in press), 'Exploring the relationship between heterogeneity and generic management trends in hospitality organizations', *International Journal of Hospitality Management*.

Bitner, M. J., Booms, B., and Tetreault, M. S. (1990) 'The service encounter: diagnosing favorable and unfavorable incidents', *Journal of Marketing*, vol. **54**, pp. 71–84.

Bowen, D. E., and Lawler, E. E. (1992) 'The empowerment of service workers: what, why, how, and when', *Sloan Management Review*, Spring, pp. 31–9.

Deming, W. E. (1982) 'Improvement of quality and productivity through action by management', *National Productivity Review*, Winter, pp. 12–22.

Drucker, P. F. (1991) 'The new productivity challenge', *Harvard Business Review*, November/December, pp. 69–79.

Garvin, D. A. (1984) 'What does product quality really mean?' *Sloan Management Review*, Fall, pp. 25–43.

Hinton, T. D. (1991) *The Spirit of Service*, Kendall/Hunt Publishing, Dubuque, IA.

Kotschevar, L. H. (1975) *Management by Menu*, Wm C. Brown in cooperation with the National Institute for the Foodservice Industry, Dubuque, IA.

Levitt, T. (1972) 'Production line approach to service', *Harvard Business Review*, September–October, pp. 41–52.

Parasuraman, A., Zeithaml, V., and Berry, L. (1985) 'A conceptual model of service quality and its implications for future research', *Journal of Marketing*, vol. **49**, pp. 41–50.

Parasuraman, A., Zeithaml, V., and Berry, L. (1988) 'SERVQUAL: a multiple item scale for measuring consumer perceptions of service quality', *Journal of Retailing*, vol. **64**, no. 1, pp. 12–37.

Peters, T. J., and Waterman, R. H. (1982) *In Search of Excellence*, Harper and Row, New York.

Pirsig, R. M. (1974) *Zen and the Art of Motorcycle Maintenance*, Bantam Books, New York.

Power, C., and Zinn. L. (1991) 'Services: their wish is your command', *Business Week*, 25 October, pp. 126–7.

Sutton, R. I., and Rafaeli, A. (1988) 'Untangling the relationship between displayed emotions and organizational sales: the case of convenience stores', *Academy of Management Journal*, vol. **31**, no. 3, pp. 461–87.

Webb, E., Campbell, D. T., Swartz, R. D., and Secrest, L. (1966) *Unobtrusive Measures*, Rand McNally, Chicago.

Zeithaml, V. (1981) 'How consumer evaluation processes differ between goods and services', in Donnelly, J. H., and George, W. R. (eds), *Marketing of Services*, American Marketing Association, Chicago, pp. 186–90.

Zeithaml, V., Berry, L. L., and Parasuraman, A. (1988) 'Communication and control processes in the delivery of service quality', *Journal of Marketing*, vol. **52**, pp. 35–48.

Zeithaml, V., Parasuraman, A., and Berry, L. L. (1985), 'Problems and strategies in services marketing', *Journal of Marketing*, vol. **49**, pp. 33–46.

Zeithaml, V., Parasuraman, A., and Berry, L. L. (1990) *Delivering Quality Service: Balancing Customer Perceptions and Expectations*, The Free Press, New York.

16

Towards a strategic total quality framework for hospitality firms

Eliza Ching-Yick Tse

SERVICE QUALITY AS A DIFFERENTIATION TOOL

Today's US economy is best described as a service economy, with approximately 76 per cent of all US workers employed in service industries (Quinn *et al.*, 1990). After a boom period in the last decade, many service businesses are experiencing consolidation and are struggling for market share (Allen, 1988). As the hospitality industry approaches maturity, the environment it faces is increasingly volatile and complex. The expansion and growth strategies in the 1980s left many hospitality firms too thinly spread, especially in the areas of human and operational resources. As with other firms in the service sector, this has contributed to the neglect of the quality of services offered by hospitality firms (Schlesinger and Heskett, 1991). Along with customers expressing dissatisfaction, many operators have been left with high employee turnover, flat or falling sales, and little or no growth in productivity.

At the same time, consumers have changed enormously in the past few years, as pointed out in a special issue on 'The tough new consumer' in *Business Week* (1993). Today's customers are more sophisticated, with complex demands to satisfy (Madu and Kuei, 1993). A sluggish world economy since 1990 has meant that consumers demand more value for the price they pay. People tend to substitute products for services, and thus the role of services in providing value is ever more important.

Value means different things to different people; it does not necessarily mean the lowest price but it does equate to the best deal for the precise mix of features required by the consumer. Today's consumers define value in terms of fair prices, intrinsic product features, service quality and convenience. This is particularly true among older Americans, for whom convenience and quality of service are more important than price (*Travel Weekly*, 1989a). In the case of California Pizza Kitchen, it learned that its customers, through focus group feedback, defined value in terms of larger portions.

Thus, in order to survive and achieve growth in the 1990s, hospitality firms are experiencing the need to differentiate themselves by offering value and re-emphasizing quality in service and product so as to establish a viable competitive position. They are also paying more attention to operational details, and to offering what the consumer perceives as value. Theoretical and empirical evidence suggests that firms that provide higher levels of service reap higher profits than those that do not (Jacobson and Aaker, 1987; Phillips *et al.*, 1983). Better sales are usually associated with better service and an effective quality assurance program (Comen, 1989). In their research, Heskett *et al.* (1990) found that some firms are good examples of what they consider as 'break-through' service providers. These firms provide evidence that service excellence pays off. As a group, they have achieved significantly higher rates of growth and higher returns on assets than the average for the largest firms in their industries. In the hospitality industry, such an example would be the Marriott Corporation.

THE NEED FOR STRATEGIC MANAGEMENT

With regard to recent growth patterns and their approach to strategic planning, service industry firms are currently at the stage where manufacturing was back in the 1950s and 1960s (Wilson, 1988). With the globalization of economic activity and the resultant intensive competition, service industry firms are re-structuring and repositioning, and new technologies are being introduced. Growth is no longer automatically assumed. Likewise, many hospitality operators find that the usual way of running their businesses (good product at a good price) is not a guarantee for survival, let alone success. Strategic planning and the development of competitive strategy is now playing a more important role. Wilson (1988) claims that strategic planning is earning its place in the management systems of service businesses; and it does appear to make a difference for the better in their efficiency and effectiveness. However, literature searches indicate that although consumer services, such as travel, lodging, restaurant, entertainment, etc., are the most developed in the more affluent of the world's economies, relatively little attention appears to have been directed to strategic management (Allen, 1988). Given the importance and growth opportunities presented by consumer services, the historical parallel with the emergence of strategic management in the manufacturing sector 20 years ago, and the fundamental differences in service business characteristics, there is a need for service businesses to take a more rigorous view of their business strategies (Olsen *et al.*, 1992).

UNIQUE CHARACTERISTICS OF SERVICE FIRMS

Strategic management in service businesses differs from manufacturing. This is because there are differences in the degree and emphasis regarding the goods and services offered in the two industries. These so-called 'serviceness' dimensions should give rise to significant differences between strategies for service firms and those for manufacturing firms. Goods and services differ along four 'serviceness' dimensions: intangibility, inseparability of production and consumption, homogeneity/heterogeneity, and perishability of product.

Until quite recently, few studies had been undertaken to investigate the differences in strategic phenomena between the manufacturing and service sectors, despite the growing magnitude and increasing competitiveness of the latter. One of the major reasons for this relative lack of attention to the service sector can be attributed to a broader conceptualization of 'product', which treats goods and services as 'products' or 'bundles of benefits' and considers the same marketing strategies for both (Lee, 1989).

Researchers generally agree that the distinctive nature of service situations is and should be one of the major determinants of strategies for service firms (Berry, 1980; Levitt, 1981; Zeithaml *et al.*, 1985). Thus, the rules and techniques of strategy based in the manufacturing environment are not immediately and completely transferable. Carman and Langeard (1980) assert that the usual determinants of profitability generally considered in strategic planning, such as the product life cycle, experience curve effects, and market share, cannot be easily applied to service firms because of the uniqueness of the service dimensions.

Thus, service businesses add value differently and so, strategically, they must plan differently (Allen, 1988). On the one hand, there is the emphasis and commitment to service quality in order to improve customer satisfaction; on the other, there is the practice of strategic management which is gaining momentum in the service sector. It is generally believed in the business community that sound business strategy leads to better organizational performance and success. However, as pointed out by Barksy and Labagh (1992), these two concepts have been developed separately. Strategic planning has not focused directly on customer satisfaction, and customer satisfaction, in general, does not have a strategic dimension. Thus, the urgent task becomes one of how to incorporate strategy into emphasis on service throughout all levels of the organization. One best way to achieve this goal is by linking the concept of service quality with the overall strategic management process.

With this objective in mind, the purpose of this chapter is to address the issues affecting service quality and changing customer expectations, as well as the need for strategic management in the hospitality industry. Characteristics of service industries that influence strategies in the hospitality industry are briefly examined. A strategic total quality management concept is discussed, and, finally, a step-by-step strategic management process, with the goal of providing service quality that customers demand, is outlined.

SERVICE QUALITY AND CUSTOMER SATISFACTION

If the 1980s was the decade of product quality, then the 1990s will be the service quality decade. Quinn and Humble (1993) indicate that both product and service quality are important. Product quality is important for recruiting customers, but service quality is key to retaining them. The ultimate goal of providing quality service and product is to achieve customer satisfaction, or as Dodwell and Simmons (1994) put it, people retention, customer acquisition and retention, and profitability.

The three parts of a successful service strategy are segmentation, customer research, and setting customer expectations (Davidow and Uttal, 1989). Figure 16.1 depicts the relationship between customers and the organization using a systems approach. It shows that effective customer segmentation based on extensive market research generates information regarding both potential and repeat customer profiles with certain levels of expectation of the product and service that the operation generates.

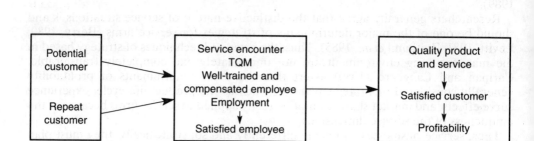

Figure 16.1 *Customer segmentation and profitability: a systems approach*

Lewis and Nightingale (1991) maintain that the key to an effective service strategy is to segment the customers to be served. According to these authors, focusing on customers is not the same as focusing on service. They indicate that service is defined relative to customers' needs. Marriott's Courtyard concept was successful because Courtyard's emphasis was a match of the customer's exact needs, not the company's idea of what service ought to be. Services must be designed for customers' needs and their willingness to pay for the services.

Once customers enter the service delivery process and the service encounter with the employee begins, it is the attention to detail in operations and emphasis on quality that meets or exceeds the expectations of the customer that results in positive encounters and happy customers. There is a positive correlation between well-trained, fairly paid employees, with lower employee turnover, and satisfied customers and a higher return rate. A long-term commitment to employee growth is necessary (Barsky and Dittmann, 1993). Page (1994) points out that a satisfied employee reduces turnover, which in turn contributes to providing quality service that leads to customer satisfaction and a loyal customer base. For the Marriott Corporation, a study was conducted by its two divisions to quantify the links among turnover, customer retention, and profitability. The study shows that reducing turnover by 10 per cent reduces customer non-repeats and yields savings greater than the operating profits of the two divisions combined (Schlesinger and Heskett, 1991).

As indicated by Reichheld and Sasser (1990), it is important for service companies to measure quality, just as their manufacturing counterparts did in the 1980s. They propose 'zero defections' to keep every customer the company can profitably serve. They feel that managers should use defections as a vehicle for continuously improving the quality and value of the services they provide to customers. It is common for a business to lose 15 per cent to 20 per cent of its customers each year. Customer defections have great impact on the bottom line. It is estimated that companies can boost profits by almost 100 per cent by retaining just 5 per cent more of their customers. Today's accounting systems do not capture the value of a loyal customer. When customers defect, they take all of the profit-making potential with them. Aside from generating additional revenue, loyal customers mean cost savings because acquiring a new customer entails certain one-time costs for advertising, promotions, and the like.

Long-time customers are also good advocates for the word of mouth free advertising they provide. Companies with long-time customers can often charge a premium for their products or services. Many customers are willing to pay more to stay in a hotel that provides quality service.

While it is possible to make mistakes in any service firm, it is fundamental and essential to commit to service recovery. Hart *et al.* (1990) discuss how the best companies turn complaining customers into loyal ones. They maintain that there are plenty of opportunities for service firms to turn angry, frustrated customers into loyal ones. The case of Club Med-Cacun provides a good example. Recovery is fundamental to service excellence and should therefore be regarded as an integral part of a service company's strategy. It is perhaps five times more expensive to replace a customer than it is to retain one. At Club Med, one lost customer costs the company at least $2,400, plus the high cost of marketing efforts to find a replacement (Hart *et al.*, 1990). Given the cost, companies should take steps to ensure that employees have the skill, motivation, and authority to make service recovery an integral part of operations. Some successful techniques for developing service recovery skills can be developed through simulated real-life situations and role playing. Sonesta Hotels uses games as part of its orientation program for new employees, so as to enhance their service skills.

TOTAL QUALITY MANAGEMENT (TQM) VERSUS STRATEGIC TOTAL QUALITY MANAGEMENT (STQM)

Following the examples of Japanese quality management, total quality management (TQM) has been a buzzword for the manufacturing sector in the USA for many years (Wood, 1993). Only in recent years have service firms realized that TQM principles can apply to the delivery of services as well.

Quality assurance is a management philosophy that strives for harmony among guests, employees and management. Its three main elements are operations planning, problem-solving teams and performance standards. It is a participative management tool used by all levels of employees that enables a hotel to achieve desired service levels. Walker and Salameh (1990) in an early study of 19 hotels showed that the rewards of quality assurance are worth the initial investment.

Quality management, or quality assurance, is different from quality control – it is a proactive process. The operation tries to prevent or avoid errors rather than fixing or correcting the problems after they have occurred (Wood, 1993; Walker and Salameh, 1990). The five tenets of TQM include: commit to quality, focus on customer satisfaction, assess organizational culture, empower employees and teams, and measure quality efforts. Quality in the case of TQM has a customer-oriented focus and is market-driven. It is often very narrow and centers primarily on the ability of the product or service to satisfy a customer's direct need. Yet it does not take into consideration the increasing awareness of the environment and the need for environmental protection. This is why Madu and Kuei (1993) proposed the concept of strategic total quality management (STQM) as an alternative.

STQM is an extension of TQM. STQM is defined as a quality management philosophy that is based on developing a 'total system' view of quality, to guide the overall performance of a firm (Madu and Kuei, 1993). From the perspective of STQM, quality is seen to be driven by external factors as well as customer and environmental needs.

STQM is a philosophy that considers socially responsible and environmentally sensitive decisions and integrates them into TQM in order to improve the global competitiveness of a firm by strengthening and enhancing its quality objectives. How is STQM incorporated within an organization? Emphasis on quality in services should not be limited to the operational level, nor should it be static, but rather focused on continuous improvement. Further it should involve the whole organization in customer- and environment-driven analyses of internal and external performance so as to drive customer defects (non-return) to zero and maximize the satisfaction of customers with the products/services of the firm.

Once senior management is committed to the concept of STQM, the company should be prepared to engage in a strategic management process with an emphasis on service quality. Strategic management is a continuous process aimed at keeping an organization appropriately matched to its environment. Irrespective of the degree of formality, whether it is the first time the company engages in the process, or whether it is part of a strategy of continuous improvement, a typical strategic management process involves the following series of steps: strategic formulation, implementation, and evaluation and control. Figure 16.2 shows that STQM is all-encompassing in that it acts as the umbrella for all decisions and activities that govern the organization, regarding direction, commitment and allocation of resources.

Senior management – strategy formulation

This phase is what Madu and Kuei (1993) refer to as the 'strategy planning and formulation' phase of the strategic cycle. The process begins with *environmental scanning* and a *SWOT analysis*. Environmental scanning involves the monitoring of the general and task environments of the business to identify both present and future threats and opportunities. Factors included in the general environment are political, economic, sociocultural, technological and ecological, whereas the task environment consists of competitors, customers, suppliers and regulatory agency. Internal analysis of the operation is an identification of the strengths and weaknesses within the business (given the current organizational structure, culture, leadership and resources), relative to the competitors. In this context, the business's environment encompasses all factors both inside (internal of the organization) and outside (external, e.g. greening of the environment, global issues, etc.). These internal and external environmental factors can influence progress toward the attainment of the objectives of the business.

A quality team headed by senior management is formed. The team's major task is to identify customer needs. This stage of the strategic cycle focuses on gaining competitive advantage. In performing the environmental analysis, customer focus should be the key. All employees in the organization need to know how their jobs affect or enhance the total satisfaction of both internal (employees) and external (paying) customers.

Quality should be both environmental and customer driven. Thus, the level of social responsibility of a firm becomes a critical factor in responding to the environmental concerns, or the so-called 'green technology'. Customers' needs have significantly changed to reflect a focus on the environment. Quality is perceived in 'totality' and includes the impact of the end product or service on the environment and its interaction with society. Some firms are perceived to be concerned and active in protecting the environment. Such is the example of three family-owned hotels in Boston. Four years ago, the management made a strong operational and financial commitment to install a policy of environmental management into its operating procedures. Today, there are more than 186 company-wide initiatives (Feiertag, 1994). The public relations aspect associated with this policy is impressive, including White House recognition and wide media coverage. The marketing plan also fully utilizes its environmental policy as a sales tool in differentiating and communicating to the customers about the properties. This in turn translates into additional convention sales for the properties.

Comen (1989) suggests that there are three considerations in designing a successful quality assurance program: conducting a thorough needs analysis, gaining commitment from senior management, and having a program champion. He points out that commitment by senior management is the single most important ingredient in a successful quality assurance program. At the same time, management must also be willing to commit money, time, physical space and competent facilitators to the program. Kirwin (1991) suggests that commitment also includes allocating funds for customer service

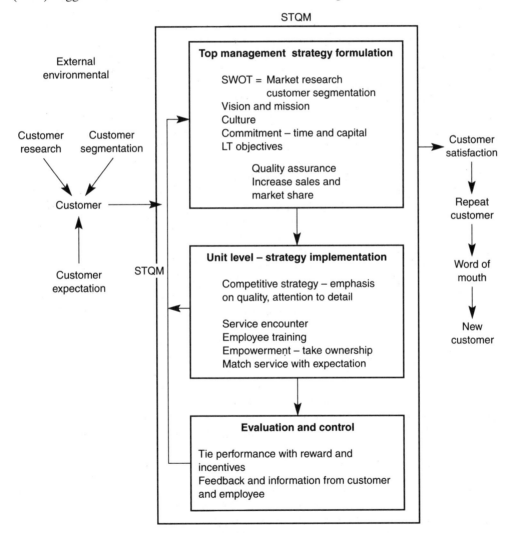

Figure 16.2 *Strategic total quality management focus on customer satisfaction*

expenses as part of the marketing budget. Moreover, operators should direct their capital budgets toward implementing those ideas initiated by customers' suggestions. Partlow (1993) points out that, for Ritz-Carlton, quality management begins with the president and chief operating officer and the other 13 senior executives who make up the corporate steering committee and the senior quality management team. Approximately one-quarter of each executive's time is devoted to quality-related matters. The same scenario can be found at Sutcliffe Catering in the UK. The commitment to service came from the board, which meets six times a year to review quality of service issues and in order to help achieve sustained customer loyalty (Page, 1994).

Thus, two ways for senior management to achieve a climate of change are through symbolism and active involvement. It is essential for senior management to reinforce communication and cooperation within and among work groups by solving problems and by providing strong, yet facilitative leadership. Further, management must provide leadership by establishing a *shared vision* so as to create long-range plans and foster a common set of values. A service vision is a statement of intent about the future, and it must then be communicated to all employees throughout the organization, especially those in the front line. The service vision, based on the detailed SWOT analysis, must be customer- and environmentally focused and it should describe how the company would like to have its products and services perceived by customers (Quinn and Humble, 1993). Five- and ten-year strategic plans should then be developed and updated annually so as to create a sense of purpose and direction.

To ensure customer satisfaction it is necessary to start with a corporate commitment to build on its *culture* and its mission. Culture can be defined as the beliefs which pervade the organization about how business should be conducted and how employees should behave and should be treated (Rue and Holland, 1989). A new culture with STQM means transferring thinking from problem-solving to that of continuous improvement and challenging people to question everything and to think differently. According to Harrison (1987), in any given organization there are four distinct corporate cultures that influence the service encounter: power (centered around the founder or chief executive of the organization), task (focused attention on primary activities inherent in the organization), role (based on the roles that members of the organization have, and person culture (based on the wants and needs of the organizations' members). Depending on the types of hotel properties and the mission of the corporation, these four cultures dictate particular service styles. For instance, in a power culture, the service emphasizes status and prestige and different customers often receive different levels of service whereas in a task culture, the customer becomes the 'target' of the service and the customers rely on the service provider's expertise and desire to do the job correctly. Managers can influence the service encounter between employees and customers by changing or emphasizing the culture of the organization (Lockwood and Jones, 1989). Davidow and Uttal (1990) stress the importance in service businesses of having a clear strategy regarding service. The essence of any customer service strategy is to segment the customers to be served. They note that a clear strategy helps sort out decisions related to product, marketing and distribution as they relate to 'good service'. A service strategy also provides an effective way to choose the optimum mix and level of service for different customer sets. Systematic research on customers' service expectations is equally important. Finally, management needs to find ways to influence customer expectations. In order to successfully position itself in terms of customer service, it becomes a constant challenge for a company to keep expectations at just the right level.

Depending on the different degree and emphasis of the service situations, Lee (1989) proposes a contingency approach to develop strategies and tactics for service firms. He suggests that, for hotels and motels, where the inseparability of production and consumption of services is very high, and thus the degree of consumer involvement in the production and delivery of services is very high, a firm should:

- pay special attention to employee quality and performance in order to employ and retain the best possible people;
- take full advantage of opportunities to customize services;
- attempt to integrate its operational and marketing functions.

Unit level – strategic implementation

Once the planning is complete and organizational change has begun, the implementation or the action can shift to the unit level. Management at the business and operating unit, levels should have access to an annual capital budget and operating plan. This is the 'do' and 'act' phase of Madu and Kuei's strategic cycle.

Schlesinger and Heskett (1991) claim that attracting and retaining today's customers demands a fundamental change from the old model of putting the people who deliver service to customers last to the new model of putting front-line workers first and designing the business system around them. A good example is Fairfield Inn, which has made service delivery the centerpiece of its competitive strategy.

Service industries offer 'products' with intangible quality components which cannot be inventoried. In short, production and consumption occur simultaneously, and front-line people shape the customer's experience through the *service encounter*. Thus, service quality can stand or fall on the relationship between providers and recipients. Accordingly, managers must have a good understanding of the variables that have an impact on the interactive process between employees and customers, such as personal characteristics, perceptions, social competence, and needs and objectives. It is the responsibility of managers to reduce stresses created by such common issues arising from role ambiguity, role conflict, role overload and role incompatibility.

Restaurant customers may not return, regardless of the quality of the food, if they dislike the treatment they received from the waiting staff (Kanter, 1991). Research on customer loyalty in service industries shows that two-thirds of customers defect because they find service personnel indifferent or unhelpful. Schlesinger and Heskett (1991) argue that understanding this truth about service quality is the first step to achieving service excellence because it makes concern for people the cornerstone of service strategy. Thus while the cost of service delivery may benefit from economies of scale in large global enterprises, the act of service delivery is still intensely local (Kanter, 1991).

One way for successful implementation of strategy to occur is through empowerment. This is where a company seeks to refocus its resource commitment and priority by empowering the front-line employees with decision-making authority and responsibility in situations where such authority has traditionally resided solely with management (Hart *et al.*, 1990). Empowering workers to take more initiatives to create or deliver the things that customers value – a spotless hotel room, a fresh, inexpensive sandwich, and many other things – is essential to quality management. Empowerment comes from the combination of a streamlined chain of command, greater decision-making latitude for employees, and the training necessary to enable workers to make good decisions (Wood, 1993). Ritz-Carlton, for instance, allows each individual employee to spend up to $2,000 to satisfy a guest (Partlow, 1993).

Lockwood and Jones (1989) present a series of strategies that employees can use in service encounters. Among them, they suggest the use of a script approach to change customers' expectations regarding the service they will receive. Script approach involves key words and phrases that both participants recognize and use, and which the employee can use to guide the customer smoothly through the service encounter. The following list gives a variety of methods proposed by various authors to enhance service encounters:

1. Computerized service management system (Records and Glennie, 1991).
2. Set up quality circle to address problem areas that affect the quality of guests' experience (Orly, 1988). The goal of quality circles is to involve hourly workers in achieving maximum quality. As a hotel management tool, quality circles offer human relations benefits as well as better service.
3. Comment cards (Wood, 1993).
4. From survey of guest comment cards from a 1,000-room hotel in San Francisco, a customer satisfaction matrix was derived, and 'customer-satisfaction scores' computed for each of the nine attributes included in the survey. Attributes include employee attitudes, location, room, price facilities, reception, services, parking, and food and beverage. The feedback provides data for segmentation analysis (Barsky and Labagh, 1992).
5. Empowering employees, lower turnover rate from 223 per cent to 160 per cent in Taco Bell (Wood, 1993). Both restaurant managers and district-level supervisors had to change from being 'policemen' to being 'coaches'.
6. Script approach or service blueprinting (Lockwood and Jones, 1989). The Disney Corporation is a good example.

Another way to empower employees is through the use of technology by subordinating technology to people. Information technology (IT) is fundamentally changing the nature of work, and is providing new opportunities to serve customers. However, there is a weak link between IT strategy and customer service. Computer applications that help in serving customers better are 'strategic', particularly for service companies. Added value is likely to come from technological improvements, styling features, product image, and other attributes that only services can create. In response to these demands, John E. Martin, President and chief executive officer of Taco Bell Corporation Worldwide, indicated that his company would place the decision-making process directly into the hands of dine-in and drive-through customers by introducing computer touch-screen-ordering technology. Moreover, Taco Bell forms strategic alliances with suppliers to gain a competitive advantage in the marketplace by providing technology that takes the concept and product to new places: airports, malls, schools, theaters, supermarkets, petrol stations, convenience stores, etc. (*Harvard Business Review*, 1993).

Records and Glennie (1991) explain how to integrate technology into the service management process by using available computer programs, and then describe the successful implementation of just such an application by the Boca Raton Resort and Club. They refer to a computerized service management system designed to integrate such tasks as budgeting, forecasting, labor scheduling, time accounting and performance reporting so that a property can maximize productivity and savings as well as its service standards.

Service excellence can be achieved through investment in training, for both managers and, more particularly, front-line employees, so as to develop an awareness of customers' concerns (Hart *et al.*, 1990). Further management should encourage staff development, skill building and cross-training so that staff can have new or expanded roles and jobs. In order to help managers to provide a conducive environment for their service employees, it is important that managers are 'retrained' and receive support to move from one management style to another and to acquire the skills of coaching and counseling, performance appraisal, quality improvement, communication, team-building and empowerment (Dodwell and Simmons, 1994). This is also a good time to learn from the field by letting the front line teach the top floor. Taco Bell is turning managers into coaches and supporters of the customer contact employees.

Regarding the organizational structure, in order to enable and pay for these changes, one way is to cut 'corporate'. Smaller, flatter companies staffed with generalists are found to be more efficient, as having fewer levels of bureaucracy accelerates decision-making in the field. To ensure service excellence, companies need to ensure the excellence of the service worker's job (Kanter, 1991).

As seen in Figure 16.2, strategic evaluation and control reflects the bottom-up approach of STQM. By providing feedback, it tests whether the firm is doing things right. This is an error-checking procedure intended to identify the sources of the problem and come up with corrective measures. This is especially important after a continuous improvement initiative has begun, so that management can monitor efforts to ensure that results are forthcoming. It is bottom-up, because this is where much information, such as customer complaint, suggestions and new ideas or local competitive positions, can be input at the unit level. Unit managers and employees are in the best position in terms of monitoring the environment, and keeping track of customer taste changes, and any potential threat of new competitor entry.

With the issue of quality of service at the forefront in the 1990s, customer feedback is an important factor in trying to maintain quality of service. Stephenson (1989) suggests using different and creative strategies for getting feedback from customers, in addition to telephone interviews and comment cards. Moreover, field surveys are conducted to detect customers' perceptions of the service they receive and the concept itself. On-line information systems for customers and suppliers can be installed to collect information, conduct competitor analysis and substitute product analysis, and make sure that both the product and service are of the best quality and also environmentally sound. It is essential to make it easy for the 'silent majority' of dissatisfied customers to register their complaints, perhaps through '800' numbers, as is the case with Marriott Corporation's 24-hour 'hot line' in its hotels, or simply through questions such as 'how was everything?', or through informal 'listening devices' like questionnaires and customer suggestion boxes.

Reichheld and Sasser (1990) suggest the need to develop mechanisms to gather information about customers, especially those ending or about to end their relationship with the company. Information sources include: reservation systems, and guest history databases. The idea is to gain insights by using defections as an early warning signal – to learn from defectors why they left the company and to use this information to improve the business. Information gathered in defections analysis tends to be concrete and specific, which is helpful for companies trying to decide on the kind of service quality investments which will be profitable. Managers can establish meaningful targets and monitor progress and also create a culture whereby employees understand the importance of keeping customers and encouraging them to pursue zero defections.

It is equally important to recognize and reward those employees who carry out the company mission – these are the 'service champions'. Thus, the reward systems should reflect consistent incentives and pay structure (s) for motivating behavior and performance. Kanter (1991) suggests raising pay in order to create the incentives to encourage professionalism. Equity ownership and performance measures that support motivation – and better pay – are other ways to foster professionalism. Reichheld and Sasser (1990) stress that training employees on the specifics of defections analysis is necessary, to motivate them by linking incentives, planning and budgeting to defection rates. Ultimately, defections should be a key performance measure for senior management and a fundamental component of incentive systems.

Intangible rewards include increased self-esteem, improved job satisfaction, prestige and job enrichment. Common tangible incentives include monetary incentives, bonuses and merit certificates. An awards program can be a helpful way of recognizing and encouraging the achievement of total customer service. Such a program can include a combination of monetary incentives, exotic vacations, gifts, and non-monetary rewards such as badges or a special parking place.

Industry examples

Many hospitality firms are beginning to experience the value of service quality management. Taco Bell has been successful in creating its 'value strategy'. Starting with the premise that customers value the food, the service, and the physical appearance of a restaurant, Taco Bell's management examined every aspect of the restaurant operation, and then fundamentally altered roles and responsibilities at every level of the corporate hierarchy. The company also uses a selection process that is designed to elicit prospective employees' values and attitudes toward responsibility, team work, etc., as well as revised job descriptions for the company's restaurant managers. With the better trained, better motivated employees, there is less need of supervision. The style of supervisory positions is also changing, from direction and control to coaching and support. Information technology provides the timely, accurate information necessary to help raise quality and sales as well as to monitor mistakes. It is the goal of Taco Bell to position the company as the employers of choice so as to attract quality personnel.

According to Michael Quinlan, chairman and chief executive officer of McDonald's Corporation, the goal for the company in the 1990s is to exceed customer expectations. McDonald's places emphasis on training and initiates 'customer care' programs where the local restaurant will conduct its own consumer focus groups, employee rap sessions, complaint racking systems, and other front-line, service-enhancing actions. The company also 'out-sources' food preparation work that does not have to be done in the restaurant.

Johnson (1991) discusses the business philosophy of Walt Disney. The management of the company felt that the culture, the environment and the performance of people, both customers and employees, contributed to the success of a quality service program. In order to gather information on customers, a research and statistics department conducts external surveys and focus groups. A guest letters department deals with both complaints and compliments. It also believes in empowering the cast members (employees) to provide the desired service level. Empowerment is the key to getting everyone to 'buy in' to the plan. The commitment begins at the senior level in terms of resource allocation and delegation of authority. An investment in reliable, efficient support systems to help employees carry their responsibilities is also deemed essential.

The Ritz-Carlton Company is the first hotel group to win the Malcolm Baldrige National Quality Award (Partlow, 1993). A focus on customer satisfaction has been built into the management processes of the organization and supported through an integrated system of information analysis, total employee participation, training, and the continuous effort to improve service and product quality. In addition, Ritz-Carlton uses advanced technology to full advantage, from automated building and safety systems to computerized reservation systems.

The following list gives examples of industry using service quality management.

1. Boca Raton Resort and Club, Florida – computerized service management system (Records and Glennie, 1991).
2. Accor Hotel Group, France (Orly, 1988) – quality-circle program.
3. Taco Bell installs quality management after consumer studies done in 1987 and 1989 to meet customers' expectations (Wood, 1993). Quality management has clearly produced results for Taco Bell.
4. Restaurant division of General Mills Corporation since the late 1970s has a comprehensive program to ensure the quality of the seafood (Wood, 1993).
5. Ritz-Carlton – winner of the Malcolm Baldrige National Quality Award (Partlow, 1993) for its quality management program.
6. Kowloon Hotel, Hong Kong – total customer service (Barsky and Dittmann, 1993).
7. Country Hospitality of Carlson Hospitality Group – 'The Promise', a commitment to provide quality product and guest satisfaction.
8. The Bristol Marriott Hotel and Scott's Hotels, UK (Dodwell and Simmons, 1994). Total – everyone being involved; quality – delighting the customer; management – organizing, not supervising.
9. Using four hotels as examples, Comen (1989) discusses in detail the 'how-tos' in developing and managing an effective quality assurance program that uses employee problem-solving teams.

CONCLUSION

However, more of the same no longer works. There is no single strategy for competing on service. Competing in today's environment requires a shift in management's mindset as well as a new appreciation of the real value of service and the value that service employees create. Further, the increase in international competition also suggests that only quality-driven companies will be able to survive in the 1990s.

REFERENCES

Allen, M. (1988) 'Strategic management of consumer services', *Long Range Planning*, vol. **21**, no. 6, pp. 20–5.

Barsky, J. D., and Dittmann, S. (1990) 'Theory S: total customer service', *Cornell HRA Quarterly*, May, pp. 88–95.

Barsky, J. D., and Labagh, R. (1992) 'A strategy for customer satisfaction', *Cornell HRA Quarterly*, October, pp. 32–40.

Berry, L. L (1980) 'Service marketing is different', *Business*, vol. **30**, pp. 24–9.

Business Week (1993) 'The tough new consumer', special issue, Autumn–Winter.

Carman, J. M., and Langeard, E. (1980) 'Growth strategies for service firms', *Strategic Management Journal*, vol. **1**, pp. 7–22.

Comen, T. (1989) 'Making quality assurance work for you', *Cornell HRA Quarterly*, vol. **30**, no. 3, pp. 23–9.

Davidow, W. H., and Uttal, B. (1989) *Total Customer Service*, Harper and Row, New York.

Davidow, W. H., and Uttal, B. (1990) 'Why you need a service strategy', *Planning Review*, January–February, pp. 10–14.

Dodwell, S., and Simmons, P. (1994) 'Trials and tribulations in the pursuit of quality improvement', *International Journal of Contemporary Hospitality Management*, vol. **6**, nos 1/2, pp. 14–18.

Feiertag, H. (1994) 'Boost sales with environment-driven strategy', *Hotel and Motel Management*, vol. **209**, no. 2, p. 8.

Harrison, R. (1987) *Organizational Culture and Quality of Service*, Association for Management Education and Development, London.

Hart, C. W. L., Heskett, J. L., and Sasser, W. E., Jr (1990) 'The profitable art of service recovery', *Harvard Business Review*, July–August, pp. 148–56.

Harvard Business Review (1991) 'How does service drive the service company?' November–December, pp. 146–58.

Harvard Business Review (1993) 'Strategy and the art of reinventing value', September–October, pp. 39–51.

Heskett, J. L., and Hart, C. W. L. (1990) *Service Breakthroughs: Changing the Rules of the Game*, The Free Press, New York.

Imai, M. (1986) *Kaizen: The Key to Japan's Competitive Success*, Random House, New York.

Jacobson, R., and Aaker, D. A. (1987) 'The strategic role of product quality', *Journal of Marketing*, vol. **51**, pp. 31–44.

Johnson, R. (1991) 'A strategy for service – Disney style' *Journal of Business Strategy*, September/October, pp. 38–43.

Kanter, R. M. (1991) 'Service quality: you get what you pay for', *Harvard Business Review*, September/October, pp. 8–9.

Kirwin, P. (1991) 'Increasing sales and profits through guest satisfaction', *Lodging Hospitality*, June, p. 66.

Lee, M. L. (1989) 'Contingency approach to strategies for service firms', *Journal of Business Research*, vol. **19**, pp. 293–301.

Levitt, T. (1981) 'Marketing intangible products and product intangibles', *Harvard Business Review*, vol. **58**, January–February, pp. 83–91.

Lewis, R. C., and Nightingale, M. A. (1991) 'Targeting service to your customer', *Cornell HRA Quarterly*, August, pp. 18–27.

Lockwood, A., and Jones, P. (1989) 'Creating positive service encounters', *Cornell HRA Quarterly*, February, pp. 44–50.

Madu, C. N., and Kuei, C. (1993) 'Introducing strategic quality management', *Long Range Planning*, vol. **26**, no. 6, pp. 121–31.

Neave, H. R. (1990) *The Deming Dimension*, SPC Press, Knoxville, TN.

Normann, R., and Ramfrez, R. (1993) 'From value chain to value constellation: designing interactive strategy', *Harvard Business Review*, July–August, pp. 65–77.

Olsen, M. D., Tse, E. C., and West, J. J. (1992) *Strategic Management in the Hospitality Industry*, Van Nostrand Reinhold, New York.

Orly, C. (1988) 'Quality circles in France: Accor's experiment in self-management', *Cornell HRA Quarterly*, November, pp. 50–7.

Page, C. (1994) 'Sutcliffe Caterings's approach to continuous improvement', *International Journal of Contemporary Hospitality Management*, vol. **6**, no. 1/2, pp. 19–24.

Partlow, C. G. (1993) 'How Ritz-Carlton applies "TQM" ', *Cornell HRA Quarterly*, August, pp. 16–24.

Phillips, L. W., Chang, D. R., and Buzzell, R. D. (1983) 'Product quality, cost position and business performance: a test of some key hypotheses', *Journal of Marketing*, vol. **47**, pp. 26–43.

Quinn, J. B., Doorley, T. L., and Paquette, P. C. (1990) 'Beyond products: services-based strategy', *Harvard Business Review*, March–April, pp. 58–67.

Quinn, M., and Humble, J. (1993) 'Using service to gain a competitive edge – the PROMPT approach', *Long Range Planning*, vol. **26**, no. 2, pp. 31–40.

Records, H. A., and Glennie, M. F. (1991), 'Service management and quality assurance', *Cornell HRA Quarterly*, May, pp. 26–35.

Reichheld, F. F., and Sasser, W. E., Jr (1990) 'Zero defections: quality comes to services', *Harvard Business Review*, September–October, pp. 105–11.

Rue, L. W., and Holland, P. G. (1989) *Strategic Management: Concepts and Experiences*, 2nd edn, McGraw-Hill Book Company, New York.

Schlesinger, L. A., and Heskett, J. L., (1991) 'The service-driven service company', *Harvard Business Review*, September–October, pp. 71–81.

Showalter, M. J., and Mulholland, J. A. (1992) 'Continuous improvement strategies for service organizations', *Business Horizons*, vol. **35**, July–August, pp. 82–7.

Stephenson, S. (1989) 'Feedback techniques tell "how I am doing"?' *Restaurant Institutions*, vol. **99**, no. 8, pp. 20–1.

Travel Weekly (1989a) 'Senior travelers say convenience and service rank above price', vol. **48**, 17 April, p. 38.

Travel Weekly (1989b) 'Hyatt quality-control plan eyes service in the 90's', vol. **48**, 19 October, p. 19.

Walker, J. R., and Salameh, T. T. 'The Q.A. payoff', *Cornell HRA Quarterly*, February, pp. 57–9.

Wilson, I. (1988) 'Competitive strategies for service business', *Long Range Planning*, vol. **21**, no. 6, pp. 10–12.

Wood, T. (1993) 'Total quality management', *Restaurant USA*, February, pp. 16–19.

Zeithaml, V. A., Parasuraman, A., and Berry, L. L. (1985) 'Problems and strategies in services marketing', *Journal of Marketing*, vol. **49**, Spring, pp. 33–46.

Index